D1388522

KEY: Freshwater fishes are printed in **red** and marine fishes in **black**.
Types of fish found in both fresh and salt-water bear a **red dot**.

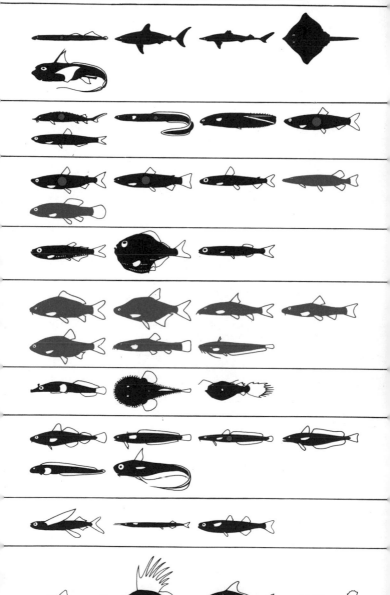

Key to the Fishes
of Northern Europe

Key to the Fishes of Northern Europe

A GUIDE TO THE IDENTIFICATION OF MORE THAN 350 SPECIES

by **Alwyne Wheeler**

Illustrated by **Peter Stebbing**

Maps drawn by **F. Rodney Fraser**

FREDERICK WARNE

Published by Frederick Warne (Publishers) Ltd, London, 1978
© 1978 Frederick Warne & Co. Ltd
Illustrations © 1978 Peter Stebbing

For Tony, Rosalind, and Mary,
my present fishing companions

Cased edition: ISBN 0 7232 2097 2
Limp edition: ISBN 0 7232 2064 6

Printed and bound in Great Britain by
William Clowes & Sons Limited, London, Beccles and Colchester
2730.478

Contents

Preface

When invited by the publishers long ago to revise the late J. Travis Jenkins's *The Fishes of the British Isles* (first edition 1925; second edition 1936) I accepted with pleasure because this was a book which had inspired me when young with a deep interest in fishes. Alas, time had rendered it so much out of date and the world of the publisher changed so much that it became evident that a completely new text, with new illustrations, was called for. In presenting the *Key to the Fishes of Northern Europe* my chief hope is that it will be as inspiring to others as Jenkins's book was to myself, and that it will lead to a better understanding and appreciation of this fascinating group of animals.

Although this book appears under the author's name, it is the result of collaboration and the help of a number of people, and I should, therefore, like to express my thanks to them. It has been a pleasure to work again with the illustrator, Peter Stebbing, whose patience and skill have contributed greatly to this volume. The support and help of my wife, Cicely Wheeler, has been a constant inspiration, as has her forbearance, and that of my children, while I have been working on the text.

Alwyne Wheeler
Theydon Bois
Essex

Introduction

This book is a complete guide to the fishes of northern Europe and it aims to facilitate identification with the minimum of technicality. Both text and illustrations are designed to draw attention to the vital distinguishing features of each species. Descriptions of the body form, fin ray and scale counts are not given except where essential, technicalities and jargon are eschewed—with the result that in the words of that inimitable teacher and fellow ichthyophile, A. F. Magri MacMahon, 'Big Brother Ichthyologist, this book is not for you'.

The body of the text is arranged under four headings. **Distinguishing features** gives the salient characteristics of each species. **Coloration** gives in brief detail the usual colour with notes on special colour changes, e.g. in the breeding season, but it must be noted that the colours of fishes are fugitive, changing on death, and always modified by the intensity of the light, tone of the background, and often with the emotional state of the fish. **Size** gives the maximum total length, weight, and where appropriate, differences between the sexes. Under **Remarks** are given details of habitat, depth range, food, breeding, and relations with man. Much of this information appears in very condensed form, necessarily so as whole books have been written about some of the species included. Each family of fishes has a general introduction.

The maps which accompany most accounts of species show the total range in which the fish has been recorded, except where otherwise stated. There are no maps for introduced species, because it is clear that further introductions might take place which would render them outdated. Maps for certain widely distributed oceanic species have also been omitted.

The scope of this book is the whole of northern Europe. All freshwater fishes found north of the Alps and Pyrenees, and eastwards to the headwaters of the Danube have been included. The traveller in France, Belgium, Holland, Germany, Austria, Denmark, Sweden, and Norway will find that any fish encountered is described. Sea fishes from north of Biscay to the Barents Sea are also included down to a depth of *c*. 1000 m (547 fathoms). Some very small oceanic fishes which are caught only by research vessels using special nets have been omitted, as have a very few species recorded once only within the area. Otherwise every fish found on the shore, in shallow water, or in the sea above the continental shelf has been included.

The fish fauna of northern Europe is not outstandingly rich. The freshwater fishes still show the effects of the ice ages which covered the greater part of the region. At their maximum the ice extended far south, and the adjacent land, the periglacial zone, was frozen for much of the year. Even those lakes and rivers which were unfrozen for as much as six months of the year were inhabited by only a few fishes such as the whitefishes, charr, sea trout, and salmon which entered the rivers from the sea. It is likely that the whole of Europe north of the Alps had no freshwater fishes other than these, except for the Rhône system, and possibly the Gironde, in southern France, where certain cyprinid and percid fishes survived. After the retreat of the ice, freshwater fishes migrated across Europe from the east, most notably from the Danube basin (which had never been so severely affected by the ice as northern Europe).

Even today, as one travels westwards from the Danube, the freshwater fish fauna gradually becomes poorer in terms of species. The eastern rivers of England were still in contact with continental rivers (notably the Rhine) until a relatively late date (the beginning of the Atlantic period, *c.* 7500 years ago, when England became separated from the continent). Ireland had become an island long before this and no true freshwater fishes are native there, or in the western rivers of England and Wales, or in the whole of Scotland. The native freshwater fishes found in these areas (as in Norway) are all species such as the salmon, trout, whitefishes, stickleback, and eel which gained access from the sea. The fact that many freshwater fishes such as pike, perch, roach, dace, and bream are now found throughout the British Isles, as well as in parts of Europe where they are not native, is due entirely to man's activities.

Europe's marine fishes likewise have suffered from human activities, but it is chiefly the species of economic importance which show this, mostly as a result of overfishing. Their distribution on the Atlantic seaboard owes less to the ice ages than to the present-day climate and oceanic circulatory systems. The northern European fish fauna is an amalgam of several biogeographical zones and as such has a certain richness. Many of the species are typically cool temperate in range, found virtually along the whole coast. Superimposed on this are two elements, the Lusitanian (so called from the Latin name Lusitania for Portugal and much of Spain) and the boreal (or Arctic) fish faunas. The Lusitanian species are those which are at the northward limit of their range, around the British Isles, either as residents or as summertime migrants, and in many cases both as residents and migrants. They are usually abundant south of Biscay and in the Mediterranean. The boreal species normally extend only as far south as the North Sea coasts. There are more Lusitanian migrants than boreal ones, which is only to be expected as the fauna is richer to the south.

In addition to these native elements, there is the massive northward movement of the Atlantic Ocean currents, known as the North Atlantic Drift, although it starts out in the western Atlantic as the Gulf Stream. This warm water, which comes from the central sub-tropical Atlantic, warms the north European coastline and is a major factor in our climate. It brings with it many warm-water fishes such as wreckfish, barrelfishes, and trigger-fish as well as exotic animals such as turtles, and it also bears tropical plant seeds. It enables the seasonal migrations of the Lusitanian element such as tunnies, bass, grey mullets, blue sharks, and Ray's bream to take place. Overall, northern Europe's marine fishes are a fascinating mixture of common, widespread species, migratory species, and rare wanderers, and among the latter may be previously unrecorded species.

How to Use the Drawings
A note by the illustrator

The paramount purpose of the drawings is to help the reader to distinguish one species from another. This has been done in the following ways:

1 All detail has been omitted except where it aids the identification of the species.

2 Red indicator lines pick out specific characteristics.

3 The numbers of spines and rays have been given by numbers printed close to the relevant fins, and the fins have been simplified to a diagrammatic style. The numbers are given systematically, as in the following examples: $1 + 36–43$ means 1 spine and 36 to 43 rays, and $16–18 + 8–10$ means 16 to 18 spines and 8 to 10 rays. That is to say the spine count is always given first.

   In some cases, scale counts have been included in the drawings, and the line of the count is indicated by dots.

4 To help avoid confusion, features which lie beyond the vertical mid-plane, i.e. on the other side of the fish as drawn, have been omitted.

It is not possible to draw fishes (or other organisms) without discovering the amazing variety of their form, not just between species, but between individuals of the same species. As a result of natural variation it becomes almost a matter of choice which individual represents the standard of the species. If the reader were to select one person to be the standard for identifying the human species, the problem becomes clear. The reader should remember that when using the key, the fish to be identified may vary from the illustrated standard.

Great attention has been paid to the natural shape of the fish and in most cases several specimens were examined before finally illustrating each species. I have drawn them as I believe they would appear in water, not because I expect many readers will have the opportunity of seeing fish under water, but showing them in this way gives a better basis for identification.

In conclusion, I would like to thank Alwyne Wheeler for his help and advice in the preparation of the drawings.

Glossary

algae   the lowest group of the plant kingdom; common in aquatic habitats, e.g. seaweeds

amphipods   small crustaceans which are laterally flattened and lack a carapace, e.g. sand-hoppers

anadromous   used of a fish which migrates from the sea to spawn in freshwater

barbel   fleshy finger-like projection richly supplied with 'taste cells' at the surface

bathymetric range   range of depths inhabited

bathypelagic   living in mid-water in the deep sea

benthic   bottom-living

bryozans   minute animals living in colonies usually covering stones or shells in a moss-like growth

capsule   membranous envelope

cartilaginous   with a skeleton composed of cartilage not bone

cephalopod   mollusc with a distinct tentacled head, e.g. squid

cetacean   member of the mammalian group including whales and porpoises

circumtropical   found throughout the tropics

commensal   animal or plant living in close association with another

copepods   minute crustaceans usually free-swimming but some are parasitic

crustacean   member of a large class of animals mostly aquatic with a hard shell

cusp   point of a tooth

demersal   close to the sea-bed, as in demersal fisheries

denticles   small teeth, as on the skin of sharks and rays

embryo   young animal before birth

euphausiids   group of small pelagic crustaceans, e.g. krill

eutrophic   a water mass enriched by organic matter

genera   groups of animals or plants having common features distinct from other groups

gill rakers   stout structures on the gill arch which prevent food items being swept out of the gill opening

gills   respiratory organs of fishes and other aquatic animals

gonads   reproductive organs

gravid   pregnant

hermaphrodite individual possessing both male and female reproductive organs

holothurian class of animals including the sea-cucumbers

hydroids minute animals which live in colonies; related to sea-anemones

hydrological concerning the study of water masses

incubation period of time eggs take to develop

inhalent opening through which water or air is drawn into a cavity

invertebrates animals without backbones

isopods small crustaceans resembling woodlice

isthmus in fishes refers to the narrowing of the throat between the gill covers

krill A type of small pelagic crustacean (*see* euphasiid)

larva young fish after hatching but still nourished by the yolk of the egg

lingual of the tongue

medusae usually refers to jellyfishes but technically is the free-swimming stage of their (and their relatives') life

meristic features of a fish which can be counted, e.g. fin-rays, scales, etc.

mesopelagic living in the middle layers of the open sea

metamorphosis change from one stage of life to another, e.g. postlarva to young fish

molluscs group of invertebrate animals most of which have hard shells

mysids small swimming shrimp-like crustaceans, often called opossum shrimps

ocellus spot of colour surrounded by a ring of other colour

ostracods small crustaceans usually living within a paired shell

oviduct canal through which egg passes from ovary

oviparous producing young by eggs shed from body before hatching

ovoviviparous producing young by eggs which develop within the body and are expelled at hatching

papilla small fleshy protuberance of the body

parasitic an organism which lives on another and is nourished by it

pelagic living at the surface of the sea

placental form of development where the embryo is nourished by a connection with its mother

plankton animal or plant life floating at the surface
polychaete a group of worms also called bristle worms, e.g. ragworm
postlarva stage of development after the yolk of the egg has been consumed
pseudoplacenta a false placenta

reticulation network of fine lines
riffle shallow stretch of river where flow is fast, usually over stones

schooling aggregation of fishes
seine a type of net
spermatozoa male fertilizing element in semen of animals
sublittoral below the level of low tide mark
swim-bladder a thin-walled gas-filled chamber within the body of some bony fishes

tendrils fine threads for attachment
tubercles small rounded hard projections

urogenital opening or canal connected with kidneys and gonads

vertebrates animals with backbones
viviparous form of development where young develop within the mother and are nourished by her
vomer bone in midline of the roof of the mouth

yolk-sac remains of egg-yolk in the hatched fish larva

Parts of a Fish

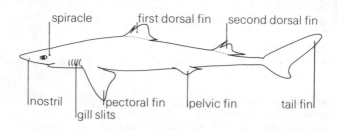

spiracle · first dorsal fin · second dorsal fin · nostril · pectoral fin · gill slits · pelvic fin · tail fin

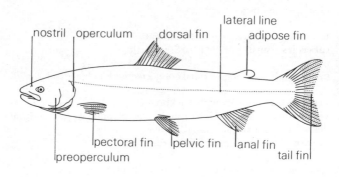

nostril · operculum · dorsal fin · lateral line · adipose fin · pectoral fin · preoperculum · pelvic fin · anal fin · tail fin

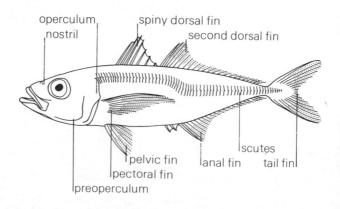

operculum · nostril · spiny dorsal fin · second dorsal fin · pelvic fin · pectoral fin · preoperculum · anal fin · scutes · tail fin

Fish and Man in Europe

Ever since man has lived in Europe he has probably affected the fish fauna to some extent. Archaeology has shown that early man lived beside rivers and lakes and captured fish for food, and pike bones are a conspicuous feature of many Mesolithic sites in Denmark and elsewhere in continental Europe. Early man was, however, living in balance with his environment and the removal of the relatively few large pike, salmon, or sturgeon that he speared or otherwise caught made no difference to the stock of the species, nor did it disturb the ecosystem. It is all too clear today that man is no longer living as part of the natural ecosystem but has, in the past millenium, altered the environment to such an extent that plant and animal life have suffered drastic change. These changes are nowhere more apparent than in northern Europe.

The pollution of many rivers and lakes is an example which immediately springs to mind and in the worst cases—and there are several in western Europe—the entire fauna has been exterminated, even if only locally in some rivers. However, pollution has many forms, all harmful to some degree although their effects vary. At one extreme are the discharges of untreated toxic waste from industrial processes and untreated domestic sewage, both of which may result in the total elimination of fish. Neither need pose a threat to the fauna as suitable treatment methods have been developed for domestic sewage and most industrial effluents, and the most intractable of the latter can be disposed of in other ways. The worst effects of pollution are usually seen in the lower reaches of rivers where toxic water may form a barrier to migratory fishes such as sturgeon, salmon, smelt, and eel.

More insidious are the milder forms of pollution which produce less dramatic but as far-reaching changes in the fish fauna. Two examples can be cited. The unnaturally acid lakes and streams of Scandinavia caused by the fall-out of waste from the upper atmosphere polluted by industrial discharges from tall chimneys elsewhere in Europe are, in places, quite uninhabitable by fish. Elsewhere they contain slow-growing, partly starved populations due to the impoverishment of the insect and crustacean life which the fish require for food. Secondly, the discharge of treated sewage effluent, the run-off of agricultural fertilizers, and natural seepage from vegetation and the soil produce an enrichment of the water by organic matter, known as eutrophication, which results in slow but profound changes in the fish fauna. In mountain lakes particularly, the outcome of eutrophication is a change in the fishes most abundant in the lake, from the domination by salmonids, trout, and charr for example, to an abundance of cyprinid fishes such as roach and bream. Even lakes as large as Lake Constance have shown such changes, and here the sequence has been from salmonids, to whitefishes, to perch and zander-dominated communities. Presumably, if eutrophication continues here the final cyprinid stage will eventually be reached.

The presumed need to control the flow of rivers has also had profound effects on the fishes. Navigation locks built in rivers to permit the passage of shipping upstream, and weirs to retain the water when normal flow was too small to allow ships to use the river, have imposed barriers to migratory fishes attempting to return from the sea to their upstream spawning-grounds. In many places they have also altered the flow of rivers so that former natural spawning-grounds have been changed, either buried under silt falling out of suspension from the slow-moving water, or washed out by fast-flowing water over the weirs. The effect on the fishes has been that migratory species such as sturgeon, salmon, and shad have been reduced in numbers and locally exterminated as breeding fish, while the cyprinid fishes, especially chub, dace, and roach, have increased in numbers.

Still waters in low-lying areas throughout Europe have been diminished by drainage schemes aimed at the betterment of agriculture, but at the expense of many specialized habitats for fishes. While agricultural drainage projects have been practised on a large scale since at least the 16th century, and are still prosecuted, a more modern threat has developed in that watery wastes have been used for the dumping of municipal rubbish. In recent years, many valuable aquatic habitats have been destroyed in this way, and others are threatened.

Mountain lakes have also been affected in several ways. Eutrophication is a severe threat to the often unique fish populations containing whitefishes and charr. More direct effects result from the regulation of water-level in those lakes which have been adapted as sources of drinking water supply, or which provide water for hydroelectric schemes. In such lakes the water-level fluctuates considerably and the shallow shore, which is the most productive in terms of plant and animal life, and which often serves as a spawning-place for many species of fish, is periodically left dry. This reduces the richness of both flora and fauna, and affects the size and condition of the fish population as well as changing the balance between one group of fishes and another.

Mainland Europe, and to a lesser extent the British Isles, now contain well-established populations of exotic, mostly North American freshwater fishes. Many of these were imported in uninformed attempts to improve the fishing, although in some cases the motives of the people concerned are hard to understand. As a result, North American catfishes and freshwater basses are now widely distributed in parts of Europe, often to the detriment of native fishes. In England fishes such as the wels and zander have been introduced from the continent; the latter has spread at a considerable rate and will eventually become established throughout lowland England. The introduction of exotic fishes has, when adequately studied, usually proved to be detrimental and should be regarded not as fishery improvement but as biological pollution.

Even more widespread has been the redistribution of native fishes within Europe. Large-scale movements of fish from one area to another have been carried out, usually as a means of improving fishing waters, but the result has been the spread of diseases and parasites, and the establishment of many fishes far outside their original area of distribution. This has contributed to the decline and sometimes the local extinction of some of Europe's rarest fishes.

Overall, the effects of man's activities have been wide reaching and often seriously damaging. Throughout northern Europe the obstruction of rivers and pollution of estuaries have seriously affected migratory fishes. The sturgeon is now a rare fish where once it was common, salmon and the shads are locally extinct and uncommon in places where once they were abundant, and the North Sea houting is very probably extinct. In highland and other lakes populations of charr and whitefishes have been reduced and, in some cases, extinguished by the combination of man-induced changes in their habitat. In many parts of Europe the changes in river habitats have been adverse for such fishes as the salmon, trout, and grayling. On the other hand, fishes such as the carp family members, roach, bream, dace, and carp, and the perch, zander, and pike have extended their ranges and have found the man-made changes in the freshwaters of Europe to their advantage. The balance therefore seems to have been that such fishes have become more abundant and more widely distributed, while the salmonoids, such as salmon, trout, charr, whitefishes, and grayling have diminished. Unchecked, the process would continue and could result in an impoverished fauna for most of Europe, except for the northernmost and extreme western extremities. It is consequently a matter of urgency for all aspects of water use, fishery management, and proposals for changes in aquatic habitats of any kind to be scrutinized for the effects they may have on Europe's diminished fish fauna.

Lampreys

The lampreys and lamperns are members of one of the major groups of truly primitive fishes, the superclass AGNATHA. They lack jaws, fin rays, paired fins, and scales. Most are freshwater species, although some migrate to the sea to feed; all breed in freshwater.

They are elongate, slender fishes with relatively small eyes, a distinctive series of openings along the sides of the anterior body, each opening to a separate gill pouch, and a characteristic sucker-like oral disc mouth.

The prides or larvae live buried in mud; the eyes and the oral disc are not developed until metamorphosis. Four species occur in northern European freshwaters and all are members of the family Petromyzonidae.

Lamprey *Petromyzon marinus*

Distinguishing features   Sucker large, teeth in the oral disc arranged in radiating rows, small teeth numerous, large sharply pointed teeth in front of disc, tooth-plate with 7–9 large, sharp cusps. Both dorsal fins well separated. Adults have large eyes. (Coloration also distinctive in adults.)

Coloration   Olive or yellow brown, heavily mottled with black or dark brown on the back; lighter ventrally.

Size   Maximum length *c.* 91 cm (36 in.); average for mature adults around 60 cm (24 in.). Maximum weight *c.* 2.5 kg (5 lb 8 oz). Larvae grow to maximum length of 20 cm (8 in.).

Remarks   A migratory species which breeds and passes an extended larval life in freshwater and migrates to the sea to feed. Moderately widespread in freshwater, it is encountered most frequently in estuaries and inshore waters, but rarely in any numbers. Often found in the open sea attached to basking sharks, and occasionally to sperm whales. Adults are parasitic on fishes including shad, cod, haddock, and saithe; salmon are also said to be attacked.

The lamprey is now much scarcer in western Europe than it was formerly, and in much of its range today it is rare. Pollution of the

Lamprey

lower reaches of major rivers and the construction of dams and weirs have played a great part in this decline.

The lamprey is not much used for food, although locally it was at one time considered to be a delicacy; its flesh is very rich and oily.

Lampern   *Lampetra fluviatilis*

Distinguishing features   A circular mouth with few distinct and sharply pointed teeth; tooth-plate on the front of the disc with two well-separated teeth, lower (i.e. posterior) tooth-plate with 7–10 pointed cusps. Dorsal fins separate, the second dorsal close to the origin of the tail fin. In adults the eyes are distinct.

Coloration   Uniformly coloured. Live specimens have a delicate greeny-brown back, merging into golden yellow sides, and a whitish belly. Some are leaden grey in colour, dead white ventrally.

Size   Maximum length 50 cm (20 in.); average length *c*. 30 cm (12 in.). Females grow larger than males. Maximum length of larvae 13 cm (5 in.).

Remarks   A migratory lamprey which comes into rivers from the sea in August–November, and in spring in northern rivers. In the sea it appears to live in estuarine and inshore waters. In freshwater the adults are found in rivers and streams; the larvae occur in small brooks.

The lampern has markedly decreased in numbers during historical times. Obstruction of rivers by weirs, navigation locks, and pollution have taken a heavy toll, and in some rivers in which it was once abundant it is now a rare fish. A good food fish, it is fished for locally and eaten fresh or smoked. It is also used as an anglers' bait today.

Brook lamprey   *Lampetra planeri*

Distinguishing features   Circular mouth complete but with weak blunt teeth, the tooth-plate in front smooth, the posterior plate in the oral disc with 5–9 weak, rounded cusps. The dorsal fins are joined at their bases and weakly so to the tail fin. The eyes are rather large and clearly visible in adults.

Coloration   Dark brown above, sometimes almost slate grey, shading to yellowish or white on the underside.

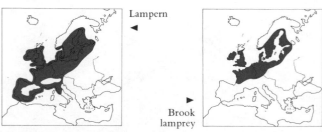

Lampern ◀

▶ Brook lamprey

Petromyzon marinus
lamprey

Lampetra fluviatilis
lampern

Lampetra planeri
brook lamprey larva

Lampetra planeri
sexually mature ♂

sucker discs

P. marinus

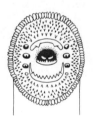

E. danfordi

L. fluviatilis

L. planeri

Size Attains 25 cm (9¾ in.), occasionally larger. Maximum length of larvae 12 cm (4½ in.).

Remarks A non-migratory lamprey living in small streams and the upper reaches of rivers. It is rarely, if ever, found in large rivers or close to the sea. The larvae are usually found buried in rich organic mud and among the roots of emergent vegetation; they feed on minute organisms filtered from the mud. Adults do not feed. Probably the most common lamprey in northern Europe.

Danubian lampern *Eudontomyzon danfordi*

Distinguishing features The circular mouth is well supplied with small teeth; the most anterior tooth-plate with two sharp cusps, well separated from one another; the posterior tooth-plate broadly curved with large cusps. The lingual tooth-plate has numerous small cusps and a large cusp in the mid-line. The body is deepest anterior to the dorsal fins which are not joined together.

Coloration Light golden brown above, fading to yellowish on the belly.

Size Adults attain a length of 30 cm (11¾ in.); larvae grow to about 19 cm (7½ in.).

Remarks Found only in the head waters of the river Danube and its tributaries. The adults are found in the lower reaches of tributary rivers but migrate upstream to spawn. The larvae are confined to the small brooks and streams especially in muddy bottoms. The adults are parasitic on fishes (mainly bullhead, loach, and salmonid young) which share its small-river habitat. The parasitic stages last only a few months.

Hagfishes

Hagfishes are one of the two living families (Myxinidae) of the superclass AGNATHA, which is well known from fossils. They are primitive fishes which lack vertebrae, jaws, true fin rays, paired fins, and scales. The mouth is a slit surrounded by fleshy barbels but with a toothed tongue. Some species at least are hermaphrodite.

They are all marine, occurring in temperate and tropical oceans. One species lives in northern European seas.

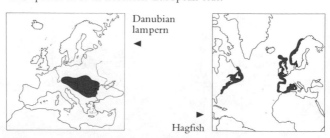

Danubian
lampern
◄

►
Hagfish

Eudontomyzon danfordi
Danubian lampern

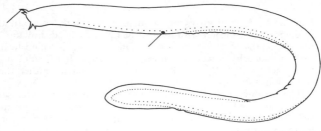

Myxine glutinosa
hagfish

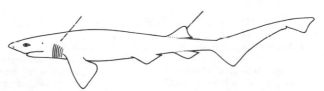

Hexanchus griseus
six-gilled shark

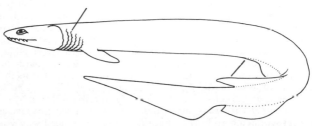

Chlamydoselachus anguineus
frilled shark

Distinguishing features Eel-like but without eyes, jaws, gill covers, pectoral or pelvic fins; the body exceptionally slimy. The mouth is a narrow slit with fleshy, broad-based barbels, the anterior pair flanking the single nostril in the mid-line. A pair of ventral gill openings, placed well along the trunk; the left one is larger than, and posterior to, the other.

Coloration Pale flesh pink. Occasionally brown or greyish above, pink below.

Size Maximum attained 60 cm (24 in.). Usually around 38 cm (15 in.).

Remarks A bottom-living animal, found only on muddy grounds usually buried with merely the tip of the head showing. It lives in depths of 20–600 m (11–328 fathoms), but is found in the shallower depths only in the north of its range. It is confined to water below 13°C (56°F). Its distribution is patchy rather than continuous.

The hagfish is known to eat bottom-living invertebrates (crustaceans—which are its principal food, and polychaete worms) and also scavenges on dead fish, but is well known for attacking and boring into the tissues of fishes caught in set nets, traps, or on long-lines. Where hagfish are common, fishing by such methods may be impractical owing to the damaged catch.

Sharks

A group of rather primitively organized fishes which differ from the bony fishes in a number of ways. Sharks have a cartilaginous skeleton, lack true bones and thus fin rays (although some have a hard spine in each dorsal fin). The tail fin is asymmetrical, the upper lobe always being well developed. The skin is covered with dermal denticles, tooth-like structures with the base buried leaving the often sharply-pointed cusp sloping backwards. These denticles give sharks' skin its characteristic rough feel. All sharks have a series of gill slits each side of the back of the head varying in number from 5 (most species) to 6 or 7. The jaws are well equipped with teeth which lie in rows, one behind the other, each row gradually moving towards the front of the jaw to replace teeth damaged or worn in use. Most sharks have sharply pointed teeth, with a keen edge, but some, for example, the smooth hounds, which feed on hard-shelled organisms such as crustaceans, have blunt and rounded teeth.

Fertilization of the egg in all sharks is internal. The male possesses a pair of claspers placed on the inner edges of the pelvic fins by which spermatozoa are transmitted to the female. A number of species lay eggs within a hard horny case; the majority produce living young. Most are ovoviviparous, but a few species are viviparous.

Some 15 species occur commonly in the shallow seas of northern Europe; at least as many more live in deep water.

COW SHARKS

A family (Hexanchidae) of sharks showing many primitive features. They are world-wide in distribution and most common in deep water. All are rather elongate in body form with 6 or 7 pairs of gill slits (most sharks have 5 pairs), a single dorsal fin, a long tail fin, and the teeth in the lower jaw with several parallel cusps, giving them a comb-like appearance.

There are possibly 6 species included in the family; 1 only occurs in northern European seas.

Six-gilled shark   *Hexanchus griseus*

Distinguishing features   Six long gill slits each side which do not run under the throat. The body is relatively slender, and the upper lobe of the tail elongate, but the head is broad and the snout blunt. The single dorsal fin is placed far back, close to the tail.

Coloration   Dark brown or grey above, lighter ventrally.

Size   Maximum length 5 m (16 ft), average length *c*. 1.5–1.8 m (5–6 ft).

Remarks   A relatively uncommon midwater shark found in the warmer parts of its range in depths of 200–1000 m (109–547 fathoms), but in the cooler regions venturing nearer the surface. Mainly an open-ocean species, it is caught occasionally in inshore waters, and rarely close to the shore.

An indiscriminate predator which eats a wide range of fish (including haddock, hake, anglerfish, dab, and spurdog), crustaceans, and on one reported occasion a seal.

Ovoviviparous; the young are born at a length of *c*. 60 cm (24 in.), in litters ranging from 47–108 in number depending on the size of the female.

FRILLED SHARK

A primitive shark family (Chlamydoselachidae) which has one living representative, the rather slender-bodied frilled shark. It is possibly world-wide in the deep temperate seas but has been captured only in the North Pacific, North Atlantic, and off South

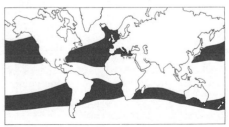

Six-gilled shark

Africa. Among its primitive features are the loose attachment of the lower jaw to the cranium, and the fact that only the first 3–4 vertebrae are calcified.

| Frilled shark | *Chlamydoselachus anguineus* |

Distinguishing features An extremely elongate shark which has small, low dorsal and anal fins opposite one another, and a rather long tail. The 6 gill slits are large and anteriorly are continuous under the throat. The teeth are three-pointed, in well-spaced rows, in large jaws.

Coloration Dark brown, or grey-brown, slightly paler ventrally.

Size Females attain a length of 191 cm (6 ft 3 in.), males 165 cm (5 ft 5 in.).

Remarks An uncommon shark living mostly in mid-water and just above the bottom in 120–1100 m (66–600 fathoms). It is ovoviviparous, the young being born in litters of up to 12. The eggs are large, and the embryo has a large yolk-sac by which it is nourished for the 12-month gestation period. Believed to be 60 cm (24 in.) at birth.

MACKEREL SHARKS

Sharks belonging to the family (Lamnidae), a group of large, dangerous, or potentially dangerous sharks. All have stout muscular, streamlined bodies, with a high lobed tail fin (such a fin is characteristic of a powerful swimming fish). These sharks have a body temperature higher than that of the surrounding water, which is also an adaptation to more powerful swimming, and a feature they share only with the spearfishes and the tunnies.

The family is world-wide in its distribution in tropical, warm temperate, and seasonally in temperate seas. It includes the man-eater or great white shark, *Carcharodon carcharias*, a species which does not occur in northern European waters. There have been no verified reports of unprovoked attacks on man by either of the 2 members of the family which do occur, although both should be regarded as potentially dangerous.

Frilled
shark

Porbeagle   *Lamna nasus*

Distinguishing features   A large round-bodied and thickset shark, with 5 moderately large gill slits. The first dorsal fin originates above the pectoral fin base; the second, which is comparatively small, lies above the equally small anal fin. A strong keel on the sides of the tail, with a smaller shorter keel beneath it at the base of the lower tail fin lobe. Teeth large and triangular with a small cusp each side at the base.

Coloration   Deep blue or greyish-blue on the back, merging gradually into pale cream on the underside. The rear edges of the dorsal fins pale.

Size   Maximum length *c*. 3 m (10 ft), and weight *c*. 226.5 kg (500 lb). The average length for British waters appears to be around 1.8–2.4 m (6–8 ft).

Remarks   A shark of the surface layers of the open ocean, it is widely distributed throughout northern European seas. It is common except towards the north of the area and in the shallower seas such as the North Sea.

It eats a wide range of surface-living and demersal fish of varying kinds. At times, it also feeds heavily on squids. It is extensively fished for with floating long-lines west of Ireland; the flesh is popular as food in Europe.

Ovoviviparous, litters of 1 to 5 have been reported. The late embryos frequently have massive yolk-filled stomachs owing to their having consumed unfertilized eggs within the oviduct. The young are born at a length of 50–60 cm ($19\frac{1}{2}$–24 in.).

Mako   *Isurus oxyrinchus*

Distinguishing features   A large shark with a rather slender shape and pointed snout. The first dorsal fin is placed vertically above the rear edge of the pectoral fin base; the small second dorsal fin origin lies in front of the anal origin. A strong keel either side of the tail, but no smaller secondary keel at the base of the lower tail fin lobe. Jaw teeth long, narrow and triangular, those on the lower jaw hanging forward clear of the lips; no basal cusps.

Coloration   Deep blue, or blue-grey with a sharp transition to the snowy white underside.

Porbeagle

9

Size Maximum length 4 m (13 ft), and weight *c.* 454 kg (1000 lb). Average in northern European waters *c.* 3 m (9 ft 9 in.) and 227 kg (500 lb).

Remarks A surface-living shark of the open ocean which only very rarely comes inshore round the British Isles. Mostly confined to the upper 20 m (11 fathoms) of the sea. Probably only a summertime visitor to northern European seas, and not common.

Eats surface-living schooling fish, mackerel, pilchard, and herring, as well as squids. In tropical waters feeds on a wide range of often large fishes, and is reputed to be dangerous to man.

Known to be ovoviviparous; an embryo of 50 cm (19½ in.) with an enormously swollen, yolk-filled stomach has been described. Not known to breed in northern European waters.

BASKING SHARK

The single member of this family (Cetorhinidae) is the basking shark, a large shark of world-wide distribution in the temperate and cool-temperate oceans. It is the second largest living fish (the largest being the whale shark, *Rhincodon typus*, a tropical species); both are plankton eaters.

Basking shark   *Cetorhinus maximus*

Distinguishing features It is distinguished by the five enormously large gill slits which occupy the whole of the sides and throat. The teeth are minute, closely set, and flattened, and the gill arches are set with long thin gill rakers (but see Remarks p. 12).

Coloration Back greyish-brown, sometimes nearly black, lighter brown vertically with grey blotches anteriorly.

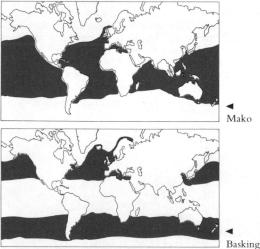

◄ Mako

◄ Basking shark

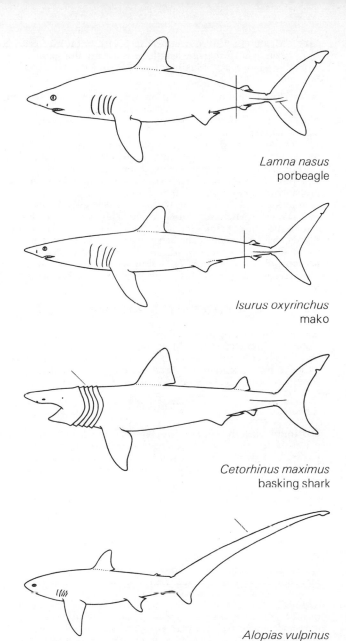

Lamna nasus
porbeagle

Isurus oxyrinchus
mako

Cetorhinus maximus
basking shark

Alopias vulpinus
thresher

Size Maximum proven length 11 m (35 ft), but it may grow to
13 m (42 ft 6 in.); average length in northern European seas is
around 7.6 m (25 ft). Maximum weight of 3000 kg (3 tons) is
estimated.

Remarks Found mainly at the surface off open ocean coasts and
far out to sea. Records of its occurrence are more numerous in
summer; it may therefore be migratory. Usually seen singly, but
occasionally in large schools.

It feeds by swimming around with its mouth wide open, sieving
the water of whatever planktonic animal life is locally abundant.

Little is known of its breeding habits. It is probably ovoviviparous. Gestation may last for $3\frac{1}{2}$ years and the young are
probably around 152 cm (5 ft) at birth.

In European waters at least, the characteristic gill rakers are shed
each winter, regenerating during spring. This may be a response to
seasonal decline of plankton during the winter months, and implies
that the shark hibernates. The basking shark has at times been fished
for locally on the Irish, Scottish, and Norwegian coasts, mostly by
harpooning or in large nets. These fisheries have never flourished or
continued for long, possibly because local stocks were exhausted or
driven away.

THRESHER SHARK

A small family (Alopiidae) of sharks, known from all the oceans in
tropical and temperate seas. Most are found in the open ocean but
occasionally come into shallow inshore waters. All are characterized
by an enormously long tail. Probably only three or four species
comprise this family; only one is known in northern European seas.

Thresher   *Alopias vulpinus*

Distinguishing features Tail fin very long, the upper lobe
equals the length of the body. The snout is short and rounded; the
teeth are small and triangular. The rather high first dorsal fin is
entirely in front of the vertical from the pelvic fin origin.

Coloration Grey-blue to nearly black on the back, white
ventrally except for the grey underside of the snout and pectoral
fins.

Size Maximum length 6 m (20 ft), more usually 3–4 m (10–
13 ft). Weight up to *c.* 127 kg (280 lb).

Remarks A surface-living shark found mostly offshore, although
occasionally coming into coastal waters. Feeds especially on
schooling fishes and squids, which it is said to herd together by
means of its tail before attacking. Specimens examined have proved
to contain large numbers of mackerel, herring, and garfish;
members of the herring family are its most common prey.

From 2–4 pups are born at a time; it is ovoviviparous. The young
are approximately 1.5 m (5 ft) at birth; the gestation period is not
known. This shark probably matures at around 4 m (13 ft).

The thresher is a rather uncommon shark in northern European waters, but it chiefly occurs along the open ocean coasts. It is reported most frequently in the summer months in British waters, which may be a result of a northwards, summertime migration. Young, evidently newly born, are occasionally captured at this season and in the autumn.

DOGFISHES

The dogfishes belong to one of the largest families of sharks (Scyliorhinidae) which comprises about 60 species. Most are small, shallow-water sharks with two dorsal fins placed towards the tail, and a long tail fin. Their build accords with their bottom-living life style. All lay eggs in brown, leathery purses, in many species with long tendrils at the corners with which they are anchored to algae or fixed objects. Many are boldly marked or coloured, including the 3 northern European species.

Dogfish   *Scyliorhinus canicula*

Distinguishing features   A small shark the tail of which is long and low, the lower lobe of the tail fin scarcely developed. The dorsal fins lie far down the back; the origin of the first is behind the pelvic fin base. The nostrils are concealed by broad flaps which are separated from one another by only a small gap; the internal nasal flap on the outer edge of the nostril is pointed.

Coloration   Back and sides sandy brown with small dark brown spots; the underside is cream coloured.

Size   Rarely grows to a length of 1 m (39 in.); more usually 60–70 cm (24–27 in.). Weights of 1.72 kg (3 lb 12 oz) are about maximal.

Remarks   A common bottom-living shark which occurs in depths of 3 to 110 m (2–60 fathoms), and less commonly down to 400 m (218 fathoms). It inhabits sandy bottoms, fine gravel and even mud. The young and newly-hatched fish are found in the shallowest depths.

The dogfish eats a very large range of bottom-living invertebrates. Its principal food consists of crustaceans including various crabs and shrimps, molluscs especially whelks, and polychaete worms. Some, mainly bottom-living, fishes are eaten.

Thresher

Dogfish

The eggs are individually enclosed in an elongate rounded capsule with slender tendrils at each corner by which they are anchored to algae or other solid structures. Reproduction continues throughout the year, but egg-laying takes place in shallow water mainly between November and July, The young hatch at a length of about 10 cm (4 in.), incubation lasts for 5 to 11 months, and sexual maturity is attained at a length of about 50 cm (20 in.).

The dogfish is an extremely common fish around the British Isles and in the seas of Europe. At times it occurs in large numbers in the catch of trawlers and it is common to find only one sex present in even large schools. The dogfish, although at one time valueless to the fisherman, is now marketed in England as 'flake' or 'rock eel' and forms a small but valuable fishery. It is occasionally caught by anglers.

Nursehound   *Scyliorhinus stellaris*

Distinguishing features   Closely resembles the common dog-fish, but the first dorsal fin is set vertically above the base of the pelvic fins. A large, broad flap covers each nostril but does not reach the upper lip; the nostrils are separated by a broad interspace. The inner nasal flap is broad.

Coloration   The back and sides are sandy brown or greyish-brown with large rounded dark brown blotches. The underside is creamy-white, but with dusky edges to the lobes of the tail and anal fins. The dark blotches are very variable in size and number; almost totally black specimens have been described.

Size   Attains a length of 152 cm (60 in.), average about 120 cm (47 in.) and a maximum weight of about 9.5 kg (21 lb).

Remarks   A bottom-living shark which is found in 1–2 m down to 63 m (35 fathoms), and occasionally deeper. It usually lives on rough or rocky grounds.

It eats a wide variety of invertebrates especially crustaceans and molluscs, and bottom-living fishes.

The eggs are enclosed in oblong smoothly rounded cases, 10–13 cm (4–5 in.) in length, each with a long curled tendril at the corners. They are deposited mainly in spring and summer, among algae around which the tendrils twine. The young take 9 months to develop and measure about 16 cm (6½ in.) at hatching.

The nursehound is the least abundant dogfish, and is common only

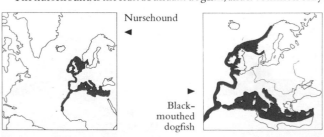

Nursehound

◄

►

Black-
mouthed
dogfish

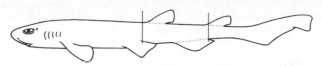

Scyliorhinus canicula
dogfish

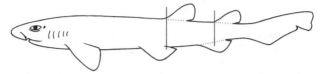

Scyliorhinus stellaris
nursehound

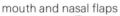

mouth and nasal flaps

S. canicula

S. stellaris

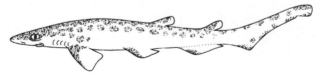

Galeus melastomus
black-mouthed dogfish

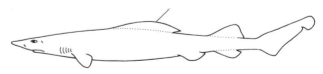

Pseudotriakis microdon
false catshark

to the south of the area. It is occasionally captured by anglers, but more often by commercial fishermen. It is also known as the bull huss and greater spotted dogfish.

Black-mouthed dogfish   *Galeus melastomus*

Distinguishing features   Snout rather broad and flattened, slightly pointed. Dorsal fins small and of equal size, the tail fin long. Nostrils with a flap, but widely separated, and spaced away from the mouth. A roughened ridge of large denticles along the back of the tail.

Coloration   Back a warm brown with rounded, large dark brown blotches, extending as a regular pattern down the sides. Ventrally creamy-brown; inside of the mouth black.

Size   Grows to 75 cm (30 in.); average length 45–65 cm (17½–25 in.).

Remarks   A bottom-living dogfish found on the upper edge of the continental slope. Most common in 200–500 m (109–273 fathoms), rarely captured in water as shallow as 55 m (30 fathoms).

Mostly shrimps and prawns are eaten, but some fish remains have been found in the stomach of this species. Lantern fish have been recorded, which suggests that it forages off the sea-bed.

The eggs are laid in summer in smooth, elongate light brown cases which have short horns at one end. The egg-case measures 6 by 3 cm (2½ by 1¼ in.). Females with up to 13 eggs have been found.

FALSE CATSHARK

A family (Pseudotriakidae) of little-known deep-water sharks, members of which have been found in the North Atlantic, North Pacific, and south-west Indian Oceans. Two species have been recognized, both rather stout-bodied, and with extremely long, low dorsal fins. One species occurs in northern European seas in deep water on the continental slope; it has been regarded, probably mistakenly, as rare.

False catshark   *Pseudotriakis microdon*

Distinguishing features   A rather heavy-bodied, large, deep-water shark which has an extremely long-based, low first dorsal fin.

False catshark

The second dorsal is similar but shorter. The teeth are minute, in closely packed mosaic rows.

Coloration   Uniformly dark brown or greyish-brown.

Size   Attains a maximum length of 3 m (9 ft 10 in.).

Remarks   A bottom-living shark found only in deep water between 300 and 1477 m (164–807 fathoms). Very exceptionally, specimens occur in inshore waters (twice on the American coast).

Live-bearing, producing two young in a litter. Young at birth are at least 85 cm (33½ in.). Females with very young embryos have been found off the Irish coast in July.

Recorded only very rarely and, until recent deep-water trawling, known only from about a dozen specimens. Experimental trawling below 500 m (273 fathoms) has resulted in a number of specimens being captured and shows that this shark is well distributed along the lower continental shelf off the British Isles. This shark is probably widely distributed in deep water in the North Atlantic.

REQUIEM SHARKS

This is the largest family (Carcharinidae) of living sharks with possibly 80–100 members. They are most abundant in tropical and warm temperate seas; those which occur in temperate seas (two only in northern Europe) are often seasonal migrants. They are all typical sharks with slender bodies, long tail fins (the upper lobe being much the longer), and five gill slits. All have sharp, triangular teeth and are entirely predatory; several species are known to be dangerous to man. Members of the family are active swimmers and are found in inshore coastal waters and on the high seas.

Tope	*Galeorhinus galeus*

Distinguishing features   A slender-bodied small shark, with a moderate first dorsal fin, but small second dorsal opposite and similar to the anal fin in size and shape. The teeth are triangular and sharply pointed. In the sides of the jaws they are oblique, with serrations on the shorter edge; in the centre of the jaws they are upright and serrated each side.

Coloration   Uniformly grey, or greyish-brown on the sides and back, white ventrally. The outer margin of the pectoral fin is light on the dorsal surface.

Tope

17

Size   Maximum length 1.67 m (5 ft 6 in.) and a weight of 33.9 kg (74 lb). A length of 1.2 m (48 in.) is more usual.

Remarks   The tope is found in shallow water, small specimens near to the shore and others down to 200 m (109 fathoms). Usually it lives in small schools, close to the bottom, although when actively feeding it is found in mid-water. It is seasonally migratory in northern waters.

This fish eats a wide range of small schooling fishes, especially whiting, pouting, and cod. It also feeds on bottom-living fishes, crustaceans, and echinoderms.

The tope is a live-bearing (ovoviviparous) shark. Between 20 and 40 pups form a litter; the number increases with the size of the mother. The young are born in late summer after the mother has moved into shallow water. They are 40 cm (15 in.) long at birth. Gestation lasts around 10 months.

Tope are a relatively popular quarry for the sea angler. Small specimens can be eaten, and their flesh is similar to the dogfishes, but large tope are rank-smelling and tough. Many of the tope caught in inshore waters are gravid females, and heavy exploitation close to shore might seriously affect the stock of this shark.

Blue shark   *Prionace glauca*

Distinguishing features   A long slender-bodied shark with a well-developed upper lobe to the tail and very long, curved pectoral fins. The snout is long and sharply pointed; there are 5 gill slits and it has no spiracle. The teeth are pointed, slightly oblique, and have serrated edges. (See also coloration.)

Coloration   The back and upper sides are a deep indigo blue, the sides clear blue, and the ventral surface white. After death this beautiful blue colouring fades to grey.

Size   It attains a maximum length of 3.83 m (12 ft 7 in.), but in European waters is usually around 2.7 m (9 ft). A maximum weight of 151 kg (333 lb) is recorded, but in European waters few weigh as much as 90 kg (200 lb).

Remarks   A surface-living shark of the open sea. It makes seasonal migrations with summertime warming of the sea which bring it into inshore waters (but not close inshore) in northern Europe.

Feeds on a wide range of fishes, mostly near-surface schooling fish

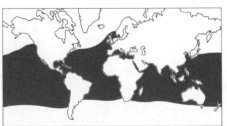

Blue shark

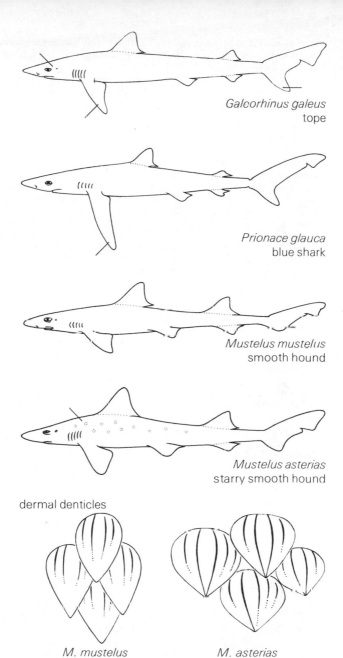

Galeorhinus galeus
tope

Prionace glauca
blue shark

Mustelus mustelus
smooth hound

Mustelus asterias
starry smooth hound

dermal denticles

M. mustelus

M. asterias

such as mackerel, herring, and pilchard. Squids of various kinds are an important part of its diet. It also follows fishing boats and feeds on discarded offal and unwanted fish.

Gives birth to live young; the embryos have a yolk-sac placental connection to the maternal uterus. Litters as large as 63 have been reported, but the number is dependent on the size of the mother. Very rarely, gravid blue sharks are caught in British waters. The young are 38–46 cm (15–18 in.) long at birth.

The blue shark is abundant offshore in the western Channel in summertime. Sport fishermen catch some 3000–5000 annually in British and southern Irish waters. They move north-eastwards during early summer, entering the Channel in June where they will be found until about the end of September. The northward migration takes them in some years into western Scottish waters in July-August, and occasionally to southern Norway and into the northern North Sea. Rarely, individuals are found as far south as eastern Scotland and Yorkshire in late summer and early winter.

The great majority of blue sharks in the north-eastern Atlantic are females; males occur in a proportion of *c.* 1:5000 in the Channel fishery. Most of the sharks are immature females. A small proportion are adults which have given birth to young, presumably in southern waters.

SMOOTH HOUNDS

A small family (Triakidae) of sharks, members of which are found in both temperate and tropical seas. They are slender-bodied, with large, broad fins, 5 gill slits, and flattened teeth arranged in rows to form a crushing mill; food is mainly crustaceans. Most are small fish and none is dangerous to man. All the members of the family bear living young, although the details of their development vary from species to species.

Two smooth hounds occur in northern European seas.

Smooth hound   *Mustelus mustelus*

Distinguishing features   A slender-bodied shark with 5 gill slits and a small spiracle each side, and 2 moderately large dorsal fins. The teeth are blunt and flattened, and lie in the jaws in a mosaic pattern. The dermal denticles (skin teeth) are relatively narrow with basal ridges but smooth ends. Nasal flaps are broad. (See also coloration.)

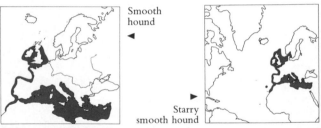

Smooth
hound
◄

►
Starry
smooth hound

Coloration   Back and sides plain grey, no noticeable white spots; ventrally creamy-white. Occasionally black blotches on back.

Size   Grows to a maximum length of 1.6 m (5 ft 3 in.), more usually between 1 m and 1.2 m (39–48 in.).

Remarks   Shallow water, from near the shoreline down to depths of 100 m (55 fathoms); most common in 5–50 m (3–27 fathoms). It is mainly bottom-living and only occasionally found in mid-water.

It eats crustaceans, including hermit crabs within their adopted mollusc shell, small edible crabs, shore crabs, and squat lobsters.

Viviparous; the embryo is nourished through a pseudoplacenta formed by the yolk-sac membrane connected to its mother. Litters of up to 15 are known, the young being about 30 cm (12 in.) in length at birth.

A rather uncommon shark in northern European waters which has only relatively recently been distinguished from the more common *M. asterias.*

Much of the information compiled by earlier biologists could have applied to either species.

Starry smooth hound   *Mustelus asterias*

Distinguishing features   A moderately slender-bodied shark with 5 gill slits and a small spiracle each side, and moderately large dorsal fins. The teeth are blunt and flattened and lie in a mosaic pattern in the jaw. Dermal denticles are broad and weakly ridged except towards the tips where the ridges (in large specimens) may wear completely. Nasal flaps are rather narrow. (See also coloration.)

Coloration   Grey above and on the upper sides, sprinkled with small white (star-like) spots. Ventrally creamy-white.

Size   Grows to a maximum length of 1.8 m (6 ft); the average length is near 1.2 m (4 ft).

Remarks   An inshore species usually found close to the sea-bed at least as deep as 70 m (38 fathoms). It seems to be most common on sand and gravel grounds.

The starry smooth hound feeds almost entirely on crustaceans including hermit crabs, edible crabs, and shore crabs, small lobsters and squat lobsters. Even hermit crabs living in whelk shells are eaten, and the remains of the commensal anemone, *Adamsia,* the mollusc shell and hermit crab have been found in the sharks' gut.

Ovoviviparous; the embryos develop within their mother, nourished by the yolk of the egg. There is no connection with the maternal membranes. Litter size varies between 7 and 15 (depending on the size of the mother); the young are about 30 cm (12 in.) at birth. The period of gestation is approximately 12 months. The young are born in summer in relatively shallow water.

The starry smooth hound is a common shark in inshore waters around the British Isles and as far north as Denmark. It is caught fairly frequently by inshore trawlers and by sea anglers.

HAMMERHEADED SHARKS

The hammerheads form a small family (Sphyrnidae) of about 10 species which all have the distinguishing hammer-like head, the sides of the head being greatly expanded with the eyes on the outer edge. They are all tropical and warm temperate marine sharks which seasonally venture into cooler waters. One species only has been reported in northern European seas, and that rarely.

The function of the distinctively shaped head is not properly explained. It has been suggested that the wide spacing of the nostrils and eyes might enhance their sensory abilities, and that the hammer head acts as a 'bow rudder' to give lift to the shark's front end when swimming.

Smooth hammerhead   *Sphyrna zygaena*

Distinguishing features   Head developed with flattened, laterally projecting 'hammer' lobes either side, with the eyes on the outer edges and the nostrils spread far apart. The front edge of the snout is smoothly rounded with notches at the level of the nostrils.

Coloration   A deep olive brown or greyish-brown above, light grey ventrally; the edges of the fins dusky.

Size   Grows to 4 m (13 ft).

Remarks   Recorded 5 times in the present century in northern European waters, and at least 7 times in the 19th century. Its status is clearly that of an extremely rare accidental vagrant from the south.

SPINY SHARKS

Representatives of 2 families of sharks (Oxynotidae and Squalidae) are distinguished by the possession of a strong spine in the front of each dorsal fin and by the lack of an anal fin. These families are widely distributed in the world's seas, mostly in the deep sea, although the spurdogs are common in shallow water on the continental shelf. The oxynotids are deep-bodied sharks with coarse spines in their skins and are distinguished by the large number of rows of teeth functional in the upper jaw. The squalids are more slender-bodied and although the skin has a rough feel, the dermal denticles are not spiny. One member of the family Oxynotidae and

Smooth
hammerhead

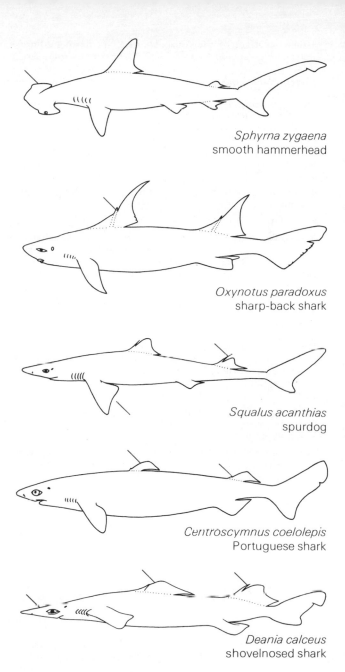

Sphyrna zygaena
smooth hammerhead

Oxynotus paradoxus
sharp-back shark

Squalus acanthias
spurdog

Centroscymnus coelolepis
Portuguese shark

Deania calceus
shovelnosed shark

8 representatives of the Squalidae occur in northern European waters; others are found in the deeper waters of the eastern Atlantic.

Sharp-back shark   *Oxynotus paradoxus*

Distinguishing features   A deep-bodied, solid-looking shark, with a high back and flattened belly giving the body a triangular cross-section. The head is small, with large spiracles, and 5 gill slits. No anal fin, the tail and dorsal fins are large and broad, and each dorsal has a strong spine running close to the front edge. The spine in both fins slopes backwards. Dermal denticles large and thorn-like.

Coloration   Dark brown on the back, slightly lighter ventrally. The inner edge of the spiracle is light.

Size   Grows to 90 cm (35 in.).

Remarks   Bottom-living on the lower continental shelf in depths of 350–600 m (191–328 fathoms), exceptionally as shallow as 92 m (50 fathoms). Recent exploration in deep water to the west of the British Isles has shown that it occurs frequently, although never in great abundance, along most of the upper slope. It is ovoviviparous, the young being born alive at a length of *c.* 25 cm (10 in.).

Spurdog   *Squalus acanthias*

Distinguishing features   The spurdog is distinguished as the only common small shark which has a spine at the front of both dorsal fins, and which lacks an anal fin. The fin spines are large, the second standing clear of the fin. Its body shape is slender with a pointed snout, large eyes, and moderate-sized spiracles.

Coloration   Dark grey above, with scattered white spots over the back and sides, forming fairly regular series on the mid-side. Ventrally lighter.

Size   Attains a maximum length of about 122 cm (48 in.), rarely in excess of 100–110 cm (39–43 in.). A maximum weight of around 9 kg (20 lb) is reached, but the normal weight is 6.3–6.8 kg (14–15 lb). Females grow longer and heavier than males.

Remarks   Found near sea-bed on soft bottoms from 10–200 m (5–110 fathoms), exceptionally down to 951 m (520 fathoms), and also near the surface. Probably it approaches the surface at night.

Sharp-back
shark
◄

►
Spurdog

Feeds on schooling fishes such as herring, sprat, pilchard, sandeels, whiting, and garfish. It also eats bottom-living species such as cod, dragonets, and flatfishes, and invertebrates including squids and crabs.

Live-bearing, the spurdog is ovoviviparous. The litter size ranges from 3–11. The pups are from 20–33 cm (8–13 in.) at birth. Both size and number at birth vary with the size of the mother. Gestation lasts between 18 and 22 months. Males become mature at 55–61 cm (22–24 in.) in length; females vary from 75–80 cm (30–31 in.).

The spurdog is a very common fish in the coastal and offshore waters of northern Europe. Typically it is encountered in large to very large, unisexual schools. Formerly this shark was regarded as a nuisance or a pest because of the damage it caused in nets and to hooked fishes, but in the present century it was caught first for the sake of its liver oil (for its liver is very large) and later for fish meal. More recently the increased demand for 'flake' for human consumption has lead to valuable fisheries. The spurdog is also caught in numbers by anglers.

Owing to the long gestation period and the rather large size at which maturity is reached, the spurdog is liable to suffer from overfishing. The level of exploitation, whether by commercial fishermen or by anglers, needs to be regulated if the size of the stock is to be maintained.

Portuguese shark   *Centroscymnus coelolepis*

Distinguishing features   The spines in the dorsal fins are so small as to be almost completely enclosed in tissue, and easily overlooked. Snout rather blunt and rounded, the body thickset and solid, and both dorsal fins relatively small; no anal fin. Upper jaw teeth have a single, erect, dagger-like cusp, the lower teeth oblique; body covered with broad, smooth denticles.

Coloration   A deep chocolate brown.

Size   Grows to 130 cm (51 in.); males rarely exceed 100 cm (39 in.).

Remarks   A deep-water shark found from 329–2718 m (154–1486 fathoms), but most commonly between 400 and 2000 m (219–1094 fathoms). Mainly bottom-living, although occasional specimens occur in mid-water.

The remains of lantern fishes, smooth-head, silver smelt, blue

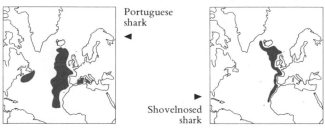

Portuguese
shark
◄

►
Shovelnosed
shark

whiting, and deep-water squids have been found in the gut. Ovoviviparous, the females have litters of up to 18 young. Large nearly full-term embryos have been found in females in early summer off the Scottish coast. Recent deep trawling has shown that off the western coasts of Ireland and Scotland this shark is moderately common, but that it lives mainly in depths below the lower limit of commercial fishing.

Shovelnosed shark *Deania calceus*

Distinguishing features A slender shark lacking an anal fin, and having a long, slender spine in front of each dorsal fin. The snout is characteristic, long and flattened from above; its length from mouth to tip is more than the length from mouth to pectoral fin.

Coloration A pale, rather dull grey.

Size Females grow to 117 cm (46 in.), and weigh about 5.25 kg (11 lb 8 oz); males are smaller, attaining only 91 cm (36 in.).

Remarks Essentially a deep-water shark which is found on the continental slope between 600 and 1450 m (328–782 fathoms), although also occasionally found up to 400 m (219 fathoms). The shovelnosed shark lives on the bottom and possibly at night in mid-water. The remains of mackerel, scad, blue whiting, lantern fishes and other mid-water fishes have been found in the gut of this shark. It also eats cephalopods and shrimps.

This shark is ovoviviparous; off the Irish coast the young are born in early summer. Gestation probably lasts at least a year. A litter may be as many as 17 pups, each around 25 cm (10 in.) in length at birth; 10–12 per litter is more usual.

This is the most abundant of the larger deep-water sharks in the eastern North Atlantic. At appropriate depths catches of up to 100 can be made in a short trawl haul. The schools are usually sexually segregated; catches mostly consist of one sex. This shark becomes more common to the south of the British Isles, but is by no means rare even off southern Iceland and the Faroes. It is possible that this shark is also found in both the North and South Pacific Ocean.

Velvet-belly *Etmopterus spinax*

Distinguishing features A small shark distinguished by having

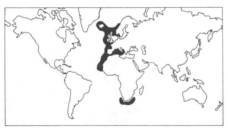

Velvet-belly

sharp spines at the front of each dorsal fin, that on the second fin the larger. Pectoral fins small and rounded. No anal fin. The dermal denticles are very fine, giving the skin a velvety feel. Gill openings small. (See also coloration.)

Coloration Dark brown, fading on the sides to grey-brown with a distinct greenish-black line along the lower side and dark on the belly. Small luminous raised pores on the skin.

Size Females grow to a total length of 60 cm (23½ in.); males attain a maximum of 50 cm (19¾ in.).

Remarks Living near the bottom on soft muddy grounds in depths of around 100 m (55 fathoms) to the north of its range and to 1000 m (546 fathoms) in the south; most abundant in 200–700 m (110–382 fathoms).

Small lantern fishes and blue whiting, squids and crustaceans have been found in its gut.

A live-bearer, litters vary in size from 6–20, according to the size of the mother. They are 12–14 cm (5–5½ in.) in length at birth, and are born in late winter to spring off the south-western Irish shelf, and through to July or August off the Faroes. Males become mature at about 33 cm (13 in.), females at 36 cm (14 in.). The life span extends to at least 3 years.

This is probably the commonest spiny-finned shark to be found in deep water in the eastern North Atlantic. It lives in large schools (occasional trawl hauls of hundreds have been made). The velvet-belly is also one of the smallest of sharks, and one of the very few sharks known to possess light-organs. Occasional specimens are caught (especially locally in the Norwegian Sea) which have a protruding clump on the dorsal fin or beneath the head. This is due to infestation by a parasitic cirripede (barnacle), *Analasma squalicola*.

Bramble shark
Echinorhinus brucus

Distinguishing features A large shark with 2 very small dorsal fins situated close together and close to the tail fin, which is itself rather large and broad. The skin is covered with rough denticles and scattered, broad-based large thorns. The jaw teeth are oblique with large central cusps, a smaller single cusp in the acute angle, and 2 cusps in the obtuse angle.

Coloration The back and sides are grey or olive brown, often with black spots; the ventral surface is yellowish-white.

Bramble shark

Size   Attains a length of about 2.7 m (9 ft) and a maximum weight of *c*. 152 kg (336 lb).

Remarks   Found close to the bottom in depths of 400–900 m (220–500 fathoms), but occurs very occasionally in shallower water. It is said to eat fishes and crustaceans.

Ovoviviparous; one bramble shark in the Mediterranean weighing 60 kg (132 lb) contained a single embryo of 164 g (5¾ oz), 29.5 cm (11½ in.) in length.

The bramble shark is exceptionally rare in the seas of north-west Europe, and very few specimens have been reported in the present century. In the 19th century there were some 40 records in British waters alone, which suggests that either the species has become scarcer, or that climatic or hydrological conditions were more suitable a century ago.

Darkie Charlie   *Scymnorhinus licha*

Distinguishing features   A relatively slender-bodied shark with 2 small dorsal fins, and no anal fin; no spines in the dorsal fins. The snout is very short and blunt, the nostrils are large, but the spiracles are even larger. Lips thick and fleshy.

Coloration   Dark brown, almost black, with the inner edge of the spiracle and corners of the mouth almost white.

Size   The usual maximum size for females is around 1.50 m (59 in.) and a weight of *c*. 20 kg (44 lb); males are smaller, attaining at the most 1 m (39 in.). A maximum of 1.82 m (72 in.) has been given.

Remarks   Usually lives close to the bottom, but it has been taken in mid-water on the continental slope in 360–1000 m (200–546 fathoms). It feeds heavily on blue whiting, less on ling, black scabbardfish, silver smelt, and occasionally on hake and smoothhead.

This shark is ovoviviparous. The embryos develop in a distinct membranous envelope. Litter sizes vary from 3–9. The young are born at a length of 30 cm (12 in.). Embryos in several developmental stages may be found at any time of the year.

This is a common shark on the lower continental shelf. Like most sharks it forms unisexual shoals; frequently a trawl haul will contain 100 or so males and only 1 or 2 females, or the converse.

Darkie Charlie

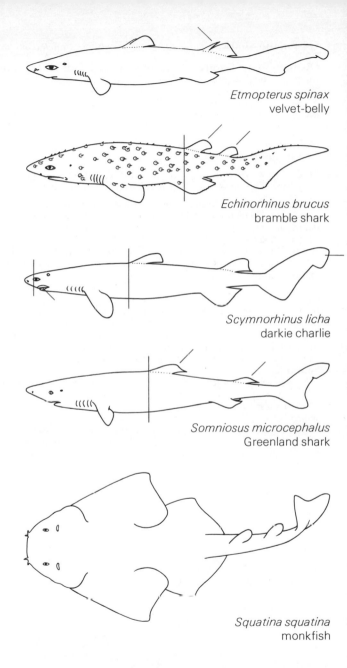

Etmopterus spinax
velvet-belly

Echinorhinus brucus
bramble shark

Scymnorhinus licha
darkie charlie

Somniosus microcephalus
Greenland shark

Squatina squatina
monkfish

Greenland shark   *Somniosus microcephalus*

Distinguishing features   Usually very large, but always with small but well-spaced dorsal fins. The first dorsal fin is placed approximately in the middle of the body. The gill slits are small. Teeth in the upper jaw are small, narrow, and knife-like, in the lower jaw so strongly oblique that the outer side forms the cutting edge.

Coloration   Dark; often deep brown, sometimes greyish with faint indistinct darker bands.

Size   Grows to at least 6.4 m (21 ft) and a weight of 1400 kg (27½ cwt). The maximum length reported is *c.* 8 m (26 ft).

Remarks   Bottom-living, but encountered near the surface especially when attracted by potential food. Most common in depths of *c.* 183–550 m (100–300 fathoms), and sometimes as deep as 1207 m (660 fathoms).

An omnivorous feeder on both pelagic and bottom-living fishes. Among the fish recorded are haddock, saithe, cod, plaice, lumpfish, redfish, catfish, halibut, Greenland halibut, and skate. Numerous molluscs, starfish, and crustaceans have also been reported. The Greenland shark was well known as a scavenger on offal and waste from whaling stations. It also eats other refuse, and one specimen in the Faroes was found to contain the hindquarters of a sheep, part of a pig, a hare, as well as a halibut, and a porbeagle shark. A more sinister report was of one caught near the Isle of May, in January 1895, which contained a seaman's boot complete with part of a human leg!

Live-bearing, but little is known of its breeding biology. A litter of 10 unborn pups has been recorded, each 38 cm (15 in.) in length. The smallest free-swimming specimens were 70 cm (27 in.)—which is likely to be close to their length at birth. The Greenland shark is relatively common in the northern seas of Europe, but around the British Isles it is an uncommon wanderer, becoming even less common to the south. Off Greenland, in the Barents Sea and Norwegian Sea as far south as the Faroes, there were numerous local fisheries for this shark, mainly producing oil from the large liver, but also meat for man, and for dogs in the far north. Most of these fisheries died out before the present century, and this shark has no value today.

Specimens of the Greenland shark frequently suffer from

Greenland shark

infestations of the parasitic copepod, *Lernaeopoda elongata*, which attaches itself to the eye and develops within the cornea.

ANGEL SHARKS

The family (Squatinidae) of the angel sharks, or monkfish, is confined to temperate zones of the world's seas. Most are relatively small, the largest growing to 1.8 m (6 ft), and live close to the sea-bed. Their general appearance is that of fishes midway between sharks and rays, but their laterally sited gill slits, mouth placed at the end of the head, rather than ventrally, and well-developed dorsal and tail fins all place them with the sharks. Only a single species occurs in northern European waters; others are found in the Mediterranean.

Monkfish	*Squatina squatina*

Distinguishing features Body greatly expanded from side to side, the pectoral and pelvic fins broad and lateral. The mouth is wide, with large nostrils each covered with a broad flap.

Coloration Sandy or greyish-brown above, finely dotted with darker markings; white on the underside.

Size Grows to a length of 183 cm (6 ft) and a weight of 32.6 kg (70 lb). Females are generally larger than males.

Remarks A bottom-living fish found on sand or mud in depths of 5–91 m (3–50 fathoms). It lies in perfect concealment usually partially buried, although it can swim powerfully and for relatively long distances off the bottom.

The monkfish feeds very extensively on bottom-living fishes, particularly flatfish such as dab, plaice, and sole, as well as rays and other fishes. Some crustaceans, especially crabs, and molluscs are eaten.

Live-bearing, technically ovoviviparous; litters vary from 9–20, the young are *c.* 24 cm (9½ in.) at birth. In the Mediterranean they are born in February to April, and later in the eastern North Atlantic. It is not known whether this species breeds in northern waters.

The monkfish is a common summertime visitor to the area as a result of northward migration.

Monkfish

Electric Rays

A family of cartilaginous fishes (Torpedinidae) related to the skates and rays, but differing principally in having a smooth skin and thick tail with a well-developed tail fin. Their most distinctive feature is the very well-developed electrical organ which comprises most of each pectoral fin, and which in a large specimen can give a painful and disabling shock.

Electric rays are found in all subtropical and temperate seas, mostly in shallow inshore waters (although a few live in the deep sea). In general they are slow-moving and inoffensive, obtaining their food by stunning other fishes with their electric discharge. Only 2 species are found in northern European waters.

Marbled electric ray   *Torpedo marmorata*

Distinguishing features   Body disc-like, rounded with very smooth skin, a thickset tail, and large, broad tail fin. The dorsal fins are nearly equal in size, and close together so that they almost overlap. Edge of each spiracle with 7 distinct large papillae pointing inwards. (See also coloration.)

Coloration   Deep brown on the back with lighter mottling over the entire upper surface; ventrally cream coloured. Occasionally, in Mediterranean examples, the back is uniformly dark.

Size   Grows to a maximum length of 60 cm (23½ in.), and a weight of 3 kg (6 lb 8½ oz).

Remarks   Entirely benthic and found on sandy and rarely muddy bottoms. Lives in shallow water from 10–30 m (5½–16 fathoms); in the Mediterranean, recorded down to 100 m (55 fathoms). Is known to eat three-bearded rockling and whiting, but most suitably-sized, bottom-living fish are potential prey.

Ovoviviparous, the female gives birth to litters of 5–8 at a maternal length of 32 cm (12½ in.), up to 32 at 50 cm (19¾ in.). This species is not known to breed in northern waters.

The marbled electric ray is not common in northern European waters, but it has been reported on numerous occasions. Most occurrences have been in the western Channel and southern North Sea, and most have been found in summer or autumn, which suggests that there is a northward migration earlier in the year.

Marbled electric ray

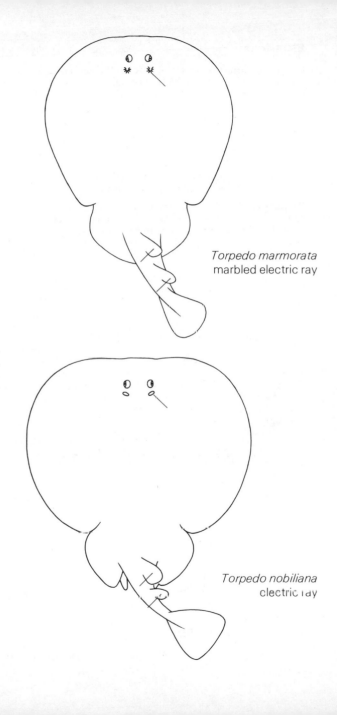

Torpedo marmorata
marbled electric ray

Torpedo nobiliana
electric ray

Distinguishing features Body disc-like and rounded, with the pectoral fins joined to the body; skin smooth. The first dorsal fin is distinctly larger than the second, and both are widely spaced. The inner edges of the spiracles are smooth.

Coloration Dorsally uniformly dark, although varying from slate grey to liver brown. The underside is white, with only a trace of dusky colour around the disc margin.

Size A large electric ray which grows to 180 cm (5 ft 11 in.), and a weight of 50 kg (110 lb 4 oz.). A weight of 70 kg (154 lb 8 oz) has been recorded for a Mediterranean specimen.

Remarks Bottom-living on mud and sand in 10 m (5½ fathoms) down to 150 m (82 fathoms), and exceptionally to 350 m (190 fathoms). Its diet has been little studied. From isolated observations, such as the specimen which contained a dogfish and poor-cod, it might be assumed that a large variety of bottom-living fishes are eaten.

Live-bearing. No reports exist of gravid females in northern European waters, but an evidently newly-born young fish has been caught in the North Sea.

This species is the more common of the 2 electric rays in northern European waters, although its distribution is mainly along the Channel and western coasts of the British Isles. Being such a large fish its electrical properties are formidable, and a big specimen can give a powerful shock (measured up to 220 volts at 8 amps). Repeated discharges become weaker. This species has been observed to spring at a passing fish, and wrapping the pectoral fins around it, stun or kill the victim which is eaten at leisure. The mouth of the electric ray is very small and clearly unsuited to attacking moving prey.

Skates and Rays

The members of this family (Rajidae) are all flattened cartilaginous fishes with broad pectoral fins which give the body its diamond shape, and a long tail. The mouth, nostrils, and the 5 pairs of gill slits are ventral, while the eyes and the spiracles are dorsal in position. The nostrils are well developed and most skates depend on

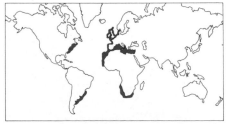

Electric ray

their sense of smell to detect food. They also possess quite well-developed electrical organs and these presumably serve to detect approaching prey, and possibly permit species recognition.

The skates are typically bottom-dwelling, their diet composed entirely of benthic animals, the dorsal surface pigmented to provide near-perfect concealment. Some, however, are semi-benthic only, foraging off the bottom and feeding on mid-water fishes; these species frequently have dark or dusky undersides.

Male skates and rays have pelvic claspers by which spermatozoa are introduced into the genital opening of the female. Fertilization is thus internal, but these fish are oviparous and the eggs are laid in dark, oblong, leathery cases, with a projection at each corner.

Some 20 species are known in the waters of the north-east Atlantic. Their identification frequently presents many problems, which are often compounded by differences in body shape or development of skin spines within the same species.

Two genera are represented in this area, *Raja* and *Bathyraja*. The former has been divided into a number of subgenera; the 3 species of *Bathyraja* are found in deep water.

Blonde ray   *Raja brachyura*

Distinguishing features A ray with a relatively short snout and the outer corners of the pectoral fins almost right-angled. In half-grown and adult fish the back is entirely prickly, only the front edges of the disc being rough in the young. The eyes are large. In adults the tail bears a line of larger spines in the mid-line; young fish have spines along the back also. Adult females may have an interrupted series along the sides of the tail. (See also coloration.)

Coloration Ventrally white. The back light brown with a few creamy-white blotches and dense dark spots which extend up to the very edge of the disc and on to the tail.

Size Grows to a maximum length of 113 cm ($44\frac{1}{2}$ in.) and a weight of 17.122 kg (37 lb 7 oz).

Remarks In coastal waters down to 100 m (55 fathoms), although most common around 40 m (22 fathoms). It is not found in estuaries and usually young specimens only are encountered in very shallow water. It lives mainly on sandy bottoms.

The blonde ray eats a wide range of crustaceans, nereid worms and fishes (especially herring, sprat, pouting, sandeels, and sole).

Blonde
ray
◀

▶
Roker

In the English Channel females with well-developed eggs occur from February to August, most from April to July. The egg-case measures 115–143 mm (4½–5¾ in.) in length, 72–80 mm (2–3½ in.) in width, the horns being long. The case is flat at one side, while the other side is convex and densely covered with loose fibres.

The blonde ray reaches the northern limit of its range around the British Isles, but is common there only on western coasts.

Roker   *Raja clavata*

Distinguishing features Distinguished by dense prickles over the entire back, and larger thorns in the mid-line from mid-disc to the dorsal fins. In sexually mature specimens these thorns are very large, with button-like bases (known as bucklers) present on the back and sides of the tail in males, and well-developed ventrally also in females. The snout is relatively short, the anterior edges of the disc sinuous, and the outer corners nearly right-angled.

Coloration Very variable dorsally, medium brown to light grey with light brown to yellowish mottling. Numerous small dark spots and yellowish patches (sometimes surrounded with dark spots to form a faint ocellus). Ventrally a pale cream colour with greyish margins.

Size A maximum length of 85 cm (34 in.), width 61 cm (24 in.). Attains a weight of 17.25 kg (38 lb). The largest specimens are always females.

Remarks The commonest ray in shallow water, it is found on muddy, sandy, or gravelly bottoms, rarely even on rough grounds. Its depth range extends to 280 m (153 fathoms), but it is most common in depths of between 10 and 60 m (5½–33 fathoms).

In the first days after hatching the young ray does not feed, but subsists on the residual yolk from the egg. Its first food consists of small crustaceans, mainly amphipods and small bottom-living shrimps. As it grows, it continues to eat crustaceans as the major constituent of the diet, including shore crabs, swimming crabs, and brown shrimps. Numerous fishes are eaten, chiefly sandeels, herring, sprat, various gadoids, and small flatfishes.

The breeding cycle appears to govern the roker's migrations. In the spring the mature females move into inshore waters, followed within a month or so by the mature males. Egg-capsules are laid in shallow water from March to August, and the embryo takes from 16–20 weeks to hatch. Newly-hatched fish [about 8 cm (3¼ in.) in width] are very abundant in the English Channel and southern North Sea through the summer months. The egg-capsule is oblong with long horns at each corner, and measures 6–9 cm (2⅓–3½ in.) long and rather less across; these capsules are often numerous in the jetsam in late summer and autumn.

After the egg-capsules have been laid the adults mate again, but the sexes soon segregate into unisexual schools.

The roker is the principal constituent of the 'skate' landed by inshore fishing vessels, the great majority taken in bottom trawls,

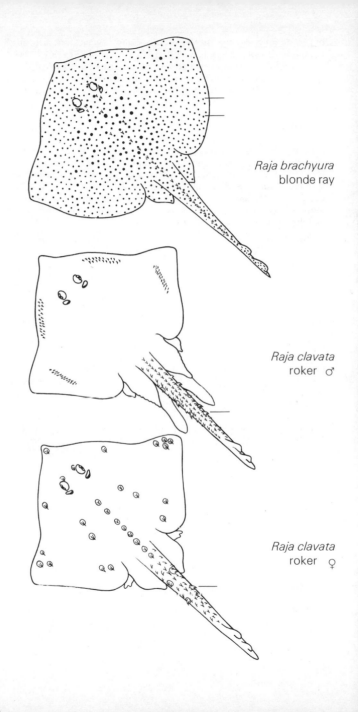

Raja brachyura
blonde ray

Raja clavata
roker ♂

Raja clavata
roker ♀

but some on lines. It is also frequently caught by anglers. Although the name thornback ray is widely used, it is to some extent a 'book name'; roker is commonly used among fishermen in East Anglia—a word derived from the Danish and possibly current since the Viking invasions. For this reason, and for its convenient shortness, it seems preferable to adopt it more widely.

Small-eyed ray   *Raja microocellata*

Distinguishing features   The snout is relatively short, and the corners of the disc are almost right angles. The only sure means of identification are the small eyes (the combined length of eye and spiracle being less than half the distance between the eyes), the presence of prickles on the front half of the disc only, and the spines in the mid-line of the body and tail being closely packed and bent at a right angle. (See also coloration.)

Coloration   Greyish to medium brown on the back with large creamy blotches and streaks which run parallel to the margins of the disc. White ventrally.

Size   Attains a length of 82 cm (32 in.) and width of 60 cm (24 in.). The males are usually smaller. Grows to a weight of at least 5.4 kg (12 lb).

Remarks   Lives in shallow water from close inshore down to depths of 100 m (55 fathoms). It seems to be particularly common on sandy grounds, and in the English Channel at least it is found mainly in certain sandy bays and outer estuaries. Egg-capsules are deposited in summer in the English Channel. They measure 8.7–9.5 cm ($3\frac{1}{4}$–$3\frac{3}{4}$ in.) in length by 5.4–6.3 cm ($2\frac{1}{4}$–$2\frac{1}{2}$ in.) excluding the horns, two of which are very long and thin, the other pair being short and strongly curved.

The small-eyed ray is comparatively scarce in northern European waters, extending as far north as the southern North Sea and Irish Sea. It makes little contribution to the commercial fishery for rays and relatively few are caught by anglers. To the south of the British Isles it is more common.

Spotted ray   *Raja montagui*

Distinguishing features   A short-snouted ray with the outer corners of the disc forming rather rounded, but nearly right angles.

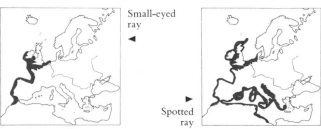

Small-eyed
ray
◀

▶
Spotted
ray

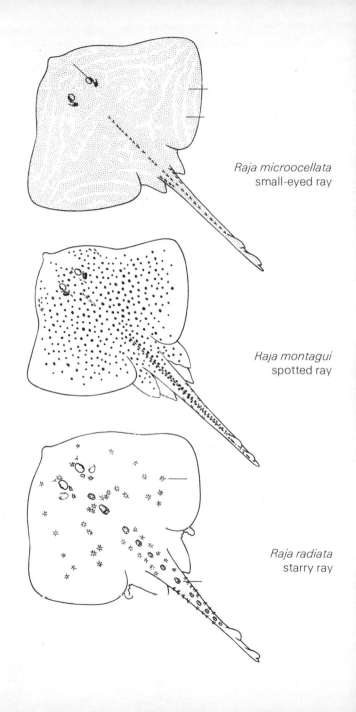

Raja microocellata
small-eyed ray

Raja montagui
spotted ray

Raja radiata
starry ray

Fine prickles occur along the upper front edge of the disc in the young and extend back to the level of the eyes in adults; the posterior parts of the disc are always bare. A mid-line row of larger spines runs from the centre of the disc to the dorsal fin and consists of closely-packed spines. Rows of spines are present along the sides of the tail in young fish, are irregular in adult females, and scattered in adult males. (See also coloration.)

Coloration Ventrally white; on the back warm brown, with numerous black spots which do not reach the margins of the disc. The black spots sometimes form a faint ocellus on the wings.

Size Attains a length of 75 cm (30 in.) and a width of 51 cm (20 in.); males are generally smaller.

Remarks The spotted ray lives in moderately deep water, mainly between 60–120 m (33–66 fathoms), although it is sometimes caught in 25 m (14 fathoms). It is most common on sandy bottoms but is occasionally caught on rough grounds.

It feeds almost entirely on crustaceans, amphipods, isopods, and shrimps when young, but the prey is larger as the ray grows and includes crabs of several kinds. Although this ray eats fishes, they are not an important element in the diet. The egg-capsules are deposited from April to July, and the embryo takes from 5–6 months to develop fully. The eggs are shed in shallow water. The egg-capsule is small, 64–77 mm (2¾–3 in.) long and 37–46 mm (1½–1¾ in.) wide. One side is smooth, the other has a fine mat of fibres, and all four horns are short.

The spotted ray is relatively common in the seas of northern Europe, but is less frequently encountered than the roker because it lives in rather deeper water. It is caught in moderate numbers by trawlers, and less commonly by anglers.

Starry ray   *Raja radiata*

Distinguishing features A short-snouted species with a rather rounded disc; the outer corners of the pectoral fins are smoothly curved. It is distinguished by the coarse prickles which cover the dorsal surface and by the large spines (12–19 in number) in the mid-line of the back and tail, each spine having a massive ridged base. Similar large based spines occur indiscriminately on the back.

Coloration The back is pale brown and faintly marbled with

Starry ray

cream and dark brown spots; the underside is white but greyish near the edges of the tail.

Size Attains a length of 76 cm (30 in.) and a width of about 50 cm (20 in.). Females are larger than males and considerably more spiny.

Remarks The starry ray lives in moderately deep water. In European seas it is most common at depths of 50–100 m (27–55 fathoms). In northern areas it is found at greater depths in colder water (in the Barents Sea at $-1.7°$ to $+4.0°C$), but rarely in temperatures below zero. The depth range for the species is from 20–1000 m (11–547 fathoms). It prefers sandy or muddy bottoms, but is occasionally found on shell or gravel.

Fishes and crustaceans make up the greater part of its diet. The egg-cases are deposited mainly between February and June, although mature females with well-developed eggs can be caught throughout the year. The egg-case is small, 42–66 mm ($1\frac{1}{2}$–$2\frac{1}{2}$ in.) in length, 25–53 mm (1–2 in.) wide, with a distinct keel at the sides, and a mass of fine filaments on the faces. Newly-hatched fish are 93–109 mm ($3\frac{3}{4}$–$4\frac{1}{4}$ in.) in length. Females mature at a length of 39 cm (15 in.), males at 42 cm (17 in.).

The starry ray is essentially a cold-water species which reaches the southern limits of its range in British waters. Although it is a common species (in appropriate depths), it is not found close inshore except in the north of its range.

Arctic skate   *Raja hyperborea*

Distinguishing features Similar in appearance to the starry ray, but differing in having a distinctly wider interorbital region and a slightly more pointed snout. The upper surface of the disc is covered with small prickles with conspicuous star-shaped bases, while the ventral surface is smooth; there is a conspicuous row of large spines (22–30) in the mid-line of the back. The tail is distinctly short.

Coloration The back is dark, usually brownish-grey frequently with light spots. Ventrally, the young are yellow-white, but adults have conspicuous dark patches often symmetrically arranged and particularly prominent on the outer edges of the disc.

Size Females attain a length of 92 cm (36 in.); males reach 86 cm (34 in.).

Remarks A cold-water ray found north of the ridge between

Arctic skate

Shetland and the Faroes. It lives on muddy bottoms in temperatures below or slightly above 0°C. Its depth range is from 280–2461 m (153–1346 fathoms), although it is only in the colder, northern extremities of its range that it lives in the shallower of these depths. Recent observations have shown that it feeds mostly on crustaceans (large numbers of euphausiids being found in the stomach) and various fishes (blue whiting, *Paralepis*, *Cottunculus*, and *Lycodes*).

The egg-capsule is moderately large, 8–12.5 cm long (3–5 in.) and 5–8 cm wide (2–3 in.); the horns at one end are much longer than those at the other. On hatching, the young ray is about 16 cm (6¼ in.) in length.

This is one of the least known of European rays. Living in deep cold water, it is not often encountered and has been little studied. Its flesh is flabby and tasteless.

Skate   *Raja batis*

Distinguishing features   The skate is one of several large, long-snouted species, the front edge of the disc being strongly concave as a result of the length of the snout. Young specimens are usually smooth-skinned, adult females have prickles on the front of the disc, and males are spiny overall on the back. Both sexes are prickly ventrally and have a row of 12–20 larger spines in the mid-line of the tail, with 1–3 spines between the dorsal fins. (See also coloration.)

Coloration   Dark olive brown to grey above with light brown blotches and darker spots. Ventrally blue-grey or ash-grey, with lines of black pores conspicuous after the mucus has been removed.

Size   The skate is the largest and heaviest European ray. Females attain a length of 2.85 m (9 ft 4 in.) and a width of 2 m (6 ft 7 in.); males attain a length of 2.05 m (6 ft 9 in.). A weight of 113 kg (250 lb) has been reported.

Remarks   The depth-range is 30–600 m (16–328 fathoms), but only young fish live in shallow water. Adults live mostly between 90–220 m (49–120 fathoms).

The skate is an active predator feeding in mid-water as well as close to the sea-bed. It feeds extensively on fishes (other rays, spurdog, plaice, angler fish, cod, haddock, and herring) and also on crustaceans.

The egg-capsules are large, 14–25 cm (6–9 in.) long and 8–14 cm (3–6 in.) wide, with a tuft of filaments at the base of each long horn;

Skate ◄

► Black skate

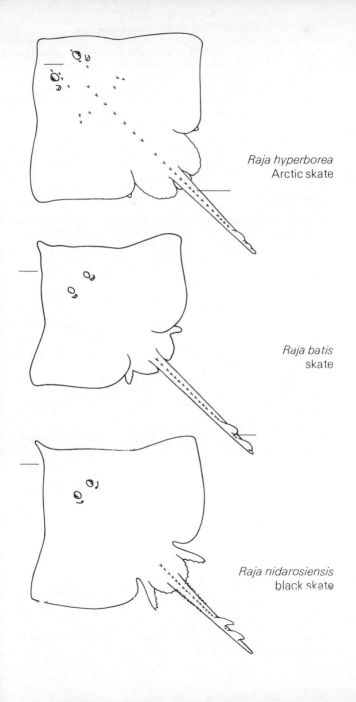

Raja hyperborea
Arctic skate

Raja batis
skate

Raja nidarosiensis
black skate

they are deposited on the sea-bed mainly between February and August. The newly-hatched young measures about 21 cm ($8\frac{1}{4}$ in.) in length. Males become sexually mature at 1.5 m (59 in.), females when slightly larger.

This species is relatively common except in the shallowest inshore waters. It is an important commercial fish caught both by trawling and on lines, but mostly to the north of its range, in the northern North Sea, and off Icelandic, Faroese, and Norwegian waters. It is occasionally taken by anglers fishing in suitable areas. Very large skate are less commonly reported than they were in the 1920–30 period, and it seems probable that fishing has affected the stock of this species.

Black skate   *Raja nidarosiensis*

Distinguishing features A long-snouted ray with the anterior margin of the disc strongly concave; the length of the snout is one-third or more the width of the disc. The whole underside is covered with fine prickles, but only the front part of the back. There is a distinct row of spines along the mid-line of the tail, including the part between the dorsal fins. (See also coloration.)

Coloration Very dark brown, often almost black above; ventrally dark grey with black pores.

Size Females grow to a length of 2 m (6 ft 7 in.), males to 1.75 m (5 ft 9 in.).

Remarks Known only from fjords on the Norwegian coast, southern Iceland and off the west coast of the British Isles mostly in 400–500 m (219–273 fathoms), exceptionally from 200 m (109 fathoms) down to 923 m (505 fathoms). Lives in depressions in the bottom of the fjord. It is said to eat fishes and crustaceans.

Gravid females have been captured mainly in winter and spring (October to April). The egg-capsule measures 182–260 mm (7–$10\frac{1}{2}$ in.) in length, 102–113 mm (4–$4\frac{1}{2}$ in.) in width. The capsule is covered with a loose network of yellowish threads.

This is one of the least-known European skates, its biology has been little studied, and relatively few specimens have been examined. It appears to be rare everywhere. It was first reported to occur off the western coast of Scotland on the evidence of a stranded egg-case identified as belonging to this species; it has since been captured in deep-water trawling to the west of the British Isles by a German research vessel.

Long-nosed skate   *Raja oxyrinchus*

Distinguishing features A large, relatively deep-water skate with an exceptionally long snout, the front edges of the disc being strongly concave. The skin on the back is smooth, except for fine prickles on the snout and anterior edges of the disc, but ventrally it is prickly. Larger spines are present on the tail, in the mid-line in juveniles, with weakly-developed lateral rows only in adults. (See also coloration.)

Coloration Dark brown or greyish, often with lighter rounded spots on the back. The underside is grey with small black dots scattered to the very edge of the disc.

Size Grows to a length of 1.50 m (59 in.); males are rarely longer than 1.20 m (47 in.).

Remarks A bottom-living fish occurring between 90–950 m (49–500 fathoms), although mostly deeper than 200 m (109 fathoms). It lives mainly on soft bottoms, often in shallow depressions in the sea-bed. It eats crustaceans, including shrimps and crabs, and fishes, among which redfish, gurnards, dragonets, and small sharks have been recorded.

The egg-capsules are *c.* 13 cm long and 7.4–10 cm wide (5 by 3–4 in.) in British waters; in the Mediterranean rather larger specimens have been found. The horns at the corners of the capsules are short, and the whole is covered with yellowish fibres. In Italian seas the eggs are deposited between February and April. The fish attains sexual maturity at 1.2 m (47 in.).

Although it is by no means uncommon in northern European waters, its biology is little known. As a relatively deep-water fish it is not often caught, except in trawls or on long-lines worked at appropriate depths.

Shagreen ray   *Raja fullonica*

Distinguishing features The snout is sharply pointed and is relatively long (about 3 times the distance between the eyes). The body is densely covered with coarse prickles on the back, which are present on the underside of the disc, but only in the region of the snout and the anterior edges. Two closely-packed series of larger spines run along the tail, but no spines in the mid-line except in the young. The dorsal fins are set well apart; there is no interdorsal spine. Jaw teeth long, slender, and pointed.

Coloration Greyish-brown on the back, often quite pale, and usually unmarked. White ventrally.

Size Grows to a length of about 1.2 m (47 in.).

Remarks Bottom-living, but actively feeding above the sea-bed, in moderately deep water 35–500 m (19–300 fathoms). Feeds heavily on fish, but some crustaceans and molluscs have been found in their stomachs.

The egg-capsule is relatively small, *c.* 9 by 4.6 cm (3½ by 2 in.),

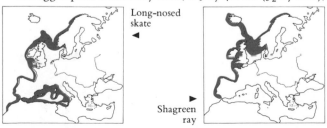

Long-nosed skate ◄

► Shagreen ray

45

amber-coloured and almost transparent. The horns of the capsule are very long, the longer pair being longer than the egg-case.

Although overall the shagreen ray is not a rare ray, its occurrence seems 'patchy' and it may be locally abundant in some areas, but is rarely encountered in others. It is believed to migrate inshore in summer; probably a feeding migration. Although it has often been reported from the Mediterranean Sea, this may have been due to earlier confusion between this species and *Raja rondeleti*, a similar but recently described Mediterranean ray.

Sandy ray   *Raja circularis*

Distinguishing features   A short-snouted ray, with rounded tips to the disc. The back is covered with rather fine prickles, except for a bare patch in the mid-line (most noticeable in large males); the underside is smooth except for the snout and front of the wings. Two rows of closely-packed, strongly-curved spines each side of the mid-line on the tail and posterior part of the body. The dorsal fins are large; their bases run together.

Coloration   Light brown or reddish-brown above, usually with 4–6 yellowish-white spots on the disc; ventrally white.

Size   Grows to a length of 1.20 m (3 ft 11 in.).

Remarks   Bottom-living, usually on sandy bottoms and in depths of 50–100 m (27–55 fathoms), although exceptionally down to 275 m (150 fathoms). The egg-capsule is transparent amber in colour, has fine threads on the sides, and measures 8.4–9 cm ($3\frac{1}{4}$–$3\frac{1}{2}$ in.) in length, 4.5–5.3 cm ($1\frac{3}{4}$–2 in.) in width. The sandy ray appears to be localized in its distribution, for even within the bathymetric range which it favours, it is found only occasionally. In the Mediterranean it seems even scarcer. The biology of this ray is very little known.

Cuckoo ray   *Raja naevus*

Distinguishing features   A short-snouted, round-winged ray, with the dorsal surface covered with fine prickles except for a rounded patch on each wing; smooth ventrally except for the snout. A double row of curved, close-packed spines either side of the mid-line and running the length of the tail and onto the body. Young specimens have a mid-line row in addition. (See also coloration.)

 Sandy ray
◄

►
 Cuckoo ray

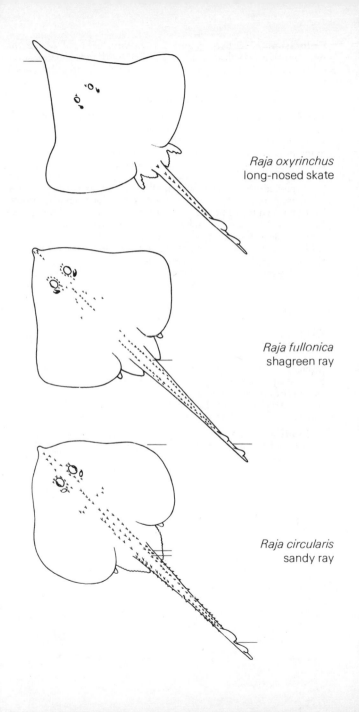

Raja oxyrinchus
long-nosed skate

Raja fullonica
shagreen ray

Raja circularis
sandy ray

Coloration The back is grey-brown with light patches on the disc, and two very distinct black and yellow rounded marks in the centre of each wing. Ventrally it is white with irregular darker marks.

Size Grows to 70 cm (28 in.) in length.

Remarks A bottom-living ray found in fairly shallow water from 20–150 m (11–80 fathoms), and probably most abundant between 70–100 m (38–55 fathoms). It is reported to feed on amphipods and shrimps, and nereid worms throughout its life, but eats increasing quantities of fishes (chiefly herring, gadoids, sandeels, and dragonets) as it grows. Fish are an important food to the adult. The egg-capsule is relatively small, and the shell more or less transparent, one pair of horns being strikingly long while the others have incurved tips. The average size is 6.3 cm long, 3.7 cm wide ($2\frac{1}{2}$ by $1\frac{1}{2}$ in.). The newly-hatched young measures 12 cm ($4\frac{3}{4}$ in.) in length. Incubation (in the aquarium) lasts for 243 days. The cuckoo ray lays eggs all the year round, possibly most in December to May; about 90 eggs are produced each year.

While this species is moderately common to the south of the British Isles (as in the English Channel), its biology is little known.

Round skate   *Raja fyllae*

Distinguishing features A small ray with very rounded outline to the disc, the young being almost circular. In adults the snout is rather more pronounced and the anterior edge is sinuous. The upper surface is coarsely prickly with the exception of bare patches on the pectoral and pelvic fin bases. Numerous long spines around the eyes and on the centre of the disc, the mid-line row of spines prominent, and 1–2 irregular rows of rather larger thorns on the sides of the tail. The tail is longer than the disc in large specimens.

Coloration Dark grey to chocolate brown above (young specimens have dark brown bands across the tail); ventrally pale grey with darker patches around the vent, on the tail, and front of the wings.

Size Attains a length of 56 cm (23 in.) and a width of 31 cm (12 in.).

Remarks A deep-water ray found mainly between 300–800 m (164–437 fathoms), although the recorded limits of its depth

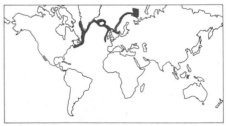
Round skate

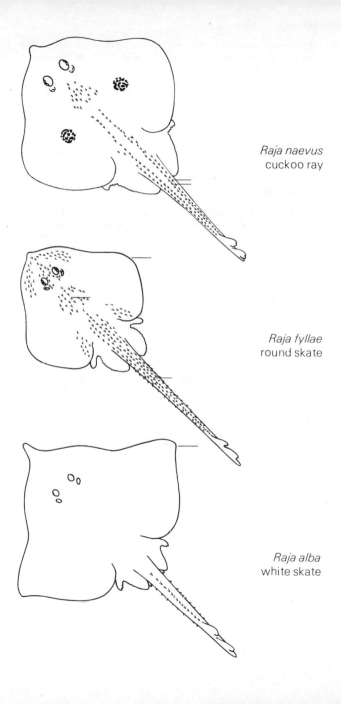

Raja naevus
cuckoo ray

Raja fyllae
round skate

Raja alba
white skate

distribution are 170–2055 m (93–1124 fathoms). It inhabits the shallower water to the north of its range, but is said to keep within temperatures of 3–6°C.

The egg-capsule is small and smooth, 4–4.4 cm (1½–1¾ in.) long, 2.4–2.8 cm (⅞–1 in.) wide. One pair of horns is very long and the tips cross. The newly-hatched young is *c.* 7 cm long, 4 cm wide (2¾ by 1½ in.).

Despite its wide distribution, the biology of this ray is virtually unknown. Although recorded to the west of the British Isles on a few occasions in very deep water, the round skate must be regarded as an Arctic species.

White skate   *Raja alba*

Distinguishing features The snout is moderately long and rather triangular in outline, while the front edges of the disc are sinuous and distinctly concave from snout to wing tip. The angles of the disc are sharp, rather less than 90°. Adults are prickly on the back but have a bare patch in the middle of the back; ventrally they are prickly in the front only. The young are smooth-skinned, and have a row of spines in the mid-line of the tail with weakly-ridged bases, and another 2 on either side of the tail.

Coloration Greyish-brown on the back, young fish reddish-brown with indistinct light spots. The underside is conspicuously white with a dusky edge around the outer and posterior edges of the pectoral and pelvic fins. In young fish this band is conspicuous and dark.

Size Grows to a maximum of 2.02 m in length and 1.51 m in width (6 ft 7 in. and 5 ft), but the usual length range is 1.5–1.8 m (5–6 ft). It attains a weight in excess of 63 kg (140 lb).

Remarks Lives in inshore waters from 40–200 m (22–109 fathoms) and exceptionally to 366 m (200 fathoms). The larger specimens tend to live in deeper water. The egg-capsule is flat on one surface, convex on the other, and of honeycomb texture. The body of the case measures 16–19 cm (6–7½ in.) long and 13–15 cm (5–6 in.) wide; the lower horns are short and hooked, the others long and flattened. The eggs are deposited in April to June (in the Mediterranean), and in late summer to the north of its range. Incubation takes 15 months, and the newly-hatched young is 29 cm (11½ in.) long.

White skate

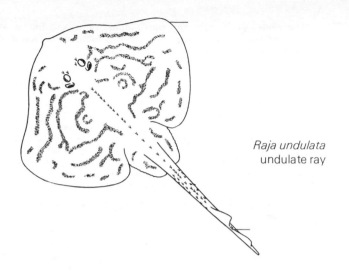

Raja undulata
undulate ray

egg-cases

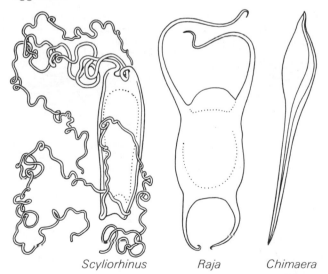

Scyliorhinus   *Raja*   *Chimaera*

The white skate is relatively uncommon in northern European waters, although in the Mediterranean it is locally common and forms part of the commercial catch of skate.

Undulate ray	*Raja undulata*

Distinguishing features   The pectoral fins are rounded and the snout is short; the back is prickly except for the rear edges of the pectoral and pelvic fins. The snout is covered with coarse prickles, but the remainder of the underside is smooth. Young fish have a complete mid-line row of spines on the back. This becomes interrupted in larger specimens, which also have irregular rows of spines on the sides of the tail. The dorsal fins are widely separated, with one or two inter-dorsal spines. (See also coloration.)

Coloration   Yellowish-brown to deep brown on the back, with long, very distinct, wavy dark bands margined with white or yellowish spots. White ventrally.

Size   Grows to a maximum length of 1.2 m (48 in.) in the Mediterranean. British specimens rarely attain 1 m (39 in.). Weights of 6.5–7.2 kg (14 lb 4 oz–15 lb 13 oz) have been reported.

Remarks   This ray is found on sandy bottoms in inshore waters, although rarely close to the shore. Its depth range extends to 200 m (109 fathoms), but it is most common between 45–100 m (25–55 fathoms). It is known to eat flatfishes (plaice and dab), gobies, and clupeoid fishes, squids, and crustaceans.

Egg-capsules are 8.2–9 cm (3–3$\frac{1}{2}$ in.) long, without the horns, and 4.5–5.2 cm (1$\frac{1}{2}$–2 in.) wide, and are opaque reddish-brown in colour. The eggs are deposited in late summer in the English Channel, in spring in the Mediterranean.

In northern European waters this ray makes little contribution to commercial fisheries or sport. Its biology is little known. It is one of the most distinctive of the northern European rays.

Stingrays

The stingrays are a large group of rays comprising several families—although representatives of 2 (Dasyatidae and Myliobatidae) are found in British seas. They are most abundant in tropical seas and

Undulate ray

locally in freshwater in the tropics, especially in South America. Their bodies are usually wide and less angular than the skates. They are characterized by the possession of a long serrated spine or spines close to the tail fin base. Glandular tissue on the underside of the spine secretes a venom which renders a stab from the spine most painful and on occasions fatal, although fatalities are not recorded in European waters.

Two species occur in northern European seas.

Stingray   *Dasyatis pastinaca*

Distinguishing features   Body shape typical of a ray, with large broad pectoral fins, but lacking a dorsal fin and having one, sometimes 2 or more, long serrated spines in the tail. The tail itself is long and whip-like with no tail fin.

Coloration   Above greyish, olive or brown, usually plain but occasionally with light blotches. Ventrally the body and wings are cream coloured, usually with grey edges.

Size   The maximum length observed in British waters appears to be 1.06 m (42 in.), with a weight of 25.4 kg (56 lb). In the Mediterranean a length of 1.4 m (55 in.) may be attained.

Remarks   Bottom-living, but always found on soft bottoms usually of sand, occasionally mud, in depths of 3.7–73 m (2–40 fathoms). It seems to be confined to shallow coastal waters and is even found in outer estuaries. The stingray feeds exclusively on bottom-living organisms such as molluscs and crustaceans, especially crabs.

Live-bearing (ovoviviparous); the embryos in later stages of development are nourished by a secretion from the uterine wall. From 6–9 young form a normal-sized litter. Breeding may not take place in northern parts of its range; occasionally young specimens occur, but gravid females have not been reported.

In northern waters the stingray becomes noticeably more common during the summer and autumn months. It is not common enough to be fished for deliberately, but is moderately common around southern Britain, and is caught by anglers and more frequently by inshore trawlers.

The 'sting' on the back of the tail is serrated on the sides and may measure up to 13 cm (5 in.) in length. The tissue lining the grooves ventrally is venom-laden and wounds from the spine are excessively

Stingray

painful. Most injuries are caused by the ray swinging its tail upwards and forwards, thus driving the spine into the leg of anyone standing on or near the fish. Specimens with 2 and sometimes more spines are not uncommon, the ventral ones being well-developed replacement spines.

Eagle ray	*Myliobatis aquila*

Distinguishing features A broad-bodied ray, with the pectoral fins long and pointed, and the forepart of the head distinct from the disc. The tail is long and whip-like with a small dorsal fin preceding a long, serrated-edged spine. The teeth are flattened and broad with a large central plate; 3 rows either side are arranged in mosaic form.

Coloration The back is grey-brown, sometimes with greenish or bronze tints; the underside whitish-cream with grey edges to the disc.

Size Grows to a length of 2 m (6 ft 7 in.), the width rather less. Attains a maximum weight of 24 kg (52 lb 8 oz).

Remarks Partly bottom-living, but frequently found swimming strongly at, or near the surface. Mainly encountered in coastal waters down to a depth of *c.* 100 m (55 fathoms). Usually on sandy or muddy bottoms. Feeds entirely on bottom-living invertebrates, particularly molluscs and crustaceans, the hard shells of which are crushed by the broad teeth.

Not known to breed in northern waters. Development is ovoviviparous, the young in a late stage of uterine growth being nourished with a fluid from the maternal membranes. Litters of up to 7 young are on record.

In northern waters the eagle ray is a relatively rare vagrant found mostly during summer and autumn, presumably as a result of northward migration. Only in the English Channel and off south-western Ireland is it at all common. Where this fish is abundant, its diet makes it a pest to shellfish beds; it has no commercial value to the fisherman.

Rat-fishes

The rat-fishes or chimaeras (family Chimaeridae) are a small group of relatives of the sharks and rays, and like them have a cartilaginous

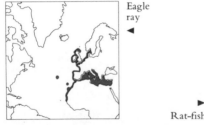

Eagle ray ◄

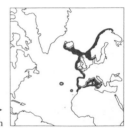

► Rat-fish

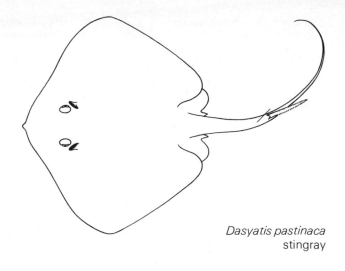

Dasyatis pastinaca
stingray

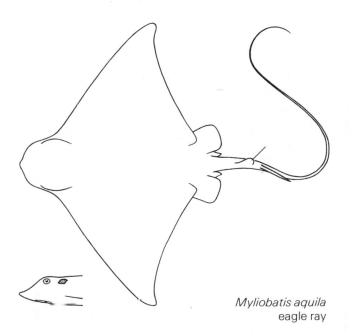

Myliobatis aquila
eagle ray

skeleton. They differ, however, in having fewer teeth; these are united in the form of plates, 2 in the upper jaw and 1 in the lower. The upper jaw is fused with the head skeleton, there is no spiracle, and only 1 gill opening each side of the head covered by a fleshy flap-like cover. The first dorsal fin has a strong spine, but otherwise all the fins are supported by fine horny rays.

Male rat-fishes have claspers with simple or compound tips and a roughened surface. They also have a curious thumb-shaped organ with a spiny end on the forehead.

The rat-fishes are all marine, and in the North Atlantic they occur on the edge of the continental shelf and in the deep sea.

Rat-fish *Chimaera monstrosa*

Distinguishing features Identified by its comparatively short snout (which is bluntly pointed), high first dorsal fin with a strong spine, very large pectoral fins, and an anal fin which is divided from the long tail fin by a notch. The eyes are relatively large. (See also coloration.)

Coloration Light creamy-brown above with darker brown patches; ventrally white. The posterior edges of the second dorsal and anal fins are dark.

Size Said to attain a length of 1.5 m (5 ft), but in waters to the west of the British Isles rarely exceeds 1.10 m (43 in.). Males seem to be slightly smaller than females.

Remarks Lives close to the bottom and in deep water from 300–500 m (164–234 fathoms), in summertime coming into shallower water and occasionally captured in 100 m (55 fathoms). Its diet has not been systematically studied, but remains of brittlestars, crabs, shrimps, and molluscs, as well as unidentifiable fishes have been found in the gut.

The rat-fish deposits its eggs singly in long, tapering, light brown capsules, mainly in spring and summer, and in fairly shallow water. The capsule is 15–18 cm (6–7 in.) long. It is said to lay its eggs 2 at a time.

Despite its abundance, and it is not uncommon to catch several hundred rat-fish in a deep-water haul, this fish is not exploited. The flesh is said to be bitter. Like many sharks and rays, it tends to form one-sex schools, although the segregation is not absolute.

Sturgeons

A group of fishes (family Acipenseridae) which possess a number of primitive features, among them a heterocercal tail (the body continuing along the upper lobe), a poorly ossified skeleton, and a spiral valve in the lower intestine. The body is elongate, with 5 rows of conspicuous bony plates running along its length, and the head is covered with hard bony plates that meet to form conspicuous sutures.

Sturgeons are confined to the rivers and seas of the temperate northern hemisphere; some live entirely in freshwater but most are anadromous, migrating into rivers to spawn. Sturgeons the world over are now greatly depleted in numbers on account of overfishing, damming of rivers, and pollution.

Some 25 species are recognized; a single species occurs in north-western Europe, while 2 others occur in the Danube basin.

Sturgeon   *Acipenser sturio*

Distinguishing features   The elongate body, asymmetrical tail, and 5 rows of characteristic bony plates along the back, sides, and belly are all distinctive. The snout is long, the nostrils well developed, the mouth small and tubular; 2 pairs of long, smooth barbels are present between the tip of the snout and the mouth.

Coloration   The back varies from greenish-brown to near black, darkening with age, while the underside is yellowish-white. In young fish the lateral bony plates are light in colour.

Size   A huge fish; females attain a length of 3.5 m (11 ft 6 in.) and a weight of 317 kg (700 lb); males are smaller. Large fish are exceptionally rare today.

Remarks   In the sea, a mainly bottom-living, shallow-water fish, although the occurrence of large sturgeon so far from their spawning rivers suggests active, probably mid-water swimming. In northern European waters it is now so rare that little can be inferred from its capture, but taken overall it appears to be caught mainly on soft bottoms, chiefly sand or mud. In the rivers in which they spawn, sturgeon stay in the lower reaches. The breeding stock enters the river in spring (April–May), the adults leaving after spawning, while the young fish stay in freshwater for up to 3 years.

In the sea, sturgeon eat molluscs, polychaete worms, crustaceans (chiefly shrimps and isopods), and fishes (gobies, sandeels, and, in the Black Sea, anchovies). The food of the young while in freshwater is composed entirely of bottom-living insect larvae, small crustaceans, and molluscs.

This fish spawns in deep, gravel-bottomed rivers, in 6–8 m (20–26 ft) of water. The eggs are sticky and black in colour and are quickly swept into the gravel. They hatch in 3–7 days at water temperatures of 19–14°C, the newly-hatched young being 9 mm in length. Depending on size, the female may contain between 800,000 to 2,400,000 eggs. In the Black Sea females attain sexual maturity at 8–14 years, the males at 7–9 years.

The sturgeon is one of the fishes used in the production of caviare. Caviare is prepared by salting the unshed eggs of the ripe female. The flesh is also excellent and locally important as food.

Possibly because of overfishing, coupled with pollution in estuaries, navigation locks, and weirs in rivers, the sturgeon is today a rare fish. A land-locked population exists in Lake Ladoga (Baltic USSR), spawning also occurs in the river Gironde (France), and river Guadalquivir (southern Spain), and possibly still in the river Elbe (Germany). Otherwise, in north-western Europe, the sturgeon is known only as a rare vagrant captured at sea. Throughout the 19th century there were numerous records of its occurrence far up British rivers, the majority in May and June, while the remainder fell between April and October. This suggests that spawning may have taken place in the larger British rivers at one time. Sea-caught fish are taken in all months of the year.

Sterlet
Acipenser ruthenus

Distinguishing features In general build similar to the sturgeon, but with a more pointed, rather upturned snout. The bony plates along the back and sides are small and those on the sides are numerous (60–70 in number). The barbels in front of the mouth are finely fringed for half their length.

Coloration Dark green or grey on the back and upper sides, fading to yellowish ventrally. The lateral row of scutes is light in colour, in young fish forming a whitish stripe down the side.

Size A small species which attains a maximum length of 1.22 m (48 in.) and a weight of 15.8 kg (35 lb). At 76 cm (30 in.) it may be 15 years of age, and weigh 2.265 kg (5 lb).

Remarks The only wholly freshwater sturgeon in Europe, it lives in rivers and large lakes, but is occasionally found in slightly salt water, as in the Caspian Sea. It eats aquatic invertebrates, especially bottom-living forms.

It spawns on clean, stony riverbeds, often well towards the head-waters, from mid-April to June. It lays between 11,000 and 140,000 eggs, which hatch in 4–5 days. The young lie in the gravel for the first few days of life before dispersing.

The sterlet is represented by two stocks, one in European Russia and eastern and central Europe, and the other in Siberia. In the Volga, the Don, and the Dnieper rivers this fish is common and forms a valuable fishery. It has also been stocked in artificial lakes and reservoirs as a potential fishery resource.

Beluga
Huso huso

Distinguishing features A very large, rather stout-bodied sturgeon which is clearly identified by its very wide mouth. The barbels on the underside of the snout are long and reach to the upper

Sturgeon ◀

▶ Sterlet

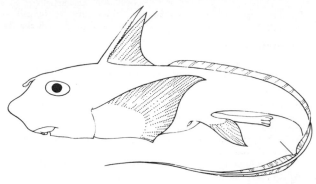

Chimaera monstrosa
rat-fish ♂

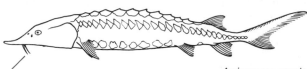

Acipenser sturio
sturgeon

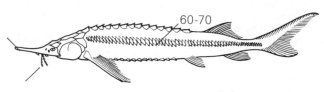

60-70

Acipenser ruthenus
sterlet

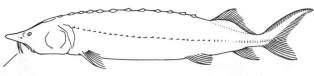

Huso huso
beluga

lip. The branchiostegal membranes (which support the gill covers ventrally) are joined together and are not united with the throat.

Coloration   Adults are dull grey-brown above, lighter ventrally.

Size   Grows to a length of *c.* 5 m (16 ft) and a weight of perhaps 1524 kg (1½ tons). Definite records exist of specimens (usually females) weighing as much as 1228 kg (1¼ tons).

Remarks   A migratory sturgeon which is found in the sea and travels far up the larger rivers of its range to breed. When adult, it feeds mainly on fishes, especially anchovies, gobies, various herring-like fishes, and members of the carp family. The young fish feed on bottom-living invertebrates.

The beluga spawns on stony river-beds in late spring. Those which have entered the river in winter travel far upstream, but spring-run fish breed near the river mouth. The young hatch in about 8 days at 13°C and begin to move downstream. Sexual maturity is attained at 14 years in males and 18 years in females, most of this time being spent in the sea. According to their size, females contain between 360,000 to 7½ million eggs.

The beluga was formerly much more common than it is today, and was fished for extensively in the Black and Caspian Seas, both as a food-fish and for caviare. It is now uncommon throughout its range.

Eels

Eels are distinctive fishes by reason of their elongate body form, and long dorsal and anal fins, which usually merge with the tail fin. None has pelvic fins, and members of several families have no pectoral fins. Some eels have scaly bodies, but the scales are small and embedded in the skin.

Eel larvae are transparent, shaped like a willow leaf, and live in the ocean's plankton. This larval type is known as a *leptocephalus*.

Several hundred species of eels are recognized world-wide in about 25 families. The majority are marine fishes distributed in all seas, except for the polar regions. Only 4 species (each belonging to a separate family Anguillidae, Muraenidae, Congridae, and Nemichthyidae) are common in northern European waters. Several other species, mostly small, live in deep water.

Beluga
◄

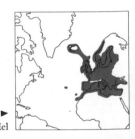

►
Eel

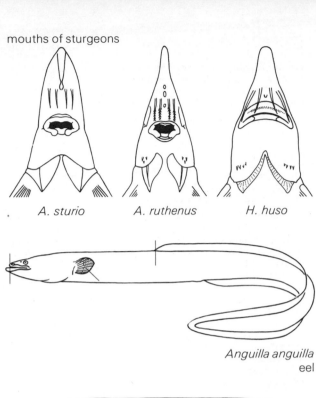

mouths of sturgeons

A. sturio   *A. ruthenus*   *H. huso*

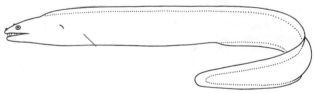

Anguilla anguilla
eel

Muraena helena
moray

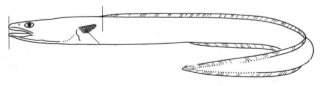

Conger conger
conger

Eel

Anguilla anguilla

Distinguishing features   In freshwater the only eel-like fish. Positively identified by its protruding lower jaw, small blunt teeth, rounded pectoral fins, and a dorsal fin origin which is closer to the vent than the gill openings. Minute scales are embedded in the skin.

Coloration   The freshwater, yellow eel stage is muddy brown above, yellowish or even golden on the sides and underside. As the fish approaches sexual maturity the back is almost black, and the belly silvery; it is then known as a silver eel.

Size   Males grow to 50 cm (19¾ in.); females grow to 100 cm (39½ in.). Specimens up to 12.7 kg (28 lb) have been recorded, but up to 4.5 kg (10 lb) is more usual.

Remarks   The eel is believed to breed in mid-Atlantic, the larvae being transported to Europe by ocean currents in 3 years. They undergo metamorphosis from larvae to elvers in coastal waters, and enter many rivers in countless millions. Many eels stay in the mouth of rivers and on the seashore. The freshwater stage is a feeding and growing phase, and as they mature sexually they descend the river to the sea—the changes in coloration and increase in the size of the eye being adaptations to life in the ocean's middle depths. Very few maturing eels have been caught in the open ocean and some of the details of their life history have yet to be elucidated.

The eel is a valuable food-fish throughout Europe, although natural stocks are poor in some inland areas and elvers have to be imported.

Moray

Muraena helena

Distinguishing features   An eel with a rather flattened deep body, pointed snout, and long very sharp teeth. The pectoral fins are absent and the gill openings are small slits high up on either side of the head. (See also coloration.)

Coloration   Dark brown or browny-purple with regular yellow mottling posteriorly, the pattern less regular towards the head. Only slightly lighter ventrally.

Size   Grows to 130 cm (51 in.).

Remarks   The moray is an extremely rare fish north of central Biscay, and has occurred fewer than 6 times in the last century. It

Moray ◄

► Conger

frequents rocky shores, small specimens living intertidally under boulders, larger ones in crevices in rock faces below low-tide level. This fish is active mainly at night.

Live morays are dangerous to handle. They bite savagely and the wounds often go septic.

Conger
Conger conger

Distinguishing features   A large marine eel which has a rounded cylindrical body, prominent pointed pectoral fins, and moderately large gill openings. The dorsal fin origin is placed well forward, vertically above the tip of the pectoral fin. The upper jaw is longer than the lower. Body scaleless.

Coloration   Dull brown above sharply set off from the light golden brown or cream on the underside. Deep-water specimens are light grey-brown, lighter ventrally but with the margins of the dorsal and anal fins black.

Size   A maximum length of 274 cm (9 ft) and a weight of 65 kg (143 lb) is attained.

Remarks   The conger is a common fish on rocky shores and offshore. Many young, small fish can be caught in deep shore pools, particularly those with dense algal cover low down the shore. In soft-bottomed areas few congers are found, but they quickly colonize sunken wrecks, harbour walls, and loose stone groynes, and many can be caught in such man-made habitats.

The conger's food consists of a wide range of mainly bottom-living fishes, large crustaceans, especially crabs, and octopuses. It breeds in the tropical Atlantic at depths of 3000–4000 m (1640–2200 fathoms). The larva is transparent and flattened, and lives at the sea's surface, drifting inshore for 1 or 2 years before undergoing metamorphosis to a small eel.

The conger is not much esteemed as a food-fish, but considerable numbers are caught by anglers.

Snipe-eel
Nemichthys scolopaceus

Distinguishing features   A fragile, slender black eel with very elongate narrow jaws resembling a snipe's bill. The dorsal fin origin is well forward on to the head (in front of the pectoral fins), and the anal fin origin is close behind the pectoral base. The tips of the 'beak'

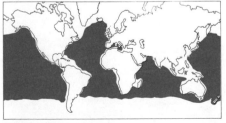

Snipe-eel

are not flattened. The tail is long and filamentous, when not broken off.

Coloration Jet black when dead; fresh specimens are dark brown with an iridescent tint.

Size The largest known specimen was 145 cm (57 in.); most caught are around 102 cm (40 in.).

Remarks The snipe-eel is a moderately common deep-sea eel, found between the surface and 1000 m (547 fathoms). It is occasionally captured in deep-fishing commercial trawls, often tangled by its jaws in the warp or netting, more commonly caught by research vessels, but occasionally found in the gut of other fishes. It feeds on small crustaceans and deep-water fishes. Its larvae are elongate, leaflike and transparent, and are found in the upper 91 m (50 fathoms), but only in the open sea.

Spiny-eels

A family (Notacanthidae) of marine fishes, mostly found in moderately deep to very deep water. Slender-bodied and eel-like in body form, they have a series of stout, sharp spines on the back, and similar spines in the anterior part of the anal fin (which continues as soft rays to the tip of the tail). Like their relatives, the thinner, long-snouted halosaurs, which have a small dorsal fin and live in deeper water, these fishes have a transparent, thin, leptocephalus larva, distinctly reminiscent of the eel larvae.

Possibly some 40 species of both families are found in the world's oceans. Only one occurs on the continental shelf of northern Europe.

Spiny-eel	*Notacanthus chemnitzii*

Distinguishing features Rounded, blunt snout with a transverse mouth placed ventrally, and with numerous small, rather flattened teeth in the jaws. The first dorsal spine is above the pelvic fin base, and the fin has 10–11 pungent spines only. The anal fin has between 20 and 21 slender spines. Adult size is also characteristic within the area.

Coloration Deep brown on the back and sides; grey-brown

Spiny-eel

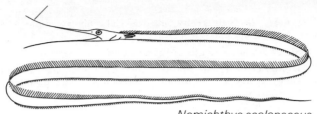

Nemichthys scolopaceus
snipe-eel

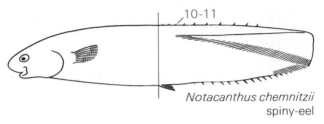

10-11

Notacanthus chemnitzii
spiny-eel

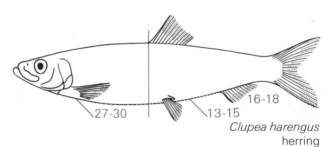

16-18

27-30

13-15

Clupea harengus
herring

heads of herring and shads

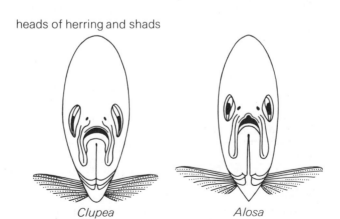

Clupea

Alosa

beneath the body cavity and head. The fins are dusky. Young specimens are pinkish-brown.

Size   Attains a length of 122 cm (48 in.).

Remarks   Large specimens of this fish are occasionally caught and landed by trawlers fishing northern grounds; young specimens have been rarely taken to the west of Ireland. The spiny-eel feeds on bottom-living invertebrates, particularly large pinkish actinarian sea anemones, and is presumed to feed in a head-down posture to do so. Ripe females have been caught in Icelandic waters in late autumn, and this may be the breeding season at these latitudes. Caught in 456–1463 m (250–800 fathoms) depth. Possibly world-wide in all temperate oceans; distribution, like its biology, little known.

Herrings and Anchovies

Members of the herring family form one of the most important of the world's fisheries resources. Most are marine fish which usually swim in schools at the sea's surface and in coastal waters. They are usually flattened from side to side, often have sharp scales on the belly, and have silvery sides. Their scales are large, easily detached, and there is no lateral line; the head is scaleless. There are possibly around 200 species of true herrings (family Clupeidae), of which 5 occur in European waters.

The anchovy is the single European representative of another large family (Engraulidae). Members of the family are world-wide in temperate and tropical seas, and of enormous economic importance. Superficially similar to herrings, they are distinguished by the very large mouth which opens to reveal a huge gape. Like the herrings, anchovies are plankton feeders.

Herring   *Clupea harengus*

Distinguishing features   Flat-sided, with large fragile scales, easily removed in handling. The belly is rounded, although in young fish it is keel-like and has a sharp edge. There are 13–15 scales between the pelvic fin base and the vent; 27–30 between the throat and the pelvics. The anal fin has 16–18 rays. The dorsal fin origin is above or in front of the pelvic fin origin. The lower jaw is prominent, the gill covers not ridged, and there is no deep notch in the mid-line of the upper jaw. (See also coloration.)

Coloration   The back is deep blue, lightening on the sides to silvery-white on the belly. The gill covers and flanks are shot with golden or rose-coloured tints.

Size   Grows to 43 cm (17 in.) and 680 g (1 lb 8 oz). A number of small races have a maximum size of around half this length and weight.

Remarks   The herring is an extremely abundant fish off northern

Europe, although now locally (as in the North Sea) overfished so that it is less economically valuable than it once was. It forms distinct breeding stocks often referred to as races, which are recognizable from their spawning grounds and seasons as well as meristic features, such as the number of vertebrae. The spring spawners shed their eggs close inshore, but others spawn in summer and autumn offshore and on the edges of ocean banks. The eggs are shed close to the bottom and form a mat, often several deep, over the gravel or shell beds of the bottom. The larvae are slender and about 0.6 cm ($\frac{1}{4}$ in.) on hatching; they are planktonic. The young fish form large schools and are particularly common inshore through their first year. In certain areas they form a substantial part of the catch of whitebait (the remainder being sprats). Despite their comparative scarcity in the North Sea today, considerable quantities of herring are still caught and they continue to be a valuable food-fish. Occasional specimens are caught by anglers. At all stages of its life the herring is preyed upon by numerous predators including sea-birds, dolphins, and other fishes.

Sprat   *Sprattus sprattus*

Distinguishing features   A small herring-like fish with flattened sides and a sharply toothed keel to the belly. The free rear-edges of the belly scales form backward-pointing teeth which are very noticeable. There are 21–23 between the throat and the pelvic fin origin, and 11–12 between the pelvic fins and the vent. The origin of the dorsal fin is behind the base of the pelvic fins. The anal fin has 18–20 rays. (See also coloration.)

Coloration   The back is dark green shading off on the sides to brilliant silver. Traces of golden colour on the gill covers and sides.

Size   Attains a maximum length of 16.5 cm ($6\frac{1}{2}$ in.); becomes sexually mature at 13–14 cm ($5–5\frac{1}{2}$ in.), at an age of 2 years.

Remarks   The sprat is an extremely abundant, small pelagic fish in northern European waters. It is particularly common in inshore coastal waters, the young especially being found in estuaries and arms of the sea. At this stage (during their first year) they are fished for as whitebait. In summer, sprats are found in depths of 10–50 m ($5\frac{1}{2}$–27 fathoms), but go deeper in winter. At all seasons they rise towards the surface at night. The sprat spawns in spring and summer, the eggs and early larvae are planktonic, and the latter drift inshore as they develop.

Herring

Sprats are extensively exploited and as well as being sold fresh, they are smoked, and preserved by canning in oil as brisling (their Norwegian name). Many tons are also processed into animal feed stuff or fertilizer.

Pilchard   *Sardina pilchardus*

Distinguishing features   Clearly herring-like in general body form, but with larger, easily detached scales, and a rounded body. The underside has a faint ridge, but nothing like the sharply-scaled belly of herring or sprat. The gill covers have distinct ridges radiating from a centre just behind the eye. The origin of the dorsal fin is in front of the pelvics and the last anal rays are elongate.

Coloration   The back is blue-green shading to gold on the sides and whitish-silver ventrally. A series of up to 4 dusky spots along the sides at the level of the eye.

Size   Attains a length of 25 cm (10 in.).

Remarks   The pilchard is a pelagic schooling fish of wide distribution in European seas, although reaching the northward limit of its range in the vicinity of the British Isles. Its abundance varies with climatic changes and their related effects on the sea, and during warm periods the pilchard may be numerous in the English Channel and the southern North Sea. It spawns in spring and summer in the open sea; the eggs are pelagic as are the early larvae. An inshore and usually northerly migration follows spawning, the schools then being found close to the coast. It was during this period that the most intensive fishery for the adult fish (as formerly off the Cornish coast) was carried out. The fishery in northern waters has now virtually died out, although small catches are still made in the English Channel and the southern North Sea. The young fish are heavily fished off the Biscay coast, and off Portugal they are canned as sardines. The largest pilchard fisheries are for related genera in the Pacific Ocean and off southern Africa.

Twaite shad   *Alosa fallax*

Distinguishing features   A large, deep-bodied, heavy-headed herring-like fish. The scales are very numerous and easily detached. The body is strongly compressed and the belly has a sharp keel, with the scales forming distinct teeth. The upper jaw is prominently

Sprat

Pilchard

68

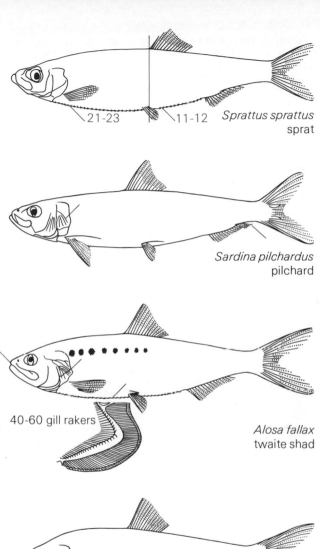

21-23   11-12   *Sprattus sprattus*
sprat

Sardina pilchardus
pilchard

40-60 gill rakers   *Alosa fallax*
twaite shad

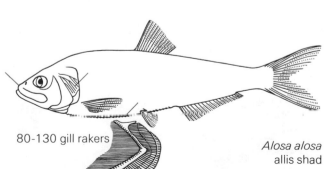

80-130 gill rakers   *Alosa alosa*
allis shad

notched in the mid-line ('hare-lipped'), and there are weak radiating ridges on the gill covers. The critical feature for identification is the number of gill rakers on the first gill arch (between 40 and 60 according to size). The gill rakers appear to be fewer in number and shorter than the red-coloured gill filaments opposite. (See also coloration.)

Coloration   The back is a brilliant deep blue shading to golden yellow on the sides and silvery on the belly. A line of 6–8 dusky round blotches runs along each side at the level of the eye, but are sometimes faint or missing.

Size   Attains a maximum length of 55 cm (22 in.) and a weight of 1.5 kg (3 lb 5 oz).

Remarks   The twaite shad is the more common of the 2 shads in northern European waters. It is migratory, making a spawning migration into the tidal reaches of rivers in which it breeds. In many rivers pollution of the lower reaches, and weirs or other obstructions have denied access for the fish, and it is now rare where once it was very common. Shad feed on crustaceans and small fishes such as sandeels, young sprats, and herring, but they do not feed during their spawning migration. It is not a prime food-fish, although it was at one time commercially exploited. A few are caught by anglers.

A land-locked freshwater population in Lake Killarney, Republic of Ireland, is known as the goureen.

Allis shad   *Alosa alosa*

Distinguishing features   A deep-bodied, heavy-headed herring-like fish. The body is strongly compressed and there is a sharp keel along the belly of the fish. The upper lip has a deep notch in the mid-line, and there are weak radiating ridges on the gill covers. The gill rakers on the first gill arch are long and numerous, apparently longer and more numerous than the red-coloured gill filaments opposite; the rakers number 80–130, depending on size.

Coloration   The back is deep blue, the sides golden shading to silver. There is usually a single dusky blotch at the upper edge of the gill cover on each side, although sometimes it is absent.

Size   A comparatively large fish which grows to 60 cm (24 in.) and may attain a weight of 2.7 kg (6 lb).

Twaite shad
◄

► Allis shad

Remarks   The allis shad is moderately rare in European waters for the same reasons that its relative is now uncommon; if anything, this species has proved more vulnerable. It enters rivers in spring running well upstream to freshwater, to spawn in May, usually at night where the current is swift. The eggs sink and lodge in the gravel bed of the stream. The adults return to the sea after spawning; the young fish drop downstream in the autumn. This fish feeds on a wide range of planktonic crustaceans, although larger specimens eat small shoaling fish. It is not commercially exploited. The fish is palatable, but marred by its boniness.

Anchovy   *Engraulis encrasicolus*

Distinguishing features   Quite unmistakable on account of its rounded protuberant snout and very long lower jaw. The body is slender and rounded in cross-section, without a keel on the belly. The scales are large, fragile and exceptionally easily detached with handling. (See also coloration.)

Coloration   On the back a clear green, sharply contrasting with the bright silvery sides and the silvery-white ventral surface. The gill covers have a yellowish tinge.

Size   A small fish which rarely attains a length of 20 cm (8 in.), and is more usually between 9 and 12 cm ($3\frac{1}{2}$–$4\frac{3}{4}$ in.).

Remarks   A schooling fish living in the surface waters of the sea and feeding on planktonic animals, especially small crustaceans and the larvae of invertebrates and fishes. In summer anchovies migrate into inshore waters and are often found in bights and in estuaries. In winter they move offshore, and in the North Sea probably migrate southwards. Spawning takes place from June to August, and the eggs and larvae are pelagic. The anchovy is not fished for in northern waters, but off southern Europe and in the Black Sea it is an important commercial fish. Much of the catch is salted down in barrels and stored; part is canned in oil. Other species of anchovies form the immensely valuable anchovy fisheries of Peru, and are an important source of animal feed and, indirectly, of fertilizer.

Whitefishes

A group (family Coregonidae) related to the salmon family and like them having an adipose fin on the back. Whitefishes are distinguished by the possession of large scales, fewer in number than any salmon, have toothless jaws and a small mouth, with a deeply forked tail. They are also silvery—hence their name. They are distributed in Arctic rivers and brackish seas, and in mountain lakes across the northern parts of Europe, Asia, and North America.

As a group they offer a most confusing situation to the taxonomist. The lake-dwelling populations have been isolated from one another since soon after the last Ice Age and have evolved as local forms in response to local conditions. In some cases the presence of 2 species in the lake has resulted in hybridization, with sometimes both parent species and the hybrid present, more usually a rather variable type intermediate between the parent species. Whitefishes are also well known for their plasticity, that is the modification of features by environmental conditions. Six species are recognized from northern Europe; more than 50 forms, subspecies or species have been recognized in the past.

Powan   *Coregonus lavaretus*

Distinguishing features   A variable species in snout shape; some forms have bluntly rounded snouts, others elongate snouts. The gill rakers on the first gill arch number 33–39 (exceptionally as few as 25); the rakers are usually smooth-edged. The upper jawbone reaches to the front of the eye.

Coloration   The back is bluish or blue-green, the sides silvery; the dorsal, anal, and tail fins are greyish, as are the tips of the pectoral and pelvic fins.

Size   Varies greatly with the habitat. In the Baltic Sea attains 70 cm (27½in.) and 10 kg (22 lb) in weight, but in many lakes, especially ones in which food is scarce, rarely reaches 20 cm (8 in.) in length.

Remarks   Widely distributed in the Baltic and North Sea basins, but found in brackish water only in the north of its range. In the British Isles (the powan, gwyniad and schellies) and in the Alps (the kilch) is restricted to mountain lakes, in many of which it has survived since late glacial times.

It feeds on planktonic crustaceans, although in brackish water it eats larger crustaceans and tends to feed close to the bottom. The migratory populations enter rivers to spawn in winter; lake populations also spawn in winter on gravelly shallows. The eggs take from 60–70 days to hatch, and the fry emerge from the gravel only in spring.

Vendace   *Coregonus albula*

Distinguishing features   It shares the features of the other whitefishes, but has a long curved, lower jaw which protrudes beyond the tip of the snout. Gill rakers on the first arch number 36–52.

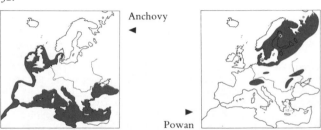

Anchovy

◀

▶

Powan

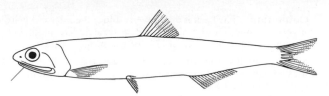

Engraulis encrasicolus
anchovy

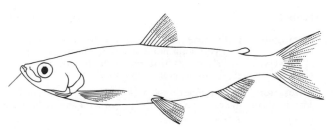

Coregonus lavaretus
powan

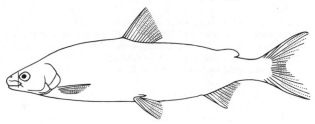

Coregonus albula
vendace

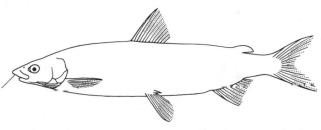

Coregonus oxyrinchus
houting

Coloration   The back is dark greeny-blue; the sides and belly are silvery to white. The dorsal, tail, and pectoral fins are dusky, but not pronouncedly dark coloured. Tip of the snout is dark.

Size   A small species which grows to 20–26 cm (7¾–10¼ in.), but may exceptionally attain 35 cm (13¾ in.). The maximum weight appears to be *c.* 1 kg (2.2 lb).

Remarks   The Scottish and English Lake District vendaces belong to this species, which is widely distributed from northern European USSR and the lakes of the Volga to the Baltic Sea basin. It is found in lakes and, in the north of its range, in rivers; only in the north and east of the Baltic does it venture into brackish water. It migrates from there into nearby rivers to spawn in early winter; the lake-dwelling populations spawn in shallow water in winter, but usually live in deep water. Most populations feed on planktonic crustaceans, but some (usually those living in eutrophic conditions) feed on molluscs and larger crustaceans.

In the Baltic countries it is fished for with traps and seines, especially when it is migrating up rivers. Some of the lake-dwelling populations are threatened with extinction as man-made changes to the environment and the introduction of predators and competitors affect them adversely.

It has recently been suggested that the Irish pollans, at one time thought to be this species, belong to the Arctic *C. autumnalis.*

Houting   *Coregonus oxyrinchus*

Distinguishing features   In its typical form this species is characterized by its very long pointed snout, and by having 35–44 gill rakers (mean 40) on its first gill arch. In other respects it resembles whitefishes in general. (See remarks.)

Coloration   Greeny-blue on the back with silvery sides and belly. The dorsal fin, the extreme tip of the pectoral fin and the snout are dark; all other fins are clear.

Size   Attains a length of 50 cm (19¾ in.) and a weight of *c.* 2 kg (4 lb 6 oz). Several stunted lake populations attain less than half of these dimensions.

Remarks   This species was originally distributed in the southern North Sea and the western Baltic Sea, and was found in the rivers Rhine, Weser, and Elbe, and large lakes in southern Sweden. It

Vendace

occurred in British waters a few times on the south-eastern coast. There is now reason to believe that the North Sea population is extinct, and the Baltic stock is reduced in numbers owing to pollution of river mouths, and obstructions in rivers.

This species is closely related to *Coregonus lavaretus*, and some authorities regard it as only a variety of that species.

Northern whitefish   *Coregonus peled*

Distinguishing features A deep-bodied whitefish with a dorsal profile humped anteriorly then straight. The snout protrudes slightly beyond the lower jaw. It has a large number (46–68) of gill rakers on the first arch, all rather long and thin.

Coloration It is rather dark in colour, with small black speckles on the head and sides of the body outlining the scales, and larger dark spots on the dorsal fin.

Size Varies with habitat; dwarf forms are often found in lakes and have a maximum size of about 27 cm (10½ in.). The river-living populations may grow to 40 cm (15¾ in.) and a weight of up to 900 g (2 lb).

Remarks This whitefish is mainly a lake-dwelling species, although in the Arctic it is also found in rivers and migrates into estuarine water. During October and November, migratory fish move upstream to shed their eggs on shallow gravel beds. Lake-dwelling populations spawn under the ice in early winter. Both types feed mainly on plankton, especially small crustaceans. In Arctic USSR this species is commercially important.

Broad whitefish   *Coregonus nasus*

Distinguishing features A deep-bodied whitefish with a rather humped back. Its most immediate distinguishing character is the deep, short maxillary (upper jawbone), its depth usually half the length. The body is flatsided, not round in cross-section. It has 20–29 gill rakers on the first gill arch.

Coloration Back olive brown to black, sides silvery and silvery-white below; the fins are pale grey, the lower fins usually paler.

Size As in all whitefishes, variable with habitat. In Siberia this species is said to attain a weight of 16 kg (35 lb); in northern Canada

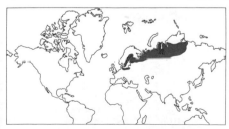

Northern whitefish

75

it is said to weigh up to 1.8 kg (4 lb). European fish generally reach 1 kg (2 lb 3 oz) and about 50 cm (19¾ in.) in length.

Remarks This is an Arctic whitefish which is found more in rivers than in lakes, and is occasionally encountered in estuaries. In northern Canada it spawns in rivers in July and August following a downstream migration in winter. It feeds on bottom-living organisms such as insect larvae, molluscs, and crustaceans. In Arctic regions it is a locally important food-fish, but it is not of prime importance in Europe.

Humpback whitefish   *Coregonus pidschian*

Distinguishing features In this species the tip of the snout projects beyond the lower jaw, the body is flat-sided not round in cross-section, and large specimens have a conspicuously humped back so that the nape appears concave in outline. Gill rakers on the first gill arch are comparatively few, 16–27 (average about 20).

Coloration Back dark brownish-green, belly silvery or with a yellow tinge; the fins may be pale or dusky.

Size Very variable with habitat; in Europe it grows to a maximum of only 50 cm (19¾ in.), and in many populations it rarely exceeds 30 cm (11¾ in.). In Asia and North America (see remarks) it grows much larger and specimens of 5.8 kg (12 lb 12 oz), aged 28 years, have been reported.

Remarks This species occurs across the northern land mass of North America, Asia and Europe—a vast range in which it exists in numerous forms and is subject to great nomenclatural confusion. It is usually referred to as the *Coregonus clupeaformis* complex. It occurs in the extreme north as a migratory fish, entering rivers in autumn

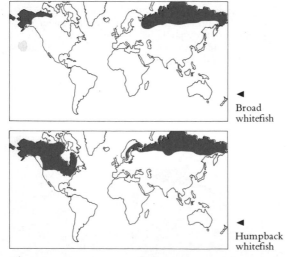

◄
Broad
whitefish

◄
Humpback
whitefish

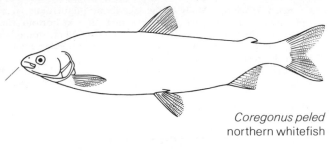

Coregonus peled
northern whitefish

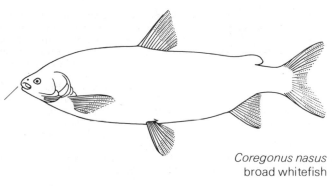

Coregonus nasus
broad whitefish

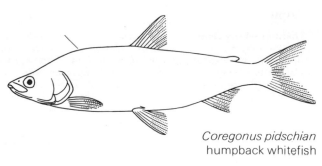

Coregonus pidschian
humpback whitefish

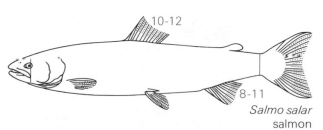

10-12

8-11
Salmo salar
salmon

to spawn in winter. Many of the lake-living populations are so-called dwarf fish living in deep water close to the lake bottom; these too spawn in winter usually in the shallows. When young this species eats plankton, but as it grows it becomes more dependent on larger, bottom-living animals for food.

In Siberia and northern USSR this is a commercially important species, as in the far north is the Canadian representative, *Coregonus clupeaformis*. The flesh is rich and fat, and commands a high price. Most of the catch is taken by gill net in lakes.

Salmon family

The members of this family (Salmonidae) are medium to large fishes with fully scaled bodies and scaleless heads; a lateral line is present. Superficially they resemble the herrings, but they are rounder bodied. No spines are present in the fins, the pelvic fins are abdominal in position, and all species have a small adipose fin on the back.

They are essentially northern hemisphere fishes, although some species have been widely introduced in the southern hemisphere. Members of the family live in freshwater, although many species make regular feeding migrations to the sea. They are also well adapted to cold water, and the charr and the related whitefishes are the dominant fishes in Arctic freshwaters.

Seven species are found in northern European waters, 4 of them having been imported from North America.

Salmon   *Salmo salar*

Distinguishing features The body is typically trout-like, elongate with slightly compressed sides, and deepest in the region of the dorsal fin. The caudal peduncle (body in front of the tail fin) is narrow and the upper and lower rays of the fin stand out from the outline; the tail fin itself is shallowly forked. The upper jawbone extends to the level of the rear of the eye, not beyond. There are 10–13 scales between the base of the adipose fin and the lateral line; 10–12 major dorsal fin rays, and 8–11 major anal rays. A few teeth are present on the palate in a staggered row, but no patch of teeth on the head of the vomer. The gill rakers on the first arch are slender and number 15–20.

Salmon

Coloration Smolts and adult salmon returning from the sea are green or blue on the back, silvery-sided, and white beneath. As the adult approaches spawning it becomes darker, brown or bronze with red spots and dark fins. Fish which have spawned are very dark in colour, often with heavy red patches. The young fish (parr) are dark above with a series of 8–11 dark, rounded parr marks on the sides, and a single reddish-orange spot between each blotch.

Size Salmon can attain a length of 1.5 m (59 in.) and a weight of 36 kg (79 lb).

Remarks The salmon is possibly the most famous fish of the North Atlantic both for its value as a commercial resource and for its sporting qualities. It has also been seen by some as a symbol illustrating the decline in the quality of the environment. Owing to obstruction in rivers, pollution, and overfishing, the range and numbers of the salmon are now much reduced both in Europe and North America.

Salmon spawn far upstream in freshwater, usually in November and December, the eggs being laid on a redd or nest hollowed out in gravel by the female. By spawning time the adult male develops a hooked lower jaw (kype). Over the redd, the large males are often joined by sexually active male parr, which join in the spawning. The eggs fall into the gravel and develop there until they hatch out in April to May; for about a month the fry live in the gravel sustained by the yolk of the egg. They begin to feed actively in midsummer and soon are schooling in the small streams they inhabit. As they grow, the parr spread out along the stream in which they may spend up to 3 years before migrating to the sea.

In the sea salmon travel widely. Substantial numbers travel to the Norwegian Sea and probably more make a trans-Atlantic migration to West Greenland; both areas are rich feeding-grounds. The offshore fishery off Greenland which has caught large quantities of European as well as North American salmon is widely seen as a threat to the survival of the species if its activities are not restricted. After 3 or 4 years (although in some cases only 1 or 2 years) the salmon return to the spawning rivers. Many die after spawning, but some will survive the downstream journey (as kelts), to spawn a second or third time.

Trout   *Salmo trutta*

Distinguishing features The caudal peduncle (region of the body in front of the tail fin) is deep, rather flattened, and the upper and lower tail fin rays seem to merge with the outline. The tail fin is square-cut, or at the most very slightly concave. The upper jawbone extends well beyond the level of the eye. The scales are small, 13–16 between the base of the adipose fin and the lateral line. There are 12–14 major dorsal fin rays and 10–12 major anal fin rays. Teeth are numerous on the palate, present both on the shaft of the vomer and as a patch on the head of the vomer. Gill rakers on the first arch 14–17, short and stubby.

Coloration   In streams brownish overall, darker on the back and silvery on the sides and ventrally, with numerous black spots extending below the lateral line. Spots often have a lighter halo; also numerous rusty red spots on the sides. Dorsal and tail fins only lightly spotted; adipose fin with an orange edge. In large lakes, larger rivers and estuaries, trout are silvery with the spotting reduced; the adipose fin is orange tinted.

Size   Maximum size variable according to habitat. In small brooks trout may not exceed 23 cm (9 in.); in larger lakes or rivers brown trout grow to 1 m (39 in.) and a weight of 8.6 kg (19 lb). Sea trout may attain 1.4 m (55 in.) and 13.6 kg (30 lb).

Remarks   The trout shares many of the biological features of its close relative, the salmon, but forms two basic types: migratory (i.e. the sea trout) and non-migratory (brown trout). There is no justification for regarding them as subspecies.

Trout spawn in winter from October to January, the eggs being shed in redds cut by the female in river gravel, usually in upstream reaches, although many spawn in the gravel below weirs. The eggs hatch in 6–8 weeks, depending on the water temperature, and the fry remain in the gravel for a further 4–6 weeks before beginning to feed. Both types of trout feed on small crustaceans and insect larvae when young. Brown trout tend to continue this diet with larger specimens eating fish extensively; sea trout feed heavily on fish and larger crustaceans in the sea.

Trout require cool water of relatively high quality to thrive, and consequently have suffered from pollution and water misuse rather more than other fishes. Their popularity with anglers, however, has led to the maintenance of large artificial populations in lakes and rivers, and fish farms raise brown trout in numbers. Owing to this farming and the trout's value as food, it is probably as abundant in northern Europe as it was originally. It has been widely spread about the world for angling purposes.

Rainbow trout   *Salmo gairdneri*

Distinguishing features   Essentially trout-like in body form and with the upper jaw extending back to the rear edge of the eye. The head is usually small, but varies with maturity and sex. The tail fin is slightly concave. Scales are very small with 15–16 in a row between the adipose fin and the lateral line; 11–12 major dorsal rays, anal fin

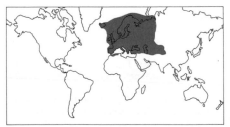

Trout

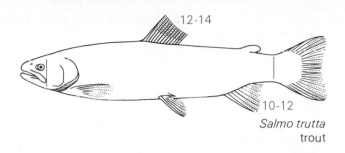

12-14

10-12

Salmo trutta
trout

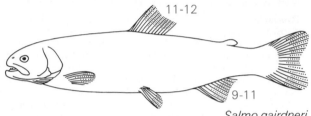

11-12

9-11

Salmo gairdneri
rainbow trout

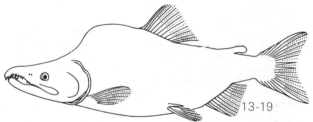

13-19

Oncorhynchus gorbuscha
pink salmon ♂

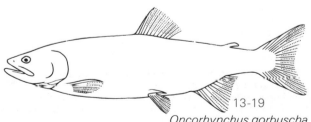

13-19

Oncorhynchus gorbuscha
pink salmon ♀

with 9–11 major rays. Gill rakers moderate, 16–22 on the first gill arch. (See also coloration.)

Coloration   Variable with type of habitat, size and sex. Rainbow trout are typically brown on the back, silvery-white ventrally with a very distinct iridescent (rainbow) stripe along the sides. The kamloops type are silvery, and the migratory steelhead is brilliantly silvery. All types are densely spotted on the back and dorsal, adipose, and tail fins.

Size   Rainbow trout attain 1 m (39 in.) and 15.9 kg (35 lb); steelhead trout grow to 1.2 m (48 in.) and 16.3 kg (36 lb); the kamloops trout usually do not exceed 2.7–3.6 kg (6–8 lb), but have been recorded at 23.6 kg (52 lb). These are North American figures.

Remarks   Native to the eastern Pacific Ocean and rivers from north-west Mexico to Alaska, mainly west of the Rocky Mountains, now introduced across North America and into many other regions including New Zealand, Australia, South America, Africa, southern Asia, and Europe. It lives in similar habitats to the brown trout, but can tolerate higher temperatures and slightly poorer quality water. Growth is rapid when adequately fed. Huge numbers are now raised on fish farms in Britain and Europe. They are bred for food as well as for stocking angling waters, for although the species has been introduced since 1890, relatively few self-sustaining populations have been established.

Three forms are recognized: rainbow trout which is typically an inhabitant of small streams; the kamloops which lives in moderately deep to deep, cool lakes with shallows adequate for food production; and the steelhead which migrates to the sea. In general, all types feed on insects and their larvae, crustaceans, and snails; some fishes are eaten as well as fish eggs. Fishes are eaten mainly by the largest trout, but rainbows will grow to large proportions on a diet of even small crustaceans if they are abundant.

Pink salmon   *Oncorhynchus gorbuscha*

Distinguishing features   Typically salmon-like in general appearance, but with a long upper jaw extending beyond the level of the eye. Scales small, 147–205 in the lateral line (more than any salmonid except the huchen in European waters). Immediately distinguished by its long-based anal fin which has 13–19 principal rays. Dorsal fin rays 10–15; gill rakers on the first gill arch 24–35; those near the middle of moderate length. Breeding males have a pronounced humpback, as well as a hooked snout, gaping mouth, and large teeth.

Coloration   In the sea, steel blue or blue-green above, sides silvery, underside white, with large smudgy black spots on the back and upper sides, and particularly on the tail fin. Breeding males have dark head and back; the sides are pale red with green-brown blotches.

Size   A relatively small salmon, growing to about 6.3 kg (14 lb) and a length of *c.* 48 cm (19 in.).

Remarks   The pink salmon is native to the North Pacific and the Arctic Oceans, and breeds in rivers from the Sacramento river, California, to the Mackenzie river, and in north-east Asia from Peter the Great Bay to the Lena river. It has been introduced to the Atlantic, both to the rivers of Newfoundland and those in the Kola Peninsula (Barents Sea). A number of specimens have been captured in Icelandic, Norwegian, and British waters, presumably strays from the Barents Sea stock which appears to be established. So far they have been captured only as single specimens, and there is no evidence that they have become more widely established.

Coho salmon   *Oncorhynchus kisutch*

Distinguishing features   Salmon-like in appearance, with a long upper jaw which extends beyond the level of the eye. Scales moderately large, 121–148 in the lateral line, which is almost straight. Anal fin long-based, with 12–17 principal rays. Dorsal fin with 9–12 principal rays; adipose fin well developed; a very obvious long scaly process in the axil of the pelvic fin. Gill rakers 18–25, coarsely toothed. (See also coloration.) Not illustrated.

Coloration   In the sea, steel-blue or greenish above, brilliant silver below. Small black spots on back, upper sides, base of dorsal fin and upper lobe only of tail fin. Breeding males are darker, blue green, with a red stripe on the sides, and leaden grey ventrally.

Size   Grows exceptionally to 14.04 kg (31 lb), more usually to around 3.6 kg (8 lb), at which weight it measures around 76.2 cm (30 in.).

Remarks   This salmon, native to the Pacific coast of North America, has been introduced into the Great Lakes of America where it is now common. Introductions have been made in French rivers where, in 1973 and 1974, a considerable number of young fish escaped confinement. In 1976 and 1977 a number of adults were caught on the coasts of Normandy, Brittany, and in the Channel Islands. The spread of this species along the French coast, and into southern British rivers, is likely.

Arctic charr   *Salvelinus alpinus*

Distinguishing features   Body trout-like in general form. Scales are very small, 123–152 in the lateral line. Upper jawbone reaches just to the level of the rear of the eye (lake charr), but just past the eye in migratory charr. 8–11 principal anal rays; 10–12 principal dorsal rays; gill rakers on the first gill arch 19–32. Teeth in the centre of the palate concentrated on the head of the vomer (front of the palate) in a patch not as a staggered row in the mid-line. (See also coloration.)

Coloration   Extremely variable: sea-run charr are steel-blue above, silvery on the sides and ventrally, although the belly may be orange-red, and with numerous red or pink spots on the sides; non-migratory populations are greeny-brown above, often reddish below, but always with reddish and white spots on the sides. In both types the leading edges of the pectoral, pelvic, and anal fins are light (but followed by reddish fin colour—not black). In spawning populations the colours, especially ventrally, are heightened, and spawning males are probably the most brilliantly coloured of all European fishes.

Size   Very variable in length and weight. Migratory charr grow to 1 m (39 in.) in length and 12.2 kg (27 lb) in weight; lake races often attain no more than 25 cm (10 in.).

Remarks   Like other members of the family, the Arctic charr is represented by 2 physiological types: a migratory form which, feeding in the sea, grows to a large size, and a freshwater form which does not migrate. The migratory type is found today only in Arctic waters, in the eastern Atlantic coming as far south as Iceland and Oslo Fjord, Norway. In most of Europe, apart from the far north, charr exist as mountain lake populations, relics of the immediately post-glacial period when migratory charr occurred further south and bred in the rivers of Europe.

Charr spawn in winter or early spring, usually in water of moderate depth, but in some lakes 2 populations are found spawning at different times and places. Anadromous or migratory forms spawn in early winter in rivers, shedding their eggs among gravel in a redd prepared by the female. In Arctic rivers the eggs and the newly-hatched young lie under the gravel, and emerge when the ice breaks up in early summer.

Growth rates vary from population to population; in general, however, growth is slow. Anadromous fish in Canadian waters attain full size at around 20 years, and 40-year-old fish are known. Lake populations are equally slow-growing. All types are carnivorous, many of the lake populations feeding throughout their lives on small planktonic crustaceans. They also eat insects, insect larvae, and molluscs; larger fish eat smaller fishes.

Charr are fine sporting fish and also extremely good to eat. Except in Arctic waters where the large anadromous type is available, they are rarely more than locally important. In Europe, on account of their localized distribution in isolated lakes, they are very vulnerable to human interference. Many small populations are believed to have become extinct because of pollution, competition from and possibly predation by other introduced fishes, and other man-made alterations to their habitat.

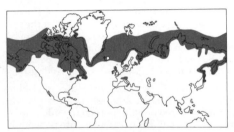

Arctic charr

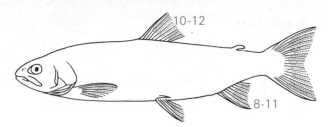

Salvelinus alpinus
Arctic charr

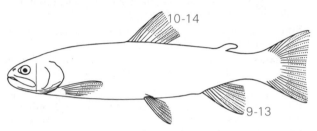

Salvelinus fontinalis
brook charr

palatine teeth

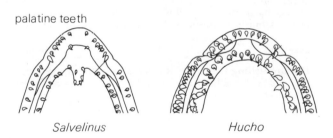

Salvelinus   *Hucho*

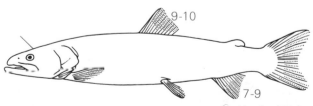

Hucho hucho
huchen

Brook charr   *Salvelinus fontinalis*

Distinguishing features Typically trout-like in body form but more closely related to the Arctic charr. Scales are very small, between 110–130 in the lateral line. Upper jaw reaches well past the level of the eye. 9–13 principal anal rays; 10–14 principal dorsal rays; 14–22 gill rakers on the first gill arch. Teeth in the roof of the mouth well developed in a patch on the vomer, not the palate. (See also coloration.)

Coloration Very variable; olive green to brown on the back, sides lighter, silvery below. Creamy spots on sides, amalgamating into wavy lines on the back. Dorsal and tail fins with black wavy lines. The front edge of pectoral, pelvic, and anal fins dead white with a black sub-marginal band.

Size May attain a maximum weight of about 4.5 kg (10 lb), but one Canadian fish weighed 6.6 kg (14 lb 8 oz).

Remarks The brook charr originates in eastern North America, approximately from Northern Canada to Cape Cod, southwards to Georgia, and westwards to the Upper Mississippi and the Great Lakes, thence northwards to Hudson's Bay. It is an excellent sport fish which has been widely introduced to western North America, South America, New Zealand, Asia, and many parts of Europe, including the British Isles. Brook charr live in cool, well-oxygenated streams and lakes, but in the extreme north of their range they migrate to the sea. They feed on insects, insect larvae, crustaceans, and small fishes mainly, but are unselective in their feeding habits. In Europe this species occasionally hybridizes with brown trout to form the boldly striped, so-called zebra trout.

Huchen   *Hucho hucho*

Distinguishing features Rather salmon-like in appearance, but thin and with the head compressed from side to side. Scales very small, between 180–200 in the lateral line, and 18–20 between the first dorsal fin and the lateral line. 7–9 principal anal rays, 9–10 principal dorsal rays; 16 gill rakers on the first gill arch. Teeth on the palate form a continuous curve (those on the vomer in line with the palatine teeth).

Coloration On the back green or greyish-blue, sides silvery with a pink sheen, white ventrally; the back and sides have many delicate

Huchen

x-shaped spots. Spawning fish have very distinct coppery-red colouring.

Size Attains a maximum of 1.5 m length (59 in.) and 21 kg (46 lb) weight. Usually about 70 cm (28 in.) and 2–3 kg ($4\frac{1}{2}$–$6\frac{1}{2}$ lb).

Remarks The huchen is native to the Danube basin, although it has been introduced successfully to eastern France. It is largely confined to the middle and upper reaches of the river, and never migrates to the sea. It spawns in early spring on gravel banks in which the female hollows a redd, the eggs being buried under the gravel. They hatch in 30–35 days, but the fry do not feed until the yolk of the egg is absorbed. The young feed on crustaceans and small fishes; adults eat a wide range of larger fishes and amphibians.

Because of its size, and edible and sporting qualities, the huchen has been heavily overfished. It has also suffered from the development of the upstream tributaries of the Danube for hydro-electric and water storage schemes. It is now locally a relatively rare fish and may be in need of protection in many parts of its original range.

Grayling

Only 4 species of grayling are recognized today: 2 are native to Mongolia, 1 is found in North America, and 1 in Europe. All are found in freshwater. Traditionally they have been placed in the family Salmonidae, sometimes as an included subfamily, but today they are correctly separated in a family on their own, Thymallidae.

All the known species have a high dorsal fin, with numerous rays, the typical adipose fin of the salmonoid fishes, numerous moderately large scales, and a forked tail fin. They have small teeth in both jaws.

Grayling   *Thymallus thymallus*

Distinguishing features Elongate but stout body with a small head and lightly toothed jaws. The dorsal fin is high and many rayed (17–24); adipose fin present. (See also coloration.)

Coloration Basically silvery on the sides and ventrally, on the back steel blue shading to silvery-green on the upper sides. The dorsal fin has several parallel rows of dusky spots on the membrane. The sides of the body have lengthwise stripes of violet. In the breeding season the colours are heightened, the dorsal fin having an orange-red margin. Young fish have dusky parr marks.

Size Rarely grows longer than 50 cm ($19\frac{3}{4}$ in.); exceptionally attains 60 cm ($23\frac{1}{4}$ in) A maximum weight of 2.5 kg (5 lb 8 oz) is reported from Europe.

Remarks The grayling is essentially a river fish found especially in clean, cool, well-oxygenated rivers, often at moderate altitudes. It also occurs in natural lakes, especially in mountain regions. Its natural distribution has been obscured by frequent attempts to introduce it for sporting purposes. In many parts of Europe pollution of streams and the building of hydro-electric plants have adversely affected this sensitive fish.

It feeds mainly on bottom-living insect larvae, crustaceans, and molluscs. It will also feed on insects at the surface. Less often the larger grayling eat small fishes. Grayling spawn in spring on gravelly shallows, the eggs being laid in a shallow redd cut by the female. Spawning is often preceded by display on the part of the brightly-coloured male. The fry hatch in 3 to 4 weeks, and disperse quickly from the redd. Growth is rapid and the young may reach 7–12 cm ($2\frac{3}{4}$–$4\frac{3}{4}$ in.) in the first year.

The grayling is a good food-fish, and much esteemed in parts of Europe, but it is best prepared and eaten when fresh as the distinctive thyme-like smell is quickly lost. It is also popular as a sporting fish.

Smelts

The true smelts, belonging to the family Osmeridae, are small relations of salmon and trout species, and like them are widely distributed in the North Atlantic, Arctic, and particularly the North Pacific Oceans. They are basically marine coastal fishes, many entering rivers and breeding in freshwater; some populations live in freshwater continuously.

Most are small fishes with slender bodies, fragile scales, and an adipose fin on the back. Two species only are found in northern European waters. No more than 10 species are known world-wide.

Smelt *Osmerus eperlanus*

Distinguishing features Similar to the trouts in general build, especially in having a rayless, adipose fin on the back. The anal fin is long-based with 12–16 principal rays. The dorsal fin is set well back. The mouth is large and the jaws have strong teeth. When fresh, it has a strong smell of cucumber.

Coloration The back is light olive green, the underside is creamy-white and there is an indistinct silvery line along the sides.

Size Attains a maximum length of 30 cm ($11\frac{3}{4}$ in.); non-migratory freshwater populations are smaller and rarely reach 20 cm ($7\frac{3}{4}$ in.).

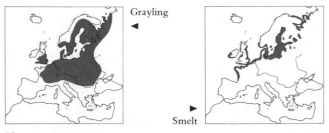

Grayling ◄

► Smelt

88

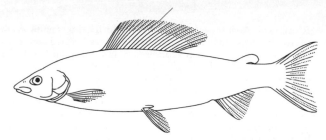

Thymallus thymallus
grayling

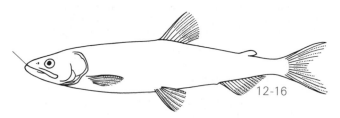

Osmerus eperlanus
smelt

12-16

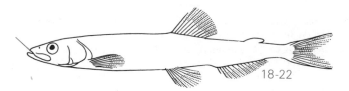

Mallotus villosus
capelin

18-22

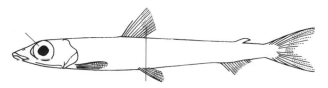

Argentina sphyraena
argentine

Remarks An inshore migratory fish which is most common close to river mouths and in the estuaries themselves. Isolated populations live in freshwater lakes in Scandinavia and European USSR (and formerly inhabited the English Rostherne Mere, where it is now extinct). These populations are relicts from migratory stocks in the immediately post-glacial period.

The smelt feeds on small planktonic crustaceans, although larger smelt mainly eat young fish. It enters rivers during winter; spawning takes place upstream in freshwater in spring, the eggs being shed over sand or gravel, or among submerged plants to which they adhere. Many of the eggs break away and float in the water suspended by the parachute-like outer membrane. Lake smelts spawn in the shallows of the lake.

The smelt has suffered greatly from the pollution of the lower reaches of rivers and more so from the erection of navigation weirs and dams in rivers. It was formerly a valuable food-fish in many rivers; where it is commonly found it is still fished for.

Capelin   *Mallotus villosus*

Distinguishing features A slender-bodied fish, with a large rayless adipose fin and a long-based anal fin (18–22 principal rays). The scales are very small, firmly attached, and pointed above the lateral line and on the belly. Males have a strongly arched anal fin base, larger fins, and ridges develop on the back and the belly before spawning.

Coloration On the back, transparent olive to bottle green; below, the sides are silvery and the belly is silvery-white. The edges of the scales have dusky specks.

Size Attains a maximum size of 23 cm (9 in.). Males are slightly larger than females in each year class.

Remarks The capelin is extremely abundant in the Arctic parts of the North Atlantic and forms a major constituent of the diet of many larger fishes, sea-birds, and cetaceans, as well as the human inhabitants of the region. It is vital to many food-chains in the Arctic.

This fish spawns in late spring and early summer in large schools on the shoreline, or in very shallow water. In many places the breeding fish ride up the shore on the crest of a wave, shed their spawn or milt into the gravel and then are swept back on the next or

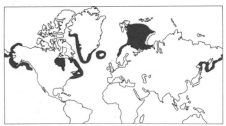

Capelin

succeeding waves. The eggs are buried in the gravel and hatch in 2 to 3 weeks. Capelin rarely live longer than 5 years. They feed almost exclusively on small planktonic crustaceans.

Argentines

A small family (Argentinidae) of marine fishes mostly found in deep water near the edge of the continental shelf. Most are relatively small fishes with large eyes, scales moderate to large, small teeth in their jaws, and an adipose dorsal fin. They are world-wide in temperate and tropical waters.

Two species only are known in the seas of northern Europe.

Argentine   *Argentina sphyraena*

Distinguishing features   A long slender fish with a pointed head, small mouth, moderately large eyes, and an adipose fin on the back close to the tail. The diameter of the eye is equal to the distance between the tip of the snout and the orbit edge. The last ray of the dorsal fin is above the base of the pelvic fins. Scales fragile, usually missing, but with almost smooth free edges; 50–54 scales between the head and tail fin. 11–14 gill rakers on the first gill arch.

Coloration   Olive green above, a prominent silvery stripe along each side, greyish-white ventrally.

Size   Attains a maximum length of 27 cm (10½ in.); females are generally longer than males of the same age.

Remarks   A relatively common, even locally abundant fish on muddy bottoms in depths of 55–200 m (30–109 fathoms). Exceptionally it has been found as shallow as 18 m (10 fathoms) and as deep as 400 m (219 fathoms). It feeds on bottom-living worms and molluscs, but principally on crustaceans and small fishes, many of them mid-water species, which suggests that this fish forages off the sea-bed, possibly at night. In its turn it is eaten by a number of other sea fishes. It has little economic value except that it has been exploited as an industrial fish for the production of fish meal. It spawns in March to July; the eggs and larvae are pelagic. This species of argentine may live to an age of 16 years.

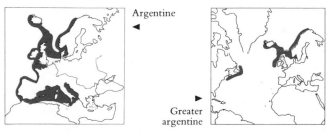

Argentine
◄

►
Greater
argentine

Distinguishing features A slender but thickset fish with a pointed head, very large eyes, small mouth and feeble teeth, and an adipose fin. The eye diameter is larger than the snout length. The last ray of the dorsal fin is in front of the pelvic fin base. The scales are moderately large, with rough edges, and not easily dislodged; 64–69 between head and tail fin. 18–22 gill rakers on the first gill arch.

Coloration Pale greeny-yellow with a marked silvery sheen on the sides and belly.

Size Attains 56 cm (22 in.) in length.

Remarks A deep-water argentine, living near the edge of the continental shelf mainly between 183 and 549 m (100–300 fathoms), exceptionally from 91–914 m (50–500 fathoms). It probably lives close to, rather than on, the bottom and is found most abundantly over muddy bottoms. It feeds on small fishes, crustaceans, and squids—many of them mid-water animals. Although it is commonly caught in deep-water trawls, its flesh is soft and insipid, and it is not marketed as food.

Pikes

A small family (Esocidae) of northern hemisphere freshwater fishes. All have similar body shape, elongate with a pointed snout, large jaws, and dorsal and anal fins opposite one another and placed close to the tail fin. Five species are recognized, only one of which is found in Europe; it is also distributed in northern Asia and North America.

Pike *Esox lucius*

Distinguishing features Unmistakable on account of its body form. The dorsal and anal fins are opposite and close to the tail fin; the pelvic fins are abdominal in position. The head is broad, although the snout is pointed; a series of large teeth in the lower jaw, dense but smaller teeth in the roof of the mouth.

Coloration Usually greeny-brown, flecked with lighter golden green to form curved lines and speckles on the back and sides. Yellowish ventrally.

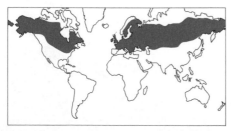

Pike

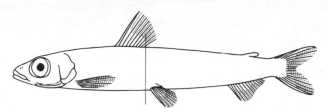

Argentina silus
greater argentine

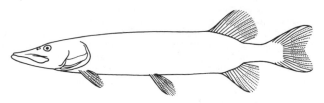

Esox lucius
pike

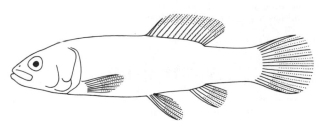

Umbra krameri
European mudminnow

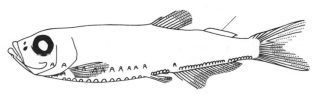

Maurolicus muelleri
pearlsides

Size   In the British Isles attains a weight of 24 kg (53 lb) and a length of 1.30 m (51 in.); up to 34 kg (75 lb) in the USSR. The largest fish are females, males rarely growing heavier than 4.5 kg (10 lb); 6.3 kg (14 lb) is probably a maximum.

Remarks   The pike is typically an inhabitant of lowland rivers and lakes, especially those which contain submerged marginal vegetation. On account of its popularity as an anglers' fish, it has been introduced to many atypical habitats and geographical regions. Its life style is predatory, lying in wait amongst vegetation and attacking its prey at great speed over a short distance. As a young fish it lives among dense vegetation and feeds on invertebrates, especially crustaceans and insect larvae. As it grows it begins to feed on larger prey and, when well grown, there are few fishes it will not eat. Large pike eat fishes mostly, but will also take waterfowl and small aquatic mammals. They feed by sight not by scent.

Both sexes mature in their second or third year. Spawning takes place in early spring at the water's edge or over flooded water-meadows, the eggs being shed over the vegetation. Often 2 or more small males accompany each much larger female. Spawning takes place during daylight. Pike live to a maximum of 15 years; in exceptionally large, probably unexploited waters, an age of 24 years has been reported.

The pike is a valuable food-fish in Europe, and both there and in the British Isles is well regarded as an anglers' fish. Unfortunately, as a predator on smaller fish, the population is never very numerous in any water and a relatively small amount of exploitation can exhaust the stock. In many parts of Europe the pike has been over-exploited and has had to be artificially restocked.

Mudminnows

The mudminnows (family Umbridae) are northern hemisphere freshwater fishes found in eastern Europe and North America. They are small fishes—up to 20 cm (8 in.) in length—with fully scaled bodies, and the dorsal fin is placed far along the back. Five species only are known; one is native to Europe, another has been introduced. All the species are notably resistant to cold and low oxygen conditions, and the Alaska blackfish, *Dallia pectoralis*, survives in Arctic conditions.

European mudminnow   *Umbra krameri*

Distinguishing features   A small, rather stout fish with scales on head and body. The dorsal fin origin is above the pelvic fins, and both these and the anal fin are well behind the mid-point of the body.

Coloration   Greenish-brown on the back, with indistinct darker vertical bars, lighter on the lower sides and yellowish ventrally.

Size Attains a maximum length of 13 cm (5 in.). Males are smaller than females.

Remarks An inhabitant of swamps and overgrown ponds and streams in which deoxygenated waters it will often thrive when all other fishes would have died. It also survives better in cold winters with heavy snowfall than most fishes. It feeds on bottom-living insect larvae, crustaceans, and molluscs. It spawns in spring, about 150 eggs being laid in a hollow guarded by the female who also removes dead or infected eggs. Females may live for 5 years, males for 3.

The eastern mudminnow, *Umbra pygmaea*, has been introduced to Europe from eastern North America. It is now found in parts of Germany, France, and Holland. Similar to the European species, it has light lengthwise stripes, a dark spot at the tail-fin base, and larger scales.

Bristlemouths

The bristlemouths are a large family (Gonostomatidae) of deep-water fishes distributed in all the oceans throughout the world. Most are small to very small, but as a group they are exceedingly abundant and play an important part in the food-chains of the sea as predators on small invertebrates and prey for many larger animals. Most species are slender and fragile, with large mouths and thin, sharp teeth; many of them have well-developed light-organs.

Several hundred species are assigned to the family; 26 are known from the eastern North Atlantic and Mediterranean, but only one is at all common over the continental shelf.

Pearlsides   *Maurolicus muelleri*

Distinguishing features A small fish with a large eye and moderately large mouth. The dorsal fin is placed vertically behind the pelvics; it has a long, very low adipose fin on the back, and the anal fin has a long base. Very obvious light-organs on the lower side of body. (See also coloration.)

Coloration Beautiful greenish-blue on the back, brilliant silver on the sides and belly; the light-organs gleam pale blue.

European mudminnow

Size Attains a total length of 65 mm (2½ in.); usually much smaller.

Remarks A mid-water fish living between 200 and 500 m (109–273 fathoms), but found only in the deeper water during daylight. At night it comes nearer the surface, and can be captured occasionally in the upper 30 m (16 fathoms) of the sea. It is fairly frequently stranded on the shore, especially on the open ocean coasts of Europe. It is preyed upon by tuna, hake and several members of the cod family; its young are taken by herring. It feeds on small crustaceans and other planktonic animals. This is one of the few deep-sea fishes to be captured regularly in shallow water; it occurs world-wide in tropical and temperate oceans.

Hatchet-fishes

A very distinctive family (Sternoptychidae) of small marine fishes living mainly in mid-water in the deep sea. All the members of the family have a deep, compressed body with a sharp edge to the belly and a narrow tail. Most are silvery on the sides with large light-organs on the belly. They are found world-wide in the oceans and are often very common, forming a major constituent in the diet of many larger, predatory fishes. Probably there are no more than 20 species altogether. Seven are found in the eastern North Atlantic, of which 3 occur at times in coastal waters of northern Europe.

Hatchet-fish   *Argyropelecus olfersi*

Distinguishing features Deep-bodied with a steeply-angled jaw and large eyes which are directed upwards. Light-organs on the lower sides and belly conspicuous. A prominent double-pointed spine in front of the pelvic fins. The caudal peduncle is short.

Coloration Back dark greyish-brown, the sides silvery-white.

Size Attains a length of 10 cm (4 in.).

Remarks A mid-water fish found from 400–600 m (219–328 fathoms) by day and from 200–300 m (109–164 fathoms) at night, and exceptionally on the surface. Moderately common on the edge of the continental shelf and occasionally close inshore on open

Hatchet-fish

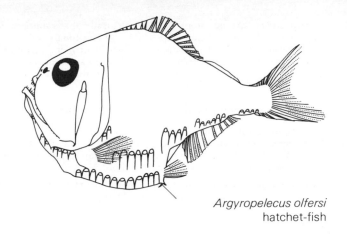

Argyropelecus olfersi
hatchet-fish

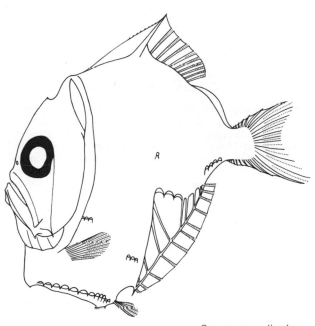

Sternoptyx diaphana
transparent hatchet-fish

ocean coasts. On occasions caught in considerable numbers. It features in the food of members of the cod and tuna families.

A related species, *A. hemigymnus*, which is smaller (maximum length 4.5 cm) is distinguished by the slender caudal peduncle. It lives in rather deeper water, but may be more abundant in certain water masses.

Transparent hatchet-fish   *Sternoptyx diaphana*

Distinguishing features   Similar in body shape to the hatchet-fish, but even deeper, so that the depth is only slightly less than the body length. The eyes are laterally placed. A thin transparent bony blade on the back in front of the dorsal fin.

Coloration   Dark olive green on the back, silvery on the sides and ventrally, with small oval blue-green light-organs in clusters on the belly and tail.

Size   Attains 5 cm (2 in.).

Remarks   Found mainly in deep water between 700 and 900 m (382–492 fathoms), exceptionally down to 3083 m (1686 fathoms), and occasionally shallower. Apparently stays at the same depth day and night. Moderately common on the edge of the continental shelf, rarely straying into coastal water. World-wide in tropical and temperate Atlantic, Indian, and Pacific Oceans; absent in the Mediterranean.

Smooth-heads

A family (Alepocephalidae) of mainly small fishes found in the deep sea, usually in mid-water. They are characterized by their small mouths, weak teeth, and small dorsal fin placed far down the body near the tail. Many of them have large thin scales on the body but smooth, rather slimy skin on the head. A considerable number of species are known, many from single specimens; 2 of the largest species occur in European waters.

Risso's smooth-head   *Alepocephalus rostratus*

Distinguishing features   An elongate fish with soft flabby texture, and smooth-skinned head. Scales large, easily dislodged but

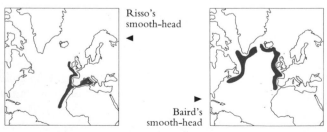

Risso's
smooth-head

Baird's
smooth-head

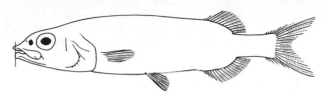

Alepocephalus rostratus
Risso's smooth-head

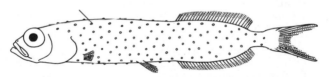

Alepocephalus bairdii
Baird's smooth-head

Xenodermichthys socialis
Atlantic gymnast

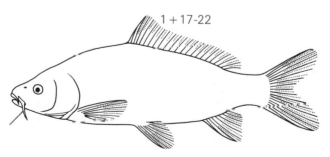

1 + 17-22

Cyprinus carpio
carp

with 53–55 scales in the lateral line. Snout concave with the upper jaw slightly longer than the lower; eyes large. 23–25 gill rakers on the first gill arch. Back with a central ridge giving it a deeper body.

Coloration Dark purplish-brown when fresh, fading to brown after death.

Size Attains a length of 70 cm (28 in.).

Remarks Deep-water fish living on the edge of the continental shelf in depths of 365–1000 m (200–546 fathoms). It is taken over soft, muddy bottoms, occasionally by deep-fishing commercial trawlers, but seems rare and is never taken in any numbers.

Baird's smooth-head   *Alepocephalus bairdii*

Distinguishing features A slender-bodied fish with soft, flabby-textured flesh, smooth head and large, very easily dislodged scales (trawl-caught fish are usually scaleless). 63–67 scales (or scale pockets) in the lateral line. Snout profile straight, jaws equal in length, eyes moderately large. 28–30 gill rakers on the first gill arch. Body round in cross-section, not ridged at the dorsal fin.

Coloration Deep purplish-brown on capture, fading to dark brown.

Size Attains length of 1.15 m (45 in.), rarely beyond 1 m (39 in.).

Remarks A deep water smooth-head found between 365 and 1000 m (200–547 fathoms), although most abundant around 600–800 m (328–437 fathoms). It is confined to soft muddy bottoms, and occurs occasionally in commercial trawl catches. Locally, possibly as a result of seasonal spawning movements, very large numbers have been captured together; several hundred were caught in April 1973, the females containing large ripe eggs. Its principal diet appears to be the bathypelagic jellyfish, *Atolla*. Despite its abundance locally it is useless as a food-fish, the flesh having a most unpleasant smell, flavour and texture.

Atlantic gymnast   *Xenodermichthys socialis*

Distinguishing features A slender, scaleless fish with a moderately small head, large eyes, and dorsal and anal fins equal-sized and opposite one another. The skin is soft and slimy, and has raised light-organs on the sides and ventral surface.

Atlantic
gymnast

Coloration   Entirely black with a deep violet tinge on the sides when fresh.

Size   Attains 15 cm (6 in.) in length.

Remarks   Occurs in mid-water from *c.* 100 to 1000 m (55–557 fathoms), but common, at times even abundant, between 366 and 732 m (200–400 fathoms). Its biology is little known and this fish is rarely seen except when it is found in the stomach of larger fishes such as blue ling and hake. It is too small to be captured in commercial fishing nets.

Carp Family

This family (Cyprinidae) is the major group of freshwater fishes in Europe, as it is an important constituent of the fauna of the freshwaters of North America, Africa, and Asia. The members are typically 'fish-shaped' with scaly bodies, no adipose fin, a single dorsal fin (occasionally with a hard spiny ray anteriorly—as also in the anal fin); many have barbels. Internally, its members have a complex connection between the two-chambered swim-bladder and the inner ear, which gives them enhanced hearing; they can also produce sounds. The family is also characterized by having no teeth in the jaws, but well-developed teeth are present on the pharyngeal bones (behind the gill chamber) which grind food against a hard, horny pad in the roof of the pharynx.

The pharyngeal teeth are a diagnostic feature in the distinction between closely related cyprinids. Unfortunately, the fish must be killed before the teeth can be extracted, and the pharyngeal bones cleaned of tissue (see p. 135). Information on the numbers of teeth and the number of rows is given for the left side first; i.e. $6+2:2+6$ means that there are 2 rows, the outer with 6, the inner with 2 teeth. The teeth of most of the common western European species are illustrated. Most species can, however, be identified with certainty on external features.

Cyprinid fishes frequently breed together and produce hybrid offspring. These usually resemble one parent more than another, but are variable between the two standards— in the roach × rudd hybrid the offspring more closely resemble roach than rudd. Wherever it is important to identify a fish thought to be a hybrid, the body should be saved entire and sent to a competent authority.

In the breeding season adult fish have a so-called nuptial livery; in males particularly, the head, paired fins, and the scales especially on the front of the body develop hard, white, conical outgrowths. The coloration may also be enhanced. After spawning the fish lose the nuptial tubercles and the colour returns to normal.

Carp	*Cyprinus carpio*

Distinguishing features   Four barbels, 2 long ones at the corners of the mouth, shorter ones on the upper lip. Dorsal fin base long

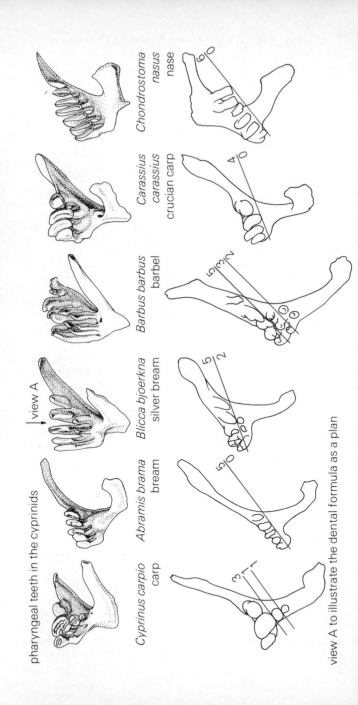

pharyngeal teeth in the cyprinids

Cyprinus carpio carp

Abramis brama bream

Blicca bjoerkna silver bream

Barbus barbus barbel

Carassius carassius crucian carp

Chondrostoma nasus nase

view A

view A to illustrate the dental formula as a plan

pharyngeal teeth in the cyprinids continued

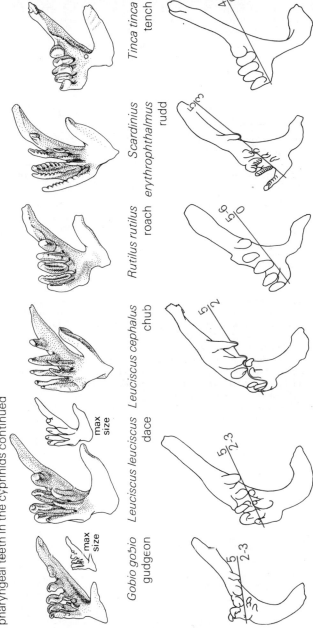

Gobio gobio gudgeon

Leuciscus leuciscus dace

Leuciscus cephalus chub

Rutilus rutilus roach

Scardinius erythrophthalmus rudd

Tinca tinca tench

with 17–22 branched rays and a strong, toothed spine in front. Dorsal fin outline concave anteriorly. King or wild carp have fully scaled bodies; leather carp are scaleless or almost so; mirror carp have exceptionally large scales along the sides and at the base of the dorsal fin. Pharyngeal teeth 3 + 1 + 1 : 1 + 1 + 3; teeth with flattened crowns.

Coloration Variable; wild carp are brownish-green on the back and upper sides, shading to golden yellow ventrally. The fins are dusky, ventrally with a reddish tinge. Golden carp are bred for ornamental purposes.

Size Growth is variable with local conditions. In south-eastern Europe (where conditions are optimum) an average length of 51–61 cm (20–24 in.) and weight of 1.8–4.5 kg (4–10 lb) is attained; in northern Europe it is rather less. A maximum weight of 32 kg (70 lb 8 oz) is recorded (Italy, 1886).

Remarks The natural conditions that suit carp are lowland lakes and rivers where there is abundant vegetation to provide food and shelter. They thrive in warm-water conditions, and require temperatures of at least 18°C to spawn. Consequently the success of populations introduced to northern Europe and the British Isles is dependent on warm weather during spring and summer.

Carp feed mainly on bottom-living insect larvae, small snails, crustaceans, and some vegetable matter. They are most active at night, and feed little at low temperatures. The diet of the young includes small planktonic crustaceans, but the larvae, after they have utilized the yolk from the egg, feed on minute rotifers and algae, and the young stages of water-fleas.

Breeding takes place in late spring in relatively shallow water overgrown with water plants. The eggs (1–1.5 mm diameter) are attached to plants and hatch in 3–8 days, depending on temperature. The newly-hatched alevins remain attached to the plants until the yolk of the egg is exhausted.

The carp is very popular as a food-fish in Europe (and elsewhere), and is well suited for raising in fish farms; carp farming is now a considerable industry. Carp is also a popular anglers' fish and many waters are stocked with large fish. Owing to its popularity as a food or sporting fish, it has been widely introduced to other parts of the world (North America, southern Africa, New Zealand, Australia, etc.).

Carp

Crucian carp
Carassius carassius

Distinguishing features The body is deep and the back distinctly high. There are no barbels at the mouth. Dorsal fin long-based with 14–21 branched rays, with anteriorly a full-length, lightly serrated spine. Anal fin with a similar, lightly serrated spine and 6–8 branched rays. Outline of dorsal fin convex. Gill rakers on the first gill arch 26–31. Pharyngeal teeth 4:4, narrow and smooth-edged.

Coloration Olive green, or reddish-brown on the back, a bronze tint on the sides fading to yellowish ventrally. Young fish have a dusky blotch on the tail. The fins are dark grey-brown, but the pelvics, anal and pectoral fins have a red tinge.

Size Grows to a maximum of 51 cm (20 in.) and 1.8 kg (4 lb); owing to its ability to thrive in food-poor conditions, its average size is much smaller, often no more than 15 cm (6 in.) and 170 g (6 oz).

Remarks Typically an inhabitant of marshy pools, overgrown lakes, and slow-flowing lowland rivers. It is very tolerant of low oxygen levels and can live in conditions which few other fish could survive. As a consequence it is often stocked in marginally viable fishery ponds, although it rarely grows well in such places. However, in good conditions it can attain a good growth rate. It is also resistant to cold and to organic pollution.

The crucian carp feeds on plants, insect larvae and, when young, on planktonic crustaceans. It breeds in May and June, but is dependent on the temperature (the minimum being 14°C). The eggs are deep gold and stick to the water plants, hatching in 5 to 7 days, although the alevins remain attached to the plant leaves for a further 2 days until the yolk is absorbed.

The crucian carp is a food-fish of some value in Europe, but is not favoured in carp fisheries as it competes for food with the faster growing carp. Hybrids between the 2 species offer some advantages in that they grow moderately well and are resistant to poor conditions. This hybrid also occurs in the wild where both species are present. It is suitable as an angler's fish in small lakes and woodland pools.

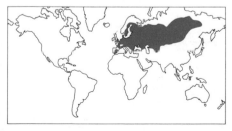

Crucian carp

Goldfish   *Carassius auratus*

Distinguishing features   Moderately deep-bodied, the dorsal
profile gently curved. No barbels at mouth. Dorsal fin long-based,
with 15–19 branched rays and a deeply serrated spine at the front of
the fin; anal fin with a similar spine and 5–6 branched rays. Outline
of dorsal fin straight to slightly concave. Gill rakers on first gill arch
35–48. Pharyngeal teeth 4:4, narrow and smooth edged.

Coloration   Goldfish, *C. auratus auratus*: when young, green-
brown above, bronze on sides, yellowish ventrally; as adult,
beautiful orange red. Gibel carp, *C. auratus gibelio*: greeny-brown
on the back and upper sides, golden on sides fading to silver or white
ventrally.

Size   Maximum length *c*. 30.5 cm (12 in.), and weight 907 g
(2 lb); usually much smaller.

Remarks   Goldfish found in European freshwaters are all the
result of the liberation of ornamental fish which have, in many
places, established viable populations. They are widespread in
lowland Europe and in England, but their distribution is impossible
to establish with certainty as introductions continue intermittently.
Some of the goldfish are ornate, long-finned varieties.

The gibel carp, sometimes called the Prussian carp, is native to
eastern Europe, but has been introduced to western Europe,
including England. It thrives in densely weeded small lakes, ponds
and the lower reaches of rivers. It spawns among vegetation in June
or July, the eggs sticking to the plants; hatching takes place in about
a week.

Tench   *Tinca tinca*

Distinguishing features   Rather thickset and elongate body
with a deep tail and rounded fins; scales very small, embedded, and
covered with heavy mucus. A pair of thin barbels, one each side, at
the corner of the mouth. Pharyngeal teeth 4:5, the tips swollen and
with a slight hook. Males have the second ray in the pelvic fin
swollen and the fin rays are longer, reaching past the vent.

Coloration   A deep greeny-brown above, often with bronze
sides and a yellowish tinge to the belly. The fins are dark brown or
grey.

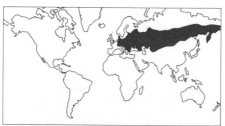

Goldfish

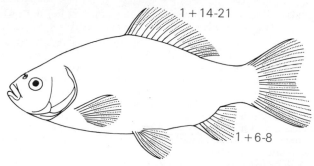

1 + 15-19

1 + 5-6

Carassius auratus
goldfish

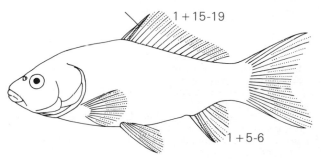

1 + 14-21

1 + 6-8

Carassius carassius
crucian carp

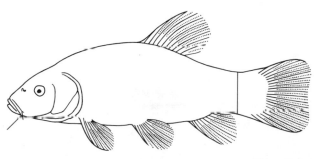

Tinca tinca
tench

Size Attains a maximum length of 70 cm (27½ in.) and a weight of *c.* 8 kg (17 lb 9 oz). Large fish are more usually *c.* 1.8 kg (4 lb).

Remarks The tench is a fish of still waters, mostly lakes and ponds, less often of the lowland reaches of rivers, where it is found in dense vegetation. It is to some extent a bottom feeder, and eats insect larvae, pond snails, crustaceans, and occasionally plant life. It spawns in shallow water in late spring and early summer, the eggs being shed among water plants often on the plants' leaves. The small, green eggs hatch in 6–8 days and the alevins remain attached for a few days. Once they have absorbed the yolk of the egg, they begin to feed actively on planktonic crustacean larvae, rotifers, and other minute animals.

The tench is very tolerant of low oxygen conditions and can survive for some time out of water. It is thus able to inhabit small, overgrown pools where many other fish would die, although it never grows to a large size in such conditions. In Europe it is raised as a supplementary crop in carp farms, and finds a ready sale as a food-fish. It is also a popular angler's fish. It has been introduced to other parts of the world, for example Australia, New Zealand, and North America.

Bream	*Abramis brama*

Distinguishing features Deep-bodied with a high back and flattened sides. The head is comparatively small, with the mouth ventral and extending into a tube when feeding. The eye is small, between 1¼ and 1½ in the length of the snout. The scales are small with 51–60 scales in the lateral line. The anal fin origin is beneath the rear end of the dorsal fin; its base is long, with 24–30 branched rays and its outline is strongly concave. Pharyngeal teeth 5:5, the teeth long and compressed.

Coloration Dark brown or greyish on the back; adults have golden brown sides, the young have silver, and are ventrally yellowish. The fins are grey or light brown, those underneath being reddish tinted.

Size An average length of 40.6–51 cm (16–20 in.) and a weight of 3.6 kg (8 lb) is attained; exceptionally a length of 80 cm (31½ in.), and 9 kg (19 lb 10 oz) in weight.

Remarks The bream inhabits slow-flowing rivers, lowland lakes, and ponds; it also occurs in the brackish areas of the Baltic Sea.

Tench

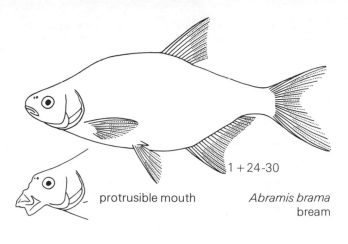

protrusible mouth

1 + 24-30

Abramis brama
bream

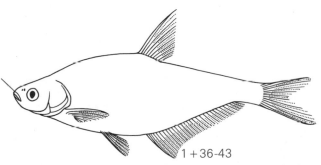

1 + 36-43

Abramis ballerus
zope

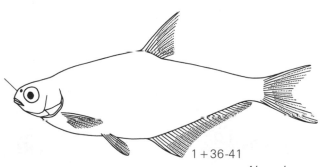

1 + 36-41

Abramis sapa
Danubian bream

It feeds, usually in schools on the river bed, swimming slowly over the bottom in a head-down oblique stance, using its protrusible mouth to pick up insect larvae, worms, and molluscs. Schools feed in shallow water at night, often with their tails 'dimpling' the water as they move.

Bream spawn in late spring and early summer among dense vegetation, often in shallow water and at night. The yellowish eggs stick to the weeds, and hatch in 3–12 days, depending on temperature. Breeding males develop numerous spawning tubercles on the head and body. Bream are affected by temperature; in the northern parts of their range, growth is very slow and maturity may not be attained until 10 years of age. Small lakes may also become crowded with small, stunted bream.

In Europe this is a commercially important food-fish. It is also a valuable fish for anglers, although all too frequently expected to grow well and provide sport in unsuitable habitats.

Zope $Abramis\ ballerus$

Distinguishing features Very compressed body, but not so high as the bream. The dorsal fin rays are long and the fin is high; the anal fin base is very long, with 36–43 branched rays. The tail fin is deeply forked. Scales are small, 66–73 in the lateral line. The eyes are moderately large (equal to the snout length). Pharyngeal teeth 5 : 5, compressed.

Coloration The back is dark blue-green, the flanks are silvery with a yellowish tinge above, and on the throat. The fins are grey, except for the pectorals and pelvics which are yellowish with dark tips.

Size Grows to an average of 30–36 cm (12–14 in.), rarely up to 41 cm (16 in.).

Remarks The zope (it is also called the blue bream) is an inhabitant of the lowest reaches of rivers and of lakes. It migrates upriver to the heavily weeded margins where it spawns in April and May, the eggs being shed during spring floods among the dead vegetation. As an adult fish it schools in open water, in cold weather retiring to deep holes; the young live in the shallows for their first year or two.

In the lower reaches of the Danube and Volga it is a valuable food-fish, but it is not considered valuable in northern Europe.

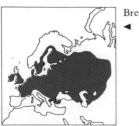
Bream ◄

► Zope

Danubian bream
Abramis sapa

Distinguishing features Compressed body, but not high as in the bream. Head small with a blunt, curved snout. Dorsal fin rays long, the fin high; the anal fin base is long, with 36–41 branched rays. The tail fin is forked, the lower lobe longer. Scales are moderately small, 48–52 in the lateral line. The eyes are moderately large. Pharyngeal teeth 5:5, compressed.

Coloration Blue-green on the back, silvery on the sides; the iris of the eye is silvery. The dorsal and tail fins are dusky.

Size Average length between 15–20 cm (6–7¾ in.), rarely to 30 cm (11¾ in.) and a weight of 0.8 kg (1 lb 12 oz).

Remarks A bottom-living, schooling fish found in lowland reaches of rivers, and in the Black and Caspian Seas, in estuaries. Its food is entirely composed of bottom-living organisms, especially midge larvae, amphipods, ostracods, and molluscs. In April to May, these estuarine inhabitants migrate upstream to freshwater, to spawn. Spawning takes place in rivers over dense vegetation.

In eastern Europe and the USSR the Danubian bream is commercially exploited on a minor scale.

Zährte
Vimba vimba

Distinguishing features Slender-bodied and only slightly compressed. A low keel runs along the back from the dorsal fin to the tail. Head small, snout projecting, always longer than the eye, and the mouth ventral. Anal fin moderately long, with 18–21 branched rays. Scales small, 57–63 in the lateral line. Pharyngeal teeth 5:5.

Coloration Grey-blue on the back, on the sides yellowish, ventrally light yellow. When spawning, the head and back are much darker, while the lips, underside of the head and body, pectoral and pelvic fins are reddish orange. Spawning tubercles are well developed.

Size Average length 20–40 cm (8–15¾ in.) exceptionally attaining 50 cm (19¾ in.) and a weight of *c.* 906 g (2 lb).

Remarks A bottom-living fish which is found in the lower reaches of rivers and in low salinity estuaries, as well as parts of the Baltic, Black, and Caspian Seas. It also lives in some lowland lakes. It is migratory in that the schools move upriver into freshwater to

Danubian bream ◀

► Zährte

spawn in May to July in shallow water. The eggs are shed directly onto a clean stony bottom, and stick to the stones or fall into crevices. They hatch in 3–10 days, according to temperature.

The distribution of the zährte is discontinuous and several sub-species are recognized in the different major drainage basins. The biology of each is slightly different.

In eastern Europe and the USSR this is a minor commercial fish, and is caught in numbers during its spawning migrations.

Silver bream   *Blicca bjoerkna*

Distinguishing features   Moderately deep-bodied, with a high dorsal profile. Head small; the eye is large, its diameter greater than the snout length. Anal fin long, with 21–23 branched rays, its origin behind the last ray of the dorsal fin. Scales moderately large, 44–48 in the lateral line. Pharyngeal teeth $5+2:2+5$, flattened and with a weak hook.

Coloration   Light olive brown on the back, the sides conspicuously silver. Fins dark, except for the pelvics and pectorals which are distinctly reddish with grey tips.

Size   Attains a length of 25 cm (10 in.), exceptionally up to 36 cm (14 in.); weight rarely in excess of 453 g (1 lb).

Remarks   An inhabitant of lowland rivers, lakes and ponds, usually found only where the current is slow in rivers, and close inshore among vegetation. It feeds both in mid-water among vegetation and on the bottom, eating insect larvae, crustaceans, small molluscs, and plants. The young feed on planktonic organisms.

The silver bream spawns in summer, in schools among the water plants. The yellow eggs stick to the weeds, and hatch in 4–6 days at a length of 4.8 mm.

This fish is not used for food, nor well regarded as a sport fish. In waters where fishery management is attempted, it may be a serious competitor with the bream and other fishes.

Schneider   *Alburnoides bipunctatus*

Distinguishing features   A small, slender fish with a moderately long anal fin (14–17 branched rays), a small head, with the mouth

Silver bream
◀

▶
Schneider

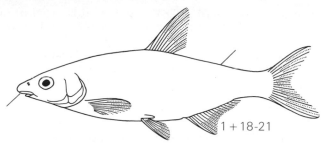

1 + 18-21

Vimba vimba
zährte

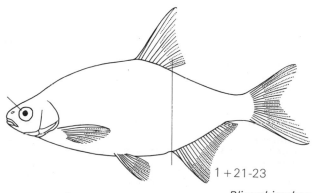

1 + 21-23

Blicca bjoerkna
silver bream

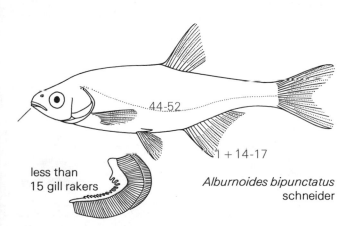

44-52

1 + 14-17

less than
15 gill rakers

Alburnoides bipunctatus
schneider

terminal and jaws equal. Gill rakers on the first gill arch short and fewer than 15. Scales moderate in size but easily detached, 44–52 in lateral line. Pharyngeal teeth 5+2:2+4 or 5+2:2+5.

Coloration   Back light olive green with faint broken stripes on upper sides; lateral line bordered above and below with a dusky stripe; yellowish silver ventrally. Ventral fins orange tinted. Colours brighter at spawning season.

Size   Mostly only up to 10 cm (4 in.), rarely to 15 cm (6 in.) in length.

Remarks   Lives in rivers, usually where the current is moderate to swift; occasionally found in clear lakes. It spawns on gravelly shallows in May and June, the eggs dropping between the stones. It feeds on small planktonic animals—chiefly crustaceans, and aquatic insects. In Europe this fish is found in the same habitat as the minnow; it is similar to the bleak but lives in faster water, even in riffles.

Bleak   *Alburnus alburnus*

Distinguishing features   Slim-bodied and very silvery in colour. The anal fin is long-based (16–20 branched rays). The head is small with the mouth strongly oblique, and the lower jaw prominent. The eyes are large. Gill rakers on the first gill arch 17–22. Scales moderate in size, easily detached, 48–55 in the lateral line. Pharyngeal teeth 5+2:2+5, serrated and hooked at the tip.

Coloration   Back and upper sides blue-green, lower sides and ventral surface brilliant silvery-white. The fins are grey, white ventrally.

Size   Usual length 12–15 cm (4¾–6 in.); exceptionally attains 20 cm (8 in.).

Remarks   A schooling fish which is often extremely abundant in slow-flowing rivers, mainly in the lowland areas, but penetrating well upstream to moderate current regions. It also lives successfully in lakes. Although it prefers clean water, it survives well in turbid, even poorly-oxygenated rivers, as it swims at the very surface where conditions are more favourable.

It feeds on animal plankton, especially small crustaceans, surface-living insects and aerial insects which fall into the water. Spawning takes place in shallow water, the eggs being shed among the stones

Bleak
◄

►
Danubian
bleak

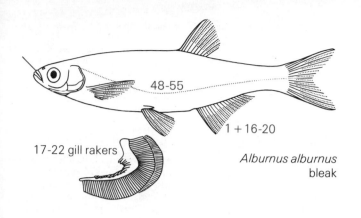

48-55

1 + 16-20

17-22 gill rakers

Alburnus alburnus
bleak

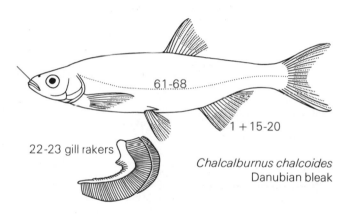

61-68

1 + 15-20

22-23 gill rakers

Chalcalburnus chalcoides
Danubian bleak

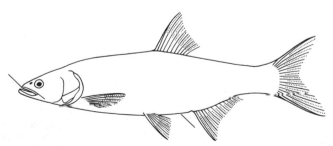

Aspius aspius
asp

or on nearby vegetation; the bleak spawns in May or June depending on the temperature.

The bleak is of little direct economic importance. It has occasionally been exploited as a fertilizer or as animal feed stuff; at one time its scales were used to produce pearl essence for the manufacture of artificial pearls. Because of its abundance it is often a valuable forage fish for larger predators, trout, zander, perch, chub, and pike, as well as for fish-eating birds.

Danubian bleak   *Chalcalburnus chalcoides*

Distinguishing features   A slender-bodied, bleak-like fish with a small head, oblique mouth, and prominent lower jaw. The anal fin is long-based with 15–20 branched rays. The eyes are large. Gill rakers on the first arch, long and crowded, 22–23 in number. Scales small, firmly attached, 61–68 in the lateral line. Pharyngeal teeth 5+2:2+5, slightly serrated.

Coloration   Olive brown on the back, shading to golden yellow on the sides, silver ventrally.

Size   Attains a length of 22–25 cm ($8\frac{3}{4}$–$9\frac{3}{4}$ in.), rarely 30 cm ($11\frac{3}{4}$ in.).

Remarks   This species is of wide distribution in the Black, Caspian, and Aral Sea basins. It enters Europe only along the Danube (subspecies *C. chalcoides mento*). In these seas it lives in brackish water and migrates into rivers to spawn. It feeds on planktonic animals, crustaceans and insects, and its life style is much like that of the bleak. In the USSR it is of some commercial importance.

Asp   *Aspius aspius*

Distinguishing features   Body slender and slightly compressed, with a sharp keel between the pelvic fins and the vent. The head is pointed with a very large, oblique mouth. The lower jaw is longer with a thickened tip which fits into a notch in the upper jaw. The scales are small, well attached; 65–74 in the lateral line. Anal fin is concave in outline, moderately long-based; 12–14 branched rays. Pharyngeal teeth 5+3:3+5, strong and smooth.

Coloration   Dark green on the back, the sides silvery with each scale centre picked out greyish, white ventrally. The fins are dark except that the pectoral, pelvic, and anal fins are deep red.

Size   Normally between 40–60 cm ($15\frac{3}{4}$–$23\frac{1}{2}$ in.) and weighing up to 3.6 kg (8 lb). Exceptional fish may weigh *c.* 9 kg (20 lb).

Remarks   The asp inhabits the middle reaches of rivers, usually where the current is moderate, and also large lakes. In the Black and Caspian Sea basins it is migratory, living in estuaries and river mouths, and migrating into freshwater to breed. It spawns in late April to May in clean running water, the eggs falling between stones. They hatch in 10–17 days depending on temperature. Young fish school and feed on small planktonic crustaceans and insect larvae, etc. The adults eat fishes, especially surface-living and mid-water cyprinids, and also amphibians. Large fish are solitary.

In eastern Europe the asp has some importance as a food-fish. It is an excellent sporting fish, although because of their life style, large specimens are not frequent.

Barbel
Barbus barbus

Distinguishing features Elongate body, almost round in cross-section but flat on the belly. Two pairs of barbels on the upper lip, one pair at the front of the snout, the other at the angles of the mouth; lips fleshy. Dorsal fin short-based but high, with a strongly serrated full-length spine; anal fin short and rounded. Scales small, deeply embedded, 55–65 in lateral line. Pharyngeal teeth $5 + 3 + 2 : 2 + 3 + 5$, teeth pointed, their tips hooked.

Coloration A warm, greeny-brown on the back, golden yellow on the sides and ventrally. The fins are dark except that the pectoral, pelvic, and anal fins are orange.

Size Attains a maximum of 7.25 kg (16 lb) weight, and a length of 91 cm (36 in.); the average length is about 50 cm (20 in.) and a weight of 2.27 kg (5 lb).

Remarks The barbel is a bottom-living fish found in the middle reaches of lowland rivers where the bed is clean gravel and the current is moderate. Outside this kind of habitat it may be found in weir pools, in the lower reaches, and in deep pools in upstream regions. Typically it is most active by night and in the half-light, moving around in small schools usually of equal-sized fish. It feeds on bottom-living invertebrates, particularly aquatic insect larvae, crustaceans, and molluscs. Spawning takes place in late spring, when the males develop prominent spawning tubercles in rows on the head and back. The yellowish eggs adhere to stones or lodge between them, and hatch in 10–15 days. In most rivers there is an upstream migration before spawning.

The barbel is a major sporting fish, and angling interests have ensured its wide distribution (as in England). Only locally is it fished for food. Its roe is slightly poisonous.

Several subspecies are recognized in Spain, Italy, and the USSR

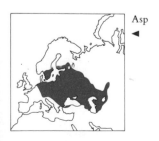
Asp ◄

► Barbel
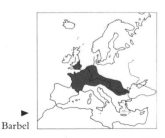

Southern barbel   *Barbus meridionalis*

Distinguishing features   Elongate body, with the back slightly arched. Two pairs of long barbels, one on the front of the upper lip, the other at the angle of the jaw. The front barbel reaches the nostril if bent towards it. Dorsal fin short-based but high, with a strong, smooth-edged full length spine. Anal fin short-based but pointed, with the longest rays in front. Scales moderate, 48–55 in lateral line. Pharyngeal teeth $5+3+2:2+3+5$.

Coloration   Warm greeny-brown above, yellowish on the sides, lighter ventrally, with dark blotches on upper sides and back. Dorsal and tail fins spotted.

Size   Attains a maximum length of 40 cm (16 in.), on average around 25 cm (10 in.), and a weight of 250 g ($8\frac{1}{2}$ oz).

Remarks   Lives in swiftly-flowing rivers and streams, mainly in lowland regions but also at moderate altitudes. It spawns in May to July on gravel shallows, usually after an upstream migration. This species is represented by several subspecies in the southern parts of its range, in each of which they have been isolated since pre-glacial times.

Gudgeon   *Gobio gobio*

Distinguishing features   An elongate but round-bodied fish with a large head. Tail moderately short and deep. The snout is prominent with a ventral mouth, thick lips and a barbel at each corner of the mouth. The scales are moderate in size, firmly attached with 38–44 in the lateral line.

Southern barbel

Gudgeon

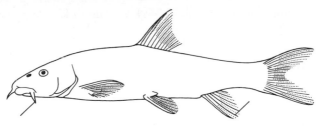

Barbus barbus
barbel

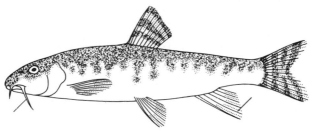

Barbus meridionalis
southern barbel

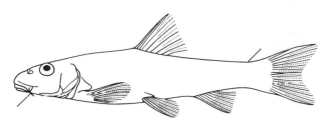

Gobio gobio
gudgeon

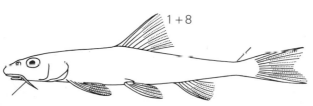

1 + 8

Gobio kessleri
Kessler's gudgeon

Coloration   Greeny-brown shading on the back to deep yellow on the sides, along which runs a series of large, rounded, dark blotches; silvery-white ventrally. The dorsal, tail, and anal fins are heavily spotted.

Size   Usually around 10–15 cm (4–6 in.), but can attain 20 cm (8 in.) in length. Maximum weight *c.* 226 g (8 oz). Females are larger than males of the same age.

Remarks   Widely distributed in a variety of habitats from lakes and slow-flowing lowland rivers to moderately fast-running rivers well upstream; also occurs in low salinity areas of the northern Baltic. It is a bottom-living fish usually living in small schools in shallow water; in winter it is found in deeper water. It feeds on bottom-living insect larvae, crustaceans, and molluscs, although young fish eat planktonic crustaceans.

Spawning takes place in early summer, usually in shallow water and at night. The eggs adhere to plants and stones, and hatch in 10–30 days depending on temperature. Few gudgeon live longer than 3 years, although exceptional 6- and 7-year-old fish have been recorded.

A minor angling fish and of little importance as a food-fish.

Kessler's gudgeon *Gobio kessleri*

Distinguishing features   Elongate but with a rounded body in cross-section and a large head. The tail is long and slender, particularly just before the tail fin. Dorsal fin with 8 branched rays. Snout prominent, lips thick with a very long barbel at each corner of the mouth. No scales on throat.

Coloration   Dark brown above, yellowish-brown on the sides, with large brown blotches running along the sides. Prominent dark spots on dorsal and tail fins.

Size   Length usually up to 12 cm (4¾ in.), occasionally to 13 cm (5 in.).

Remarks   Found only in the lower Danube basin, including the estuary and other Black Sea rivers. Its habits are similar to the European gudgeon except that it tends to be confined to the lower reaches of rivers.

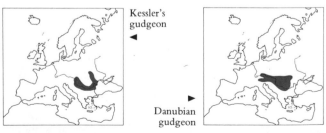

Kessler's gudgeon ◄

Danubian gudgeon ►

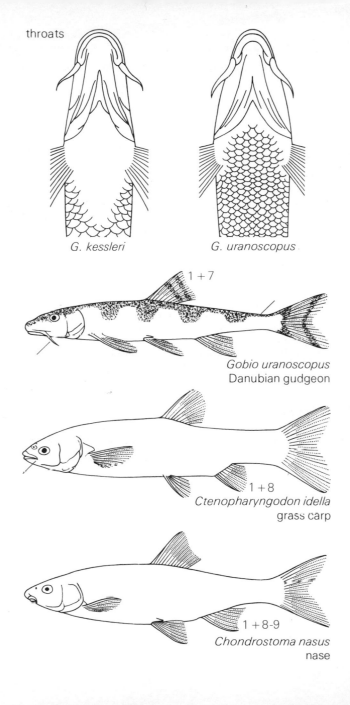

throats

G. kessleri

G. uranoscopus

1 + 7

Gobio uranoscopus
Danubian gudgeon

1 + 8

Ctenopharyngodon idella
grass carp

1 + 8-9

Chondrostoma nasus
nase

Danubian gudgeon

Gobio uranoscopus

Distinguishing features   Elongate but with a rounded body in cross-section. The tail is long and slender, especially just in front of the tail fin. Dorsal fin with 7 branched rays. Snout prominent with thick lips and very long barbels, 1 at each corner of the mouth. Throat scaly.

Coloration   Dark brown above, the colour forming a series of large dark blotches along the flank continuous with the back colouring. Silver ventrally.

Size   Average length 10–12 cm (4–4¾ in.), maximum *c.* 15 cm (6 in.).

Remarks   Like the gudgeon, a bottom-living fish which lives on gravel or stony bottoms. It is more common in the upper reaches of rivers and their tributaries than in the main stream. Feeds on bottom-living insect larvae, crustaceans, and small molluscs.

Grass carp

Ctenopharyngodon idella

Distinguishing features   Slender-bodied, but with a large, broad head, eye small, mouth terminal and very wide, reaching back to the front of the eye. Dorsal and anal fins short-based, the former rounded in outline and its origin in front of the pelvic fin origin, the anal with 8 branched rays. Scales moderately large, 43–45 in the lateral line. Pharyngeal teeth usually 2 + 5 : 4 + 2, flattened with folded sides and a groove on the grinding surface.

Coloration   Back dark greeny-brown, the sides with a golden tinge, with each scale dusky at the base; fins dark.

Size   Attains a length of 1.25 m (48 in.) and a weight of *c.* 35 kg (77 lb).

Remarks   The grass carp is native to the river Amur and the region to the south, including much of China. It has been introduced to many parts of central and eastern Europe and the USSR (and even to England experimentally). It feeds entirely on plant matter once it is more than a few inches in length (until then it eats animal plankton) and is introduced as a means of keeping under control plant growth in navigation and drainage channels. In some

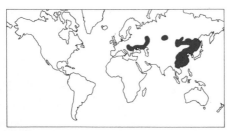

Grass carp

parts of Europe it is propagated in fish farms; it is not known to breed in western or northern Europe.

Nase
Chondrostoma nasus

Distinguishing features A slender-bodied fish with a small head and very rounded protuberant snout. The mouth is characteristic, being a horizontal slit with sharp-edged, horny lips. The anal fin is short-based with 10–12 branched rays. Scales moderate in size, 57–62 in lateral line which is almost straight. Pharyngeal teeth 6:6, narrow and knife-shaped.

Coloration Back grey-green, shading lighter on the sides, the belly yellowish-silver. Pectoral, pelvic, and anal fins reddish, the others grey.

Size Attains a length of 50 cm (20 in.), more usually between 25 and 40 cm (10–16 in.), and a maximum weight of 1.79 kg (4 lb).

Remarks The nase is most abundant in the swiftly-flowing middle reaches of rivers just below the mountainous zones. Lower downstream it is locally common below weirs and obstructions in the river where the flow is temporarily turbulent. It forms large schools, especially in winter, when it congregates in deeper water before making an upstream migration to spawn. It spawns in spring, usually in small tributaries on clean gravel bottoms; the eggs adhere to the stones. Its principal food is algae and other vegetation (its lips are well adapted to scrape algae off rocks).
It is fished for commercially where it is found in large numbers, and may be locally valuable as a food-fish.

Soiffe
Chondrostoma toxostoma

Distinguishing features Slender-bodied with a small head and very prominent protuberant snout. The mouth is horseshoe shaped, entirely ventral and has sharp-edged horny lips. The anal fin is short-based, with 8–9 branched rays; the scales are moderate in size, 52–56 in the lateral line, which is almost straight. Pharyngeal teeth 6:6, compressed and knife-shaped.

Coloration Olive green on the back, shading to yellowish on the sides and silvery ventrally. The ventral fins are yellowish, the dorsal and tail fins olive.

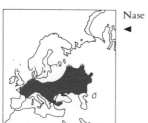

Nase
◄

►
Soiffe

Size Usually attains a length of 20–25 cm (8–10 in.), exceptionally 30 cm (11¾ in.).

Remarks Found in smaller rivers than the nase, where the current is moderate and the water clear. It feeds on algae and water plants, and spawns in spring further upstream than its larger relative.

The Spanish stock is recognized as subspecifically distinct (*C. toxostoma arrigonis*) from the French stock. A related species, *C. genei*, is found in northern Italy.

Moderlieschen   *Leucaspius delineatus*

Distinguishing features A slender fish with large, thin, easily detached silvery scales. The lateral line pores are found on at most the first 10 scales. The head is small, with a large eye, and a strongly oblique mouth. The anal fin is longer-based than the dorsal, with 10–13 branched rays; a sharp keel between the pelvic fins and the vent.

Coloration Back olive, the sides silvery-white; an intense silver-blue stripe running along the sides. The fins are pale.

Size Average length 6–8 cm (2½–3¼ in.), maximum *c.* 12 cm (4¾ in.). Females are larger than males of the same age.

Remarks The moderlieschen is a small schooling fish which typically inhabits small ponds and lakes, and less often the lowland reaches of rivers where the current is very slow. It spawns in summer, the female developing a small tube-like pore at the genital opening by means of which the eggs are looped around water plants. The males have very distinct spawning tubercles on the head and gill covers.

Bitterling   *Rhodeus sericeus*

Distinguishing features A rather deep-bodied fish with moderately well attached scales, although the lateral line pores are present on only the first 5 or 6 scales. The head is small, the eye moderate and the mouth is transverse. The dorsal fin is relatively long, with 8–9 branched rays.

Coloration Warm grey-brown on the back, the sides are silvery with a pinkish flush, and towards the tail there is a bright metallic

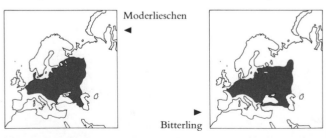

Moderlieschen ◄

► Bitterling

ventral views of mouths

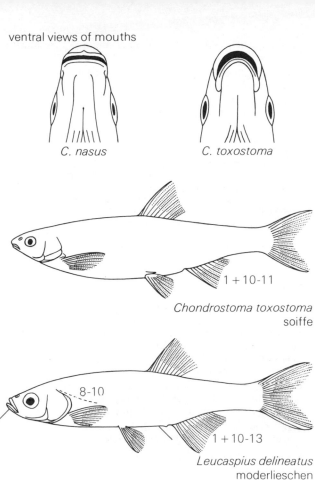

C. nasus   *C. toxostoma*

1 + 10-11

Chondrostoma toxostoma
soiffe

8-10

1 + 10-13

Leucaspius delineatus
moderlieschen

1 + 8-9

5-6

Rhodeus sericeus
bitterling

streak. Ventrally silvery. At spawning, the males are much more brightly coloured.

Size Usually attains a size of 6–7 cm ($2\frac{1}{2}$–$2\frac{3}{4}$ in.), but may grow to 9 cm ($3\frac{1}{2}$ in.).

Remarks The bitterling is typically a fish of small lakes, ponds, and overgrown lowland rivers. It feeds on a wide range of small animals, especially planktonic crustaceans, plant plankton, and vegetation. Its breeding habits are unique amongst European fishes in that the female develops a long (often of body length) egg-depositing tube from the genital opening. The eggs are laid within the gill chamber of freshwater mussels and are fertilized by the male ejecting sperm into the inhalent current of the mussel's gills. The eggs are moderately large (c. 3 mm) and develop within 3–4 weeks, protected by the mussel. Breeding male bitterling are brilliantly coloured and have conspicuous white tubercles on the head; they adopt a territory around a mussel which is defended against intruders. The bitterling often acts as host to the parasitic young stages of the mussel.

Dace   *Leuciscus leuciscus*

Distinguishing features A rather slim-bodied fish with a narrow head and a small mouth. The dorsal fin, which originates above the pelvic fin base has 7–8 full length branched rays; the anal fin has 8–9 branched rays. The outer edge of both fins is concave. Scales in the lateral fin 48–51; pharyngeal teeth $5+2:2+5$ (occasionally 3 in the inner row).

Coloration Greenish-olive above, the sides silvery, and silver-white ventrally. The iris of the eye is yellow. The fins are greyish, but the pectorals, pelvics and anal fins are yellow to pale orange.

Size Generally attains a length of 15–25 cm (6–10 in.), exceptionally to 30 cm ($11\frac{3}{4}$ in.), and a weight of 600 g (1 lb 5 oz).

Remarks A fish which is typically found in the middle reaches of rivers and in brooks, although it also occurs in lakes and lowland rivers but never numerously. It requires a moderate current and clean water, and is usually present in large schools. It feeds on insects, both larval and flying adults, and will take quantities of terrestrial arthropods which fall into the water. Crustaceans and some

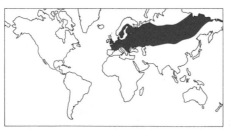

Dace

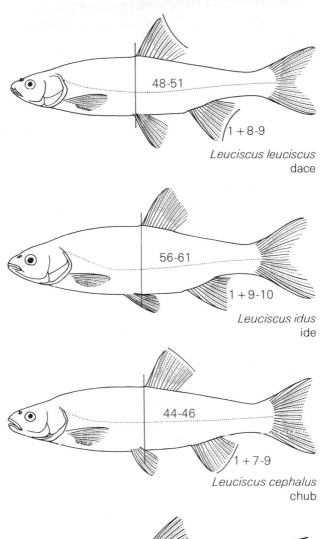

48-51

1 + 8-9

Leuciscus leuciscus
dace

56-61

1 + 9-10

Leuciscus idus
ide

44-46

1 + 7-9

Leuciscus cephalus
chub

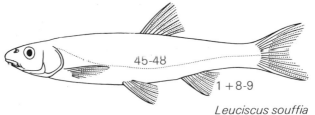

45-48

1 + 8-9

Leuciscus souffia
soufie

vegetation are also eaten. The dace spawns early in the spring, often at night and usually in gravel shallows below a riffle. The eggs are small (1.5 mm), pale orange in colour and take up to 25 days to develop at 13°C. They mature mostly in their second year; few dace live longer than 7 years.

Although small, the dace is a moderately popular angling fish; it is not used for food.

Ide   *Leuciscus idus*

Distinguishing features   A moderately slender-bodied fish with a broad head and 'humped' back. The snout is blunt and the mouth oblique. The dorsal fin origin is just behind the base of the pelvic fins and has 8 branched rays; it has a straight free edge. The anal fin is concave on the free edge, with 9–10 branched rays. Scales are moderately small with 56–61 in the lateral line. Pharyngeal teeth cylindrical and smooth, 5 + 3 : 3 + 5.

Coloration   On the back greenish-brown, the lower sides silvery, the belly white; ventral fins are reddish. The ornamental golden orfe is a deep orange variety of the wild fish.

Size   Average length 30–43 cm (11¾–17 in.), and a weight of *c.* 680 g (1 lb 8 oz); exceptionally grows to 1 m (39 in.) and a weight of *c.* 4 kg (8 lb 12 oz).

Remarks   In Europe the ide is a fish of the lower reaches of large rivers, lowland lakes, and the brackish estuaries of rivers. It lives in schools in clean deep water, although it comes into shallow fresh-water to spawn in April and May. It spawns over sandy or gravel areas, the eggs being attached to water plants and stones. Before and after spawning the adults migrate from or to the deep water. It feeds, when adult, on the larger insect larvae, crustaceans, and molluscs; large ones even consume small fishes. Young ide eat small planktonic crustaceans.

In eastern Europe the ide is fished for commercially. Elsewhere it has become rather rare owing to pollution in river mouths and possibly overfishing. It is popular as an angler's fish and the golden variety is very suitable for keeping in lakes and ponds. Several rivers in Britain contain ide as a result of escapes or the release of unwanted fish.

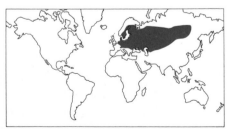

Ide

Chub *Leuciscus cephalus*

Distinguishing features Rather thickset about the head and 'shoulders' but basically slender; the head is very broad, the snout blunt, and the mouth large. The dorsal fin is placed just behind the base of the pelvic fins; it has 8–9 branched rays and a convex free edge. The anal fin is rounded and conspicuously convex; it has 7–9 branched rays. Scales 44–46 in the lateral line; pharyngeal teeth 5 + 2 : 2 + 5.

Coloration Dark green or grey-brown on the back, the sides silvery, ventrally silvery-white; each scale is dusky edged. The fins are dark except for the pelvic and anal fins which are yellowish, even orange.

Size On average between 30–50 cm ($11\frac{3}{4}$–$19\frac{3}{4}$ in.); exceptionally it may attain 61 cm (24 in.). Weights range from an average of *c.* 2.7 kg (6 lb) to a maximum of 7.25 kg (16 lb).

Remarks The chub is a river fish found most abundantly in the middle reaches, but extending upstream into more typically fast-flowing trout streams as well as downstream to the lowland reaches. This versatility also enables it to thrive in large lakes. It is a schooling fish, particularly when young, but large chub are often solitary. When young, it feeds mostly on aquatic invertebrates, mainly insects, their larvae, and crustaceans. The larger fish feed on larger prey; many small fishes are eaten as well as crayfish and lamperns, and very occasionally water voles and frogs.

The chub spawns in May–June, usually in shallow water on gravel beds, often in the smaller tributaries. The eggs are sticky and adhere to plants and stones. The young hatch in 8–10 days. Chub grow slowly and live for up to 12 years.

This is a popular sporting fish, but quite valueless as food because of its soft flesh and numerous bones.

Soufie *Leuciscus souffia*

Distinguishing features Slender-bodied with a small, pointed head (its length about equal to the body depth at the dorsal fin). The dorsal and anal fins are short-based, with slightly convex free edges, 8–9 branched rays in both. The scales are moderate in size, 45–48 in the lateral line; pharyngeal teeth 4 (or 5) + 2 : 2 + 4 (or 5). (See also coloration.)

Chub
◄

►
Soufie

Coloration   Grey-green on the back with a conspicuous dark, greeny-blue stripe along the sides; silver ventrally.

Size   Generally between 12 and 15 cm (4¾–6 in.) in length; grows exceptionally to 25 cm (10 in.).

Remarks   A fish which lives in the small streams of the head waters of continental rivers; it is also found in lakes. It is known to inhabit lakes as high as 2000 m. It lives in large schools, feeding on insects, crustaceans, and even algae. It spawns from April to July, later at higher altitudes, the eggs being shed into the gravel. Throughout its range a number of isolated populations exist which are sufficiently different to be recognized as subspecies.

Ziege   *Pelecus cultratus*

Distinguishing features   Highly characteristic body form with elongate body, strongly curved belly, which forms a sharp keel, and straight back. The lateral line is wavy, the anal fin long-based (24–28 branched rays), and the pectoral fin long and pointed. The mouth is large and strongly oblique.

Coloration   Top of head and back light greeny-blue, the sides silvery with a pinkish tinge. The fins are colourless.

Size   Grows to 25–40 cm (10–15¾ in.) on average; can attain 51 cm (20 in.) and a weight of 1.5 kg (3 lb 4 oz).

Remarks   This interesting cyprinid fish lives in brackish water, in lagoons, and in the lowest reaches of rivers. It is a pelagic, schooling fish which migrates from salt water upstream to spawn amongst vegetation from May to July. It feeds on fishes, particularly surface schooling young herring, gadoids, and gobies; in freshwater, especially when young, it eats surface-living insects, crustaceans, and smaller fishes. The Baltic populations are confined to river mouths; the Black and Caspian Sea populations make extensive migrations upriver. In the east it is exploited on a small scale as a food-fish.

Minnow   *Phoxinus phoxinus*

Distinguishing features   A small slender-bodied fish with short-based, rounded dorsal and anal fins. The scales are minute and the lateral line is short and interrupted to form an incomplete line. (See also coloration.)

Ziege

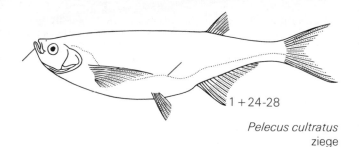

1 + 24-28

Pelecus cultratus
ziege

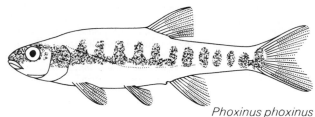

Phoxinus phoxinus
minnow

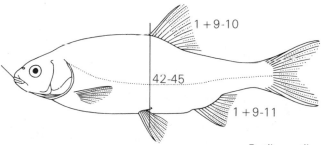

1 + 9-10

42-45

1 + 9-11

Rutilus rutilus
roach

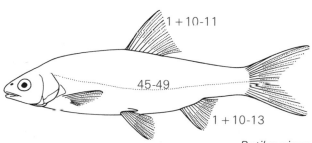

1 + 10-11

45-49

1 + 10-13

Rutilus pigus
Danubian roach

Coloration   Back and upper sides olive brown, ventrally whitish; along the sides a series of dark blotches, the last, at the base of the tail fin, most conspicuous. Young fish are lighter. Breeding males have brilliant red undersides and black throats.

Size   Rarely more than 8 cm (3¼ in.), but very exceptionally growing to 12 cm (4¾ in.). Females are larger than males of the same age.

Remarks   Typically a fish of the upper reaches of rivers, even in mountainous regions (up to 198 m altitude in the Alps). It is also common in high altitude lakes and in small lowland streams where the water is clean and moderately fast flowing. It schools at or near the surface in summer; in winter it retires to deeper water, and in times of high river flow hides under stones or close to the banks.

It spawns in spring (May or mid-July) on gravelly shoals, often just below a riffle; the eggs are shed among the stones. They hatch in 5–10 days depending on temperature. The minnow feeds on a wide range of aquatic animals, principally insect larvae and crustaceans, but it will eat algae and plants, and often leap for flying insects.

It is often extremely abundant in suitable rivers and makes an important contribution to the food-chain of freshwaters. It is eaten by many fish-eating birds, and larger fishes. Locally, in parts of Europe, it is caught for human consumption by means of traps or seine nets.

Roach   *Rutilus rutilus*

Distinguishing features   A moderately deep-bodied cyprinid with a rather short head. The dorsal fin is high, has 9–10 (rarely 11) branched rays; its origin is above the base of the pelvic fins. The scales are relatively large, 42–45 in the lateral line. Anal fin moderate, with 9–11 branched rays. Pharyngeal teeth 5:6; the smaller ones slightly hooked.

Coloration   Iris of the eye red; back dull bluish or greeny-brown, the sides intensely silvery, sometimes brassy-yellow. The fins are grey-brown except for the pelvic and anal fins which are orange to bright red; the pectoral fins have reddish tints.

Size   Depending on local conditions of food availability and density of population, average roach attain a length of 35 cm

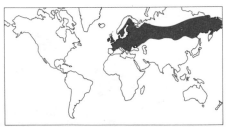

Minnow

($13\frac{3}{4}$ in.) and a weight of 1 kg (2 lb 3 oz); exceptionally specimens attain 53 cm (21 in.) and up to 1.8 kg (4 lb).

Remarks The roach lives in lowland rivers and lakes, being possibly more common where the current is slow, but thriving as well in moderately quick streams. Because of its adaptability it can live in canals, ponds, and in mildly polluted water, and has thus become widely distributed across virtually the whole of Europe. It is also found in brackish water in the Baltic, Black, and Aral Seas. Several subspecies have been recognized from eastern Europe.

It is unselective in its diet and eats insects, insect larvae, crustaceans and snails, as well as vegetable matter; almost all smaller animals are eaten if abundant. The roach spawns in spring (April–June), shedding its eggs amongst the dense vegetation in shallow water. The yellow eggs (1–1.5 mm in diameter) stick to the plants and hatch in 9–12 days, at 12–14°C. Growth rate varies enormously with food supply, and many roach populations living in barely suitable conditions consist of stunted old fish. However, where food is plentiful and conditions are good the roach can show good growth; an age of 12 years is occasionally attained.

Because of its abundance and ability to survive in poor conditions the roach is an important fish in the economy of rivers and lakes. It is important prey for fish-eating birds, and for other fishes such as pike, perch, eel, and chub. It is a popular sporting fish for the angler and (mainly in eastern Europe) is regarded as a food-fish.

Danubian roach   *Rutilus pigus*

Distinguishing features Moderately deep-bodied, with a short head. It is very similar to the roach, but distinguished by its rather smaller scales, 45–49 in the lateral line, 10–11 branched rays in the dorsal fin, 10–13 in the anal fin.

Coloration Green-olive on the back, brassy-yellow on the sides, silver ventrally. The dorsal fin is light brown; the other fins are reddish. Males are especially brilliant in the breeding season.

Size Grows to *c.* 30 cm ($11\frac{3}{4}$ in.), exceptionally to 40 cm ($15\frac{3}{4}$ in.).

Remarks Of restricted distribution, one subspecies is recognized from northern Italy, *R. p. pigus*, and another from the upper Danube, *R. p. virgo*. This fish lives in moderately deep water in slow-flowing reaches of large rivers, and feeds on bottom-living animals. It spawns in spring, shedding its eggs on water plants.

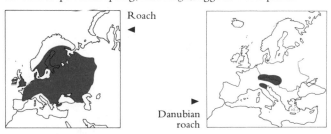

Roach ◄

► Danubian roach

Distinguishing features A deep-bodied cyprinid with a small head. The mouth is moderate in size and steeply angled. Dorsal fin origin well behind the base of the pelvic fins, with 8–9 branched rays; anal fin short-based with 10–11 branched rays. Scales moderate, 40–45 in lateral line. A sharp keel between the pelvic fins and vent. Pharyngeal teeth 5 + 3 : 3 + 5; strongly serrated.

Coloration Deep greeny-brown on the back, often with bronze-yellow sides and belly; young fish are more silvery. All the fins are reddish, the ventral ones brilliant, blood red. The iris of the eye is golden with a red fleck above.

Size An average length of 30 cm (11¾ in.) and weight of 0.8 kg (1 lb 12 oz) is reached in good conditions; exceptional specimens reach 45 cm (17¾ in.) and 2 kg (4 lb 6 oz). They are more usually stunted, rarely weighing more than 113 g (4 oz).

Remarks The rudd is typically an inhabitant of lakes and backwaters of rivers; it is unusual to find it even in lowland streams where the flow is slow. Rudd often colonize and live well in small man-made lakes (peat cuttings, marl and gravel pits), canals, and drainage channels. They swim in schools near the surface or in mid-water, and eat considerable quantities of surface-living and even aerial insects, as well as crustaceans, insect larvae, and some plant material. Young rudd eat small algae and crustaceans.

The rudd spawns from April to June around submerged vegetation and reed-beds. The eggs stick to the plants and hatch in 8–15 days depending on the temperature. They respond quickly to the availability of food. In small food-poor waters they grow slowly, and swarming stunted populations of rudd are well known. In suitable conditions they grow well. Rudd may live for 10 years.

This fish is caught by anglers, but is not considered to be a prime sporting fish (although it has a place in waters where other fish might not survive). Its role as predator on insects and crustaceans, and as prey for larger fishes is considerable in lowland lakes.

Loaches

A family (Cobitidae) of small, mostly slender-bodied fishes, related to the carp family. All are freshwater fishes distributed from the

Rudd

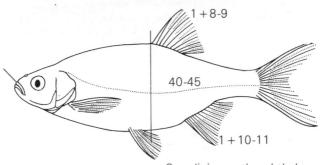

1 + 8-9

40-45

1 + 10-11

Scardinius erythrophthalmus
rudd

extracting pharyngeal teeth bones

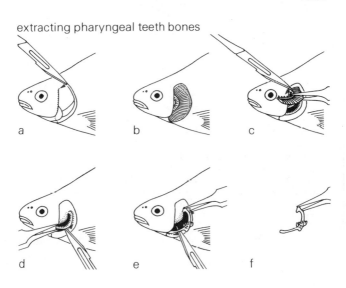

a

b

c

d

e

f

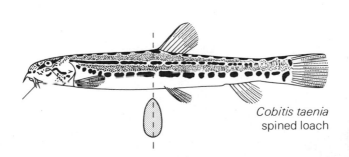

Cobitis taenia
spined loach

British Isles eastwards across Europe and Asia. They attain a peak of abundance and diversity in tropical Asia and from there several popular aquarium fish originate. Most loaches are slender with a single dorsal fin, no spines in the fins, and a wealth of barbels around the mouth.

Three species only are found in northern Europe.

Spined loach *Cobitis taenia*

Distinguishing features The body is elongated and very compressed from side to side; the head is small with very small barbels around the mouth. A small double pointed spine beneath each eye, usually retracted into the skin. (See also coloration.)

Coloration Light brown on the back, sandy brown on the sides and lighter on the belly. A conspicuous regular row of rounded dark blotches running along each side.

Size Usually up to 11.5 cm ($4\frac{1}{2}$ in.), exceptionally to 13.5 cm ($5\frac{1}{4}$ in.).

Remarks A loach which is typically found in slow-flowing, even stagnant rivers and drainage canals. It is either buried under the surface mud or hidden in the dense growth of blanket-weed, a filamentous alga, at the surface of the mud. Also found in lowland lakes and reservoirs which are connected to such rivers. It is probably active at night, or in conditions of low light intensity.

It feeds on small crustaceans, especially ostracods and copepods, and rotifers. It spawns from April to June, the eggs being deposited on algae. Little is known of its biology.

This loach can be kept in aquaria, but is not active enough to be an attractive pet-fish. It gulps air at the surface in poorly oxygenated conditions, absorbing the oxygen in its gut.

Numerous subspecies and related species have been described in Europe and northern Asia.

Weatherfish *Misgurnus fossilis*

Distinguishing features Long slender, almost eel-like body, cylindrical in form with a small dorsal fin closer to the tail than the head, and a small head with 5 pairs of barbels around the mouth. The barbels on the upper lip are long, and the lower ones difficult to see.

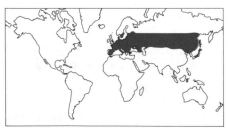

Spined loach

Coloration Dark grey-brown above, lighter ventrally with several lengthwise dark stripes along the body.

Size Usually up to 15 cm (6 in.), in eastern Europe reaching 35.6 cm (14 in.).

Remarks An inhabitant of lowland ponds, marshes, and the backwaters of rivers. It lives in overgrown, muddy waters where few fish would survive owing to sparsity of dissolved oxygen. It is well equipped for this habitat as it can breath air at the surface, absorbing the oxygen through the much-folded lining of the gut. Its presence in small ponds is often betrayed by noisy gulping at the surface. It is also very sensitive to changes in barometric pressure, becoming restless before a thunderstorm.

The weatherfish breeds in April to June, the reddish-brown eggs being shed over water plants. Hatching takes place in 8–10 days and the newly-hatched larvae have long external gills, an adaptation to life in poorly oxygenated waters.

Stone loach   *Noemacheilus barbatulus*

Distinguishing features A comparatively slender-bodied loach with a cylindrical anterior body and flattened tail. The head is moderate in size, with 6 long barbels around the mouth. No spine beneath the eye.

Coloration Greeny-brown above, yellowish-brown on the sides, yellow ventrally. Indistinct and irregular darker blotches on the sides.

Size Generally about 10 cm (4 in.) long, exceptionally grows to 15 cm (6 in.).

Weatherfish

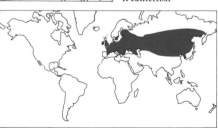

Stone loach

Remarks An inhabitant of running water, most commonly in small rivers, but occurring in lowland reaches and, possibly more often, in upland streams. It is also found in gravel-shored lakes, and in brackish water in the Baltic. It is active at night and in dull light, but usually spends the daytime hidden under stones or in dense weed-beds. It feeds on bottom-living invertebrates, mainly crustaceans, insect larvae, and worms.

The stone loach spawns in April to June, the dull white eggs being shed in 2 or 3 batches among stones and in weed-beds. The eggs hatch in 14–16 days at temperatures from 12–16°C. It attains a maximum age of 7 years.

This fish has no direct economic importance, but is a frequent food of trout, eels, and large chub, and is also eaten by aquatic birds and mammals.

Catfishes

Two families of catfish are represented in northern Europe: the wels or sheat-fish belongs to the Siluridae and is native, while the bullheads or North American catfishes (Ictaluridae) have been introduced. All the species concerned are freshwater fishes, with a broad head and abundant barbels around a wide mouth. They are mainly found in lowland rivers and lakes, living close to the bottom. The silurids are distributed across Europe and Asia, while the ictalurids are North American and are found from Canada to Guatemala. Numerous species belong to both families.

Wels   *Silurus glanis*

Distinguishing features Elongate body with a broad head, wide mouth with three pairs of barbels, the longest on the upper lip. A long anal fin, dorsal fin very short-based; adipose fin absent.

Coloration Dull brown or green on the back, variously mottled with yellow and creamy ventrally.

Size Usually around 1 m (39 in.) in length and a weight of 10 kg (22 lb), but exceptionally attaining 3 m (9 ft 10 in.) and 200 kg (441 lb). An old record from the river Dneiper reported 5 m (16 ft 6 in.) and 300 kg (675 lb).

Wels

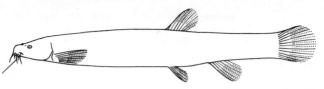

Misgurnus fossilis
weatherfish

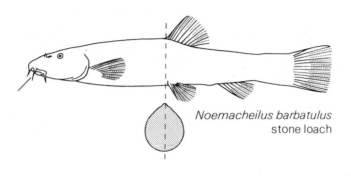

Noemacheilus barbatulus
stone loach

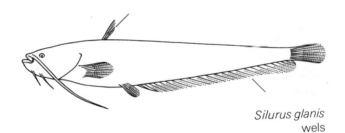

Silurus glanis
wels

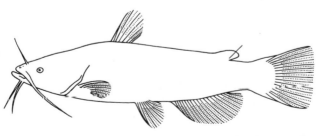

Ictalurus melas
black bullhead

Remarks An inhabitant of slow-flowing deep lowland rivers and adjacent still waters, such as lagoons, marshes, and lakes. It can live in brackish water in both the Baltic and Black Seas. It is largely nocturnal, although in deep, clouded water it may be active on dull days during daytime, but mostly it feeds at sunset and just before dawn. It keeps close to the bottom or lies under tree roots or in hollows in the bank.

It feeds on fishes, mainly eels, burbot, tench, bream, and roach, but also takes ducklings, water voles, and amphibians. When young it eats smaller prey—chiefly invertebrates and young fish.

The wels spawns in mid-May to mid-July, the eggs being laid in a shallow depression in the bottom excavated by the male. The eggs are *c.* 3 mm in diameter, stick together in a large mound, and are guarded by the male until they hatch. The early young feed on small planktonic animals. Growth is rapid after the first year and the wels commonly lives for 20 years.

In eastern Europe and the USSR the wels is of considerable importance as a commercial fish. Much of the catch is of wild fish, but in Hungary at least it is stocked in fish farms and raised for marketing at 3–4 kg (6 lb 8 oz–8 lb 12 oz). It is an attractive by-product as it can be fed on unwanted fish from other farming operations. Elsewhere, as in England—where it is introduced—it is a rather uncommon but favoured angling species.

Black bullhead   *Ictalurus melas*

Distinguishing features Moderately stout-bodied with a broad head, wide mouth with 4 pairs of barbels, the longest being the pair on the upper jaw which are flattened at the base. The dorsal fin is short-based, the anal fin only relatively long, and a long low adipose fin is present; tail fin rounded. The trailing edge of the pectoral fin spines only faintly barbed at the base. Anal fin with 17–21 rays.

Coloration Back dark brown, the sides greenish with a golden tinge, ventrally yellow or dull white. Dorsal fin membrane black. Males at spawning jet black above with bright yellow belly.

Size Usually up to 30.5 cm (12 in.) in length and up to 425 g (15 oz) in weight. Exceptional North American specimens of 61 cm (24 in.) length and 3.6 kg (8 lb) have been reported.

Remarks The black bullhead inhabits small lowland streams, lakes, ponds, and parts of larger rivers where the bottom is silty. It is

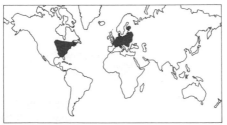

Black
bullhead

a hardy species and can stand moderately high temperatures and poor conditions of oxygenation. In Canada it spawns in summer; the female first excavates a nest in which the eggs are laid. The nest contains from 200–6000 eggs (depending on the female's size); they are pale cream in colour and clump together in a mass. Both male and female fan and protect the eggs which, at normal temperatures, hatch in five days. The newly-hatched young form a tight school and are guarded by one of the parents.

The black bullhead is widespread in Europe (and occurs sparsely in England), where it was introduced in the late 19th century.

Brown bullhead *Ictalurus nebulosus*

Distinguishing features   Very similar to the preceding species, but the trailing edge of the pectoral fin spines is stongly barbed almost to the tip. Anal fin with 21–24 rays. (Not illustrated.)

Coloration   Back and upper sides brown, often mottled, ventrally yellowish white. Dorsal fin membrane dusky.

Size   Usually between 20 cm and 36 cm (8–14 in.) in length.

Remarks   The brown bullhead is widely distributed in eastern and central North America, and has been distributed by man elsewhere in the New World, New Zealand, and Europe. It occurs in the rivers and lakes of Belgium, the Netherlands, and probably north Germany, and has been imported accidentally into England.

Its biology is very similar to that of the black bullhead.

Clingfishes

A group of small fishes, mostly marine, found in tropical and temperate seas and some tropical freshwaters, and world-wide in distribution. They have a powerful sucking disc on the underside, formed partly from the pelvic fins, by means of which they cling to the underside of rocks. They are rather flattened fishes with almost triangular heads, and upward directed eyes; their bodies are scaleless, the fins generally small and without spines.

Members of this family (Gobiesocidae) are often hard to find and are frequently overlooked; 4 species are found in northern European waters.

Small-headed clingfish *Apletodon microcephalus*

Distinguishing features   A small clingfish with a short head, a quarter of the length of the body. Dorsal and anal fins short-based (dorsal 5–6 rays; anal 5–7 rays), neither joined to the tail fin. Teeth in jaws small in front, with 1–3 larger curved canines at the sides.

Coloration   Variable, usually reddish-brown on the back with lighter patches, sometimes greenish. Males have a dark spot on the dorsal and anal fins, and a purple patch on the throat.

Size   Attains 4 cm (1½ in.) in length.

Remarks   This clingfish lives on the lower shore and in inshore waters down to a depth of 25 m (14 fathoms). It is little recorded, but has been found widely and at times comparatively commonly; it is probably much more common than present records suggest.

It breeds in spring and early summer, the eggs being laid in a hollow within the holdfast of the kelp and other marine algae. After a short planktonic stage following hatching, the young fish of 15 mm (½ in.) can be found among algae in autumn. Its biology is largely unknown.

Two-spotted clingfish   *Diplecogaster bimaculata*

Distinguishing features   A small clingfish with a fairly small head although it is more than one quarter of the body length. Dorsal and anal fins short-based (dorsal, 5–7 rays; anal, 4–6 rays), neither joined to the tail fin. Teeth in jaws uniformly small, not enlarged at sides.

Coloration   Variable, but often bright red or reddish with blue or brown spots, yellowish ventrally. Males have two purple spots, circled with yellow on the nape.

Size   Attains 4 cm (1½ in.) in length.

Remarks   A moderately common species which lives on the lower shore and in inshore waters to a depth of 55 m (30 fathoms). It is most abundant on stony grounds, but is also found on soft ground often clinging to a mollusc shell. It spawns in spring and early summer, the eggs being laid on the inside of a shell or under stones, and are guarded by an adult. The eggs are golden yellow and 1.6 mm in diameter. The larvae and postlarvae are pelagic during summer. The food of the adult consists of small crustaceans.

Shore clingfish   *Lepadogaster lepadogaster*

Distinguishing features   A moderately large species with a long snout and 'duck-billed' appearance, and a fringed flap at the edge of the front nostril. Dorsal and anal fins long-based (dorsal, 16–19 rays; anal, 9–10 rays) and joined to the tail fin.

Small-
headed
clingfish

◀

▶

Two-
spotted
clingfish

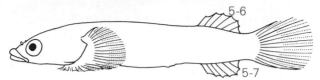

5-6

5-7

Apletodon microcephalus
small-headed clingfish

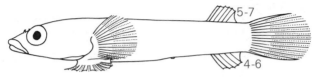

5-7

4-6

Diplecogaster bimaculata
two-spotted clingfish

teeth of clingfishes

A. microcephalus

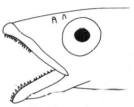

D. bimaculata

16-19

9-10

Lepadogaster lepadogaster
shore clingfish

13-16

9-11

Lepadogaster candollei
Connemara clingfish

Coloration Background colour varies from pink through rose to deep red, with yellow-rimmed blue eye-spots on the top of the head.

Size Attains a length of 6.5 cm (2½ in.).

Remarks This is the most frequently encountered of the clingfishes in intertidal habitats in northern European waters. In places it is locally abundant on boulder shores at mid-tide level and below, especially where the shore is partly sheltered. It is always found clinging to the underside of the stones, or amongst kelp growing on rocks low down the shore. It breeds in summer, the golden eggs being laid in clusters on the underside of a boulder and guarded by a parent. The larvae and later fry are planktonic for a short period.

The Mediterranean stock is recognized as a distinct subspecies.

Connemara clingfish   *Lepadogaster candollei*

Distinguishing features A moderately large species with a long, rather flattened snout. A very small skin flap at the edge .of the anterior nostril. Dorsal and anal fins long-based (dorsal, 13–16 rays; anal, 9–11 rays), but neither is joined to the tail fin.

Coloration Males are usually reddish on the back with deeper toned spots on the head. Females are mostly yellowish-green.

Size Attains a length of 7.5 cm (3 in.).

Remarks This clingfish is usually found on rocky shores at extreme low-water mark and in pools, as well as below tide level amongst the holdfasts of kelp and thongweed. It is usually found clinging to the underside of stones or amongst the algae holdfasts. It lays its eggs on the underside of stones; they are guarded by one of the parents. The breeding season extends from April to July, and the larvae and postlarvae live for a short while in the plankton. It is rarely found and little is known of its biology.

Angler Fishes

Angler fish are so-called because they possess a fishing lure at the tip of a specially modified dorsal ray with which they can entice prey close to their capacious jaws. All angler fish have large jaws with

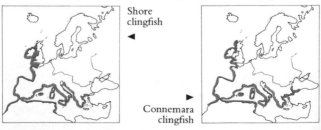

Shore
clingfish
◄

►
Connemara
clingfish

well-developed teeth, loose scaleless skin, rather small fins and generally bizarre body form. They are all marine fishes, some of them inhabiting the deep-sea. Three families are represented in northern European waters: 2 shallow water anglers (Lophiidae) and 2 deep-sea species (Himantolophidae and Ceratiidae), both of which are very rare.

Angler   *Lophius piscatorius*

Distinguishing features   The broad, rather flattened head, short, rather thickset tail, and the very large mouth with long teeth are distinctive. First rays of the dorsal fin separate and elongate. There are 2 (sometimes 3) points to the spine above the gill opening; there is no skin flap on the upper edge of the eye. Second dorsal fin rays 11–12; anal rays 9–10; pectoral rays 24–26; vertebrae 29–30. (See also coloration.)

Coloration   Very variable on the back, ranging from reddish-brown to greeny-grey with irregular markings. Ventrally, dead white with distinct black edges to the pelvic fins and dusky pectoral and anal edges.

Size   Attains a maximum length of 2 m (6 ft 6½ in.) and a weight of *c.* 40.8 kg (90 lb). Specimens in excess of 1.20 m (47 in.) are uncommon.

Remarks   A common, bottom-living fish from 2–3 m (6½–10 ft) below tide mark down to 548 m (300 fathoms), although it is most common below 18 m (10 fathoms). It lives on sandy, shell, or gravel bottoms and is found less abundantly on muddy or rough grounds. The angler fish feeds on a wide range of smaller fishes, mostly associated with the sea-bed, which have been enticed close to its mouth by delicate movements of its fishing lure.

Spawning takes place in spring and early summer over deep water offshore. The eggs are shed in ribbon-like gelatinous sheets which may be as much as 9 m (29 ft 6 in.) long and 3 m (10 ft) wide. The eggs are carried within this sheet in a single, or occasionally double, layer. They hatch when the larvae are about 4.5 mm long. A little later the larvae are free-swimming with most remarkable elongation of the fin rays. These gradually shorten comparative to the growth of the body. The young fish live on the sea-bed when they are about 8 cm (3¼ in.) in length.

The angler fish is not fished for deliberately, but accidental

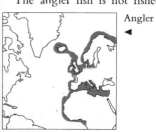

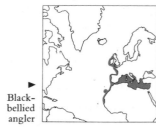

Angler
◄

Black-
bellied
angler
►

captures are beheaded and the fleshy tails marketed. They have tasty flesh, if rather fibrous, and reminiscent of crustacean meat.

Black-bellied angler   *Lophius budegassa*

Distinguishing features   Similar externally to the more common angler, but always with three points on the spine above the gill opening, and a small fleshy flap above the upper edge of the eye. Second dorsal fin with 8–9 rays; anal fin with 8–9 rays; pectoral rays 22–24; vertebrae 25–26. (See also coloration.)

Coloration   Usually light sandy brown above and dead white ventrally; the colour of the back is very variable. The inner face of the pelvic fins is white, in the largest specimens pale grey. The lining of the body cavity is black and this shows through the belly skin as dull grey.

Size   Attains a total length of 82 cm (32¼ in.).

Remarks   This is a bottom-living fish which is found usually on sandy bottoms between 100 and 300 m (55–164 fathoms), although occasionally it is caught in shallower water. It breeds, in the Mediterranean, in autumn and winter, the larvae and postlarvae being planktonic and common through to spring. It feeds in a similar manner to the more common angler fish, but there is little recorded on details of its diet. This species has only recently been recognized in northern European waters and is little known.

Deep-sea angler   *Ceratias holboeli*

Distinguishing features   A large, gross, flabby-skinned angler with the skin densely covered in sharp, pointed bony spines giving it a rasp-like feel. Adult females have a small eye and a long fishing ray rising on the head. The dorsal, anal and tail fin rays are very thick and fleshy; there are 4 rays only in the 2 former fins. Adult males have much reduced fins and are found attached to the females.

Coloration   Dark brown to black, the skin is often abraded leaving grey patches.

Size   Females grow to 120 cm (47 in.); males to 6 cm (2½ in.)

Remarks   This deep-sea angler is occasionally captured on the deeper fishing grounds of the N. E. Atlantic, in depths of 121–1000 m (66–546 fathoms). Its biology is little known. Larval stages are pelagic round-bodied fishes with loose skin, but the males never grow large and as sub-adults attach themselves by their jaws to a maturing female. Eventually the male becomes parasitic on the female, their vascular system uniting so that the male is nourished by its mate. They are sparsely distributed in all oceans.

Atlantic football-fish   *Himantolophus groenlandicus*

Distinguishing features   A moderately large, almost spherical-bodied angler with the skin studded with large spines which have

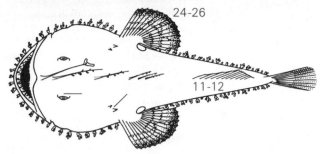

24-26

11-12

Lophius piscatorius
angler

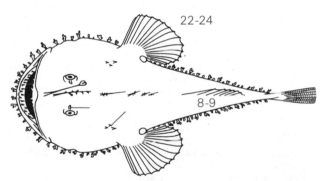

22-24

8-9

Lophius budegassa
black-bellied angler

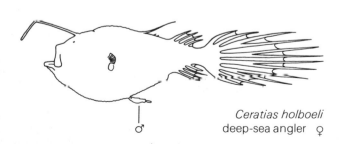

♂

Ceratias holboeli
deep-sea angler ♀

broad bases. On the snout a thick fishing rod ends in a massive lure with a short bulb-like organ in the centre and long tentacles around it. Dorsal, anal, and tail fins with stout, relatively short rays.

Coloration Deep brown to jet black; the tips of the lure tentacles and the central bulb shining white.

Size Attains 61 cm (24 in.) in length.

Remarks Occasionally captured on the deeper fishing grounds of the European Atlantic. Like the other deep-sea anglers, this is a mid-water fish preying on a range of animals that are attracted to its luminous lure. The adults live at 100–300 m (55–164 fathoms); the young have been caught near the surface and at depths of 3000 m (1640 fathoms).

It is sparsely distributed in all oceans.

Cod Fishes

The members of the cod family (Gadidae) are (with one exception) all marine fishes. Most are found in the cool temperate waters of the northern hemisphere, generally on or close to the continental shelf. Few are found in the deep sea and then only near the surface or in the southern hemisphere. Their fins lack spines, and they usually have 2 or 3 dorsal and 1 or 2 anal fins; a barbel on the chin is normal, and they all have small to minute scales.

Approximately 100 species are known world-wide, but no more than 30 live in European waters.

Cod   *Gadus morhua*

Distinguishing features A stout-bodied codfish with a long chin barbel, relatively small eye, 3 dorsal fins all close together at the base and rounded in outline, and 2 anal fins. The first anal fin originates behind or beneath the interspace between first and second dorsal fins. Upper jaw overhangs the lower. Lateral line continuous, with a smooth curve above the pectoral fin.

Coloration Background colouring variable, greenish or sandy brown with darker or lighter mottling on back and sides. White ventrally. The lateral line is conspicuously light.

Size Historical records of 90 kg (200 lb) fish exist, but the

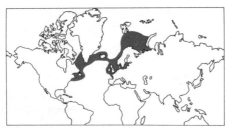

Cod

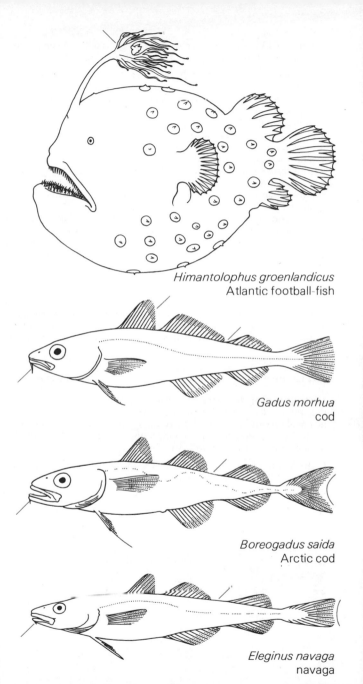

Himantolophus groenlandicus
Atlantic football-fish

Gadus morhua
cod

Boreogadus saida
Arctic cod

Eleginus navaga
navaga

maximum likely today is around 45.3 kg (100 lb). Average cod measure about 120 cm (47 in.) and weigh 11.3 kg (25 lb).

Remarks   The cod is widely distributed in a variety of habitats from the shoreline to well down the continental shelf, in depths of 600 m (328 fathoms). To the south of its range it is found in shallow water only during the winter, and there, as elsewhere, it is the younger, smaller fish which live close inshore. It usually schools at least 30–80 m (16–44 fathoms) above the bottom, although it forages for food on the sea-bed and in mid-water.

The food of the cod consists of a wide range of crustaceans, worms, brittlestars and fishes especially, among which are included herring, sandeels, capelin, and smaller gadoid fishes. When young, cod feed mainly on small crustaceans, as they also do when pelagic postlarvae.

The cod spawns in February to April in water about 200 m (109 fathoms) deep, the eggs being widely spread by currents. The adults make considerable migrations to reach the spawning grounds, for although there are numerous such grounds, the cod in the North Atlantic exists as a number of more or less isolated populations or races. These discrete stocks can be overfished individually, even when cod are common elsewhere.

The cod has been exploited ever since man began to fish in the seas of Europe. Its value as a prime food-fish is enormous, and when salted and dried it keeps for wintertime use, or export, so that its consumption is not confined to the Atlantic seaboard of Europe or North America.

Arctic cod   *Boreogadus saida*

Distinguishing features   A rather slender codfish with 3 dorsal fins and 2 anal fins, all of which are separated with large spaces. The first anal fin origin is behind the origin of the second dorsal fin. Tail fin forked. Lateral line not continuous, a sharp dip beneath the second dorsal fin origin and wavy thereafter.

Coloration   Light brownish above, the upper sides are lighter with a yellowish tint; the belly is silvery.

Size   Attains a length of 46 cm (15 in.).

Remarks   A small Arctic cod which is commonly found in close proximity to the polar ice, both far out to sea and in inshore waters.

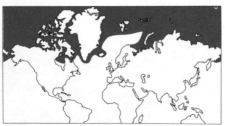

Arctic cod

Found in almost fresh water in river mouths. It spawns from November to February, relatively few eggs being produced by each female. Its food consists principally of crustaceans, mainly shrimps and copepods.

It is an important food-fish for many of the larger mammals and birds of the Arctic seas. It has also been exploited in a minor way as an industrial fish, but has great potential for increased catches.

Navaga   *Eleginus navaga*

Distinguishing features Moderately deep-bodied, with a short chin barbel, 3 dorsal and 2 anal fins—all well spaced out—and a square-cut tail fin. The lower jaw is shorter than the upper. The lateral line is continuous only to the beginning of the second dorsal fin where it curves sharply downwards and becomes interrupted.

Coloration Back and sides grey with brownish and dark spots on the back; ventrally silvery-white.

Size Usually grows to only 35 cm (13¾ in.) but occasionally attains 42 cm (16½ in.) in length.

Remarks A northern codfish found only on the Arctic coasts of Europe; a relative, *E. gracilis*, is found in similar situations in the Arctic Pacific. The navaga is found close to the ice and on the continental shelf in shallow water, occasionally entering outer estuaries. It spawns over sandy or rocky bottoms in 8–10 m (4–6 fathoms), usually in January. The eggs sink to the sea-bed.

It feeds mainly on crustaceans and worms, but eats small fishes as well, including stickleback, capelin, sandeels, and small gadoids. It is in turn eaten by a wide range of larger fishes and Arctic mammals, and the young by sea-birds. It is also commercially fished for by the Soviet fishing fleet.

Silvery pout   *Gadiculus argenteus*

Distinguishing features A small open-sea gadoid with 3 dorsal and 2 anal fins, each well spaced from the next, low, and with fragile fin rays. The eyes are large; the mouth is steeply angled, and the snout and forehead have clearly visible cavities under the skin. The scales are large and fragile.

Coloration Mainly dull and silvery; small dark marks on the head.

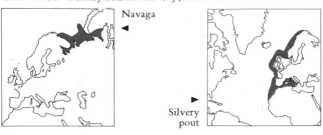

Navaga ◄

► Silvery pout

Size   Attains a maximum length of 15 cm (6 in.), more commonly 13 cm (5 in.).

Remarks   A deep-water, open-sea fish which is most common in depths of 200–500 m (109–273 fathoms) over the edge of the continental shelf. It occurs in large schools. It breeds from midwinter to spring, the later further north, the eggs and larvae being pelagic; spawning occurs in deep water. The silvery pout rarely lives for as much as 3 years.

It has no particular economic importance, but it is eaten by a number of larger valuable fishes.

The stock in the N. E. Atlantic is recognized as a subspecies, *G. argenteus thori.*

Haddock   *Melanogrammus aeglefinus*

Distinguishing features   Three dorsal fins, 2 anal; the first dorsal is triangular in shape with long fin rays. Head relatively small, eye moderately large, chin barbel very short, jaws with the lower jaw distinctly shorter than the upper. (See also coloration.)

Coloration   Dark greeny-brown on the back, greyish-silver on the sides, white ventrally. A conspicuous rounded black blotch between the pectoral base and the lateral line; the lateral line is black.

Size   Attains a maximum length of 76 cm (30 in.) and a weight of 4.53 kg (10 lb), although the usual commercial length is between 38–63.6 cm (15–25 in.). The largest recorded was caught off Iceland; it was 112 cm (44 in.) and weighed nearly 16.76 kg (37 lb).

Remarks   The haddock lives close to the sea-bed in depths of 40–300 m (22–164 fathoms); it feeds almost exclusively on bottom-living animals, chiefly brittlestars, worms, and molluscs. Occasionally it eats small fishes (capelin and sandeels) and also herring eggs. The larval and postlarval haddock feed on copepods and their larvae, and later on small crustaceans.

Haddock spawn between February and June, but mostly in March and April. The eggs are buoyant and spherical, 1.2–1.7 mm in diameter, and float at or near the surface. The fry are pelagic and are frequently found accompanying large jellyfishes. Young haddock begin to live close to the bottom at a length of about 5 cm (2 in.).

To some extent this is a migratory fish; in the north of its range it

Haddock

is found in inshore shallow waters during the summer and retires to deep water in winter. In the warmer, southern end of its range, the reverse is true. Haddock also from time to time enjoy favourable years when survival of the larvae and fry is particularly good, and a strong year class is established which results in great abundance often followed by apparent extension of the range.

The haddock is an important commerical fish throughout the North Atlantic. It is marketed fresh, smoked, or frozen.

Whiting   *Merlangius merlangus*

Distinguishing features   A slender-bodied codfish with a narrow rather pointed head; the upper jaw is longer than the lower. Three dorsal fins, all closely joined at their bases; 2 anal fins, the first long, its origin beneath the middle of the first dorsal base. Medium to large fish are without a chin barbel; a minute barbel in young fish.

Coloration   The back is sandy to greeny-blue, the sides and belly are conspicuously white, silvery when alive. A distinct black spot at the upper base of the pectoral fin.

Size   Usually around 30–40 cm (11¾–15¾ in.), but occasionally attaining a length of 70 cm (27½ in.). Attains a weight of 3.0 kg (6 lb 10 oz).

Remarks   The whiting is a very common fish in shallow inshore waters. It is most abundant between 30 and 100 m (16 and 55 fathoms), exceptionally down to 200 m (109 fathoms). It lives both in mid-water in these depths and inhabits sandy as well as muddy bottoms. The smallest fish are found close inshore. Young whiting of 3 cm (1¼ in.) are often found sheltering amongst the tentacles of live jellyfishes.

Adults feed on small fishes especially sandeels, young herring and sprats, young gadoids, shrimps, and other crustaceans. The young fish eat more crustaceans than fishes. The whiting breeds between January and July, but mostly in spring, in shallow water, and without making extensive migrations.

The whiting is a valuable food-fish which is extensively fished in European seas. It also forms an important constituent of the diet of other, larger fishes and sea-birds. The Black Sea population is recognized as a subspecies, *M. m. euxinus.*

Whiting

Blue whiting _Micromesistius poutassou_

Distinguishing features A slender-bodied codfish with 3 dorsal fins all separated by long gaps, and 2 anal fins, the first of which is very long-based, its origin in front of the first dorsal fin origin. The head is pointed, and the lower jaw is slightly longer than the upper. No chin barbel.

Coloration Back blue, sides and belly silvery-white. The back fades to grey soon after death.

Size Attains 45 cm (17¾ in.) in length, more usually around 35 cm (13¾ in.).

Remarks The blue whiting is an oceanic fish living mainly in mid-water over the edge of the continental shelf. It is most abundant 100–300 m (55–164 fathoms) below the surface in depths of 1000 m (547 fathoms) or more. Occasionally it is captured in shallow inshore water. Its food consists mainly of crustaceans, but small fishes are eaten also. It is an important food-fish for many larger fishes such as ling, cod, hake, opah, and deep-water sharks.

It is fished commercially for processing as fish meal, and is potentially an important economic fish, the full value of which has yet to be attained.

Poor cod _Trisopterus minutus_

Distinguishing features A small codfish with 3 dorsal fins and 2 anal fins all touching at their bases or very close. The origin of the first anal fin is beneath the space between the first and second dorsal fins or anterior to it. The upper jaw overlaps the lower; the eye diameter equals the snout in length. Chin barbel long; three-quarters or more of eye diameter. About 28 gill rakers on the first arch.

Coloration Back yellowish-brown, the sides lighter—even coppery coloured; the belly is silvery grey. Upper base of the pectoral fin with a small black spot.

Size Usually measures between 15–20 cm (6–8 in.) exceptionally reaching 26 cm (10¼ in.).

Remarks The poor cod is extremely abundant in coastal waters of 25–300 m (14–164 fathoms), although it is not so common close

Blue whiting

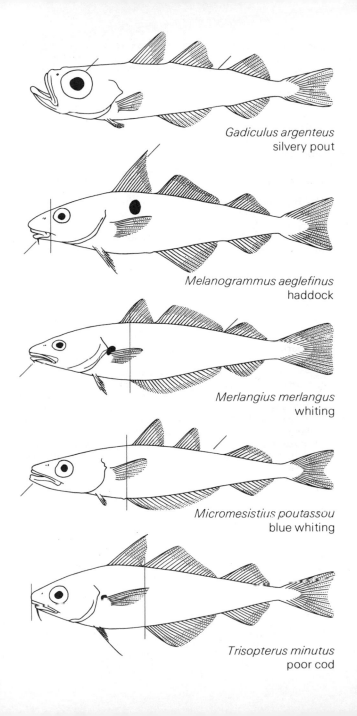

Gadiculus argenteus
silvery pout

Melanogrammus aeglefinus
haddock

Merlangius merlangus
whiting

Micromesistius poutassou
blue whiting

Trisopterus minutus
poor cod

inshore as its relative the bib. It occurs in schools, close to the bottom and in mid-water. It spawns in winter and spring (the latter further north) usually in depths of 50–100 m (27–55 fathoms). It feeds on crustaceans of various kinds, but the larger ones also eat fishes.

The poor cod is too small to be fished for as a food-fish, but is caught in great quantities for processing as fish meal. It is also a frequent food-fish for larger fishes and small cetaceans, such as dolphins.

The Mediterranean is inhabited by the subspecies *T. minutus capelanus*.

Norway pout   *Trisopterus esmarkii*

Distinguishing features   A small codfish with 3 dorsal fins and 2 anal fins; the latter fins touch at the base and the dorsals have small interspaces. The first rays of the anal fin are beneath the end of the first dorsal. The lower jaw is slightly longer than the upper; eye diameter slightly longer than snout; chin barbel short and rather thin.

Coloration   Back yellowish-brown shading to silvery white beneath. A small dusky spot on the upper edge of the pectoral fin base.

Size   Attains a maximum length of 25 cm (10 in.), more usually between 13 and 19 cm (5–7½ in.).

Remarks   An extremely common small gadoid in northern European waters; it is most common offshore in depths of 80–200 m (44–109 fathoms), although it also occurs in numbers in 40 m (22 fathoms), especially in the north. It spawns in deep water over the edge of the continental shelf mainly in March to May. Sexual maturity is reached at the end of the first (rarely) or second years.

It feeds mainly in the daytime on crustaceans and fishes. Because it is abundant, it is an important link in the food-chains of the sea both as predator, and as prey for fishes, cetaceans, and many sea-birds. It is too small for human food, but is used extensively for fish meal to feed farm animals and fish in farms.

Bib   *Trisopterus luscus*

Distinguishing features   A moderately large, deep-bodied cod-fish with 3 dorsal fins, and 2 anal fins, the bases of which all overlap.

Poor cod ◄

► Norway pout

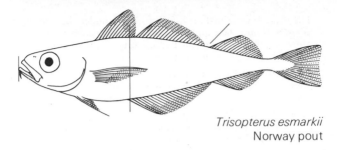

Trisopterus esmarkii
Norway pout

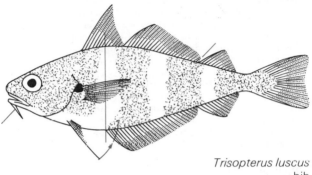

Trisopterus luscus
bib

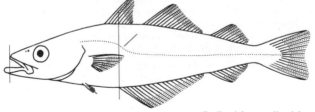

Pollachius pollachius
pollack

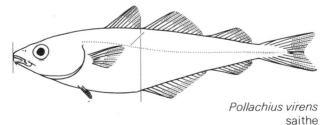

Pollachius virens
saithe

The origin of the anal fin is well forward under the middle of the first dorsal fin. The chin barbel is long, the eye diameter equals the snout length, and the pelvic fins are long, reaching back to beyond the vent. (See also coloration.)

Coloration   Back a beautiful coppery-brown, yellowish on the sides and white beneath. Four or 5 darker cross-bands over the upper body. A conspicuous black spot at the base of the pectoral fin.

Size   Attains a length of about 41 cm (16¼ in.), more usually between 20 and 32 cm (8–12½ in.). Maximum weight attained about 2.5 kg (5 lb 8 oz).

Remarks   A very common fish in inshore waters, particularly in rocky areas where large schools form about reefs or wrecks. Small bib are very abundant in shallow water over sand. Its depth range extends from about 3 to 300 m (1½–164 fathoms), the largest fish living at the greatest depths. It spawns in moderately shallow water in March to April.

Its food consists mainly of crustaceans, particularly shrimps, small squids, and fishes. It is not greatly exploited, its flesh being soft and spoiling quickly, but it is fished for locally. Quantities of young fish are caught to process into fish meal; larger ones are caught by anglers.

This fish is known also as pout or pouting, the three names being used about equally.

Pollack   *Pollachius pollachius*

Distinguishing features   Typical of the cod family in body form, with 3 dorsal fins and 2 anal fins, the first of which is long and originates beneath the first dorsal fin. The lower jaw protrudes beyond the upper; there is no chin barbel. Lateral line with a sharp curve over the pectoral fin, dipping to the mid-line posteriorly. Gill rakers on the first gill arch, 26–27.

Coloration   Dark brownish-green on the back, shading to yellowish-green on the sides, white beneath. The lateral line is dark.

Size   Attains a length of 130 cm (51 in.) and a weight in excess of 11 kg (24–25 lb). Usually around 50 cm (19¾ in.) and 4 kg (8 lb 13 oz).

Remarks   The pollack is widely distributed in European waters,

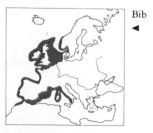

Bib

Pollack

particularly in inshore areas. Large fish are most abundant near rocks or on rough ground, swimming in schools; smaller specimens tend to be less restricted and occur over sandy shores and even in estuaries. Its depth range is from the surface to 200 m (109 fathoms).

It feeds mainly on fishes, especially sandeels, and members of the herring and cod families, and on large numbers of crustaceans. The young eat crustaceans. It spawns between January to April in deep water at 100–200 m (55–109 fathoms); the eggs and larvae are pelagic and drift shorewards. Young of the first year are particularly common close inshore.

Pollack are caught by nets, but more are captured on lines or are taken by anglers. Their flesh is dry, rather coloured, but edible.

Saithe   *Pollachius virens*

Distinguishing features   Similar to the pollack in build and number of fins; the first anal fin originates beneath the space between first and second dorsal fins. The jaws are equal in young fish; the lower jaw protrudes slightly in adults, which also lack the chin barbel (it is minute in the young). The lateral line is straight from gill cover to tail. 35–40 gill rakers on the first gill arch.

Coloration   Very dark green on the back and upper sides, sharply giving way to dull silvery sides and belly. The lateral line is creamy coloured.

Size   Grows to 130 cm (51¼ in.), and 14 kg (31 lb 13 oz) in weight. Mostly captured at around 70–80 cm (27½–31½ in.).

Remarks   The saithe is widely distributed in the North Atlantic, living in large schools near the surface and in mid-water in depths of 200–250 m (109–137 fathoms). From Scotland northwards the young fish are particularly abundant in inshore waters; in their first year they may be found in intertidal pools, and in their second close to the shoreline. These young feed on small crustaceans and fishes, especially sandeels, herring, and capelin (in the north). Larger saithe feed almost entirely on fishes, especially members of the cod and herring families.

Saithe spawn from January to April in depths of 100–200 m (55–108 fathoms). The eggs and larvae drift near the surface and are carried from the deep-water spawning grounds to the shallower nursery areas.

This is a very important commercial fish, caught mainly by

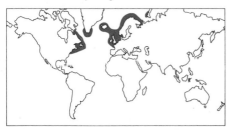

Saithe

Scandinavian, German, and Russian vessels, in trawls and seines. The catch is sold fresh, frozen, smoked, and even dried and salted. It is also taken in some numbers by anglers.

Few other fishes have as many widely-used names: coalfish, coley, billet, black pollack, and glasshan or glosshan are samples. In North America this fish is called the pollock.

Burbot
Lota lota

Distinguishing features The only codfish living in freshwater. It has the typical cod-family chin barbel, and nostrils with raised rims. Two dorsal fins, the first short and rounded in outline, the second long; a single anal fin. Scales small and embedded.

Coloration Dull greeny-brown above with darker mottling, the blotches extending on to the sides. Yellowish ventrally.

Size Attains 1 m (39½ in.), most commonly about 51 cm (20 in.).

Remarks The burbot inhabits the lowland reaches of rivers and lakes in their flood plains. It is found in brackish conditions in the Baltic Sea. Its life style is sedentary, usually hiding among tree roots or in crevices, under the bank or among the roots of water plants by day, and being most active in the early evening and at dawn.

Young fish eat invertebrates, chiefly bottom-living insect larvae, crustaceans, and leeches; adult burbot eat large quantities of fish as well as crustaceans and insects. The burbot spawns in winter (December to March); the females contain up to 3 million eggs. The eggs fall to the bottom and develop among the gravel of the spawning bed.

The burbot is occasionally caught by anglers in continental Europe; it is also locally fished for as food, as its flesh is of fine quality and the liver is especially valued. In England, the burbot was moderately abundant in the fens and rivers between Yorkshire and Cambridgeshire, but is now rare and almost extinct.

Torsk
Brosme brosme

Distinguishing features Rather heavy-bodied with a single long-based dorsal fin, and a single anal fin, both joined at their bases to the tail fin. A long chin barbel. The lateral line curves sharply down at the level of the vent to follow the mid-line. Scales minute, embedded in thick skin.

Burbot

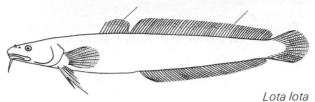

Lota lota
burbot

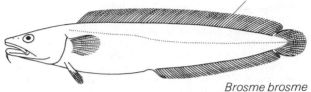

Brosme brosme
torsk

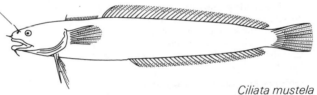

Ciliata mustela
five-bearded rockling

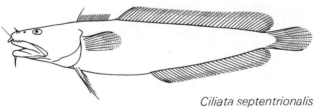

Ciliata septentrionalis
northern rockling

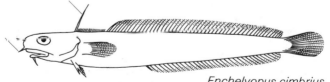

Enchelyopus cimbrius
four-bearded rockling

Coloration   Greyish-brown, lighter on the sides and ventrally; dorsal, tail and anal fins with a dark submarginal band and white edges.

Size   Grows to a maximum length of 110 cm (43¼ in.), and weight of 12 kg (26 lb 8 oz); more usually about 50 cm (19¾ in.).

Remarks   The torsk lives in deep water mainly at depths of 200–500 m (109–273 fathoms), but exceptionally from 50 m–1000 m (27–547 fathoms). It lives alone or in small schools, close to the sea-bed, especially where it is rocky. Its food consists of crustaceans, molluscs, and other bottom-living fishes.

It spawns at about 200 m (109 fathoms) from April to July (the later spawnings being further north). The female is very prolific and may lay between 2 and 3 million eggs, which develop close to the surface. It lives for a maximum of about 20 years.

The torsk is fished for by lines and trawl, chiefly by Norwegian and Soviet boats. Mostly it is dried and salted as stock fish; less is marketed fresh or frozen.

Five-bearded rockling   *Ciliata mustela*

Distinguishing features   A small, slender-bodied codfish with 2 dorsal fins, the first merely a single long ray followed by a fringe of low rays, the second dorsal fin long; a single anal fin. Five barbels, one on the chin, a pair on the front of the upper lip, and a pair on the anterior nostrils. Head short, its length less than a fifth of the body length.

Coloration   Dark brown above, sometimes with a reddish tinge; lighter grey-brown below.

Size   Grows to 25 cm (10 in.).

Remarks   A common fish in the intertidal zone on all kinds of shores, living in rock pools and pools formed by pilings on sand and mud. Also occurs down to 20 m (11 fathoms) on muddy, sandy and shell gravel bottoms. It breeds in winter and early spring in deeper water; the eggs and larvae are pelagic. This rockling eats small crustaceans, and occasionally small fishes. Young rocklings are silvery with greenish backs and live near the surface until they come close inshore; this juvenile stage is the mackerel-midge stage. It is eaten by numerous sea-birds and being particularly abundant in spring, is frequently an important diet for the nestlings of such birds as terns and puffins.

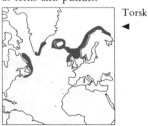

Torsk ◀

▶ Five-bearded rockling

Northern rockling   *Ciliata septentrionalis*

Distinguishing features   Two dorsal fins, the first a low fringe of
fine fin rays (the first longest), the second long-based; a long-based
anal fin. Five barbels around the mouth, one on the chin, a pair on
the front of the upper lip, a pair on the anterior nostrils; small lobes
along the fold of skin above the upper jaw. Head long, its length
more than a fifth of the body length.

Coloration   Medium brown above and on the sides; lighter
ventrally.

Size   Grows to 18 cm (7 in.)

Remarks   A little-known rockling which is found mainly below
tide mark level, although it is occasionally caught on the shore. It
seems most common in depths of 10–50 m (5½–27 fathoms),
sometimes down to 90 m (49 fathoms). It lives among rocks and on
sandy and muddy bottoms.
   Its food consists of small crustaceans and worms. As this rockling
has frequently been found in cod stomachs, it evidently features in
the diet of this fish, at least locally.

Four-bearded rockling   *Enchelyopus cimbrius*

Distinguishing features   Slender-bodied with a long-based
dorsal fin of uniform height preceded by a low first dorsal fin of fine
rays, the first of which is very long (as long as the head length). A
single long-based anal fin. Four barbels; one on the chin, one in the
mid-line of the upper jaw, and a pair on the anterior nostril's rim.

Coloration   Dull reddish-brown or sandy above, grey on the
sides, white ventrally; bluish-grey over the body cavity. A rounded
dark blotch at the far end of the dorsal and anal fins.

Size   Attains 41 cm (16¼ in.); usually 25–30 cm (10–12 in.).

Remarks   A bottom-living rockling which is generally captured
on muddy or sandy bottoms in 20–250 m (11–137 fathoms); it has
been caught as deep as 550 m (300 fathoms). In the northern parts of
its range it is found in the shallower of these depths; to the south it is
usually caught in deep water. In general, it is not a common fish.
   It feeds chiefly on crustaceans, and to a lesser extent on worms and
molluscs. It breeds in deep water in late spring and summer; the eggs
and larvae are pelagic.

Northern
rockling
◀

▶
Four-
bearded
rockling

Big-eyed rockling
Antonogadus macrophthalmus

Distinguishing features   A slender-bodied rockling with the low fringe-like first dorsal fin preceded by a longer ray, which is typical of the rocklings. Second dorsal fin long-based, of uniform height; anal fin similar but shorter. Eyes large; mouth large, gape extending well beyond eye level; front teeth of upper jaw fang-like, 2–4 in number.

Coloration   Back mottled with medium brown; the sides reddish, pink ventrally.

Size   Attains at least 13 cm (5 in.), possibly 25 cm (10 in.).

Remarks   A deep-water rockling found on the bottom between 146 and 510 m (80–279 fathoms), always well offshore. It is apparently rare, for it has been reported on few occasions, but this is probably because it is difficult to catch in most kinds of fishing net. Its biology is virtually unknown. A closely related, apparently larger species is found in the Mediterranean.

Shore rockling
Gaidropsarus mediterraneus

Distinguishing features   Typical rockling shape with a low fringe of fine rays in the first dorsal fin, preceded by a single long ray. Second dorsal and anal fins long-based, of uniform height. Three barbels, one on the chin, one on each anterior nostril. Pectoral fin with 15–17 rays. (See also coloration.)

Coloration   Uniform dull brown or reddish-brown on back and sides; lighter ventrally.

Size   Attains a maximum length of 35 cm (13¾ in.) and a weight of *c*. 500 g (1 lb); mostly between 15.2 and 25.4 cm (6–10 in.).

Remarks   A common rockling on rocky shores, in tide-pools and under algae-covered rocks. It is unusual to find it on other than rocky bottoms. It is found at least as deep as 27 m (15 fathoms), but it may live deeper than that on rocky reefs.

It spawns offshore in early summer, the eggs and larvae being pelagic. Juvenile fish are clear greeny-blue above, brilliantly silvery below and on the sides, and live near the surface. They change to a bottom-dwelling life when they drift inshore at a length of *c*. 4 cm (1½ in.). These young fish first become common in shore pools in late September and October.

Big-eyed rockling ◄

► Shore rockling

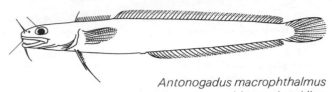

Antonogadus macrophthalmus
big-eyed rockling

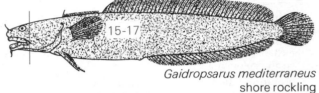

Gaidropsarus mediterraneus
shore rockling

Gaidropsarus vulgaris
three-bearded rockling

C. mustela

C. septentrionalis

E. cimbrius

Gaidropsarus

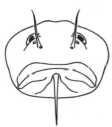

The shore rockling feeds principally on crustaceans, especially amphipods and small shore crabs, small worms, and occasionally fishes.

This rockling is often very abundant in intertidal situations and must play a considerable part in the ecology of rocky shores. It frequently is an intermediate host of the sea-bird trematode worm parasite *Cryptocotyle* sp; its skin bears the black cysts of the worm larva.

Three-bearded rockling   *Gaidropsarus vulgaris*

Distinguishing features   Possesses a low fringe of rays in the first dorsal fin preceded by a longer ray, and a second dorsal and anal fin both long-based and of uniform height. Three barbels, one on the chin and one on each anterior nostril. Pectoral fin rays 20–22. (See also coloration.)

Coloration   Body basically salmon pink, occasionally light brown with bold dark brown cross-bars and blotches on the back and upper sides. Pinkish ventrally.

Size   Attains 53 cm (20¾ in.); mostly about 40 cm (15¾ in.) in length, and 0.75 kg (1 lb 10 oz) in weight.

Remarks   This, the largest of the rocklings, is found mostly offshore between depths of 9 and 50 m (5–27 fathoms). It lives near rocks but often inhabits open ground, especially coarse gravel and sandy bottoms. It has been captured as deep as 150 m (82 fathoms).

It feeds mainly on crustaceans, but also eats smaller bottom-living fishes. It spawns in winter (January to February); the eggs and larvae are pelagic, as are the juveniles which have the distinctive mackerel-midge stage, when they have brilliantly silvery sides and belly, and clear green backs. They become bottom-living before they are 6 cm (2½ in.) long.

Occasionally captured by anglers, this rockling has no commercial value; it is too relatively uncommon to play much part in the food-chains of the sea except that the mackerel-midge young are preyed upon by several fish-eating sea-birds.

Silvery rockling   *Onogadus argentatus*

Distinguishing features   The low fine first dorsal fin rays are preceded by a long ray, usually twice as long as the eye diameter.

Three-bearded rockling ◄

► Silvery rockling

Second dorsal and anal fins long-based and low. Three barbels; one on the chin, one on each anterior nostril. Vertebrae 46–49. (See also coloration and depth range.)

Coloration Uniformly light reddish-brown, paler ventrally; the second dorsal, anal, and pectoral fins with orange edges.

Size Attains a maximum length of 45 cm (17¾ in.).

Remarks This rockling is found only in deep water on the lower continental shelf of the northern Atlantic Ocean and the Norwegian Sea. Its extreme depth range is 150–1400 m (82–766 fathoms), but it is common only below 500 m (273 fathoms). As an adult it lives on soft bottoms; the juvenile is a pelagic mackerel-midge, green on the back, silvery beneath. The juveniles are at times extremely abundant off the north-west coasts of Europe.

Ling   *Molva molva*

Distinguishing features The lings are long-bodied cod-like fishes with a single barbel on the chin, 2 dorsal fins (the first short-based and rounded in outline with 14–15 rays, the second long and of even height) and a single anal fin. In this species the lower jaw is not prominent, the eye is moderately small (about 1.5 times in the snout length), and the pelvic fins are short and do not reach as far back as the pectoral fins. (See also coloration.)

Coloration Dull browny-green and mottled on the back, lighter below; a dark spot on the hind edge of the first dorsal fin, similar but fainter spots on the second dorsal and anal fins; the edges of these fins light.

Size Attains a length of 2 m (6 ft 6 in.) and a weight of 35 kg (77 lb); usually 1 to 1.5 m (39 to 59 in.) in inshore waters.

Remarks The ling is essentially a deep-water fish occurring most abundantly in 300–400 m (164–219 fathoms) depth, although large numbers live in shallower water than this where the bottom is suitable, on open ocean coasts. It is most common on rocky grounds, but also colonizes the numerous wrecks found in inshore waters. Its food is mainly fishes including Norway pout, cod, and blue whiting, but it eats numerous larger crustaceans.

It breeds between March and July, most of the spawning grounds lying to the north of the British Isles. A single female may produce up to 60 million eggs which float at the surface while they develop.

Ling are mainly caught on lines, both by commercial fishermen and anglers; few are captured in trawls. It is a valuable commercial fish especially in northern European countries. Some of the catch is marketed fresh, a little is smoked, but most is salted and dried for local consumption and export to southern Europe.

Blue ling   *Molva dypterygia*

Distinguishing features Body very long and slender. A rather short barbel on the chin, and the lower jaw protrudes beyond the upper; eye large, nearly equal to snout length. The pelvic fins are moderately short and do not extend beyond the tips of the pectorals. First dorsal fin rounded but short-based (with 12–14 rays); second dorsal and anal fins long-based and low.

Coloration Plain greeny-brown above, lighter ventrally; dusky patches at the ends of the second dorsal and anal fins, the fin edges pale.

Size Attains a maximum length of 1.5 m (5 ft), and a probable maximum weight of 17 kg (37 lb 8 oz).

Remarks The blue ling is a deep-water species which generally lives at greater depths than its relative, although occasionally the two species are caught together. It is most abundant between 400–550 m (219–301 fathoms), but is found down to 1000 m (547 fathoms). It spawns in the deeper part of this bathymetric range, but is slow-growing, taking 5–6 years to attain sexual maturity. Spawning takes place in April-May.

It is exploited commercially on a small scale, especially by Scandinavian and Icelandic vessels; and is caught mainly on long lines. Occasionally it is taken by trawling in deep water. Its flesh is palatable and is marketed fresh as well as salted.

Spanish ling   *Molva macrophthalma*

Distinguishing features Elongate, the body long and slender. A rather short barbel on the chin, and the lower jaw projects forward and beyond the upper; eye large, almost as long as snout length. The pelvic fins are very long and continue well beyond the tips of the pectoral fins. First dorsal fin short-based and rounded with 10–12 rays; second dorsal and anal fin long and low.

Coloration The back and upper sides are greeny-brown, the belly silvery-yellow. The dorsal, anal and tail fins are greyish with light blue edges; the pelvic fins are blue.

Size Attains a length of *c.* 90 cm (36 in.) and a weight of around 7 kg (15 lb 7 oz).

Remarks This ling is the only species to be found off southern Europe and reaches the limit of its northern distribution off southern Ireland, being rare further north. It is a deep-water fish, living in 200–1000 m (109–547 fathoms), usually over muddy bottoms. It

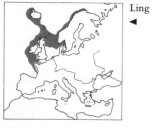

Ling ◀

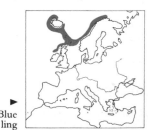

▶ Blue ling

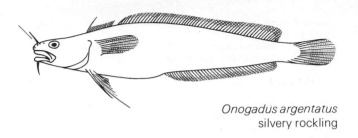

Onogadus argentatus
silvery rockling

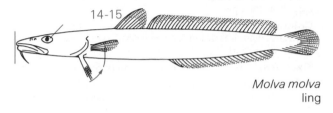

14-15

Molva molva
ling

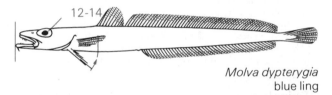

12-14

Molva dypterygia
blue ling

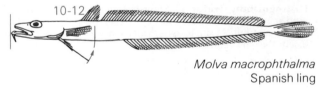

10-12

Molva macrophthalma
Spanish ling

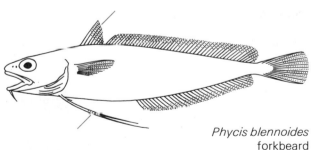

Phycis blennoides
forkbeard

spawns along the edge of the continental shelf in deep water. Its biology is little known.

In the Mediterranean and off the Spanish coast, where it is common, this ling is fairly important commercially.

Forkbeard   *Phycis blennoides*

Distinguishing features   Moderately stout-bodied but tapering sharply towards the tail. Two dorsal fins, the first short-based, triangular in shape, the second like the anal fin long-based. Pelvic fins very long, a single branched ray extending beyond the vent. A barbel on the chin.

Coloration   Warm greyish-brown above, light grey or silvery ventrally. The dorsal, tail, and anal fins have dusky edges and the lateral line is dark.

Size   Grows to 75 cm (30 in.), but rarely over 60 cm (24 in.).

Remarks   Usually occurs on muddy or sandy bottoms in depths of 100–350 m (55–191 fathoms), but occasionally is captured close inshore in shallower depths. A schooling fish, which is often caught in large numbers, the forkbeard mainly feeds on crustaceans and occasional fish. It spawns in spring and early summer.

Although considerable quantities are caught to the south-west of the British Isles, it is not an important food-fish. Its flesh is soft, but palatable. It is, however, important commercially in the Mediterranean. Off northern Europe its occurrence to the north of England is sporadic.

Tadpole-fish   *Raniceps raninus*

Distinguishing features   Stout-bodied and broad-headed, the head about as broad as it is long; a small barbel on the chin. The first dorsal fin minute (3 small rays), the second dorsal and anal fins long-based. (See also coloration.)

Coloration   Uniform dark above, varying from leaden brown to liver-coloured; the mouth and lips are white, the edges of the fins light in colour. Ventrally greyish.

Size   Attains a maximum length of 30 cm (11¾ in.), mostly around 15 cm (6 in.).

Remarks   A small, solitary, bottom-living fish found in shallow

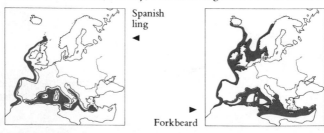

Spanish ling ◄

Forkbeard ►

water, in the region immediately below tide marks in the north, usually somewhat deeper to the south, and down to 100 m (55 fathoms). It is most common among algae-covered rocks, but is also captured over sandy and muddy bottoms. It is little-recorded rather than rare.

Its food is composed mainly of shrimps and sometimes small fishes and worms. It spawns in late summer and early autumn, usually inshore. The eggs are small and pelagic as are the larvae; the young live on the sea-bed from a length of about 2 cm ($\frac{3}{4}$ in.).

Hakes

The hakes are a group of cod-like fishes which were included in the cod family but are now regarded as distinct enough to be accorded family status as the Merlucciidae. They are widely distributed on the continental shelf of most temperate seas, both in the northern and southern hemispheres; they are important food-fishes. They are slender fishes with a large head and long jaw but no chin barbel, 2 dorsal fins, the first being short-based, and a single anal fin.

One species only is found in European seas.

Hake	*Merluccius merluccius*

Distinguishing features Slender body, head large, jaws well developed with large curved teeth. First dorsal fin triangular in shape, second dorsal and anal long-based and with a shallow dip about two-thirds of their length. Lateral line straight; scales moderately large.

Coloration Blue-grey on the back, silvery on the sides and silvery-white ventrally. Inside the mouth and gill cavity black.

Size Attains 1.80 m (6 ft) in length, but is rarely in excess of 1 m (39 in.); a weight of 11.3 kg (25 lb) has been recorded, but 5 kg (11 lb) is probably near the average maximum today.

Remarks The hake is a moderately deep-water fish which inhabits the middle and lower continental shelf in depths of 165 to 550 m (90–300 fathoms), but may be in shallower water in summertime. It lives near the bottom rather than on it and makes feeding forays into mid-water at night. Its food consists principally of fishes and squids, but young hake eat crustaceans in quantity.

Tadpole-
fish
◄

►
Hake

Spawning takes place in spring and summer (the later further north) at around 200 m (109 fathoms); the eggs and larvae are pelagic and tend to drift into inshore waters where the young are found during their first year of life.

The hake is an important food-fish which is caught mainly in trawls, although it can also be taken on a hook. It appears to have been heavily overfished and is now relatively scarce; large specimens are very uncommon.

Pearlfishes

A small family (Carapidae) of slender-bodied fishes, few exceeding 25 cm (10 in.) in length, but found world-wide in tropical and temperate seas. Many of the species whose biology is known live in association with invertebrate hosts, taking refuge within the body cavity of sea-cucumbers, tunicates, sea-urchins, and clams. Occasionally specimens are found 'fossilized' within the nacrous layers of the clam's shell. Pearlfishes pass through an extended larval life during which they are pelagic, the very elongate larva having a long-lobed filament from the front of the dorsal fin.

One species only occurs in northern European waters, but others are known from the Mediterranean.

Pearlfish	*Echiodon drummondi*

Distinguishing features   The very elongate shape is characteristic, as is the absence of pelvic fins, and the placement of the vent on the throat. The anal fin is longer and better developed than the dorsal fin. The mouth is large, and there is a pair of fang-like teeth in the front of each jaw.

Coloration   A pale pink with tints of silver on the body and gill covers, dark mottling faintly along the dorsal fin and tail.

Size   Attains a maximum length of 32 cm (12½ in.).

Remarks   The biology of this fish is little known. It is evidently widely distributed, but only locally common in deep water on the lower continental shelf in 146–275 m (80–150 fathoms). It has been captured on fishing grounds where the sea-cucumber, *Parastichopus tremmulus*, is common and may live in semi-parasitic association with it; on the other hand, many specimens of the holothurian have

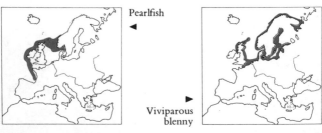

Pearlfish

◄

►

Viviparous
blenny

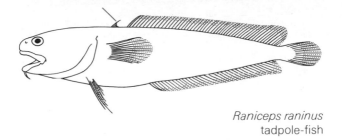

Raniceps raninus
tadpole-fish

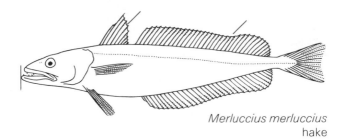

Merluccius merluccius
hake

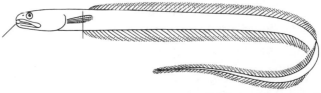

Echiodon drummondi
pearlfish

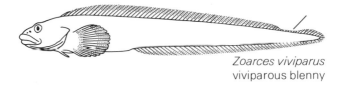

Zoarces viviparus
viviparous blenny

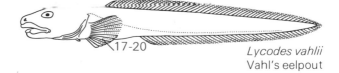

17-20

Lycodes vahlii
Vahl's eelpout

been examined without revealing a single pearlfish. The early planktonic larvae are relatively common in northern European waters.

This pearlfish may, like some of its relatives, feed on the internal organs of its invertebrate host, but small crustaceans have also been found in its gut, so it evidently catches active prey as well.

Eelpouts

The members of this family (Zoarcidae) are found in cool temperate to polar seas both in the Arctic and the Antarctic. In the northern hemisphere they are represented by numerous species which live from the shoreline down to 1000 m (547 fathoms) and more. Several of these are found in the Barents Sea region, but only 4 are at all common in shallow water south of the Arctic circle.

Eelpouts all have rather elongate bodies, the dorsal and anal fins fusing with the tail fins, large fan-like pectoral fins and short stumpy pelvic fins on the throat. They also have rather broad, large heads and protuberant lips.

Viviparous blenny   *Zoarces viviparus*

Distinguishing features   Long-bodied but rather stout at the abdomen, the head broad and lips thick. Dorsal fin long but with a low section of short spines close to the tail; the anal fin is also long and the fin continues around the tail. Skin slimy with deeply embedded small scales.

Coloration   Usually dull but very variable with the nature of the habitat. Often greyish-brown above, yellowish below with a series of dusky bars along the body. Frequently deep brown above.

Size   Attains a maximum length of 50 cm (19¾ in.), usually growing to *c.* 30 cm (11¾ in.).

Remarks   This is the most common member of the family, and the most southerly in distribution in European seas. It is common on the shore between tide marks and down to 40 m (22 fathoms) at the most. It is found on rocky shores under stones, amongst algae and in pools; in deeper water it occurs on muddy and sandy bottoms. It also occurs in estuaries, in the north in low salinities.

It is well known as a viviparous fish. Mating takes place in August-September, the eggs develop within the female for 3–4 weeks before hatching, and then continue to grow, nourished by special tissues of the ovary. The young are born fully formed in December-February and at a length of about 4 cm (1½ in.). The viviparous blenny feeds mainly on small crustaceans, occasional fish and molluscs.

In the Baltic countries it is fished commercially with traps and seines; its flesh is tasty with considerable fat content. It is eaten fresh or smoked.

Vahl's eelpout
Lycodes vahlii

Distinguishing features   Slender-bodied but with a broad head, lips thick and fleshy. Dorsal fin long, of uniform height, continuous with the tail and anal fins. Lateral line on lower side of body, belly covered with embedded scales. Pectoral fin with 17–20 rays; its base covered with scales.

Coloration   Brownish, lighter ventrally, with 8–13 dark cross-bands in young, fading and breaking up in adults; always a dark spot or up to 3 spots at front of dorsal fin. Internal lining of body cavity black.

Size   Attains 52 cm (20½ in.); European specimens rarely more than 35 cm (13¾ in.).

Remarks   Found in deep water from 170–365 m (93–200 fathoms), most abundantly in 200–300 m (110–164 fathoms) on muddy bottoms at bottom temperatures of 2–3°C and full salinity. It feeds on small crustaceans, molluscs, worms, and brittlestars. Spawns in summer, producing few (less than 100) large eggs.
   The European populations are regarded as the subspecies *L. vahli gracilis; L. vahli vahli* occurs off West Greenland and North America.

Esmark's eelpout
Lycodes esmarkii

Distinguishing features   Long-bodied with a large heavy head, thick fleshy lips. Dorsal fin long and of uniform height, continuous with the tail and anal fins. Lateral line double, running along the side and along the belly, which is covered with embedded scales. Pectoral fin with 22–23 rays—its base scaleless.

Coloration   Body dark greenish-brown, ventrally yellow-white; the back and upper sides with 7 or 8 double yellowish cross-bands each forming an inverted Y-shape.

Size   Attains a maximum of 75 cm (29½ in.), but mostly 50–65 cm (19¾–25½ in.).

Remarks   Lives on muddy bottoms in deep water in 275–550 m (150–300 fathoms), in the deeper depths at the south of its range. It does not live in the near polar temperature water of the far north or great depths, preferring temperatures of 2–5°C. It spawns in autumn,

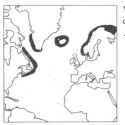

Vahl's
eelpout

◀

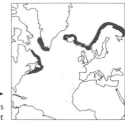

▶

Esmark's
eelpout

175

producing relatively more eggs than other eelpouts (about 1200), but they are similarly large (6 mm). It feeds mostly on small echinoderms such as brittlestars and sea-urchins. It is of no fishery value but is occasionally captured in trawls.

Sars's eelpout   *Lycenchelys sarsii*

Distinguishing features Very slender-bodied, with only a moderately large head on which large pits open to the surface around the jaws. The dorsal and anal fins are long, low and continuous. The body is scaly all over, although the scales are small and embedded. The dorsal fin origin is over the end of the pectoral fins.

Coloration Back and upper sides reddish-brown sharply divided from the light ventral surface. Back usually with rounded blotches.

Size Maximum length 18.4 cm ($7\frac{1}{4}$ in.), usually around 15 cm (6 in.)

Remarks Widely distributed along the Scandinavian coast on muddy bottoms at depths of 150–600 m (82–328 fathoms), but most common between 200 and 350 m (109–191 fathoms). A common fish in the deep Norwegian fjords. It eats worms, crustaceans, and small molluscs.

Rat-tails

A family of fishes (Macrouridae) related to the cod fishes, living in deep water conditions on the continental slope in all oceans from subarctic to Antarctic. Their general body shape is elongate, with a large head, very short trunk, and a long rat-like tail. Most species have a barbel on the chin, a short-based first dorsal fin, very low or poorly-developed second dorsal fin, and a very distinct large anal fin which runs from the vent to the tail tip.

Some rat-tails have a light-producing organ in the mid-line of the belly. The light is produced by luminous bacteria in the organ and a clear patch of skin permits the light to shine through. Some species even have a lens-like patch of tissue to intensify the light. Many rat-tails are capable sound-producers, the males having drumming muscles attached to the swim-bladder, which produce the noise.

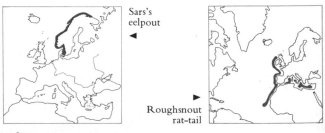

Sars's eelpout ◄

► Roughsnout rat-tail

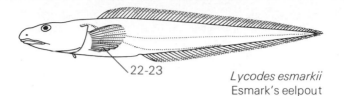

Lycodes esmarkii
Esmark's eelpout

Lycenchelys sarsii
Sars's eelpout

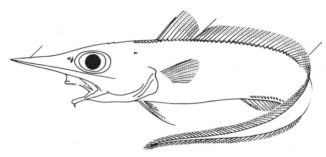

Trachyrhynchus trachyrincus
roughsnout rat-tail

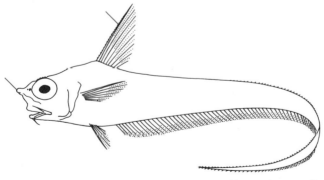

Nezumia aequalis
smooth rat-tail

Most rat-tails live close to the sea-bed, their body form being adapted to swimming with the head, with its sensitive barbel, lower than the tail.

Some 15 species live in the seas of N. W. Europe; the 6 species which live in relatively shallow water are listed here.

Roughsnout rat-tail   *Trachyrhynchus trachyrincus*

Distinguishing features   Typical of the family in general body shape, except that the first dorsal fin is low and rounded with no hard spiny rays, and the second dorsal rays are longer than those of the anal fin; the 2 dorsal fins are close together. Snout sharply pointed; chin barbel small; scales large and spiny.

Coloration   Plain pale brown above, slightly lighter ventrally.

Size   Attains 51 cm (20 in.).

Remarks   Common in deep water, 550–1100 m (300–601 fathoms) from off western Ireland southwards. Found mainly on the lower continental shelf on muddy bottoms. Feeds on small crustaceans.

Smooth rat-tail   *Nezumia aequalis*

Distinguishing features   A rather deep-bodied rat-tail with a steep dorsal profile. The first dorsal fin is short-based but high with a serrated spine in front. A weak ridge running across the cheek below the eye with large scute-like scales in 2 rows, smaller scales beneath the ridge. Body scales moderately large, with fine spines on their surface; vent in a scaleless black patch. Snout with 3 bosses, 1 central and 1 each side, bluntly pointed; mouth moderately small.

Coloration   Dark bluish-grey on the back, sides and belly slightly silvery, head brownish. The naked area around the vent jet black; the tip of the first dorsal, pelvic fins, and anal fin black.

Size   Attains a maximum length of 41 cm (16¼ in.).

Remarks   A relatively deep-water rat-tail which has been caught at depths of 200–2320 m (109–1269 fathoms), but in European waters is taken mainly between 640–1000 m (350–547 fathoms). A fairly common species on muddy sea bottoms.

Smooth
rat-tail

Softhead rat-tail   *Malacocephalus laevis*

Distinguishing features   Moderately deep-bodied, with a large head, rounded snout, and large jaws with curved teeth. The eye is particularly large. First dorsal fin high, the spiny ray with a smooth edge; second dorsal low and poorly developed. Scales small, each with fine teeth giving a sand-papery feel. Two small clear 'windows' between the pelvic fins; the vent closer to the anal fin than the pelvics.

Coloration   Greyish on the back, silvery reflections on the sides, black tissue around the gill covers, dark along the ventral mid-line. Light-organs between the pelvic fins.

Size   Attains 56 cm (22 in.) in total length.

Remarks   A relatively shallow rat-tail which lives on the upper continental slope mainly in depths of 300–750 m (164–410 fathoms), although ranging from 200–1000 m (109–547 fathoms). It is known to feed on small crustaceans and, from its dentition, it might be assumed to catch and eat larger, more active, prey such as squids and fishes. A common rat-tail off the European Atlantic coast.

Hollowsnout rat-tail   *Coelorinchus caelorhinchus*

Distinguishing features   Slender-bodied with a short-based rather high first dorsal fin with a strong but smooth first dorsal spine; second dorsal fin very weakly developed. Snout sharply pointed with a strong ridge running beneath the eye; orbit oval, longer than high. A scaleless black area in mid-line of abdomen; vent close to anal fin origin.

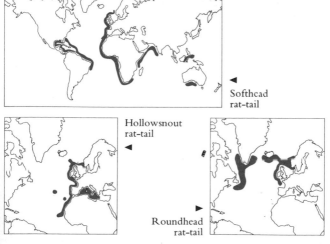

◄ Softhead
rat-tail

Hollowsnout
rat-tail
◄

► Roundhead
rat-tail

Coloration Dull grey-brown to slate-grey on the back and sides; black ventrally, around the gill cover, over the body cavity and to the anal fin origin.

Size Grows to 38 cm (15 in.).

Remarks Found mainly in depths of 200–500 m (109–273 fathoms) with an absolute range of 140–732 m (77–400 fathoms). It is relatively common on the continental shelf of N. W. Europe. Four other sub-species are found in the Atlantic Ocean; only *C. caelorhinchus caelorhinchus* is shown on the map.

Roundhead rat-tail *Coryphaenoides rupestris*

Distinguishing features Head rounded, with blunt snout and large almost terminal mouth; no noticeable bony ridge running beneath the eye. First dorsal fin high with the first spine serrated on front edge. Scales moderately large with numerous small spines; throat region naked.

Coloration Dull brown on back and upper sides, silvery on lower sides and belly; throat and gill chamber membranes dull brown.

Size Attains 1 m (39½ in.).

Remarks Widely distributed in the North Atlantic in depths between 400 and 1200 m (219–656 fathoms), usually in shallower depths further north. Its food consists mainly of deep-water prawns, amphipods, and lantern fishes. It breeds in summer, producing at least 16,000 eggs. Its biology is little known.

Rough rat-tail *Macrourus berglax*

Distinguishing features A heavy-headed rat-tail with a long trunk, the anal fin origin being posterior to the origin of the second dorsal. First dorsal fin high with a strongly serrated spine. A strong, rough-edged ridge along the head below the eye; scaleless beneath the ridge; head and body scales all with a long central spine and smaller spinules (giving the fish a rasp-like surface).

Coloration Greyish overall, slightly darker beneath the head.

Size Attains 1.10 m (43¼ in.), probably more.

Remarks A common fish in the subarctic waters of the North Atlantic which lives in moderately shallow depths of 200–600 m

Rough
rat-tail

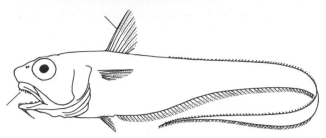

Malacocephalus laevis
softhead rat-tail

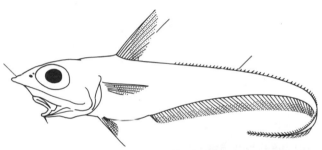

Coelorinchus caelorhinchus
hollowsnout rat-tail

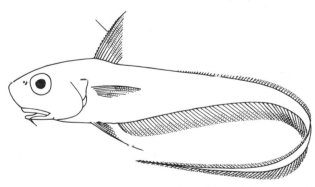

Coryphaenoides rupestris
roundhead rat-tail

(109–328 fathoms), in the far north even as shallow as 100 m (55 fathoms). It feeds on capelin, prawns and amphipods, molluscs, and brittlestars, and is occasionally taken on hooks set on long lines for halibut and other fish. It is quite palatable, but of limited use to commercial fishermen on account of the wasteful large head and long tail. It is believed to spawn in winter to spring.

Flying-Fishes

The flying-fishes are mainly tropical marine fishes which venture into temperate seas in the warmer seasons of the year. Together with the wholly tropical halfbeaks they comprise the family Exocoetidae. They live near the surface of the sea, feeding on surface-living organisms and escaping from predators (such as the dolphin fish) by 'flying'. In fact, they do not fly but glide as long as their outstretched fins can sustain the body weight; the propulsive force is provided by active under-surface swimming. Two major groups of flying-fish are recognized: the four-winged group are skilful and accomplished gliders having enlarged pelvic and pectoral fins; the two-winged group with enlarged pectoral fins only are poor 'fliers' by comparison. In northern European waters only one species has been identified more than once; it belongs to the former group. Isolated captures of other species have been noted.

Atlantic flying-fish   *Cheilopogon heterurus*

Distinguishing features Both pectoral and pelvic fins well developed, lower lobe of the tail fin elongate. Dorsal fin conspicuously longer-based than anal fin, the first ray of the anal beneath the 6th or 7th dorsal ray. 13–14 dorsal rays; 8–10 anal rays; 30–38 pre-dorsal scales.

Coloration Deep blue on the back, silvery on the sides and belly. The pectoral and pelvic fins are greyish with a poorly-defined lighter band running across their width.

Size Attains 31 cm ($12\frac{1}{4}$ in.).

Remarks This is the only flying-fish to have been positively identified more than once in northern European waters. Most of the numerous 19th-century records attributed to other species were

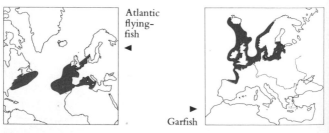

Atlantic flying-fish ◄

Garfish ►

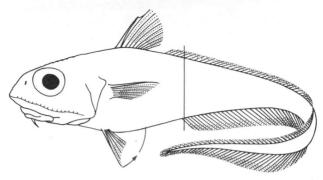

Macrourus berglax
rough rat-tail

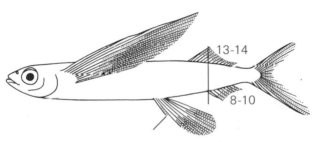

13-14

8-10

Cheilopogon heterurus
Atlantic flying-fish

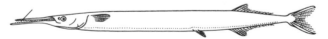

Belone belone
garfish

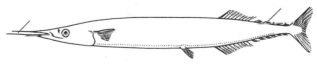

Scomberesox saurus
skipper

probably referable to this species. It is a surface-living fish which is also found in the Pacific Ocean and probably in the Indian Ocean as well. The distribution shown is of the Atlantic subspecies *C. heterurus heterurus*. In the Mediterranean it breeds in spring (May to July), and the eggs have numerous fine threads over their surface, one of which is greatly elongate. The young have a fringed chin barbel at first. This fish occurs in northern waters in late summer to early winter only.

Garfish and Skipper

Two similar-looking fishes which belong to separate families (Belonidae and Scomberesocidae). Both are surface-living predatory fish with a long, slender body and elongate jaws. The garfishes are mainly marine tropical and warm temperate fishes, although some live in tropical freshwaters. Numerous species are known worldwide, many of them closely alike in appearance, and most live in shallow inshore waters. In contrast, the skippers are few in number (4 species are recognized) and live in the open ocean, mostly in temperate zones, where they play an important role as predators on surface plankton and as prey for larger oceanic fishes and sea-birds.

Garfish *Belone belone*

Distinguishing features The long slender body and elongate, many-toothed jaws are distinctive, as are the relatively long-based single dorsal and anal fins. The lateral line runs along the lower sides from head to tail.

Coloration Brilliant greeny-blue back and upper sides, the sides and belly gleaming silver with yellowish patches.

Size Attains a maximum length of 94 cm (37 in.), and a weight of 1.30 kg (2 lb 14 oz).

Remarks A surface-living mainly offshore species which comes into the shallow waters of northern Europe in late spring and can be found close inshore throughout summer and autumn. North of the British Isles it is a rare straggler. Its food comprises most small surface-living fishes, especially the young of the herring and cod families, as well as sandeels. It also eats small squids and crustaceans. It spawns in coastal waters in May–June, the eggs having numerous long threads at the surface which tangle in algae, flotsam, and, when fresh, anything they touch. The young fish have short jaws on hatching; the lower jaw elongates first and stays longer than the upper until the fish reaches 9 cm ($3\frac{1}{2}$ in.) in length.

The garfish is not commercially exploited although its flesh is of good quality. It is a fine sporting fish on light tackle, often leaping out of the water when first hooked.

Mediterranean and Black Sea garfish are related subspecies *B. b. gracilis* and *B. b. euxini* respectively.

Distinguishing features Long and slender-bodied, with slender jaws, but relatively small teeth. The body is compressed and deeper than wide. Dorsal and anal fins rather small, both followed by a series of small finlets. The lateral line runs along the ventral surface from head to tail.

Coloration A beautiful clear green above, shading suddenly to bright silver with a yellowish tinge on the lower sides and belly.

Size Attains a maximum length of *c.* 50 cm (19¾ in.).

Remarks A surface-living fish of the open ocean which occasionally penetrates north-eastwards up the northern European coast and into the North Sea. It is found in coastal waters in late autumn and early winter. It feeds on small shrimp-like euphausiids and other crustaceans, and on small near-surface fishes. The skipper spawns in the open sea; the eggs have numerous rather short threads on their surface. The newly-hatched fish has jaws of equal length; the lower jaw protrudes and is longer until the fish is 15 cm (6 in.) in length; beyond that length the upper jaw grows longer.

The skipper is a widespread species and common in warm temperate and tropical seas. It is an important food for many larger fishes and sea-birds, and is being fished for increasingly for human food.

It occasionally strands itself in large numbers on the North Sea coasts.

Sand-Smelts

A large family of small fishes (Atherinidae) which are widely distributed in tropical and warm temperate seas world-wide, and in many regions in freshwater. They are schooling fishes of shallow inshore waters; in northern European seas they are largely seasonal in their occurrence. They are mostly rather slim fish with 2 dorsal fins, the first of which has slender spines, the body is fully scaled, the eye large and the mouth protrusible. Sand-smelts have a silvery line running from head to tail along the body, which results in them being known as silversides.

Two species only are known in northern European waters.

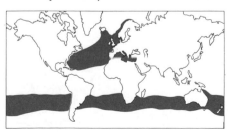

Skipper

Sand-smelt   *Atherina presbyter*

Distinguishing features   Slender-bodied with 2 dorsal fins, the first with 7–8 slender spines. Head small, its length more than 4–5 times in body length. Scales relatively small, 53–57 between the upper base of the pectoral fin and the tail fin. 48–52 vertebrae; 13–16 branched rays in the anal fin.

Coloration   Back and upper sides clear green, with black speckles around the edges of the scales. An intense silver line along the sides; ventrally white or silvery-white with iridescent reflections.

Size   Attains a maximum length of 21 cm (8¼ in.) and weight of 73 g (2 oz 9 dm); mostly *c*. 15 cm (6 in.).

Remarks   The sand-smelt is a common inshore and estuarine fish which becomes more common during summer (presumably as a result of northward migration). It is most abundant on sandy and muddy bottoms in 0–20 m (0–11 fathoms), and can easily be caught in shore seines. Young fish are occasionally found on the British coast in summer in rock pools and saltings' pools, high up the intertidal zone, swimming in tight schools, and are believed to have hatched in such locations.

Breeding takes place in late spring to midsummer. The eggs are nearly 2 mm in diameter and have short filaments by which they attach to marine algae and submerged plants. Sand-smelts feed on small crustaceans and rarely on young fish. Their jaws are strikingly protrusible.

This species is not fished for commercially although its flesh is palatable. It is a frequent prey of terns, and no doubt other predators.

Big-scale sand-smelt   *Atherina boyeri*

Distinguishing features   Similar to the preceding species, but has a larger head; its length is less than 4.5 times in the body length; the body appears deeper and a little shorter. Scales moderate, 44–48 between the upper base of the pectoral fin and the tail fin. 43–45 vertebrae; 11–13 branched rays in the anal fin.

Coloration   Greenish on the back with the scales outlined with dark dots; intense silver band on the sides, and silvery-white ventrally.

Size   Attains a maximum of 9 cm (3½ in.).

Sand-smelt ◄

► Big-scale sand-smelt

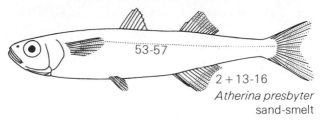

53-57

2 + 13-16

Atherina presbyter
sand-smelt

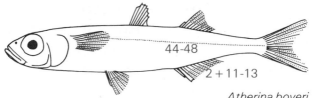

44-48

2 + 11-13

Atherina boyeri
big-scale sand-smelt

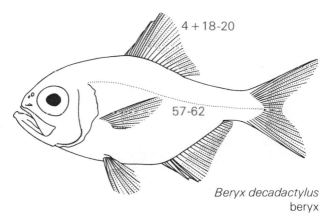

4 + 18-20

57-62

Beryx decadactylus
beryx

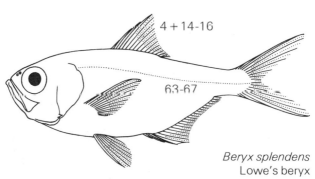

4 + 14-16

63-67

Beryx splendens
Lowe's beryx

Remarks Rare in northern European waters and still to some extent little known. In the British Isles it was first reported on the Cornish coast in 1846, and not found again until the mid-1950s, when it was caught in warm-water marine docks at Swansea and Barrow-in-Furness. Subsequently it has been caught on the coast of Holland and in the Severn estuary. It is an estuarine species which appears to be attracted to low salinity, although it occurs also in the sea and in freshwater. Its food is mainly small crustaceans with occasional worms and molluscs.

The Berycoids

Deep-water oceanic fishes found along the lower continental shelf, occasionally in large quantities, but in general little known. The 3 species included here belong to 2 families, Berycidae and Trachichthyidae, but other members of the latter family also occur in the deep sea near Europe. Members of both families are world-wide in their distribution and are marine, mostly deep sea, fishes.

Beryx	*Beryx decadactylus*

Distinguishing features A deep-bodied fish with a deep head and large eye. The pelvic fins each have a single strong spine and 10–13 branched rays. 57–62 scales in the lateral line; belly not sharply scaled. Dorsal fin with 18–20 branched rays. (See also coloration.)

Coloration Deep orange-red on the back and upper sides, clear orange elsewhere with a purple sheen over the body cavity.

Size Attains 61 cm (24 in.).

Remarks This is the most common member of the family in European seas and is captured at depths of 200–550 m (109–300 fathoms). It probably lives close to the bottom, but not actually on the sea floor, and the young live in mid-water. The young have conspicuously heavy spines on the head which are lost with increasing age. Its food is composed mainly of deep-water prawns, with fishes and squids taken occasionally.

In northern European waters this fish is not exploited by fishermen, although sometimes large hauls are made and landed. Its flesh is extremely well flavoured and palatable; in southern European waters (where it lives in shallower depths) it is regularly marketed in small quantities. This species is also believed to occur in the North Pacific.

Beryx

Lowe's beryx
Beryx splendens

Distinguishing features Less deep-bodied (body depth more than 2.5 times in body length), the head is relatively deep but the eye is comparably smaller than in the more common species. Dorsal fin with 14–16 branched rays. Scales smaller, 63–67 in the lateral line. (See also coloration.)

Coloration Clear rose-red with orange tints ventrally, inside the mouth and gill cavity bright red.

Size Attains a maximum length of 46 cm (18 in.) usually around 34 cm (14 in.)

Remarks A rare fish in northern European waters, but relatively common in the warmer seas to the south. It is marketed in small quantities in southern Europe and in other warm temperate regions. It lives in depths of 100–400 m (55–219 fathoms) and is world-wide in warm temperate seas. N. E. Atlantic distribution only is shown on the map.

Rough-fish
Hoplostethus mediterraneus

Distinguishing features Deep-bodied with a large head, heavily spined and distinctive because of the deep cavities covered by transparent skin. A series of strong spines along the belly from pelvics to vent. Branched rays in dorsal fin 15–18, in anal fin 9–11; eye relatively small.

Coloration Rose-red on the back and fins, pale pink on sides and belly; dull black of body cavity shows through the skin. Inside mouth and gill cavity deep mulberry black.

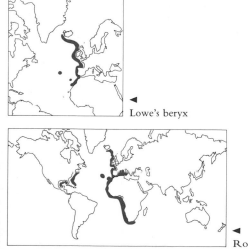

◄ Lowe's beryx

◄ Rough-fish

Size   Attains a length of at least 30 cm (11¾ in.), usually around 20 cm (7–9 in.).

Remarks   This species lives in deep water at depths of 200–500 m (109–273 fathoms), but not on the sea-bed, probably keeping about 50 m (27 fathoms) above it. It is extremely common at appropriate depths to the west of the British Isles, but it is not commercially exploited. It is also found in the Indian Ocean.

Dory and Boar-Fish

These fishes are the only representatives in shallow seas in N. W. Europe of the order Zeiformes. They belong to 2 families Zeidae and Caproidae. Members of the former family are world-wide in temperate and warm-temperate seas, mostly in shallow water, although some are found in the deep sea. All have deep compressed bodies with a large head and a highly protrusible large mouth. The members of the family Caproidae are smaller and found in moderate depths in all the oceans; they are also deep-bodied but with rather a small but protrusible mouth; mostly they are brick red in colour. Members of both families have heavy spines in their dorsal, anal, and pelvic fins.

Dory	*Zeus faber*

Distinguishing features   Deep body, massive head with large, highly protrusible jaws. 9–10 strong spines in the first dorsal fin, 3–4 similar spines in front of the anal fin. A double series of large spiny scales running around the outline of the belly and back.

Coloration   Dark yellowish-brown on the back, often with lighter yellow lines meandering along the sides; silvery-grey ventrally. A conspicuous black blotch surrounded by a yellow ring on the sides. Anal and pelvic fin membranes black.

Size   Usually up to 40 cm (15¾ in.) and a weight of 2.5 kg (5 lb 8 oz); exceptional specimens, always females, attain 66 cm (26 in.) and 6 kg (13 lb 4 oz).

Remarks   The dory is an inshore fish living mainly in 10–50 m (5½–27 fathoms), although exceptionally it is reported close to the surface and as deep as 200 m (109 fathoms). It usually lives a solitary

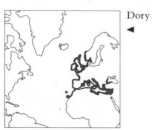

Dory
◄

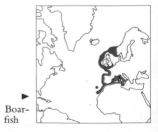

►
Boar-
fish

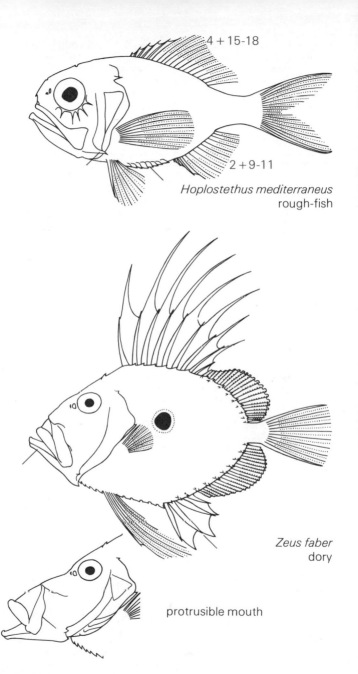

4 + 15-18

2 + 9-11

Hoplostethus mediterraneus
rough-fish

Zeus faber
dory

protrusible mouth

life or is in a small school. It feeds on a wide range of fishes which are individually sighted and stalked in a head-on posture until they are close enough to be engulfed by the sudden protrusion of the jaws, often being swept in with the inflow of water. It breeds in summer in the English Channel, but probably does not spawn further northwards.

Its flesh is extremely well flavoured and flaky, with a good texture. It is the subject of a small fishery in northern European waters, but what is captured always commands a high price. To the south of the Channel it is fished more extensively but its habits are such that large landings are rare.

Boar-fish   *Capros aper*

Distinguishing features   Rather deep-bodied but with a moderately small head and pointed snout. The mouth is small but the jaws are very protrusible. The dorsal fin spines are long and strong, as is the first pelvic spine, but the anal fin spines are relatively short. The scales are small and finely toothed and the body has a sand-paper like feel to it.

Coloration   Usually deep red with yellowish markings; in shallow water yellow or straw coloured.

Size   Attains a maximum length of 16 cm ($6\frac{1}{4}$ in.), but usually about 10 cm (4 in.).

Remarks   Evidently common locally in deep water on the lower continental shelf in 100–400 m (55–219 fathoms). It is thought to live among the yellow and pink coral growing on the rock faces in these depths. However, it is occasionally captured in large numbers on sandy grounds, and in areas such as the western English Channel it may be fairly common for a period of 2 or 3 years and then suddenly disappear. It spawns in summer, the eggs and larvae are planktonic, but spawning takes place only as far north as the British Isles. It feeds entirely on small crustaceans.

Opah

The unique representative of the family Lampridae, a fish which is found world-wide in tropical and temperate seas. Despite its total dissimilarity of body form, its closest relatives are the deal-fishes and

Opah

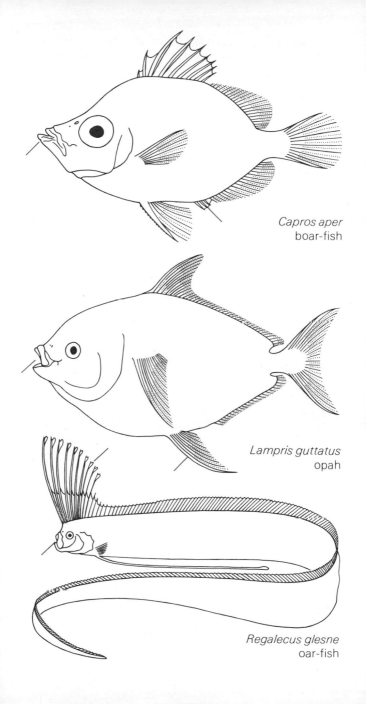

Capros aper
boar-fish

Lampris guttatus
opah

Regalecus glesne
oar-fish

the oar-fish which share the basic similarity of protrusible jaws. The fins in all 3 have no spines, although in the opah the rays are solid and stout.

Opah   *Lampris guttatus*

Distinguishing features   Unmistakable on colour alone, but having a deep though thickset body, long-based dorsal and anal fins, the former with a high lobe, and long, curved pectoral and pelvic fins. Mouth protrusible but toothless.

Coloration   Deep blue on the back shading through to green to pinkish-silver on the belly; rounded milky-white spots on the body. The fins are all blood red.

Size   Grows to at least 1.5 m (5 ft) in length and a weight of 73 kg (161 lb). Specimens of up to 272 kg (600 lb) have been reported.

Remarks   This striking fish is known mainly from chance captures in fishing nets and occasional strandings. Its normal life style is as a mid-water fish in the open sea at 100–400 m (55–219 fathoms) depth—a relatively little explored region. It feeds mainly on squids and fishes, including blue whiting, silvery pout, and hake. Although not often captured in European waters and therefore not commercially fished for, its flesh is of excellent flavour. Very rarely specimens are caught by anglers.

Oar-fish and Deal-fish

In northern European seas these 2 slender, thin-bodied fish represent the families Regalecidae and Trachipteridae. Both are similar in appearance and share with the opah the highly distinctive jaws and protrusible mouth. The oar-fish is a mid-water fish world-wide in distribution but little known. Deal-fishes are more common, and a number of species are recognized.

Oar-fish   *Regalecus glesne*

Distinguishing features   Long, slender, compressed body with a long-based dorsal fin, the front rays of which are high and form a crest. Pelvic fin rays also elongate; these and the long dorsal rays

Oar-fish

have fleshy membranes at their tips. Head bones paper-thin and virtually transparent.

Coloration   Body is silvery with interrupted oblique dusky bars. Fins deep red.

Size   Attains 7 m (23 ft).

Remarks   Presumed to be a mid-water fish in the open ocean, although most specimens described have been caught at the surface or found stranded—presumably sick fishes. Its preferred depth range seems to be 300–600 m (164–328 fathoms), at which depths it feeds mainly on euphausiid crustaceans (shrimp-like 'krill'), and when young it is eaten by deep-feeding tunas and lancet-fishes. Adults are rarely caught in their natural habitat.

Deal-fish   *Trachipterus arcticus*

Distinguishing features   Long, slender and compressed body with a long-based dorsal fin, the longest rays of which are just past the mid-point of the body. Pelvic fins minute; anal fin absent; tail fin merely a fan of 8 long, upwardly directed rays. Head bones paper-thin and fragile.

Coloration   Bright silvery overall with 1–5 rounded dark blotches along the upper sides; fins all orange-red.

Size   Attains a length of 2.5 m (8 ft 2½ in.).

Remarks   A mesopelagic fish which appears to be most common at depths of 183–914 m (100–500 fathoms), although paradoxically most that have been examined were stranded on shore or caught at the surface of the sea. It probably rises nearer to the surface at night. Occasionally small schools are reported, but mostly it is captured solitarily. It feeds on deep-water fishes, squids, and shrimps. It is not a very common fish and is quite useless as food.

Sticklebacks

Well-known and often common fishes across the temperate regions of the northern hemisphere. Some species live in fully marine conditions, others are confined to freshwater, but the majority can thrive in salt or freshwater and are often abundant in slightly saline conditions. Most sticklebacks are small, with scaleless, torpedo-

Deal-fish

shaped bodies, and a series of sharp spines along the back and a strong spine in each pelvic fin. In all species the males build a nest and guard the eggs and young fish.

Only 8 members of the family Gasterosteidae are recognized; 3 occur in N. W. Europe.

Stickleback *Gasterosteus aculeatus*

Distinguishing features Small fishes with 3 (exceptionally fewer) long isolated spines on the back—the third lying close to the second dorsal fin. Anal fin rather small. Pelvic fin spine long and strong; only a single small soft ray. Body naked or with a varying number of bony plates along the sides.

Coloration Variable; usually dark brown-green on the back and silvery on the sides. Males in the breeding season have brilliant red throats and blue eyes. Marine specimens are bluish above and clear silver on the sides.

Size Mostly about 5.1 cm (2 in.), exceptionally up to 10 cm (4 in.).

Remarks A very widely-distributed and often abundant fish in lakes, rivers and coastal waters of northern Europe. In freshwater its normal habitat is in shallows of 0–1 m (0–3 ft 3 in.) usually on clean bottoms, but in heavy river flows it takes shelter in deeper water or among bankside vegetation. In estuaries it usually lives close to the river bank, and in the sea it is common in coastal waters in tidal pools, but usually among marine algae. It is common only in fully marine habitats from Scotland northwards.

The stickleback breeds in spring and early summer, the male constructing a nest of plant fibres in a hollow on the bottom (whether in freshwater or marine habitats). Within the nest the eggs are laid; the male aerates them and removes infertile eggs. The nest is central to the male's territory, which is strongly defended by the brightly-coloured fish. Growth varies with local conditions. In environments poor in food even 3-year old fish may be only 5 cm (2 in.) in length, but in large rivers and even more in the sea this may be the length at the end of the first year. Few sticklebacks survive for more than 3 years.

Its diet is very varied but is necessarily confined to small organisms. Crustaceans and small larval insects are important, but worms, molluscs, young fishes, and a small quantity of plant

Stickleback

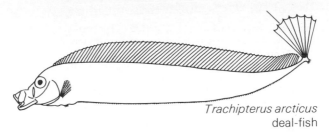

Trachipterus arcticus
deal-fish

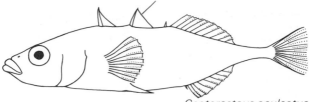

Gasterosteus aculeatus
stickleback

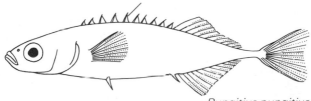

Pungitius pungitius
nine-spined stickleback

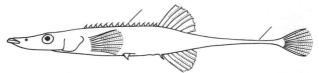

Spinachia spinachia
fifteen-spined stickleback

Macroramphosus scolopax
snipefish

material are also included. The stickleback is preyed upon by a wide variety of fish-eating fishes, birds, and mammals.

Sticklebacks with bony plates on the sides, from pectoral fin to tail fin, occur mainly in the sea and in the coastal parts of Europe and North America. Those without such plates are usually found in inland freshwaters. Many sticklebacks in the British Isles at least have a few such plates along the side, behind the pectoral fin.

Nine-spined stickleback   *Pungitius pungitius*

Distinguishing features Rather slender body, with 8–10, usually 9, short isolated spines along the back. Second dorsal and anal fins of virtually equal length and shape. The caudal peduncle is long and narrow.

Coloration Dark olive green to brown on the back, lighter ventrally, sometimes even silvery. In the breeding season males have a black throat and white or pale blue pelvic fin spines.

Size Attains a maximum length of 7 cm (2¾ in.), but usually less than 5 cm (2 in.).

Remarks Widely distributed but rather local; although it is widespread in the whole of northern Europe, it appears to be absent from large areas. It is found in fresh or at the most slightly brackish water, not in the sea, and is most common in densely vegetated situations. Ponds or rivers which in summer appear to be choked with vegetation are a typical habitat. The male builds a nest in the aquatic plants usually at least 7.7 cm (3 in.) above the bottom; in the nest the females (often more than one) lay their eggs. The male protects the eggs and later the young fish. This stickleback grows to about 3.5 cm (1½ in.) in the first year of life, at the end of which it is sexually mature. Its maximum life span is 3 years. The nine-spined stickleback feeds mainly on small crustaceans, insects and their larvae, and occasionally young fish.

Fifteen-spined stickleback   *Spinachia spinachia*

Distinguishing features Very long slender body with an elongate, pointed snout and very slim caudal peduncle. A series of 14–16 (mostly 15) short, isolated spines runs along the back. Second dorsal and anal fins short-based and almost triangular in shape. Pelvic fin spine minute.

Nine-spined stickleback

Coloration Brownish or greenish-brown on the back and upper sides with irregular darker bars. On the underside yellowish. Dorsal and anal fins with a brown blotch on the anterior fin rays and membrane.

Size Exceptionally attaining a length of 20 cm (8 in.), usually around 15 cm (6 in.).

Remarks A wholly marine stickleback which is found in shallow coastal waters down to depths of *c.* 10 m (5 fathoms). It is particularly abundant amongst marine algae and eel-grass, and is occasionally found in tidal pools. It spawns in spring and summer; the male builds a fist-sized nest in seaweed well clear of the bottom and at half-tide level or below. Up to 200 eggs are laid in the nest, each about 2 mm in diameter; they hatch in 18–21 days.

Its food consists mainly of crustaceans, chiefly copepods and small amphipods.

Snipefishes

A small family (Macroramphosidae) of marine fish found mostly in temperate and tropical seas world-wide. They are usually encountered at moderate depths. Snipefish are long-snouted, with a rather compressed, deep body, and small fins, except for the massive dorsal fin spine midway along the back. One species only occurs in northern European seas.

Snipefish	*Macroramphosus scolopax*

Distinguishing features Relatively small, deep-bodied and compressed, with a long snout terminating in a small mouth. The large dorsal fin spine is massive, serrated on its rear edge, and when laid back extends beyond the level of the tail fin origin. Scales rough-edged.

Coloration Rose-red on back and sides, silvery over the body cavity. The colour fades soon after death.

Size Attains a length of 15 cm (6 in.); rarely longer than 12 cm (4¾ in.).

Remarks A relatively rare fish in northern European waters, the snipefish is known there as an occasional wanderer from the south. It

Fifteen-spined stickleback
◄

► Snipefish

is most abundant in depths of 100–250 m (55–137 fathoms), exceptionally as shallow as 25 m (14 fathoms) and as deep as 600 m (328 fathoms); found in schools in mid-water. Its food is composed almost entirely of small planktonic crustaceans, but its biology is in general little known.

Pipefishes

A well-known family (Syngnathidae) of mainly marine, shallow-water fishes which also includes the seahorses. The family is widely distributed in tropical and warm-temperate seas, and in the tropics in freshwater, and while most are inhabitants of shallow, coastal waters, some species are pelagic and live in the open sea. Structurally they are generally similar, their bodies being encased in a segmented, usually hard armour, the fins being reduced (except for the dorsal fin, which is the main means of propulsion), and the snout being prolonged with a small mouth at the tip. Members of the family have additional interest in that the males incubate the developing eggs, either in a shallow groove on the underside of the tail, or protected by folds of soft skin, or, as in the case of the seahorses, within a brood pouch.

Eight species occur in northern European waters; several others are known from the Mediterranean.

Greater pipefish
Syngnathus acus

Distinguishing features A pipefish with pronounced body rings, those of the tail being distinctly 4-sided. Pectoral and tail fins well developed. The snout is rounded in cross-section, and long (more than half the head length); head profile rises over eye and has a conspicuous lump in the mid-line of the nape. Abdominal rings 17–21; tail rings 39–43; dorsal fin rays 36–45.

Coloration Light brown above, often with a greenish tinge, and dusky bars along the body. Creamy-yellow under the abdomen, darker towards the tail.

Size Attains 47 cm (18½ in.); the largest common pipefish. Males mature at *c.* 30 cm (11¾ in.).

Remarks A moderately common species in shallow water over muddy or sandy bottoms. It is confined to coastal waters down to

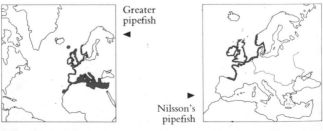

Greater pipefish ◄

► Nilsson's pipefish

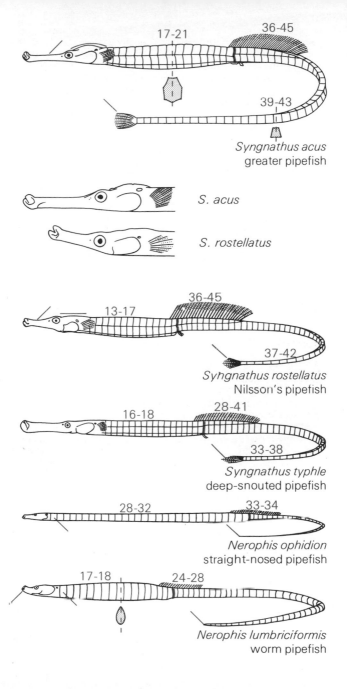

17-21
36-45
39-43

Syngnathus acus
greater pipefish

S. acus

S. rostellatus

36-45
13-17
37-42

Syhgnathus rostellatus
Nilsson's pipefish

16-18
28-41
33-38

Syngnathus typhle
deep-snouted pipefish

28-32
33-34

Nerophis ophidion
straight-nosed pipefish

17-18
24-28

Nerophis lumbriciformis
worm pipefish

depths of 20 m (11 fathoms), occasionally deeper, and is also found in outer estuaries. Its food consists of small planktonic organisms, particularly small crustaceans and postlarval fishes. They are stalked visually and snapped up by a rapid movement of the head, with the mouth opened wide and the tubular snout expanded at the same instant to create a suction.

Males brooding eggs are found mostly in June and July, but occur a month either side of this period. The brood-pouch is a double fold of skin arising from the sides of the anterior tail and meeting in the mid-line. The young are released from the pouch at a length of 22–35 mm (1–1.5 in.).

Nilsson's pipefish   *Syngnathus rostellatus*

Distinguishing features   A common pipefish with distinct body and tail rings and well-developed pectoral and tail fins. The snout is rounded in cross-section and relatively short, less than half the head length; the head profile rises over the eye, but there is no conspicuous ridge along the nape. Abdominal rings 13–17; tail rings 37–42; dorsal fin rays 36–45.

Coloration   A warm brown on the back with darker mottling to form cross-bars; ventrally it is creamy with silvery reflections.

Size   Attains a maximum of 17 cm ($6\frac{3}{4}$ in.); males mature at 10 cm (4 in.).

Remarks   The most abundant pipefish on sandy bottoms in northern Europe. It lives in shallow water of 1–10 m ($\frac{1}{2}$–$5\frac{1}{2}$ fathoms), exceptionally down to 18 m (10 fathoms) on sand or mud, and among floating algae or eel-grass usually just above the sea-bed. It is particularly abundant in estuaries.

Like other pipefishes its food is composed almost entirely of small, planktonic crustaceans, although other larvae are also eaten. The males carry the eggs in a pouch under the tail. 'Pregnant' males can be found most commonly in June to August; the young fish are free-swimming from a length of *c.* 14 mm ($\frac{1}{2}$ in.). This is the pipefish most frequently captured in shrimping nets, especially push-nets on the shore.

Deep-snouted pipefish   *Syngnathus typhle*

Distinguishing features   A pipefish with distinct body and tail rings, and pectoral and caudal fins well developed. The snout is laterally flattened, not round in cross-section, and is relatively deep. The head profile is smooth, not arched above or behind the eye. Abdominal rings 16–18; tail rings 33–38; dorsal fin rays 28–41.

Coloration   Usually light greeny-brown, sometimes plain brown; the ventral surface is pale brown.

Size   Reaches a maximum length of 30 cm ($11\frac{3}{4}$ in.); males are mature at 12 cm ($4\frac{3}{4}$ in.).

Remarks   A moderately common and widespread pipefish which is abundant only locally. Typically it lives among eel-grass on sandy shores, and around thong-weed on rocky shores. It is confined to coastal waters between 4 and 20 m (2 and 11 fathoms) and in low-salinity regions such as the middle Baltic Sea.

The food of this species is mainly small, planktonic crustaceans, but it eats a larger proportion of young fishes than the other pipefishes. Males may be captured carrying eggs in their pouch from June to August; incubation lasts for about 4 weeks and the young are 25 mm (1 in.) when they are first free-swimming.

Straight-nosed pipefish   *Nerophis ophidion*

Distinguishing features   Body rounded in cross-section, the rings without angles and visible only as segments. Dorsal fin present, 33–34 rays; no tail, anal, or pectoral fins. Snout moderately long, equal to half length of head; profile straight and not noticeably concave. Abdominal rings 28–32.

Coloration   Greeny-brown on the back, light green on the sides; large females have long bluish lines along the belly.

Size   Females attain a length of 30 cm ($11\frac{3}{4}$ in.); males grow to 25 cm (10 in.).

Remarks   This distinctive pipefish is widely distributed in European waters, usually at depths of 5–25 m (3–14 fathoms), although occasionally found shallower than this. It is particularly associated with the long-stranded, greenish-brown algae of the sublittoral zone, and with eel-grass. It is also common in low salinity areas such as the northern Baltic Sea.

Males carry the eggs attached to the concave belly; they are not enveloped within skin flaps. Males with eggs are most abundant from May to August; the young hatch and are free-swimming while still relatively undeveloped at *c.* 9 mm in length. Both young fish and adults feed on crustacean larvae.

Worm pipefish   *Nerophis lumbriciformis*

Distinguishing features   Body rounded in cross-section, the rings without angles; pectoral, anal, and tail fins absent. The snout is short and strongly concave in outline, the mouth and tip of the snout being tilted upwards. Dorsal fin rays 24–28; body rings 17–18. (See also coloration.)

Coloration   Dark overall except under the throat and anterior

Deep-snouted pipefish

◄

►

Straight-nosed pipefish

belly which have lighter markings. The basic coloration is dark green or brown to match the algae in which it lives.

Size   Attains a length of 15 cm (6 in.); males are usually smaller.

Remarks   Relatively common in shallow water, but confined to rocky areas where marine algae are abundant. It is frequently found under stones or in rock pools at low tide, but it closely resembles, both in colour and body-form, the intertidal algae *Ascophyllum*, *Bifurcaria*, and others. It seems to be confined to the tidal zone.

The males carry the eggs in a shallow groove on the belly, and are found with eggs in June to August. On hatching, the young are about 10 mm ($\frac{3}{8}$ in.) and live in the plankton for a short while, but can be found on the shore in September and October at 3–4 cm (1$\frac{1}{4}$–1$\frac{1}{2}$ in.) in length—presumably then a few months old.

Snake pipefish   *Entelurus aequoreus*

Distinguishing features   Very long and slender-bodied with the body rings smooth and the body rounded in cross-section. Pectoral and anal fins absent, tail fin minute—the rays only slightly developed. Dorsal fin with 37–47 rays, mostly in advance of the vertical from the vent.

Coloration   Pale brown or yellowish-brown, each body ring picked out with a pale blue band with faintly darker edges.

Size   Females grow to 61 cm (24 in.), males to 40 cm (15$\frac{3}{4}$ in.).

Remarks   An open-sea species which is found in deeper water than most pipefishes. It is commonest between 10–100 m (5$\frac{1}{2}$–55 fathoms), among kelps and other large, deep water seaweeds. Large and young specimens are found well offshore in the surface of the sea, and the species must be to some extent oceanic. It is relatively rare.

Males carrying eggs on the hollow underside are found in June–July. The fry are *c.* 12 mm ($\frac{1}{2}$ in.) long on hatching and are planktonic for a short while.

Seahorse   *Hippocampus ramulosus*

Distinguishing features   Characteristic shape, with head set at an angle to the rather stout body and prehensile tail, which lacks a tail fin. The snout is long, more than one-third of the head length, its

Worm pipefish

◀

▶

Snake pipefish

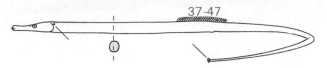

37-47

Entelurus aequoreus
snake pipefish

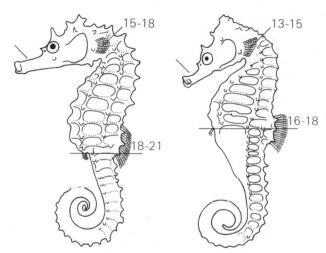

15-18

13-15

18-21

16-18

Hippocampus ramulosus
seahorse

Hippocampus hippocampus
short-snouted seahorse

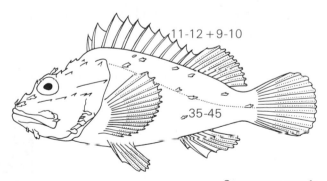

11-12 + 9-10

35-45

Scorpaena scrofa
scorpion-fish

dorsal profile straight. Dorsal fin with 18–21 rays; pectoral fin 15–18 rays. Skin appendages often absent.

Coloration Medium brown to dusky, usually with small white spots.

Size Attains a length, from crown of head to tip of tail, of 15 cm (6 in.).

Remarks A rare visitor to northern European waters and possibly only occurring as a result of a northerly summertime migration. It is found in inshore waters amongst eel-grass and fine algae, but has also been captured floating in the open sea near the surface. Males with eggs in the brood-pouch are found in May to August, and occasionally young fish have been caught in the English Channel in late summer. Seahorses feed almost entirely on small crustaceans.

Short-snouted seahorse   *Hippocampus hippocampus*

Distinguishing features Unmistakable seahorse body form but with a short snout, its length not more than one-third of the head length, and with a concave dorsal profile. Diameter of eye more than half the snout length. Dorsal fin with 16–18 rays, pectoral fin with 13–15 rays.

Coloration Warm brown overall, except that the inner surface of the tail is paler. No lighter spots.

Size Grows to 16 cm (6¼ in.).

Remarks This seahorse is exceptionally rare in northern European waters, and even in the Mediterranean is less common than *H. ramulosus*. There, it breeds from April to October, and newly-born young are found in September and October. Its biology is unknown in northern waters, and its occurrence is exceptional.

Scorpion- and Red-Fishes

A family (Scorpaenidae) of marine fishes which are distributed world-wide except for the Antarctic seas. In temperate seas they are well represented by the red-fishes, which are present as numerous species in the North Pacific with only a few Atlantic representatives.

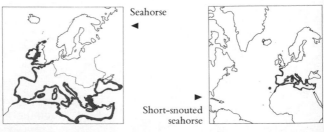

Seahorse ◄

► Short-snouted seahorse

In the tropics and in warm temperate seas there are numerous scorpion-fishes, some of them with venomous spines in their fins. The 4 northern European members of the family have strong spines in the dorsal and anal fins, are fully scaled, and all have a bony ridge across the cheek below the eye.

Scorpion-fish   *Scorpaena scrofa*

Distinguishing features A stout-bodied scorpion-fish with 11–12 strong dorsal fin spines, a scaleless head and pectoral fin base, and the membrane coming close to the tips of the pectoral fin rays. Head large and spiny; scales on body large, 35–45 in lateral line; numerous small skin flaps on head and body, but not conspicuously large above the orbit.

Coloration Usually dark reddish-brown with dusky mottlings, very variable with the fish's immediate surroundings.

Size Attains 51 cm (20 in.).

Remarks The scorpion-fish is a very rare vagrant in northern European waters. In the western Mediterranean it is common on sandy or stony grounds in 20–100 m (11–55 fathoms), and the only records of its occurrence in the English Channel have been of fish caught in similar depths. It feeds mainly on prawns and other crustaceans, and fishes.

Blue-mouth   *Helicolenus dactylopterus*

Distinguishing features A relatively narrow-bodied fish with 11–12 strong dorsal fin spines, scales between the eyes and on the gill covers and cheeks. The lower 9 pectoral fin rays have the outer third of their length free of the fin membrane. Head moderately large and

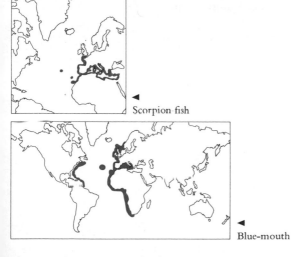

◄ Scorpion-fish

◄ Blue-mouth

spiny; scales on body large, 26–30 in the lateral line. No fleshy flaps on head or lateral line; the bony ridge beneath the eye not massive. (See also coloration.)

Coloration Predominantly red overall, lightening to rose pink ventrally. Inside the mouth and gill cavity dark leaden blue.

Size Attains 46 cm (18 in.) in length and 1.5 kg (3 lb 5 oz) in weight.

Remarks A common fish on the lower continental shelf to the west of the British Isles, but becoming less common off the western Norwegian coast. It lives on mud and sandy mud in depths of 200–800 m (109–437 fathoms); exceptionally, specimens are taken in shallower water.

It feeds on crustaceans, mainly shrimps, and fishes—especially lantern fishes, but eats cephalopods and other near-bottom invertebrates. It hunts close to, but not on, the sea-bed. The bluemouth is of little commercial importance as a food-fish although locally, as in Portugal and the western Mediterranean, it is marketed.

Red-fish   *Sebastes marinus*

Distinguishing features A thickset, heavy-headed fish with a protruberant chin. The dorsal fin has 15 strong spines and 14–16 soft rays; the anal fin has 3 spines and 8–9 soft rays; the membrane of the pectoral fins extends almost to the tips of the rays, which number 19–20. Spines on the preoperculum are flattened, the ventral spines downward pointing.

Coloration Bright red except for the belly which has a pink or rose flush, and the gill cover which is dusky.

Size Attains 1 m (39½ in.) in length and 15 kg (33 lb) in weight, at a considerable age. Few specimens today live long enough to exceed 50 cm (19¾ in.).

Remarks A common fish in the colder regions of the North Atlantic, the red-fish is most abundant on the continental shelf in 100–400 m (55–219 fathoms), less commonly down to 500 m (273 fathoms). Below that depth it is largely replaced by *Sebastes mentella*, which extends to 1000 m (547 fathoms).

Both species are viviparous. The red-fish mates in northern waters (the European stocks in the Barents Sea) in late summer,

Red-fish

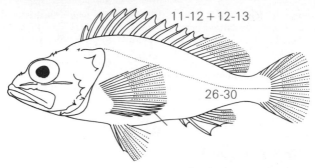

11-12 + 12-13

26-30

Helicolenus dactylopterus
blue-mouth

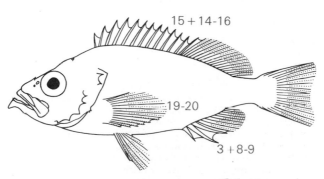

15 + 14-16

19-20

3 + 8-9

Sebastes marinus
red-fish

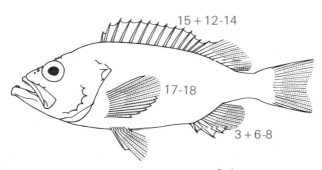

15 + 12-14

17-18

3 + 6-8

Sebastes viviparus
Norway haddock

and the females migrate southwards to the neighbourhood of the Lofoten Islands to liberate their larvae in May and June. Other North Atlantic stocks are presumed to make similar breeding migrations.

Adult red-fish eat large quantities of fishes, particularly herring, capelin, and members of the cod family. The early young are plankton-feeders, and later eat large quantities of crustaceans. Red-fish are eaten by sperm whales. They are also caught in large numbers by vessels from northern Europe, and to a lesser extent from North America.

Norway haddock   *Sebastes viviparus*

Distinguishing features A rather heavy-bodied red-fish with a large head and slightly protuberant chin. The dorsal fin has 15 strong spines and 12–14 soft rays; the anal fin has 3 spines and 6–8 soft rays; 17–18 rays in the pectoral fin, the membrane of which continues to the tips of the rays. Spines on the preoperculum flattened, all pointing towards the tail.

Coloration Rosy-red on the back and sides, pink ventrally. A dusky patch on the gill cover and 3–4 dusky bars across the back. Inside of mouth is pink.

Size Attains 30 cm (11¾ in.); usually up to 25 cm (9¾ in.).

Remarks The Norway haddock is found in inshore waters of 40–100 m (22–55 fathoms) and only occasionally occurs in deeper water. It is also the most southerly-ranging member of its genus in European waters. It tends to prefer rocky sea-beds, although it occasionally occurs on sand or even mud.

It feeds on a wide range of smaller fishes and crustaceans. The young are born as well-developed larvae at a length of 4–5 mm, and up to 30,000 young may be produced by a single fish. It has little commercial importance although small numbers may be caught on occasions; it is sometimes caught by anglers.

Gurnards

A family (Triglidae) of marine fishes known as gurnards or gurnets, and in North America called sea robins. The family is of world-wide distribution in tropical and temperate seas, usually in shallow water. The head is covered with a bony armour, often with strong spines on the gill covers and elsewhere. The lower 3 rays of the pectoral fins are separate, thickened, and well supplied with sense organs. They are used to locate food items buried in the sea-bed, and are extended forward and bent like fingers, while the fish creeps slowly along the bottom. Gurnards also make audible noises by special muscles attached to the swim-bladder. No doubt this helps in keeping schools in contact especially at spawning time.

Six species are known in northern European waters.

Piper   *Trigla lyra*

Distinguishing features   The snout is produced to form 2 flattened plates, 1 each side, with distinct forward-pointing teeth. A massive spine immediately above the pectoral fin; other head spines well developed. Fine, rough-edged scales on the body; lateral line smooth, but dorsal profile with sharp spines.

Coloration   Bright red, the sides rosy fading to pinkish-silver on the abdomen.

Size   Attains a length of 44.5 cm (17½ in.).

Remarks   The piper lives on the upper continental slope in deep water of 300–700 m (164–383 fathoms); it is the only gurnard to be found in such deep water in northern Europe. It lives on the sea-bed on muddy bottoms. Its biology is virtually unknown.

Tub gurnard   *Trigla lucerna*

Distinguishing features   The snout is produced to form 2 lobes bearing small spines on the front edge; it is pointed in profile. The eye is small, about 1.5 times the depth of the cheek. Lateral line scales are not enlarged or spiny; the body scales are small. The pectoral fins reach well past the vent. (See also coloration.)

Coloration   The back and upper sides range from bright red to pink; the underside is orange or white. Pectoral fins brilliant peacock blue, with red at the edge, and green spotted.

Size   Attains a maximum length of 75 cm (29½ in.), usually between 50–60 cm (19¾–23½ in.), and a weight of 5.2 kg (11 lb 8 oz). The largest European gurnard.

Remarks   A relatively abundant gurnard in inshore waters of 20–150 m (11–82 fathoms), extending in decreasing numbers to 200 m (109 fathoms). Small specimens are frequent in shallow water from 2–20 m (1–11 fathoms). It lives occasionally solitarily, more often in small schools, on mud and muddy-sand bottoms.

It feeds on a wide range of crustaceans and bottom-living fishes. It probably eats more fish than other gurnard species; sandeels, small flatfishes, gobies, and dragonets are all eaten in numbers. Swimming crabs and brown shrimps are also important food. A moderately important food-fish, especially in continental Europe; its flesh is white and tasty. Also caught in numbers by anglers.

Norway haddock ◄

► Piper

Red gurnard   *Aspitrigla cuculus*

Distinguishing features   A rather stout-bodied gurnard with
moderately large scales. The lateral line has no spines and each pore
is covered by a large, laterally expanded scale. The snout ends in 3
short spines each side, and is slightly concave in profile. Pectoral fins
only just reach the vent.

Coloration   Deep red overall, except that ventrally it is pinkish-
silver. The ventral fins are pale but darken towards their tips.

Size   Attains a length of 40 cm (15¾ in.) and a weight of *c.* 900 g
(2 lb). This is one of the smallest European gurnards.

Remarks   A shallower-water species found mostly on the
Atlantic coast in depths of 20–250 m (11–137 fathoms). It is a
relatively uncommon fish, except locally. It is found on a variety of
different sea-beds, usually on sand, or sand and gravel, but also on
mud and even rocks. It spawns in summer.
  Its food consists principally of crustaceans, especially shrimps and
swimming crabs, but it also eats fishes and bottom-living invertebrates. Its diet suggests that it is a more active fish than most
species of gurnard.
  It is captured in some numbers by trawlers to the south of the
British Isles; it is also occasionally caught by anglers.

Long-finned gurnard   *Aspitrigla obscura*

Distinguishing features   Relatively slender-bodied with a
pointed snout, convex or straight profile, and a single small spine on
each side of the mid-line at the tip of the snout. The second dorsal fin
spine is greatly elongate, thickened at the base and twice as long as
the remaining spines. The lateral line is covered by large flexible
scales.

Coloration   Reddish on back and sides shading to pinkish on the
underside; the lateral line is pearly-pink in colour.

Size   A small gurnard, it attains a maximum length of 36 cm
(14¼ in.).

Remarks   An extremely rare fish in northern European waters. It
appears to live in shallow inshore waters in 15–55 m (8–30 fathoms)
depth, mainly on rough rocky grounds. It feeds on crustaceans,

Tub
gurnard
◄

►
Red
gurnard

212

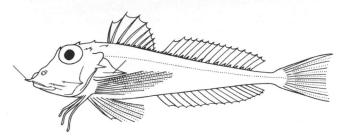

Trigla lyra
piper

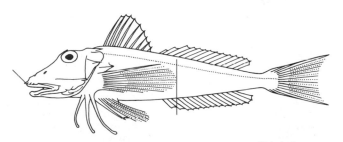

Trigla lucerna
tub gurnard

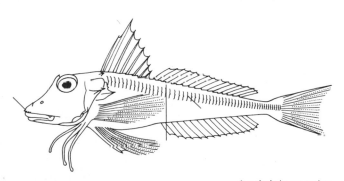

Aspitrigla cuculus
red gurnard

principally shrimps and mysids, and also eats some molluscs. Its biology is virtually unknown.

Grey gurnard   *Eutrigla gurnardus*

Distinguishing features   A relatively slender-bodied gurnard with a sharply-pointed snout; the head profile is straight. The eyes are large, their diameter as great as the depth of the cheek, except in very large fish. The pectoral fins are short and do not reach the vent. The lateral line has sharply-pointed, bony scutes, but in the largest specimens these spines are less noticeable. (See also coloration.)

Coloration   The back and upper sides grey, or greyish-brown with small white or creamy spots; ventrally dull white. A dusky blotch on the first dorsal fin.

Size   Attains a maximum length of 45 cm (17¾ in.); usually around 30 cm (11¾ in.). Maximum weight *c.* 1.2 kg (2 lb 10 oz).

Remarks   In general, this is an offshore gurnard, although it is occasionally caught in very shallow water. Usually it lives at depths of 20–50 m (11–27 fathoms), exceptionally from 10 m to 150 m (5½ to 82 fathoms). It is most common on sandy bottoms but also occurs, with decreasing frequency, on mud, shell, and rocky bottoms.

It eats bottom-living crustaceans, for example brown and pink shrimps, and small crabs, and fishes such as gobies, dragonets, small flatfishes, and sandeels. It spawns in April to August in moderately deep water. Its maximum life span rarely exceeds 6 years, and it attains sexual maturity at between 2 and 3 years.

The grey gurnard is not deliberately exploited as a food-fish in northern Europe, although a considerable quantity is captured incidentally in trawling. It is marketed in small quantities.

Streaked gurnard   *Trigloporus lastoviza*

Distinguishing features   A stout, heavy-bodied gurnard with a blunt snout and near vertical profile to the head. The lateral line scales have very slight spines, and the body is crossed by distinct ridges of skin originating at the lateral line.

Coloration   Dull red, even reddish-brown above, with darker

Long-finned gurnard

◄

►

Grey gurnard

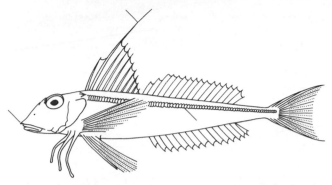

Aspitrigla obscura
long-finned gurnard

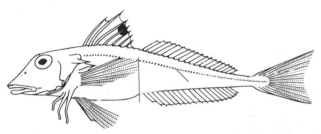

Eutrigla gurnardus
grey gurnard

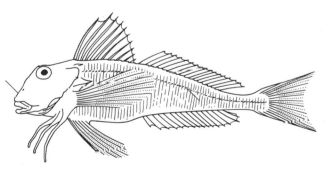

Trigloporus lastoviza
streaked gurnard

patches; ventrally creamy coloured. The pectoral fins are greyish with a red tinge and rows of large blue spots.

Size   Grows usually to *c*. 36 cm (14 in.), and a maximum of 40 cm (15¾ in.).

Remarks   A rare fish north of the English Channel, and not common even there, the streaked gurnard is mainly an occasional late summer migrant from the south to most of northern Europe. It lives in moderately deep water, 40–100 m (22–55 fathoms), and is thus not often caught close inshore. It seems to inhabit sand and muddy grounds especially where they are interspersed with rocky patches. It feeds exclusively on crustaceans, especially swimming crabs.

Sculpins and Bullheads

Fishes which are exceptionally abundant and well distributed in the shallow seas of the northern hemisphere, particularly in the North Pacific from which they have spread to the Atlantic. A few species are found in freshwater. They have rather stout bodies, and broad spiny heads. They are scaleless, but some species have small spines in the skin, or bony plates running along the sides. In most, probably all, species the sexes are distinguished by coloration and the presence of a long urogenital papilla in males.

Nine species are included here as represented in the northern European fauna of which 2 are freshwater fishes. Only 4 or 5 are at all widely distributed in this region. The first 2 species treated belong to the family Icelidae, the remainder to the Cottidae.

Two-horn sculpin   *Icelus bicornis*

Distinguishing features   A small, northerly bullhead with a roughly spiny head and 2 well-separated dorsal fins. Large spines on preoperculum, the lower 2 forward-pointing and short, the third long, branched at the tip and pointing backwards. Two lateral lines both with large scales bearing spines on their posterior ends. Anal fin base shorter than dorsal.

Coloration   Yellowish with brown spots most numerous on the back.

Size   Attains 12 cm (4¾ in.).

Streaked gurnard

Remarks A northern sculpin which lives on the sea-bed on mud, or mud and stones, mainly between 40–180 m (22–98 fathoms), exceptionally shallower than this, and also down to 560 m (306 fathoms). Young fish are, however, found in coastal waters even in the *Laminaria* zone just below low-tide mark.

Atlantic hook-ear sculpin *Artediellus atlanticus*

Distinguishing features A small, northerly species with a smooth head and 2 dorsal fins. The head has a number of raised bumps, but no spines except for 1 on the edge of the preoperculum which is large and curved to point upwards. Lateral line without large scales, no ridges in the skin on the lower body.

Coloration Greeny-brown with dark spots on body forming prominent bands in adult males. Fins with dark and light bands.

Size Attains 13 cm (5 in.), usually around 10–11 cm (4–4¼ in.); the largest specimens are males.

Remarks An Arctic fish found only in the extreme north of northern Europe. It inhabits muddy bottoms in 35–410 m (19–224 fathoms), but in the shallower of these depths only in the far north. It feeds on polychaete worms and molluscs. The European subspecies, *A. atlanticus europaeus*, is distinguished from the western North Atlantic form, *A. atlanticus atlanticus*, (which is also said to occur near Iceland and the Faroes).

Moustache sculpin *Triglops murrayi*

Distinguishing features A moderately small northern fish with 2 well-spaced dorsal fins, and the head with numerous fine spinnules

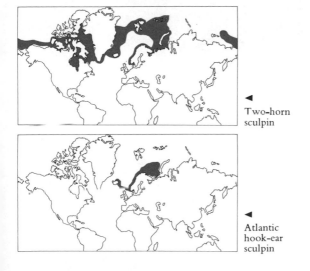

◄
Two-horn
sculpin

◄
Atlantic
hook-ear
sculpin

and a few spines. The lower half of the body has many diagonal rough-edged ridges, which begin at the lower lateral line. Two lateral lines with spiny scales, the lower curved downwards above the pectoral fin. Anal fin base shorter than second dorsal fin.

Coloration   Brownish above with dark cross-bars which break into speckles on the sides. Black spot on the first dorsal fin.

Size   Attains 17 cm (6¾ in.), usually up to 14 cm (5½ in.). Males are smaller than females.

Remarks   Found in moderately deep water usually between 50–250 m (27–137 fathoms), exceptionally to 300 m (164 fathoms), and in shallower water in far north. Mostly it is captured on sandy bottoms. It feeds mainly on polychaete worms and small crustaceans. It is frequently found in cod stomachs in northern waters.

Four-horn sculpin   *Myoxocephalus quadricornis*

Distinguishing features   A broad-headed sculpin with 3 strong spines on the preoperculum, 1 on the gill cover and another just above it. Membrane from the gill covers free, forming a flap across the throat. Adults have rounded spongy knobs on the head, and bony tubercles along the lateral line.

Coloration   Grey-brown above, yellowish or cream ventrally. Knobs on head yellowish-grey.

Size   Attains 36 cm (14¼ in.); males grow to 23 cm (9 in.).

Remarks   In Europe this fish is known only in the Baltic Sea, and the Barents and White Seas in the extreme north. However, freshwater populations are found in the lakes of Sweden, Finland,

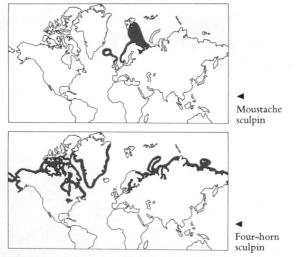

◄
Moustache
sculpin

◄
Four-horn
sculpin

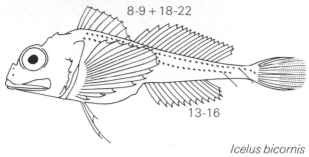

8-9 + 18-22

13-16

Icelus bicornis
two-horn sculpin

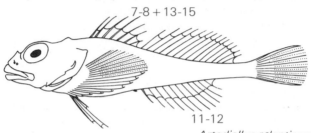

7-8 + 13-15

11-12

Artediellus atlanticus
Atlantic hook-ear sculpin

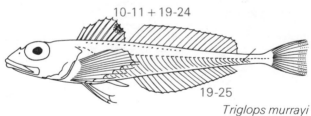

10-11 + 19-24

19-25

Triglops murrayi
moustache sculpin

Myoxocephalus quadricornis
four-horn sculpin

and the Baltic USSR. These are relicts of populations which lived in the region when the Baltic was a fully marine sea, soon after the last Ice Age.

In the sea it lives in the coastal zone, as deep as 15–20 m (8–11 fathoms). It feeds on isopod crustaceans and fishes, especially smelt, Arctic cods, and capelin. It spawns in early winter and the fry hatch in spring. It has no commercial value to fisheries.

Bull-rout   *Myoxocephalus scorpius*

Distinguishing features   A large, broad-headed sculpin with only 2 relatively short spines on the preoperculum and another on the gill cover. Membrane from the gill covers forms a flap under the throat. The sides on either side of the lateral line have numerous small spines in the skin.

Coloration   Greeny-brown above often blotched with darker colour. Ventrally cherry red (males) to orange (females) with conspicuous round white spots. Rounded spots extend onto the sides.

Size   Generally females grow to 30 cm ($11\frac{3}{4}$ in.), males to 25 cm (10 in.); in Arctic seas this species may attain 60 cm (24 in.).

Remarks   Widely distributed in shallow water of 4–60 m (2–33 fathoms) along most sea coasts of northern Europe. Only in the extreme north of its range is it found between tide marks. It inhabits a wide range of sea bottoms from sand and mud to rocks; it is commonly caught near harbour walls. It spawns from December to March, the clumps of eggs being deposited between rocks on the bottom; they are guarded by the male. They hatch in from 5 to 12 weeks, depending on the sea's temperature. The bull-rout feeds on a wide range of bottom-living fishes and crustaceans, including commercial species, but makes little difference to their numbers, for it is only locally abundant.

Sea scorpion   *Taurulus bubalis*

Distinguishing features   A relatively small sculpin which has a very long, strong spine on the preoperculum (longer than the eye diameter). The membrane running from the gill covers ventrally is

Bull-rout

Myoxocephalus scorpius
bull-rout

Taurulus bubalis
sea scorpion

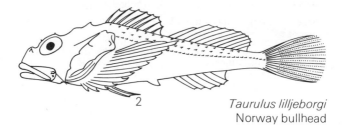

Taurulus lilljeborgi
Norway bullhead

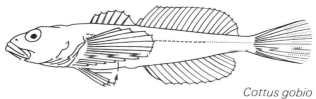

Cottus gobio
bullhead

joined to the throat and does not form a flap. Always a small flap of skin at the angle of the mouth on the upper jawbone. Lateral line spiny, but no spines on skin either side of it. Three distinct rays in each pelvic fin.

Coloration   Variable with type of habitat: usually greeny-brown with yellowish underside. Occasionally deep red.

Size   Attains 17.5 cm (7 in.); males are generally smaller.

Remarks   A common fish on rocky shores and in the immediately sublittoral zone, but apparently always in association with rocks and algae. Found down to 30 m (16 fathoms).

Its food consists almost entirely of fishes and crustaceans, mainly those species which are found in the same habitats, e.g. blennies, gobies, amphipods, prawns, and shore crabs. It breeds in early spring, the eggs being deposited in clumps amongst algae. The young are pelagic shortly after hatching, but return to the sea-bed at a length of 13–14 mm.

Norway bullhead   *Taurulus lilljeborgi*

Distinguishing features   Similar to the sea scorpion and, like it, it has a long upper preopercular spine, but equal to the eye diameter. Membrane from the gill covers joined to, not forming a flap across, the throat. A small barbel at the corner of the mouth. Lateral line spiny, distinct spines in the skin above the lateral line and on the back. Pelvic fins with 2 soft rays only.

Coloration   Reddish-olive overall with 4 dark bands on the back and upper sides. Distinct black spot on the first dorsal fin. Breeding males have a band of red across the head and red patches on the sides.

Size   Attains a maximum length of 7.4 cm (3 in.), but usually grows to only 5.0–5.5 cm (2–2¼ in.).

Remarks   Lives in close association with rocks and algae, and in the south of its range is mostly captured in moderately deep water of 20–90 m (11–49 fathoms). However, it has been caught on the shore near low-tide mark, especially in pools with dense *Corallina* growths. It breeds in spring in deep water, the eggs being laid in clumps on the sea-bed. Probably they are guarded by the male. The larvae are planktonic at first but return to the bottom at 10–14 mm long.

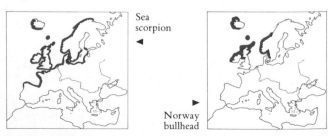

Sea scorpion ◀

Norway bullhead ▶

Bullhead
Cottus gobio

Distinguishing features   A small freshwater fish with a broad, flattened head and a relatively short spine on each preoperculum. The lateral line continues to the tail fin, although the pores are not visible beyond the second dorsal fin. Pelvic fins pale coloured, the outer ray as long as, or longer than the inner ray; neither reaches the vent.

Coloration   Variable with habitat; usually brown or greenish-brown, variously mottled. Paler ventrally.

Size   Usually not more than 10 cm (4 in.); exceptionally in the north of Europe up to 17 cm (6¾ in.).

Remarks   The bullhead is abundant in streams, small rivers, and larger lakes, especially those with stony beds. It can be found in water of 10 cm (4 in.) to 9 m (30 ft), although it is most abundant in shallow regions. In daytime it hides under rocks and stones, or in dense plant beds, but becomes active at night and then makes forays over the river bed. It feeds mainly on crustaceans, especially gammarids (freshwater shrimps), and bottom-living insect larvae. It is frequently accused of eating salmon and trout eggs on the grounds that it can be found in their redds; its effect as a predator is very slight.
It spawns in March–May in a cavity excavated beneath a large stone. The eggs are attached to the underside of the stone and are guarded by the male for 3–4 weeks, until they hatch. The fry scatter on hatching and shelter in the crevices amongst the stones. They become sexually mature in their second year and live for 5 years at most.
The bullhead is eaten by some fishes such as chub and burbot, occasionally by trout, and by aquatic birds such as the heron and the kingfisher.

Alpine bullhead
Cottus poecilopus

Distinguishing features   Very similar to the freshwater bullhead. The lateral line ends beneath the second dorsal fin. The pelvic fins are long, reaching beyond the vent. They are well marked, and the innermost ray is short—much less than half of the outer ray.

Bullhead

◀

▶

Alpine bullhead

Coloration Greeny-brown on the back with darker cross-bars, lighter ventrally, but mottled with dark patches; pelvic fins with numerous cross-bars.

Size Grows to 14.5 cm ($5\frac{3}{4}$ in.), but usually between 8.5–10.0 cm ($3\frac{1}{4}$ in.).

Remarks Found only in Scandinavia and eastern Europe. A closely related form is distributed across the USSR to the Pacific coast. It lives in stony-bottomed streams, mostly in the upland reaches, although in Europe it is found in lowland rivers. Its biology is similar to that of the bullhead.

Poachers or Pogges

A small family (Agonidae) of mainly Arctic marine fishes represented by 2 species only in the European Atlantic. The North Pacific contains a greater number of species. All have a body armour of several rows of overlapping plates, small fins, and rather small mouths. All live in shallow seas.

Hooknose	*Agonus cataphractus*

Distinguishing features Head and body encased in hard bony plates; body flexible to a limited degree. A strong spine on each gill cover and a pair of strong hooks on the snout. Many short barbels on the underside of the head. Pelvic fins short.

Coloration Dull brown on the back with 4 or 5 darker saddles; ventrally creamy-white. Pectoral fins tinted orange in breeding season.

Size Exceptionally attains 20.7 cm ($8\frac{1}{4}$ in.), usually only 10–15 cm (4–6 in.).

Remarks A common fish in inshore waters especially on sandy or muddy shores. Found at depths of 20–270 m (11–148 fathoms); young specimens live in even shallower water of 2 m (6 ft 6 in.) on offshore banks. The hooknose is commonly captured in shrimp and sprat trawls, but has no economic value.

It breeds from February to May, when the female deposits clumps of eggs between the branching holdfasts of kelp and other brown seaweeds. The eggs may take as long as 12 months to hatch. The

Hooknose

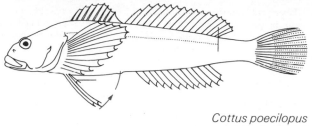

Cottus poecilopus
alpine bullhead

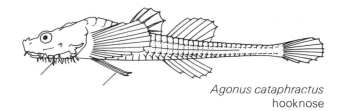

Agonus cataphractus
hooknose

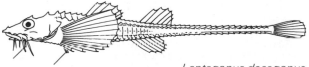

Leptagonus decagonus
Atlantic poacher

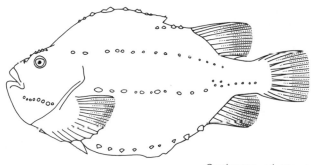

Cyclopterus lumpus
lumpsucker

larvae are planktonic at first, but at a length of 20 mm begin to live on the bottom. The hooknose feeds primarily on small crustaceans, with brittlestars, polychaete worms, and small molluscs being eaten on occasions. The name pogge is sometimes used in books for this species, but it is hardly a vernacular name.

Atlantic poacher   *Leptagonus decagonus*

Distinguishing features   Head and body encased in hard bony plates, each plate with a spine; tail very elongate. A few long barbels under the head, one branched in the middle of the lower jaw and 4 straight ones at each corner of the mouth. Pelvic fins long.

Coloration   Body brownish-grey with several darker cross-bands; lighter ventrally.

Size   Maximum attained 22.3 cm ($8\frac{3}{4}$ in.); usually up to 20 cm (8 in.).

Remarks   An Arctic species which is confined to the extreme northern parts of Europe. It has been found mainly in depths of 120–350 m (66–191 fathoms), exceptionally as shallow as 100 m (55 fathoms) and down to 900 m (492 fathoms). It lives on muddy or muddy-sandy bottoms, often among stones. Its food consists mainly of benthic crustaceans although some pelagic species are also eaten.

Lumpsucker and Sea-Snails

Members of this family (Cyclopteridae) are marine fishes found mainly in cool temperate and polar seas, and in the deep sea. They are stout-bodied, some like the lumpsucker having 2 dorsal fins and large bony plates in the skin, while others have a single dorsal fin, loose skin, either smooth or with fine prickles in it. All except some deep-sea species have a well-developed sucker-disc on the thorax.

Three species only are found on the continental shelf in northern European waters; others live in deep water further offshore.

Lumpsucker   *Cyclopterus lumpus*

Distinguishing features   Unmistakable in that the body is rounded with rows of large, coarsely-spined plates on the sides. The

Atlantic poacher

226

sucker disc on the belly is large; second dorsal and anal fins short-based and about equal in length. First dorsal fin reduced in adults; in the young it forms a high crest.

Coloration Variable; greyish or greenish-brown on the back, paler ventrally. Males show orange or reddish tints on the belly in the breeding season.

Size Females are usually 30–40 cm ($11\frac{3}{4}$–$15\frac{3}{4}$ in.) long with a maximum of 60 cm ($23\frac{1}{2}$ in.), and weight of 5.5 kg (12 lb); males attain 50 cm ($19\frac{3}{4}$ in.), but are usually 25–30 cm (10–$11\frac{3}{4}$ in.) in length.

Remarks A common fish in the seas north of the English Channel. Primarily a bottom-living species living among rocks from low-water mark on the shore down to 200 m (109 fathoms), but the larvae and young are planktonic and many of the non-breeding adults live bathypelagically. The young are often attached to floating algae or other flotsam; adults are frequently caught in mid-water trawls.

The lumpsucker makes an inshore migration to spawn at, and below, low-tide mark on rocky shores. The eggs are laid in loose clumps between seaweeds and rocks from February to May, and as late as July and August to the north. The male guards the eggs and keeps water flowing through the egg mass.

It feeds mainly on small crustaceans, polychaete worms, and fishes. During spawning migrations it does not feed. In its turn, the lumpsucker is eaten by the angler fish, halibut, Greenland shark, and frequently by sperm whales. Males guarding egg clumps are also vulnerable to sea-birds at low tide. It is fished for in a small way, mostly for the sake of the roe which, salted and dyed, is offered for sale as a substitute caviare.

Sea-snail *Liparis liparis*

Distinguishing features A small, round-bodied, tadpole-like fish with a long-based dorsal fin (33–35 rays). Anal fin also long-based but shorter (27–29 rays); both fins joined to the tail fin, the anal more noticeably. Skin loose and flabby, covered with minute prickles. Sucker disc on belly well developed.

Coloration Usually dull brown above, lighter below; variably patterned with stripes, patches, and bars of darker brown.

Lumpsucker

Size Exceptionally grows to 18 cm (7 in.) in the far north; usually attains a length of 10–12 cm (4–4¾ in.).

Remarks A relatively common fish in shallow inshore waters of 5–150 m (3–82 fathoms), but never found in intertidal habitats. In the North and Irish Seas it is common on mud and muddy-sand; elsewhere it is reported to live on rocky grounds. It breeds in winter (January to March), the eggs being laid in hazelnut-sized clumps among hydroids, or short algae or bryozoans. The eggs hatch in 6–8 weeks and the larvae are pelagic. The sea-snail feeds mainly on crustaceans, especially shrimps, and worms, and small fish.

Montagu's sea-snail   *Liparis montagui*

Distinguishing features A small, round-bodied plump fish with loose, gelatinous skin covered with minute prickles. A rounded, well-developed sucking disc on the belly. Dorsal fin long-based, low anteriorly, with 28–30 rays; anal with 22–26 rays. Neither fin is joined to the tail fin, but the anal comes close to the base of the tail fin rays.

Coloration Variable with habitat; often brownish, sometimes pink, reddish, or even green.

Size Exceptionally to 10 cm (4 in.); rarely longer than 6 cm (2½ in.).

Remarks A shallow water sea-snail most frequently captured in intertidal pools or under seaweed on rocky shores; it is probably confined to the shore. It spawns in late spring, or early summer to the north of the British Isles. The eggs are laid in small clumps on red algae, or on the hydroids on the holdfasts of brown seaweed. The early young are pelagic, but at *c.* 1.2 cm (½ in.) they begin to live on the sea-bed. Both young and adults cling by their sucker disc to the underside of a rock, with their tail curled around to the snout. They feed on small crustaceans only.

Sea Perches

A family of marine fishes (Serranidae) most abundant in tropical and warm-temperate seas, with only 2 representatives in northern Europe. In general, they are large predatory fishes with big heads and wide mouths, fully scaled bodies, 2 dorsal fins (the first with

Sea-snail

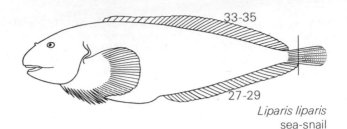

33-35

27-29

Liparis liparis
sea-snail

28-30

22-26

Liparis montagui
Montagu's sea-snail

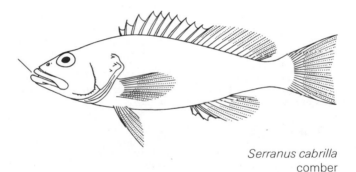

Serranus cabrilla
comber

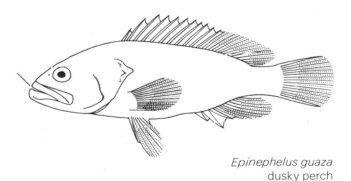

Epinephelus guaza
dusky perch

strong spines), but often joined to form a single fin, and an anal fin with 3 strong spines in front. Many sea perches are hermaphrodite, in some species developing both male and female gonads simultaneously. Others are functional males early in life, changing sex to female later. The comber exhibits this latter form of hermaphroditism.

Comber   *Serranus cabrilla*

Distinguishing features   Strong spines in the first dorsal fin which is joined to the second, soft-rayed, dorsal. Preoperculum with fine teeth on its edge. Gill cover with three flat spines but no heavy ridge running across it. Small teeth, set in jaws, densely packed and not depressible. (See also coloration.)

Coloration   Back and sides brown with 7–9 darker vertical bars; head with pale blue or greenish stripes along the lower side, often continuing along the sides. Tones vary with depth and sexual development.

Size   Grows to a length of 30 cm (11¾ in.) and a weight of *c.* 0.5 kg (1 lb).

Remarks   A relatively uncommon fish in northern waters. It is found from 20–55 m (11–20 fathoms) and to the south of Biscay in deeper water. In the Mediterranean it is caught in small quantities in trawls, and can be seen over sea-grass beds, as well as around rocks and on clear patches. In northern Europe it is mainly captured by anglers on the edges of rocky patches. It feeds on a wide range of smaller fishes, squids, and crustaceans. It breeds in July to August in the English Channel, but most of the fish in this area are probably recruited by migration from the south.

Dusky perch   *Epinephelus guaza*

Distinguishing features   First dorsal fin strongly spiny and joined to the second fin. Preoperculum with a toothed edge; gill cover with three flat spines but with no strong ridge across it. Strong, sharp teeth in the front of the jaws, all depressible (not firmly fixed). Scales very small, extending across the head and lower jaw.

Coloration   Deep brown with irregular light blotches on the

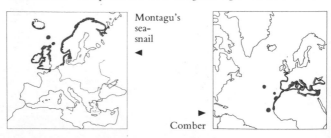

Montagu's
sea-
snail

◄

►

Comber

back and freckles on the sides; yellowish under chin and belly. Dorsal fin with an orange edge, the others with a light edge.

Size Attains a maximum length of 1.4 m (4 ft 7 in.), and a weight of *c.* 13.6 kg (30 lb).

Remarks This is a rare fish in northern European waters, and it has been recorded only on rare occasions as far north as Ireland. It is common in the Mediterranean in 8–200 m (4½–109 fathoms) among rocks in which there are caves or crevices big enough to hide in; it is usually solitary, but large caves may be inhabited by more than one fish. It feeds mainly on fishes and crustaceans.

Sea Basses

A family of spiny-finned fishes (Percichthyidae) found world-wide in both tropical and temperate freshwaters, and in the sea. In many ways these fish are similar to the sea perches, with which family they were associated for many years. The family includes the well-known North American giant sea bass, *Stereolepis gigas*, the striped bass, *Morone saxatilis*, and its freshwater relatives, but in European waters the only two representatives are the bass and the wreckfish or stone bass.

Bass *Dicentrarchus labrax*

Distinguishing features Two dorsal fins separated by a short space; the first fin is strongly spiny; 8–9 spines. Body streamlined, relatively shallow with large scales. Forward-pointing spines on the lower edge of the preoperculum; no heavy ridge across gill cover.

Coloration Greeny-grey on the back with brilliantly silver sides, and silvery-white belly. A dusky patch on the gill cover. Small fish are faintly dark spotted.

Size Attains a length of 1 m (39½ in.), usually around 60 cm (23½ in.), and a maximum weight of *c.* 9.06 kg (20 lb).

Remarks A relatively common fish in the sea around England and Wales, Ireland and the southern North Sea coasts; it becomes much rarer to the north. It is an active swimming, schooling fish in inshore waters, commonly entering estuaries and penetrating upstream into almost freshwater, a habitat of the young especially.

Dusky perch

231

Although it may be captured in offshore waters, it is usually found in close proximity to reefs. It is to some extent a migratory fish, the North Sea populations, in particular, being summertime migrants from the south or south-west.

The bass feeds on a wide range of fishes, especially members of the herring family, sandeels, and other small schooling fishes. It also eats considerable quantities of squids and various crustaceans. Young bass mainly eat small crustaceans, but soon graduate on to a fish diet.

The bass breeds from March to mid-June, mostly in May, near the British Isles in inshore waters. The eggs and early larvae are pelagic. It is a long-lived fish (large specimens may exceed 20 years of age), and its breeding success in the northern extremities of its range is limited. Heavy exploitation, whether by anglers or by commercial fishermen, can lead quickly to decreased catches. The bass is an extremely valuable fish commercially and is very popular also with sports-fishermen.

Wreckfish   *Polyprion americanus*

Distinguishing features   A heavy-bodied fish with a rather pointed head and protruding lower jaw. The dorsal fins are united into a single fin, although the first 11 fin elements are strong spines. Scales small, 90–100 in the lateral line, the vertical fins with high scaly sheaths. Cheeks scaly, the lower preopercular edge spiny, a heavy ridge running across the gill cover.

Coloration   The back and upper sides are dark brown, shading to yellowish on the sides and ventrally. Often blotchy on the back.

Size   Attains a length of 2 m (79 in.).

Remarks   The wreckfish is an uncommon fish in northern European waters, but one which occurs fairly regularly. Its habit of accompanying drifting wreckage, often in schools, is possibly the reason for its occurrence here as it follows flotsam blown from the south-west into northern latitudes. Those found in this region are mostly young fish; the large adults live solitarily in deeper water close to the bottom. They attain a weight of at least 45 kg (100 lb). Most wreckfish are caught, or seen, near the surface; larger fish live at depths of 100–200 m (55–109 fathoms), occasionally deeper. They are marketed in southern Europe as food-fish.

Found also in the western Atlantic and Indian Ocean; the map shows European distribution.

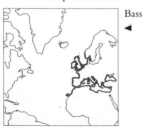
Bass
◄

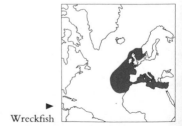
► Wreckfish

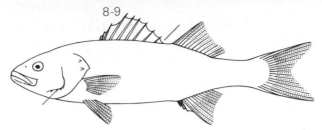

8-9

Dicentrarchus labrax
bass

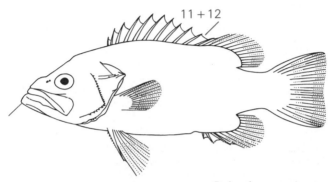

11 + 12

Polyprion americanus
wreckfish

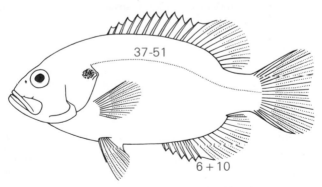

37-51

6 + 10

Ambloplites rupestris
rock bass

American Sunfishes

A family (Centrarchidae) of freshwater fishes originally confined to the North American region, but now widespread in temperate freshwaters in Europe, Africa, and elsewhere. Most of the sunfishes, as they are known in North America, are deep-bodied, rather thickset fishes with a dorsal fin composed of strong spines continuous with the branched-rayed fin. The body is fully scaled and the lateral line is complete. The larger species are popular anglers' fishes, while the smaller ones, being fairly colourful, are often kept in cold-water aquaria. Four species are found in Europe owing to stocking for angling purposes and the release of pet fish.

Rock bass   *Ambloplites rupestris*

Distinguishing features A deep-bodied freshwater fish with a continuous dorsal fin containing 10–12 stout spines. Anal fin with 5–7 (usually 6) short, strong spines. The anal fin base is more than half the length of the dorsal fin base. Scales large, 37–51 in lateral line.

Coloration Back and upper sides golden brown to olive, ventrally silvery to white; each scale below the lateral line with a dusky spot, forming faint lengthwise stripes. Eye usually bright red to orange; a dark spot on the edge of the gill cover.

Size Attains 30 cm (12 in.) in length; 566 g (1 lb 4 oz) in weight.

Remarks Native to eastern central North America; in Europe found only in a single lake in southern England. This population thrived for at least 20 years and there is no evidence that it has declined recently. In North America the rock bass inhabits rocky bottomed areas in shallow water lakes, and the lower reaches of streams. Its food is largely composed of aquatic insects, crayfish, and small fishes. Like other members of the family the male digs a shallow nest, up to 61 cm (24 in.) in diameter, in the bottom of which the eggs are laid; the male guards the eggs and later the young for a short while.

Pumpkinseed   *Lepomis gibbosus*

Distinguishing features A very deep-bodied laterally compressed fish, its head length much less than its body depth. Dorsal fins continuous, the first with usually 10, sometimes 11 strong spines; anal fin short, its base distinctly less than half the dorsal fin base, with 3 strong spines only. Scales large, 35–47 in lateral line.

Coloration Back and upper sides golden brown to olive, lower sides golden with irregular wavy blue-green lines, ventrally bronze to orange-red. Dusky bars on the sides. The gill cover with a wide black spot near the edge with a narrow border of yellow and a small, half-moon shaped red spot on the extreme edge.

Size Grows to 25 cm (10 in.) and attains 481 g (1 lb 1 oz) in weight.

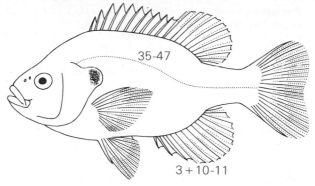

35-47

3 + 10-11

Lepomis gibbosus
pumpkinseed

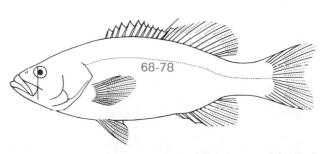

68-78

Micropterus dolomieui
small-mouth bass

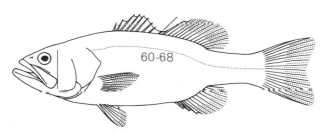

60-68

Micropterus salmoides
large-mouth bass

Remarks The pumpkinseed is native to the freshwaters of eastern North America, but has been widely redistributed by man even in that continent. In Europe it was introduced in the early 1900s and is now widespread north of the Pyrenees and Alps, its range extending as far east as the Black Sea and north to the Baltic. In England it is established in several lakes in Somerset, Sussex, London and Essex. In North America it lives in small lakes, the shallow weedy bays of larger lakes, and the quiet, slow-moving waters of streams. It is often seen in schools at the surface exposed to the sun. It feeds on insects and aquatic invertebrates. Its gay colouring makes it a good fish for the aquarium. In Canada it is an important commercial food-fish.

Small-mouth bass   *Micropterus dolomieui*

Distinguishing features A relatively slender-bodied fish, with the head length greater than the body depth. Scales small, 68–78 scales in the lateral line. Dorsal fin continuous, the first section with 10 stout spines joining the soft-rayed fin with only a shallow dip between them. Anal fin with 3 strong, rather short spines and 10–12 rays. Pelvic fins joined together by a broad membrane and weakly joined to the body. Upper jaw extends back to rear edge of eye, not beyond.

Coloration Back and sides brown, shading to golden green; faint dusky bars running across sides and radiating from the eye.

Size In North America attains a length of 68.6 cm (27 in.) and 5.4 kg (11 lb 15 oz); smaller in Europe.

Remarks Originally the small-mouth bass was distributed in the freshwaters of eastern central North America, but its value as a sporting fish led to its becoming widespread throughout that continent, Europe and elsewhere. In England it was introduced on numerous occasions from 1878 onwards, but unsuccessfully. In continental Europe it is established on the Franco-Belgian border, in Denmark, southern Sweden, and Finland. In North America this fish prefers open water over rocky or sandy bottoms in rivers and lakes. It feeds on aquatic insects, crustaceans, and fishes, the size of the prey increasing as the fish grows.

Large-mouth bass   *Micropterus salmoides*

Distinguishing features A rather slender-bodied fish with the head length greater than the depth of the body. Scales small, 60–68 in the lateral line. Dorsal fin continuous but deeply notched, the first section low with 10 short, stout spines. Anal fin with 3 strong, but short spines and 10–12 soft rays. Pelvics not joined together, but conspicuously joined to the body by a membrane. Upper jaw extends back to beyond the eye level.

Coloration Back and top of head deep green to olive, sides fading to golden green, white on the belly. A solid broad, black lateral stripe from eye to tail, most conspicuous in the young, becoming broken or inconspicuous with age.

Size   Attains a maximum length of 82.7 cm (32½ in.) and a weight of 10.08 kg (22 lb 4 oz); usually up to 53 cm (21 in.) and 2.27 kg (5 lb).

Remarks   The native range of this species included the lower Great Lakes of North America and the Mississippi river system, but because of its great popularity as a sporting fish it has been introduced to many parts of North America as well as Europe, South America, and South Africa. In Europe it is now widespread west of the Danube basin, and its range includes most of Germany, France, the Low Countries, and Denmark. Introduction from France in 1934 resulted in the establishment of a population in Dorset which still survives. The effect of the introduction in Europe has been severe, as this species is predatory on young native fish and competes very successfully with native predatory species. In Britain at least two North American fish parasites have been introduced with it.

In America it is most common near the surface of small shallow lakes, the shallow bays of larger lakes, and less often in rivers. It rarely lives below 6.1 m (20 ft) depth, and prefers well-vegetated regions. Large bass eat fishes mainly, but the smaller specimens eat a wide range of insects and crustaceans as well.

Perch Family

A family (Percidae) of freshwater fishes originally confined to the temperate waters of the northern hemisphere, but representatives have been introduced to Australia, New Zealand, and South Africa. The family is best represented in North America, where numerous small species (the darters) live. All perch-family members have 2 dorsal fins, the first composed of sharp spines, the second with mainly branched rays. In most species the fins are separate. The anal fin has 2 sharp spines in front of the branched rays. The body is covered with rough-edged scales.

Eight species are included here; several others have restricted distributions in the Black Sea basin.

Perch   *Perca fluviatilis*

Distinguishing features   Body moderately deep, head short, snout rounded and blunt. Dorsal fins separate, although joined at the base by a membrane. Teeth small but very numerous; no large canines. Pelvic fins set close together, the space between them less than two-thirds the width of the base. (See also coloration.)

Coloration   Back greeny-brown becoming golden green on the sides, and cream to white on the belly. Dark vertical bars across the upper sides, a black spot at the end of the first dorsal fin. Ventral fins orange.

Size   Attains a maximum length of 51 cm (20 in.) and a weight of 4.75 kg (10 lb 8 oz); more usually *c.* 35 cm (13¾ in.) and 1.20 kg (2 lb 10 oz).

Remarks The perch is a common fish in lowland lakes and ponds, and rivers where the current is slow. It also occurs in the brackish Baltic Sea. In general it is not found at high altitudes, although introduced populations exist in lakes up to 1000 m. Typically it is a fish found in small schools when young, lying among submerged tree roots or close to bridges, landing-stages, and weed-beds; its barred markings allow it to merge with such backgrounds. Occasionally huge schools of large fish may be seen in clear lakes outside the breeding season.

It spawns in April and May, usually in shallow areas. The eggs are moderately large (2.0–2.5 mm) and are shed in long threads wound among plants, tree roots, and any obstruction in the water. In deep barren lakes the eggs may be shed over stones, but still in the form of long lacy threads. The eggs hatch in 8 days at 13°C, and the young measure about 8 mm at hatching. Once the egg yolk has been absorbed, the fry feed on minute plankton, later graduating to larger organisms. From a length of *c.* 15 cm (6 in.) they feed to an increasing extent on fishes (mainly sticklebacks, smaller perch, roach, and other small cyprinids). In many food-poor lakes they grow extremely slowly and form stunted populations in which the largest individuals rarely attain 15 cm (6 in.) in length.

The perch is well-known as an angler's fish. In Europe it is fished for and marketed as a food-fish; its flesh is very good eating. These inland fisheries are operated by means of hooks, traps, and to some extent by netting.

The North American yellow perch is closely related.

Ruffe   *Gymnocephalus cernuus*

Distinguishing features Body moderately deep, head short, snout blunt and rounded. Teeth small, no large canines in jaws. Dorsal fins united, the first fin spiny, the fin outline notched at its junction with the soft dorsal. 11–16 spines in the first dorsal fin; 11–15 rays in the second. Head scaleless, with large cavities beneath the skin.

Coloration Back and sides greenish-brown, liberally spotted with darker colour, the lower sides yellow, ventrally white. The ventral fins are yellowish; dorsal and tail fins dark spotted.

Size Exceptionally up to 30 cm (11¾ in.) and a weight of 500 g (1 lb 2 oz); usually around 15–18 cm (6–7 in.). Females tend to be larger than males.

Perch

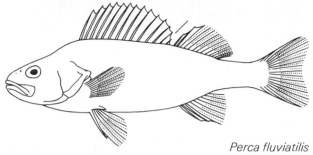

Perca fluviatilis
perch

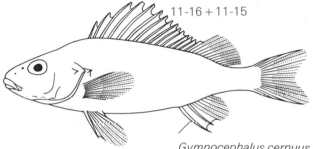

11-16 + 11-15

Gymnocephalus cernuus
ruffe

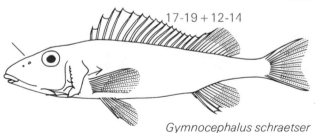

17-19 + 12-14

Gymnocephalus schraetser
schraetzer

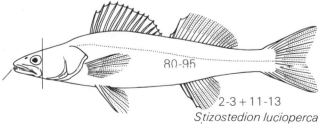

80-95

2-3 + 11-13
Stizostedion lucioperca
zander

Remarks   The ruffe is essentially a fish of lowland rivers and lakes. It is able to tolerate the slight salinity of much of the Baltic. It lives close to the bottom in small schools, feeding during daylight on bottom-living insect larvae (chiefly bloodworms), and crustaceans. Spawning takes place in March to May; the eggs are adhesive and stick to vegetation or stones on the bottom. Growth is fast at first, but slows down with sexual maturity at about 2 years; their life span seldom exceeds 5 years.

At one time ruffe fishing was important in eastern Europe; today this fish is not exploited as food, nor is it regarded as a sporting fish.

Schraetzer   *Gymnocephalus schraetser*

Distinguishing features   Similar to the ruffe but with longer, more pointed snout (eye diameter goes $1\frac{1}{2}$ times into snout length). Dorsal fins united, the posterior spines only slightly lower than the branched rays; 17–19 spines in the first dorsal fin; 12–14 rays in the second dorsal. Head scaleless with large sensory cavities under the skin. (See also coloration.)

Coloration   Pale olive brown on back and upper sides, yellow laterally and white below. Narrow dark lengthwise stripes on body, the upper ones interrupted; spiny dorsal fin with dark spots in 2 rows.

Size   Attains a maximum length of 30 cm ($11\frac{3}{4}$ in.) and weight of 250 g ($8\frac{3}{4}$ oz), usually around 15–25 cm (6–10 in.).

Remarks   A little-known fish, native to the Danube river, and found from Bavaria to the delta of that river in the Black Sea. It is relatively rare and lives in deep water in the slow-moving reaches of the river, close to the sandy bed. It feeds on bottom-living crustaceans and insect larvae. It spawns in April–May, when the eggs are shed over clean gravel beds in fairly rapid water.

Zander   *Stizostedion lucioperca*

Distinguishing features   Body elongate, the snout pointed, head length greater than depth of body or equal to it. Upper jaw extends past eye level, small teeth in jaws and several large fangs in front also. Two dorsal fins, the first spiny and separated by a narrow interspace from the second. Pelvic fins widely spaced, the distance between them almost as great as the base of one fin. 84–95 scales in the lateral line.

Ruffe

Coloration Greenish-grey or brown on the back and sides becoming lighter on the lower sides and white on the belly. Young fish have 8–10 indistinct dusky bars on the sides; these are faint in the adult. Dorsal and tail fins dark spotted.

Size Attains a maximum length of 130 cm (51¼ in.) and a weight of 12 kg (26 lb 8 oz); usually about 60 cm (23½ in.).

Remarks The zander is native to eastern Europe, but has been introduced to the Rhine catchment and to England. It is now widespread in France and western Europe, and is rapidly extending its range in eastern and central England. It is a predatory species most abundant in large lakes and lowland rivers, preferring cloudy water and avoiding weed-beds. It hunts most actively at dawn and dusk, remaining inactive at other times, usually close to the bottom. When young, it keeps in small schools, but becomes solitary when larger. Its food comprises fishes of all kinds which inhabit the same water: small bream, bleak, roach, perch, and on the continent whitefish. The young feed on aquatic insects and crustaceans. The zander spawns in April to June over sandy or stony bottoms, or among the roots of larger aquatic plants. Spawning grounds are in shallow water and are used year after year.

The zander (which is also known as pikeperch) is a valuable sporting fish, and in inland Europe an important food-fish. Here considerable effort is made to increase the stock in fish farms. Its introduction to England and release in open waterways was made by fishery interests without consideration for the wider issues involved.

Volga zander   *Stizostedion volgensis*

Distinguishing features Similar to the zander, but with the cheeks entirely scaled. Young fish have weak canine teeth in the jaws; the adults have none. 9–10 branched rays in the anal fin. Scales slightly larger, 70–83 in the lateral line.

Coloration Grey-green above, fading on sides to whitish ventrally; 8 to 10 broad dusky stripes across back and sides which persist through life. Dorsal and tail fins spotted.

Size Attains a maximum length of 50 cm (19¾ in.) and a weight of *c.* 2 kg (4 lb 6 oz).

Remarks The Volga zander (also known as the Black Sea or eastern zander) lives only in the lowland reaches of rivers in deep

Schraetzer ◄

► Zander

water over stony or sandy bottoms. It feeds actively, mainly in the evening and at night, during daylight remaining concealed close to the bed of the river, or under the bank overhangs. It feeds mainly on fish of relatively small size, but when young it eats aquatic crustaceans and insect larvae. It is often confused with the zander, but is by no means rare in the lower Danube basin, and the Caspian Sea rivers.

Zingel   *Zingel zingel*

Distinguishing features   Body slender, rounded in cross-section with a long caudal peduncle, but its length less than the base of the second dorsal fin. Dorsal fins well separated, the first fin with 13–15 slender but sharp spines. Pelvic fins broad and set far apart.

Coloration   Back and top of head brown or yellowish-brown, sides lighter, belly yellow; four irregularly-shaped dark brown bars running across the back and sides.

Size   Length up to 40 cm (15¾ in.), rarely longer than 25 cm (10 in.).

Remarks   Lives close to the bottom in swiftly-flowing rivers, in shallows. During daylight it lies quietly among stones, but it becomes active at night when it hunts for the bottom-living invertebrates on which it feeds. It breeds in April to May on gravelly river beds.

Streber   *Zingel streber*

Distinguishing features   Body slender, rounded in cross-section and with a long, slender caudal peduncle (longer than the base of the second dorsal fin). Dorsal fins well separated, the first fin with 8–9 slender spines. Pelvic fins set far apart and broad.

Coloration   Back and top of head brown, sides yellow, belly pale yellow. Four sharply-defined, bold dark bands slant forward across the back and sides. When spawning, its body is a metallic green.

Size   Length up to 22 cm (8¾ in.), weight to 200 g (7 oz); usually around 15 cm (6 in.).

Remarks   A bottom-living fish which is found in swiftly-flowing rivers, mainly in deep water, although occasionally entering moderate shallows. It is active at night when it feeds on benthic

Volga zander ◀

▶ Zingel

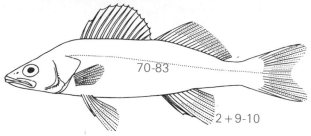

70-83

2 + 9-10

Stizostedion volgensis
Volga zander

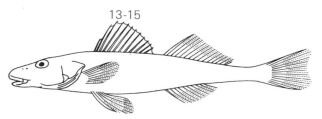

13-15

Zingel zingel
zingel

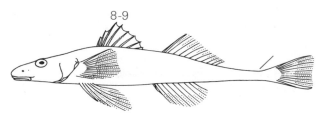

8-9

Zingel streber
streber

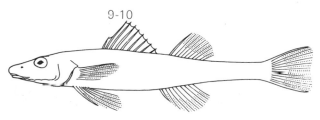

9-10

Zingel asper
Rhône streber

invertebrates; by day it lies close to the bottom. It spawns in March to April.

Rhône streber *Zingel asper*

Distinguishing features Body slender, rounded in cross-section with a slender caudal peduncle (longer than the second dorsal fin base). Dorsal fins well separated, the first with 9–10 slender spines.

Coloration Warm brown above, olive on sides and ventrally. Four boldly defined cross-bars on sides.

Size A maximum length of 20 cm (8 in.) is attained.

Remarks This species is closely related to the Danubian streber and should properly be regarded as a subspecies only. It lives on the river bed in relatively shallow water and requires fast-flowing water. Its biology is virtually the same as the streber.

Bulls-Eye

The only member of the family Apogonidae to occur in northern European waters. The family is large and mainly confined to tropical and warm temperate seas; the cardinal fishes, for example, are typical members of the coral reef community. Most are small shallow-water fishes with large eyes, big scales, and two dorsal fins, the first of which is spiny. Many of the tropical cardinal-fishes brood their eggs in the male's mouth. The bulls-eye is exceptional as it lives in deep water in the temperate zone of the Atlantic and grows to a large size.

Bulls-eye *Epigonus telescopus*

Distinguishing features Slender-bodied but rounded and even thickset anteriorly. Eye very large and reflects with a pale greeny yellow light when freshly caught. Two dorsal fins, well separated; the first with slender, rather fragile spines; anal fin with 2 slender spines in front of 9–10 branched rays. 48–53 scales in the lateral line.

Coloration Deep brown in colour, lighter ventrally; when captured in nets the scales are frequently dislodged and it appears light brown. For eye colouring see above.

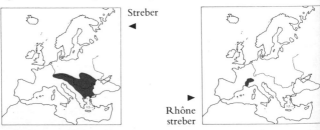

Streber

Rhône streber

Size Attains 76 cm (30 in.) in length; most caught are less than 38 cm (15 in.).

Remarks A deep-water fish found in mid-water, not on the sea-bed. It lives at depths of 183–914 m (100–500 fathoms). It has never been reported to occur close inshore. Its food has been little studied, but it is thought to feed on fishes such as lantern-fish, and deep-water crustaceans.

It is caught comparatively rarely (although recent deep trawling off the western Irish coast has shown that it is common).

Shark Suckers

A family (Echeneidae) of marine fishes of most distinctive appearance and habits. They are all rather slender fishes with protruding lower jaws and a unique sucker disc on top of the head which is formed from a modified spiny dorsal fin. The fish uses this disc to adhere to larger fishes, sharks, whales, and turtles. Most shark suckers are tropical fishes, and some are adapted to a certain type of host; 8 species are known. Several of those which are always found with the same species of host are known to clean their host of parasites; others feed on free-living food. Only a single species is known from northern European waters.

Remora   *Remora remora*

Distinguishing features Immediately recognizable because of the sucker disc on the top of the head (looks like a venetian blind with a central bar); 17–19 pairs of laminae in the disc which does not extend past the pelvic fin tips. 31–35 gill rakers on the first gill arch.

Coloration Uniformly dark greyish-brown, the pectoral fins light at their tips.

Size Attains 46 cm (18 in.). Those found in northern European waters are rarely more than 15 cm (6 in.).

Remarks A rare fish in the eastern North Atlantic and occurring only because of the northerly migrations of the blue shark, and possibly other sharks from the sub-tropical Atlantic. The only specimens reported have been caught attached to blue sharks, and porbeagle (once); also occasional sightings close to sailing ships. This species is known to feed on its host's skin parasites, but will also leave the host to make quick forays to pick up small fishes or

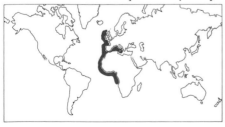

Bulls-eye

crustaceans. It does not feed on the scraps from the shark's meals.

It does not spawn near the British Isles; the only reported captures have been of small, probably young fish. World-wide in tropical oceans; the map shows European distribution.

Jacks and Scad

A large and important family (Carangidae) of marine fishes, known as jacks, pompanos, and scads or horse mackerels. The members of the family have different body shapes; some are narrow-bodied, others deep-bodied, while the pompanos (mostly tropical species) are almost plate-like in shape. Many of these fishes have a line of heavy scutes running along the side of the body; most have 2 dorsal fins, and 2 separate spines in front of the anal fin.

Some 200 species are recognized in the family; most are found in tropical and warm temperate seas. They include many valuable food and sporting species. Only 1 species (the scad) is at all common in northern European seas; 4 others are rare visitors.

Scad *Trachurus trachurus*

Distinguishing features   Slender-bodied and elongate, but with a heavy, rather long head. A series of wide bony scales along the lateral line, flexible in front, becoming sharp-edged and hard towards the tail. First dorsal fin with long spines all united by membrane, separate from second dorsal fin. Two spines in front of anal fin, joined together by membranes, but free of the anal fin.

Coloration   The back is dark grey-blue with greenish tints, the sides silvery with a golden flush, white ventrally; a dusky spot on the edge of the gill cover.

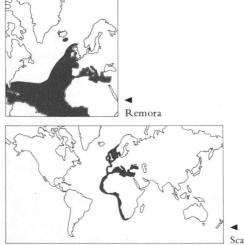

◄ Remora

◄ Scad

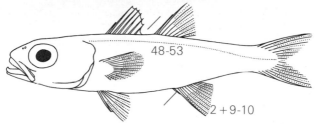

48-53

2 + 9-10

Epigonus telescopus
bulls-eye

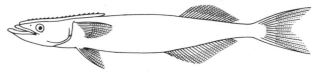

Remora remora
remora

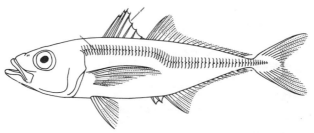

Trachurus trachurus
scad

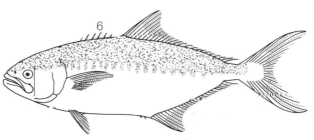

6

Campogramma glaycos
vadigo

Size Attains 50 cm (19¾ in.) in length and *c.* 1.5 kg (3 lb 5 oz) in weight; most are about 25 cm (10 in.) long.

Remarks A pelagic, schooling fish of wide distribution and great abundance. Although it can be taken close inshore (young ones in particular), it is more typical offshore, near the surface; it rarely swims deeper than 100 m (55 fathoms). Young fish in their first year are commonly found swimming in small groups beneath large jellyfishes.

Young scad feed on planktonic invertebrates. As they grow larger their diet changes to include fishes, but larger crustaceans are eaten in quantity. Fully grown, they feed on schooling fishes and small squids. Spawning takes place in summer in the North Sea, and earlier to the south of Biscay.

The scad or horse mackerel is not a prime food-fish, although in Biscay and the Mediterranean it is fished for commercially and canned in oil in large quantities, as well as being sold fresh or smoked. In northern European waters it is fished mainly for reduction to fish meal. The scad is an important food for several other fishes and sea-birds, particularly gulls.

***

Vadigo   *Campogramma glaycos*

Distinguishing features Torpedo-shaped body with long-based dorsal and anal fins, each with a high lobe in front; tail fin lobes long, fin deeply forked; first dorsal fin 6 short, separate spines; pectoral fins relatively long. Mouth large, jaw extends past eye, teeth large. (See also coloration.)

Coloration Greeny-grey above extending to the lateral line in a striking series of zig-zag lobes; ventrally white with a rose flush on flanks. Fins greyish.

Size Certainly attains 65 cm (25½ in.), possibly 1 m (39½ in.).

Remarks A near-surface inhabitant found in coastal waters but not close inshore. It feeds heavily on fishes (especially scad), and squids. It is a warm-water fish, most commonly found in the Mediterranean and the tropical eastern Atlantic; most abundant off Morocco. It is a very rare vagrant north of Spain.

***

Pilot fish   *Naucrates ductor*

Distinguishing features Torpedo-shaped body, rather rounded

Vadigo

248

in cross-section, with a fleshy keel either side of the caudal peduncle. Anal fin rather short-based (about equal to head length), 2 short spines anterior to the fin; 4–5 short, unconnected spines in front of dorsal fin. (See also coloration.)

Coloration Dark grey-blue on back and top of head continuing as 5–7 broad bands down sides and on to belly. Tail fin with a dark bar and white tips.

Size Very rarely exceeds 35 cm ($13\frac{3}{4}$ in.) in length, but has been reported to grow to 70 cm ($27\frac{1}{2}$ in.).

Remarks An open sea fish which is well known for the habit of the juveniles of accompanying larger animals (sharks and turtles mainly), sailing boats, and even driftwood. This is a habit common to many members of the family (see scad p. 248). They often swim in small schools, keeping a loose formation close to the shark's head. Large pilot fish are solitary. When young they eat pelagic crustaceans, but the adults eat fishes and squids.

It is a rare wanderer in northern European waters, its occurrence there is presumably the result of having accompanied some larger animal or vessel from the south or south-west.

Amberjack   *Seriola dumerili*

Distinguishing features A slender-bodied, rather torpedo-shaped fish with a curved head profile and deeply forked tail. The anal fin is shorter than the second dorsal fin; both have slightly higher rays in the front part of the fin. The 5–7 spines in the first dorsal fin are united by a membrane; pectoral fin short.

Coloration Back and upper sides deep blue with violet tints, sides yellow, belly pale yellow.

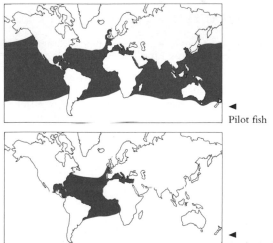

◄
Pilot fish

◄
Amberjack

Size   Grows to over 1 m (39½ in.) in length and a weight of *c.* 50 kg (110 lb).

Remarks   A surface-living fish found in small schools often in the strong currents off rocky outcrops and islands. It is a powerful swimmer which makes considerable annual migrations. Very large specimens are often solitary; the young are frequently found accompanying jellyfishes. It is of wide distribution in the tropical and warm temperate Atlantic (and is possibly found world-wide). It is exceptionally rare in northern European waters.

Derbio   *Trachinotus ovatus*

Distinguishing features   A deep-bodied very compressed fish with a small head and strongly forked tail. The mouth is small and does not extend beyond the front of the eye. A series of 5–6 short, separate spines in front of the dorsal fin (a forward-pointing spine is sometimes also visible). Pectoral fin short and rounded.

Coloration   Back pale blue, the sides and belly silvery with yellowish tints. Tips of the dorsal and tail fins black; a series of 5 dusky blotches along the sides.

Size   Usually about 30 cm (11¾ in.) in length; exceptionally up to 50 cm (19¾ in.).

Remarks   A rare fish in northern European waters, but one which is common enough to the south and in the Mediterranean. It is a surface-living species which occasionally comes into coastal waters in the course of its migrations. It feeds on small fishes, especially schooling ones such as the members of the herring family and cod family.

Ray's Bream and Pomfrets

A family (Bramidae) of moderate to large marine fishes found world-wide except in polar seas. Most live in the surface to middle layers of the ocean, often in the open ocean, although Ray's bream (the most abundant European species) lives on the edge of the continental shelf. All are deep-bodied fishes with well-developed fins, but no sharp spines in them. As a group they show striking changes in body form, and fin and scale shape from juvenile stages to

Derbio

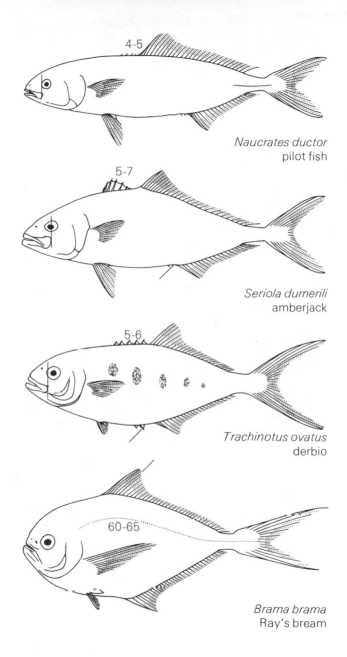

Naucrates ductor
pilot fish

Seriola dumerili
amberjack

Trachinotus ovatus
derbio

Brama brama
Ray's bream

adult, which has in the past meant that young fish and adults were regarded as separate species.

Four species have been recognized in northern European seas; only one is at all common.

Ray's bream   *Brama brama*

Distinguishing features   Deep-bodied, but narrow towards the tail; profile of head steep. Pelvic fins placed beneath the pectorals. Dorsal and anal fins moderately long and low, except that the front rays are elongate to form a lobe. Pectoral and tail fin lobes long. Body scales smooth and relatively small, more than 60 in the lateral line.

Coloration   When alive or freshly dead, dark greeny-brown on the back with silvery reflections on the sides and ventrally; pectoral fins yellow. The silver dulls after death and the fish looks plain brown.

Size   Attains a maximum length of 66 cm (26 in.); more usual at lengths of 40–55 cm (15¾–21¾ in.). Weight attained is *c.* 3.50 kg (7 lb 11 oz).

Remarks   Ray's bream is a common, if irregular visitant to the seas of northern Europe, but it is abundant enough to support an important commercial fishery on the Atlantic coast of Spain and Portugal. It lives in the open sea in mid-water, probably as shallow as 73–91 m (40–50 fathoms), but deeper further north. Its range is subject to the temperature of water masses, and it migrates northwards from the Iberian peninsula; in some years by midsummer it is caught off Ireland, and by autumn it is west of Scotland and Norway. In the winter months it returns southwards, but frequently

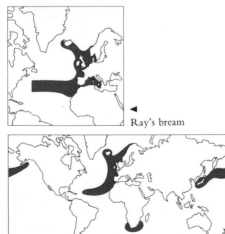

Ray's bream

Rough pomfret

great numbers become trapped in the too shallow, too cool North Sea, and are stranded on the coast. The causes of these abundant years are not clearly understood.

Ray's bream feeds on a wide range of crustaceans and fishes, but seems to be unselective in that it eats what is most abundant. Its flesh is frequently infested with the cestode worm, *Gymnorhynchus reptens*, which spoils it (at least aesthetically) as food. It is otherwise a good food-fish.

Rough pomfret   *Taractes asper*

Distinguishing features   Body relatively shallow, but with the head profile sloping gently upwards to dorsal origin. Pelvic fin beneath pectorals. Anterior rays in both dorsal and anal fins high, remaining rays short (in fish longer than 10 cm). Scales large, 41–45 in lateral line; scales near the tail have sharp hooks; young fish have hooks on all the scales.

Coloration   Dark brown on back, yellowish on sides; probably with silvery reflections when alive.

Size   Attains at least 45 cm (17¾ in.) in length.

Remarks   A relatively uncommon bramid which is probably distributed world-wide in the middle layers of the oceans. Off Spain and Portugal it is caught occasionally on lines set for Ray's bream at about 80 m (44 fathoms). In northern European waters large adults are captured rarely, although to the south young and old can be caught, which suggests that the northern specimens are not part of the breeding stock. Large specimens were originally thought to be a distinct species, *Taractes raschi*.

Long-finned bream   *Taractichthys longipinnis*

Distinguishing features   Body very deep, with a steep, rounded profile to both head and breast region. Pelvic fins small, situated beneath the bases of the pectoral fin. Dorsal and anal fins long-based, the anterior rays in both prolonged into very high lobes. Scales large, 44–46 in a series down the side; young fish have a spine on each scale towards the tail.

Coloration   Dark brown dorsally, silvery on sides and belly; pectoral, anal, and tail fins light, dorsal lobe dark.

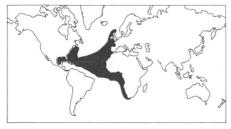

Long-finned
bream

Size Attains 1 m (39½ in.) in length and a weight of over 45 kg (100 lb); most specimens are less than half this length.

Remarks A large oceanic fish which probably swims in small schools in the upper layers of the sea. Despite its wide distribution in the tropical and warm temperate Atlantic Ocean, it is extremely rare in northern European waters, the only known specimens having been stranded. A related species occurs in the Pacific Ocean.

Silver pomfret   *Pterycombus brama*

Distinguishing features A rather slender-bodied but compressed fish. Pelvic fins small, placed in front of the level of the pectoral fins. Dorsal and anal fins very long, the origin of the dorsal above the rear edge of the eye, and of the anal below the pectoral fin base; rays in both long (but frequently broken). Scales large (45–49 in lateral line) thin and papery, but with weak hooks on them; scaly sheaths at dorsal and anal bases.

Coloration Dark brown above, lighter ventrally with silvery reflections.

Size Attains 41 cm (16¼ in.) in length.

Remarks An inhabitant of the open Atlantic Ocean living in the upper layers of the sea. It is occasionally caught by the line fishermen off Spain and Portugal at depths of around 128 m (70 fathoms); it is not a deep-sea fish. Numerous adult specimens have been stranded or caught alive on the Norwegian coast; they are presumed to have migrated from the south-west. The species spawns in the Gulf Stream waters off Florida and the Caribbean. Little is known of its biology.

Sea-breams

A family (Sparidae) of marine fishes found around the world in tropical and temperate seas, although few occur in the eastern Pacific Ocean. Most are deep-bodied, fully-scaled fishes, except that the snout is scaleless. Their teeth show many adaptations to their varied diet from the flattened molars of shellfish eaters, through the conical teeth of general predators, to the sharp-edged incisors of plant browsers.

Sea-breams, which are elsewhere also known as porgies and

Silver pomfret

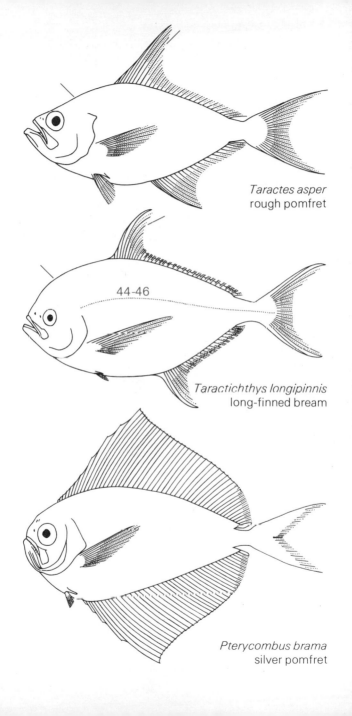

Taractes asper
rough pomfret

44-46

Taractichthys longipinnis
long-finned bream

Pterycombus brama
silver pomfret

teeth of sea-breams

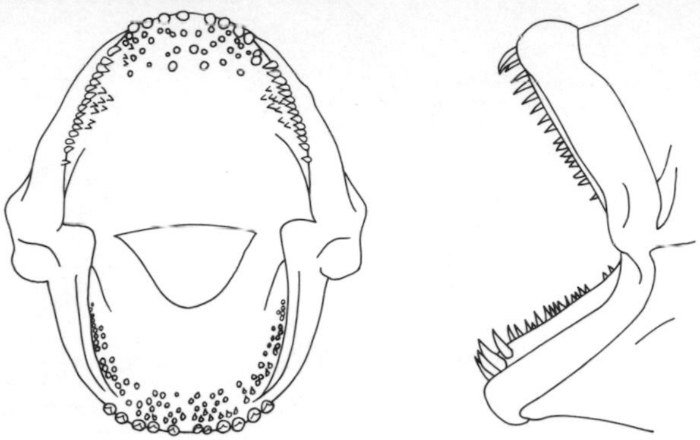

Spondyliosoma

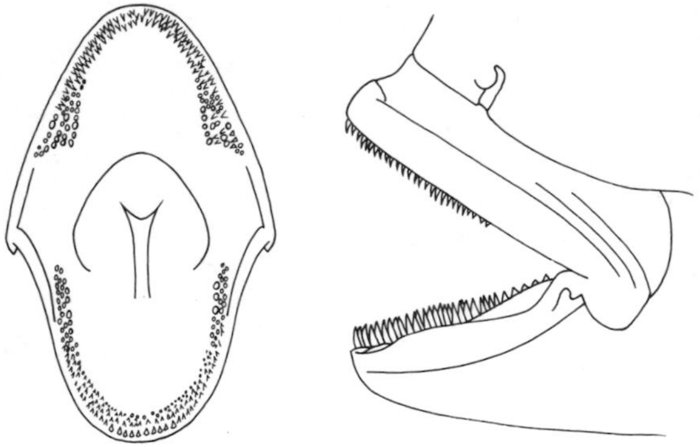

Pagellus

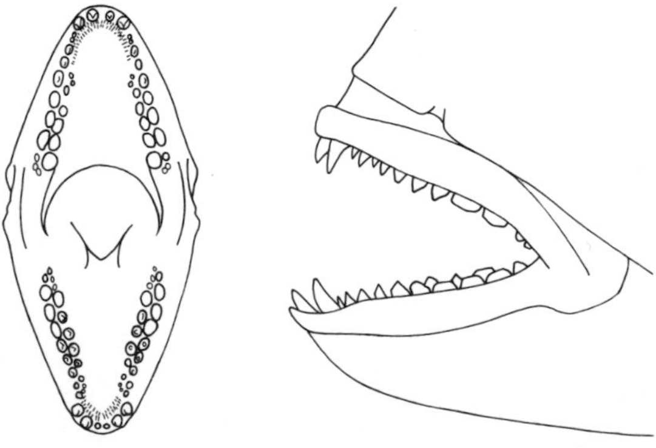

Sparus

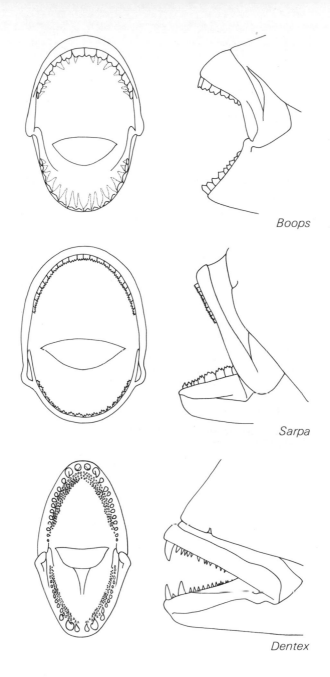

Boops

Sarpa

Dentex

snappers, include many important game and food-fishes. Eight species have been reported in northern European seas, but only 2 are at all common.

Black sea-bream   *Spondyliosoma cantharus*

Distinguishing features A rather deep-bodied sea-bream with a relatively small head, and jaws which extend at most to the front of the eye. The teeth are sharply pointed, slightly curved and not markedly large; teeth in front and sides of jaws similar in shape, slightly larger in front. (See p. 256.)

Coloration Back greyish, sides silvery-grey with 6 or 7 dusky vertical bars; fins greyish, the edge of the tail fin dusky.

Size Exceptionally it attains a length of 51 cm (20 in.); mostly it is about 35 cm (13¾ in.). Attains a weight of *c.* 3 kg (6 lb 10 oz).

Remarks A relatively common sea-bream in northern European waters, although north of the English Channel it is probably a summertime migrant. It is particularly common around wrecks, or rocky outcrops, although in the Mediterranean it is found typically over sand and sea-grass beds. It is one of the few nest-building sea breams; the male digs a depression in the sandy sea-bed in which the female sheds her eggs. Here they are guarded by the male until they hatch; the young tend to form a loose school around the nest for several weeks after hatching. The black sea-bream spawns in April and May in the eastern English Channel.

It is locally a popular fish with anglers, and small quantities are caught by commercial fishermen, but it is not sufficiently abundant generally to be an important food or sporting fish.

Red sea-bream   *Pagellus bogaraveo*

Distinguishing features A typical sea-bream shape, relatively deep-bodied with a short head. This species has a large eye, its diameter greater than the snout length; the cheek depth is less than eye diameter. The scales on the top of the head extend forward only to the middle of the eye. The pectoral fin is long. The mouth extends back to the level of the eye margin; the teeth in front of the jaws are curved, sharp but not elongate; in the sides of the jaws there are 2 to 3 rows of rounded, rather small molars. (See p. 256 and coloration.)

Black
sea-bream

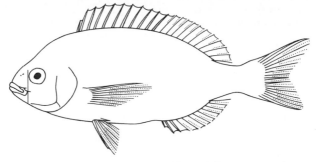

Spondyliosoma cantharus
black sea-bream

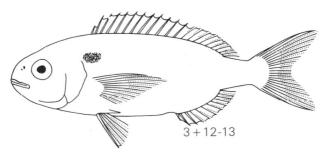

3 + 12-13

Pagellus bogaraveo
red sea-bream

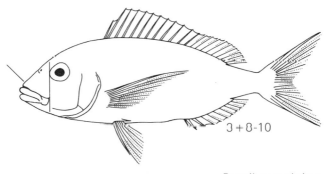

3 + 8-10

Pagellus erythrinus
pandora

Coloration Large fish are rose or reddish-grey, the sides silvery with a pink flush and the fins greyish-red; there is a rounded dusky blotch on the upper side between the dorsal fin origin and the gill cover. Young fish are paler and may lack this blotch.

Size Attains a maximum of 51 cm (20 in.), more often around 35 cm (13¾ in.) in length, and a weight of *c.* 4.50 kg (9 lb 15 oz).

Remarks Relatively common in the seas to the south and west of the British Isles, but less so further north, although occurring fairly regularly. It is a schooling species, the young in particular forming large schools, while the adults are encountered in smaller groups. The young come into inshore waters, usually over or close to rocks and rough ground or wrecks, and it may be as shallow as 35 m (19 fathoms), while the larger fish live as deep as 100–200 m (55–109 fathoms). Most of the fish in northern seas are warm-season migrants from the south.

The red sea-bream's food is mainly fish, although large ones also eat large decapod crustaceans and occasionally squid. It breeds in late summer and autumn (to the south-west of Britain), earlier to the south. It probably grows very slowly, but little is known of the biology of this species.

It is a very good food-fish, but not caught in sufficient numbers to be commercially important, except in Biscay. It is also occasionally caught by anglers.

Pandora   *Pagellus erythrinus*

Distinguishing features Moderately slender-bodied with a relatively small head, and a rather pointed snout. The mouth is large, reaching the level of the orbit; the eye is small, its diameter less than the snout length. Scales on the head extend to the level of the

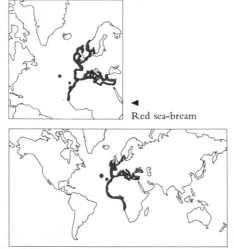

Red sea-bream

Pandora

front of the eyes. Teeth in front of jaw sharp, curved, but not very long; in the sides of the jaws small rounded molars.

Coloration   Orange-red on the back and upper sides, pinkish below fading to silver. Lateral line picked out in pale blue, blue also present on the back and the base of the dorsal fin. Eye and pectoral fin yellow. Edge of the gill cover red; inside of the mouth black.

Size   Most usual length 15–25 cm (6–10 in.), exceptionally to 60 cm (23½ in.).

Remarks   A very rare fish in northern European seas, although common in the Mediterranean and southern Biscay from whence the northern fish migrate in the summer months. Young specimens form schools in shallow water over sandy bottoms. The adults live on sand or mud, particularly near rocky outcrops between 15 and 120 m (8–66 fathoms). The pandora eats small fishes and bottom-living invertebrates, particularly crustaceans and small molluscs.

Spanish sea-bream   *Pagellus acarne*

Distinguishing features   Body distinctly slender, its dorsal profile smoothly convex, but with a rather blunt snout. The mouth is large and extends back to the level of the eye; eye diameter moderate, roughly equal to the snout length, cheek narrow. Scales extend on the top of the head to the rear of the eyes. Teeth in front of jaw relatively small, sharp and curved; in sides small rounded molars. (See also coloration.)

Coloration   Pale rose-coloured above, sides and belly silvery, fins reddish; mouth is golden or orange internally. Dusky spot at pectoral base.

Size   Grows to a maximum length of 35 cm (13¾ in.), but usually around 25 cm (10 in.).

Remarks   An inshore sea-bream which lives close to the bottom in depths of 20–100 m (11–55 fathoms) on sand or sand-and-mud. Young specimens live closer inshore in shallower water than adults. This fish feeds mainly on crustaceans, but other invertebrates are eaten. In northern European waters it is extremely rare and the few records were mainly of adults in late summer, presumably the result of a northerly migration.

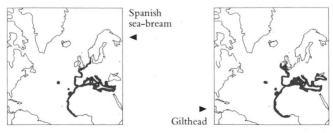

Spanish
sea-bream
◄

Gilthead ►

Gilthead
Sparus aurata

Distinguishing features A deep-bodied sea-bream with a strongly arched back, relatively small eye (diameter less than snout length) placed high on the side of the head, and deep cheeks. The teeth in front of the jaws are strong, curved and pointed—much larger than those lying behind them—while in the sides of the jaws there are large, flattened, rounded crushing teeth. (See p. 256 and coloration.)

Coloration Back dark grey-blue, the lower sides and belly silvery, with a dusky blotch at the origin of the lateral line. The edge of the gill cover is scarlet, and a bright golden stripe runs across the forehead between the eyes; both fade on death.

Size Attains a maximum length of 70 cm (27½ in.). Weights of up to 2.5 kg (5 lb 8 oz) have been reported.

Remarks A shallow water species which lives in schools over sand or mud in depths of 30 m (16 fathoms). The young fish live in shallower water still. In the Mediterranean it comes closer inshore in spring, often entering river mouths and lagoons, and thriving in the low salinity water. It migrates offshore to breed in deeper water in winter. In northern European waters it is a rare fish, the biology of which has been little studied. It is unlikely to breed in northern waters, those specimens which do occur having been recruited from southern stocks. Its food is heavily biased in favour of molluscs, especially mussels and oysters, and crustaceans. It is an important food-fish to the south but, at times, a pest to shellfish culture.

Couch's sea-bream
Sparus pagrus

Distinguishing features A deep-bodied sea-bream with a high, rounded dorsal profile to the head, the eye is relatively small and the cheek deep. In front of the jaws 4–6 very strong teeth with sharp, curved teeth behind and at the sides; at the back of the jaws there are 2 rows of flattened crushing teeth, the inner row being larger.

Coloration Rosy in general, darker on the back, silvery sides. Fins pinkish; tail fin tips white with a dark margin in central section of fin.

Size Very occasionally reaches 75 cm (29½ in.) in length; frequently up to 50 cm (19¾ in.).

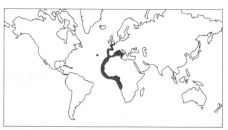

Couch's
sea-bream

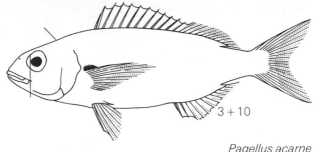

3 + 10

Pagellus acarne
Spanish sea-bream

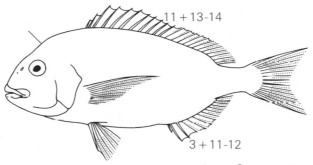

11 + 13-14

3 + 11-12

Sparus aurata
gilthead

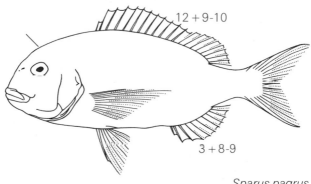

12 + 9-10

3 + 8-9

Sparus pagrus
Couch's sea-bream

Remarks An extremely rare wanderer to the seas of northern Europe. To the south of Biscay, and in the Mediterranean, it becomes more common although it is nowhere abundant. It lives over sand, or muddy bottoms where algae coat the surface, and in sea-grass beds at 20 m (11 fathoms) and below; the young fish are found in shallower water. A general offshore migration into deeper water occurs in winter. It feeds heavily on molluscs and crustaceans.

Bogue
Boops boops

Distinguishing features A slender-bodied sea-bream, its body only slightly oval in cross-section; the eyes are moderately large but the mouth is small. Pectoral fins short. Teeth compressed, incisor-like, each with several rounded cusps in upper jaw (see p. 257). 14–16 spines in the first dorsal fin.

Coloration Greeny-blue or greyish on back, paler on the sides with a yellowish tinge. Lateral line dark with faint dusky lines parallel to it on the lower side. A small dusky spot at the base of the pectoral fin.

Size Attains a maximum length of 38 cm (15 in.), but usually about 25 cm (10 in.).

Remarks An uncommon sea-bream in northern European waters but to the south, and in the Mediterranean, it is extremely common. Here it lives in schools, often containing 100 or more fish, from close inshore (*c.* 2 m) down to depths of 150 m (82 fathoms), on sandy bottoms—especially on sea-grass beds and close to rocks. It is said by some authors to eat planktonic organisms, especially copepods and young fish, but its teeth seem to be clearly adapted to browse on algae, sea-grass, and encrusting growths. In northern waters its diet has not been studied and it is rarely captured. Elsewhere it is a valuable food-fish.

Saupe
Sarpa salpa

Distinguishing features Body moderately deep, profile smoothly rounded making the body oval. Mouth small, not reaching eye level; teeth flattened incisors, in a single row in both jaws, notched at the edge in the upper jaw, triangular and serrated in the lower jaw (see p. 257). 11–12 rather stout spines in the dorsal fin. (See coloration.)

Bogue

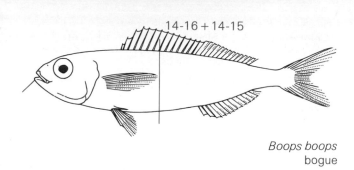

14-16 + 14-15

Boops boops
bogue

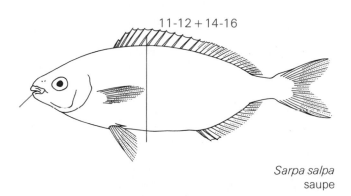

11-12 + 14-16

Sarpa salpa
saupe

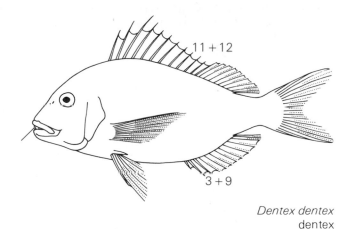

11 + 12

3 + 9

Dentex dentex
dentex

Coloration Greyish-blue on the back fading to silvery on the sides, with 10–12 lengthwise golden yellow stripes and a yellow eye. A dusky spot at the pectoral fin base.

Size Adults are usually about 30 cm (11¾ in.) in length; exceptionally they attain 45 cm (17¾ in.).

Remarks An extremely rare fish in northern European waters which has been recorded only a very few times. To the south, in the warm temperate and tropical Atlantic, and in the Mediterranean, it is common. It is a shallow water species, rarely found below 15 m (8 fathoms) and can be seen swimming in characteristically tight, compact schools sometimes with very many fish together. It feeds by grazing on the fronds of algae and sea-grass, eating mainly the growths on the surface of the plant.

Dentex
Dentex dentex

Distinguishing features A moderately slender-bodied sea-bream with a large head. The upper profile is steep (large males have a conspicuous hump on the forehead); the eyes are relatively small and set high on the head; the snout is long. Mouth large, 4–6 large, curved teeth in the front of the jaws, smaller but strong teeth behind (see p. 257).

Coloration Bluish-silver above, paler on the sides, but with small blue spots (which quickly fade on death); pectoral and ventral fins pink.

Size Attains 1.2 m (47 in.) and *c.* 12 kg (26 lb 8 oz).

Remarks A rare fish in northern European waters owing its status there to occasional migration of large fish from the south. It usually lives in small schools on rocky grounds at around 200 m (109 fathoms), but comes into shallower water in spring. It is entirely predatory on fishes and cephalopods. In southern Europe it is a valued but rather uncommon food-fish.

Shade-Fishes

A large family (Sciaenidae) of mainly marine fishes found worldwide in tropical and temperate seas. Probably as many as 200 species are known, many of them valuable food-fishes locally. They are

Saupe

distinguished by possessing 2 dorsal fins, the first short with weak spines, the second very long-based with numerous branched rays; the anal fin is generally short-based. Their most striking attribute is their marked ability to make sounds, the large swim-bladder acting as a resonating chamber amplifying the noises produced by adjacent muscles. Many shade-fishes (they are also known as drums or croakers) live in estuaries or other murky waters and their ability to locate one another by sounds (for they can hear acutely) is clearly an advantage.

Only 1 species occurs in northern European waters; 4 others occur in the Mediterranean and off southern Europe.

Meagre	*Argyrosomus regius*

Distinguishing features   A long-bodied fish and heavily scaled, the scales extending onto the head and tail fin, and obliquely inserted into scale pockets. Second dorsal fin long-based; anal fin conspicuously short-based. Mouth large, extending to eye; no barbel under chin.

Coloration   Silvery-brown on the back, paler on the sides with golden tints especially on the lateral line; inside the mouth is golden yellow.

Size   Attains a length of 2 m (6 ft 7 in.) and a weight of *c.* 65 kg (143 lb).

Remarks   A rare fish in northern European waters which occurs, presumably, as a result of stray fish wandering from the south. In the Mediterranean it lives in shallow water over sandy bottoms, and the young especially can be found in estuaries and low-salinity lagoons. It feeds on smaller, schooling fishes, especially sardines and grey mullets, and other mid-water fishes.

The deep rumbling sounds that it produces can be heard at a distance of 30 m (98 ft) or so in water. It is an extremely good food-fish, and a splendid fighting fish for the angler, but large specimens are now very rare in European seas in general.

Red Mullets

A family (Mullidae) of fishes of world-wide distribution in tropical and warm temperate seas. Around 60 species are known and all are

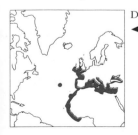

Dentex ◄

► Meagre

moderately slender with blunt snouts and rounded heads, 2 dorsal fins (the first spiny), large scales, and a pair of conspicuous barbels on the chin. These barbels are the reason for their alternative name— goat fishes. Most of them are reddish with yellow tints. They live mainly in shallow inshore waters close to the sandy or muddy sea-bed in which they detect buried invertebrates by means of their barbels.

One species only occurs in northern European waters; 3 others are found in the waters of southern Europe (2 of which are Red Sea immigrants into the Mediterranean through the Suez Canal).

Red mullet   *Mullus surmuletus*

Distinguishing features   Body slender and rather flattened, with a steeply arched head profile. Scales are large and fragile, 2 scales immediately below the eye on the cheek. Two long barbels on the lower jaw. (See also coloration.)

Coloration   In daytime, reddish-brown with 4–5 lengthwise yellow stripes and a darker stripe from eye to tail; at night, these stripes break up into an indistinct marbled pattern. Below a depth of *c.* 15 m they are deep red.

Size   Attains a maximum length of 40 cm (15¾ in.) and a weight of *c.* 1 kg (2 lb 3 oz).

Remarks   Through most of northern Europe's seas the red mullet is a scarce fish but in the English Channel, and at times in the southern North Sea, it is moderately common, presumably as a result of a summertime, northward migration. It lives in small schools on sandy or muddy bottoms in 3–90 m (1½–49 fathoms), although it also occurs on rocky grounds. These fish probe the soft bottom with their long barbels which are covered with sensory pores, in search of food and may vigorously excavate a pit to seize their prey. The school is sometimes followed by smaller fishes such as wrasses, which snap up small food items that are uncovered.

In the Mediterranean the red mullet spawns in summer, when the female sheds her eggs on the bottom in 10–55 m (5½–30 fathoms). The early young are blue-backed and silvery-sided planktonic creatures which live at the surface of the sea.

Red mullet is a valued food-fish, but in northern Europe it is too uncommon to be exploited. Occasional landings are made on the Channel coasts.

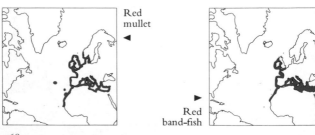

Red
mullet
◀

▶
Red
band-fish

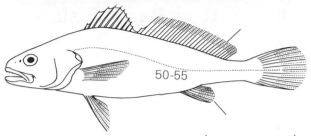

Argyrosomus regius
meagre

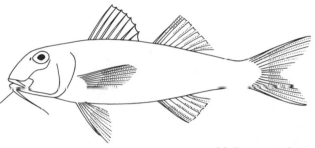

Mullus surmuletus
red mullet

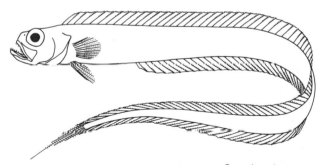

Cepola rubescens
red band-fish

Red Band-Fish

A small family (Cepolidae) of marine fishes found in the Indo-Pacific and the eastern North Atlantic. They are all basically very similar in body form, long and slender with long dorsal and anal fins, continuous with the tail fin. Many are reddish in colour. One species only is found in European waters; there are possibly 5 or 6 other representatives.

Red band-fish	*Cepola rubescens*

Distinguishing features Long slender body with long dorsal fin, originating above the gill cover. Eye large, mouth strongly oblique with well-spaced relatively large curved teeth in the jaws.

Coloration Back and sides red or orange-red, ventrally orange to yellowish. The fins are yellowish except that the anterior part of the dorsal fin is red.

Size Attains a maximum length of 70 cm ($27\frac{1}{2}$ in.), but usually around 35 cm ($13\frac{3}{4}$ in.).

Remarks Moderately common on the southern and western coasts of Britain and also off the French coast; rare in the North Sea. It lives in vertical burrows, about 6–8 cm ($2\frac{1}{2}$–$3\frac{1}{4}$ in.) wide in stiff mud at depths of 17–200 m (9–109 fathoms). It emerges from the burrow at times to feed on planktonic crustaceans, chiefly copepods, although it may take some prey by partly protruding the body from the burrow. It is occasionally eaten by other fishes, including the mid-water feeding whiting. After storms, it is sometimes stranded on shore or captured by sprat nets, presumably because the burrows have been destroyed by the sea's action.

Grey Mullets

A large family (Mugilidae) of mainly marine fishes found in all tropical and temperate seas, and in many tropical areas in freshwater. In temperate zones (as in northern Europe), they are attracted to estuaries and are sometimes found in freshwater. The numerous species are closely similar in appearance having a torpedo-shaped body, rather broad wide head, 2 dorsal fins—the first having 4 spines, and large scales. Most species feed on the rich organic layer at the surface of the bottom mud, but some browse the filamentous algae on rocks and pier pilings. They have a thick-walled gizzard-like stomach and a very long intestine, both adaptations to their nourishment-poor diet.

Three species only occur in northern European waters.

Thick-lipped grey mullet	*Chelon labrosus*

Distinguishing features Typical of the grey mullets in its body shape with a short-based, 4-spined dorsal fin. The edge of the eye is only slightly covered with clear adipose tissue; the upper lip is broad (its depth more than half eye diameter), the lower part with coarse papillae and close-packed small teeth.

Coloration Dark green or blue-grey above, with silvery sides striped with 6 or 7 lengthwise grey bands, white ventrally. Ventral fins white except for anal fin which is dusky.

Size Attains a length of 75 cm (29½ in.) and a weight of *c.* 4.5 kg (9 lb 15 oz).

Remarks A common inhabitant of coastal waters of all Europe except most northern parts. To some extent it is migratory, moving northwards with summertime warming of the sea and southwards before winter. It is particularly common close inshore in harbour mouths, estuaries, in sandy bays, and in the channels of saltings; in calm water it can be seen cruising in schools at the surface with its snout almost breaking through. It feeds on the rich organic material on the sea-bed, gulping in mouthfuls of surface mud and algae, rejecting the greater part of the indigestible mud through the gills and swallowing the plant matter, nematode worms, copepods, and other animals with a good mixture of sand. Large grey mullet also feed on molluscs and small crustaceans.

This species is of some value to the fisheries of northern Europe, as it is in the Mediterranean. It is also a good sport fish even if hard to hook and capture.

Golden grey mullet   *Liza aurata*

Distinguishing features Typical body shape of a grey mullet, but with a narrow upper lip (its depth less than half eye-diameter) and adipose eyelid very narrow. Teeth on edge of upper lip moderately large; preorbital bone (at corner of mouth) finely toothed and pointed. The pectoral fin, when folded forward, covers the rear edge of the eye. (See also coloration.)

Coloration Grey-blue above, silvery on sides with grey lengthwise stripes; a conspicuous golden spot on the cheek and gill cover. Anal fin light; no spot at pectoral fin base.

Size Attains 45 cm (17¾ in.) in length.

Remarks This is probably the least abundant of northern European grey mullets, although it is by no means rare in the English Channel and on the south-western coasts of the British Isles.

Thick-
lipped
grey
mullet
◄

►

Golden
grey
mullet

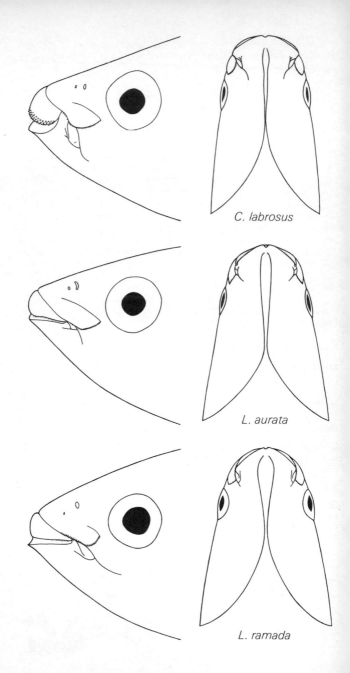

C. labrosus

L. aurata

L. ramada

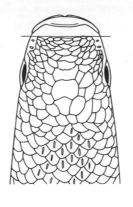

C. labrosus

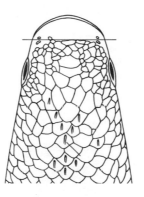

L. aurata

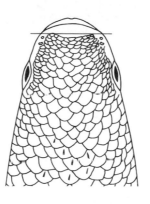

L. ramada

It enters harbours and river mouths, but rarely moves into freshwater. Its biology has not been studied in northern waters; its diet is composed of algae and bottom detritus. It does not apparently breed north of Biscay.

Thin-lipped grey mullet *Liza ramada*

Distinguishing features   Typical grey mullet body shape with a narrow upper lip (its depth less than half eye-diameter) and a narrow adipose eyelid. Teeth on edge of upper lip minute and bristle-like; preorbital bone coarsely toothed and rounded. Pectoral fin short and does not reach eye if folded forwards.

Coloration   Grey-blue above, silvery on sides with faint grey stripes running lengthwise; white ventrally. Anal fin dusky; a dark spot at the base of the pectoral fin.

Size   Attains a length of 60 cm (23½ in.) and a weight of *c.* 2.50 kg (5 lb 8 oz).

Remarks   The thin-lipped grey mullet is moderately common on the Biscay coast of France, is uncommon and mainly a summertime migrant on the Channel coasts, and is rare north of this with the exception of southern Ireland. This species stays close to the shore, enters lagoons and estuaries, and will penetrate well into the freshwaters of rivers. It is the most abundant grey mullet in freshwater in northern Europe. It is also migratory with the seasons. It spawns in the sea and has been proved to spawn on occasions as far north as southern England. Its biology is largely unknown, but is likely to be similar to that of the other mullets.

Wrasses

A large family (Labridae) which contains some 600 species distributed in tropical, warm temperate, and temperate seas. Wrasses are fully scaled, have a long-based dorsal fin the anterior rays of which are spiny, usually have stout teeth, and have well-developed pharyngeal bones with flattened teeth. Most are relatively small, shorter than 30 cm (12 in.).

In general, they are colourful fishes, the sexes having different colouring or markings. Some species (probably most) change sex with age from female to male, and the coloration changes also.

Thin-lipped grey mullet

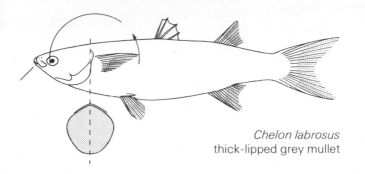

Chelon labrosus
thick-lipped grey mullet

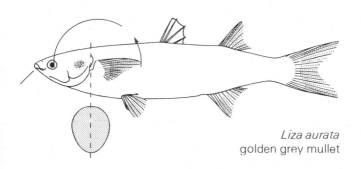

Liza aurata
golden grey mullet

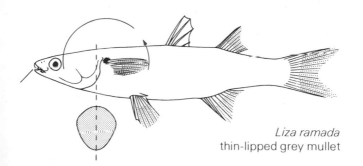

Liza ramada
thin-lipped grey mullet

Wrasses are also well known for their habit of sleeping at night, sometimes buried in sand, at other times hidden between rocks or in algae. Some also are well known as 'cleaner fishes' which pick parasites off other, larger fishes, although this behaviour has been proven in only a few European species. In general, they have little food value although they are locally marketed; the largest species have some appeal to anglers, but they are not sporting fishes.

Cuckoo wrasse   *Labrus mixtus*

Distinguishing features   A rather slender-looking wrasse with notably elongate head and pointed snout; mouth large, reaches almost to eye level. Scales rather small, not much bigger than the pupil, 45–48 in lateral line. Rear edge of preoperculum smooth. 16–18 spines in the dorsal fin. (See also coloration).

Coloration   Females and immature males yellow, reddish-orange, or red, paler on the belly, with 3 dusky blotches on the back at the rear of the dorsal fin and on the caudal peduncle. Males have a brilliant blue head, the blue continuing on the sides as streaks across the yellow or orange. When spawning, the male has a white patch on top of the head.

Size   Attains a length of 35 cm (13¾ in.) and a weight of 1 kg (2 lb 3 oz).

Remarks   A moderately uncommon wrasse in northern European waters in general, although it may be common locally especially close to rocks in 35–180 m (19–98½ fathoms). In summer it moves inshore and may be found in water as shallow as 10 m (5½ fathoms), while small specimens occur in the low tidal fringe. An offshore migration into deeper water takes place in early winter.

The male selects a nest, usually a cleared hollow in the sea-bed and displays around it, attracting females towards the nest and driving rival males away. An elaborate courtship ensues on nest building. Growth is slow and in northern waters at least, cuckoo wrasse live for a considerable span (up to 17 years). Their diet has been little studied, but is believed to comprise crustaceans, molluscs, and other bottom-living organisms.

Ballan wrasse   *Labrus bergylta*

Distinguishing features   The largest species in Europe, the ballan wrasse has a rather deep body, pointed but not elongate

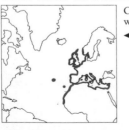

Cuckoo
wrasse

◄

►

Ballan
wrasse

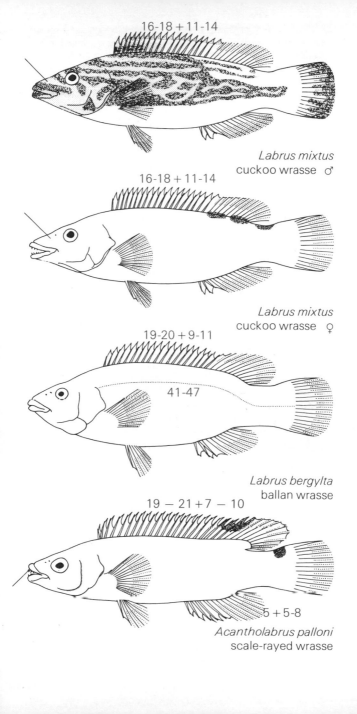

16-18 + 11-14

Labrus mixtus
cuckoo wrasse ♂

16-18 + 11-14

Labrus mixtus
cuckoo wrasse ♀

19-20 + 9-11

41-47

Labrus bergylta
ballan wrasse

19 – 21 + 7 – 10

5 + 5-8

Acantholabrus palloni
scale-rayed wrasse

snout, and a small mouth which does not reach to eye level. Scales moderately small, 41–47 scales on the lateral line, all about pupil sized. Rear edge of the preoperculum smooth. Dorsal fin with 19–20 spines.

Coloration Very variable, generally basically greenish or greeny-brown, sometimes reddish; the undersides and the fins are spotted with white and the scale edges are dark.

Size Attains a maximum length of 60 cm (23½ in.) and a weight of *c*. 3.5 kg (7 lb 11 oz).

Remarks Probably the most abundant large wrasse in the eastern North Atlantic. It is common close to rocks and around reefs from 2–3 m (7–10 ft) to about 20 m (11 fathoms), while the young are often found in shore pools provided there is abundant algae and rock. The adults are usually solitary or form small schools.

It feeds heavily on molluscs (mainly mussels), but also eats large numbers of crustaceans, especially the smaller crabs. Like several other wrasses it builds a nest of fine algae, wedged into a crevice, in which the eggs are laid in summer. After hatching, the larvae are pelagic for a short while and drift into shallow inshore water.

The ballan wrasse in northern Europe suffers in very severe winters, when many may be killed.

Scale-rayed wrasse   *Acantholabrus palloni*

Distinguishing features A slender-bodied wrasse with moderately large scales which extend up the rays of the fins and over most of the head. Five sharp spines in the anal fin, 19–21 in the dorsal fin. Mouth large, almost reaching the level of the eye; teeth in front, especially in the lower jaw sharp and protruding.

Coloration Basically greeny-brown on the back and upper sides, lighter ventrally; dusky blotches at the end of the spiny dorsal fin and on the upper edge of the tail fin base.

Size Grows to 30 cm (11¾ in.).

Remarks In northern European waters this wrasse is rare, but even to the south it seems uncommon. It lives in deeper water than most wrasses, among rocks mostly between 50 and 270 m (27–148 fathoms), exceptionally as shallow as 18 m (10 fathoms). Its diet has been little studied, but one specimen examined contained mollusc, crab, and fish remains.

Scale-rayed wrasse

Rock cook

Rock cook   *Centrolabrus exoletus*

Distinguishing features   A rather deep-bodied but small wrasse. Its mouth is small, although the thick lips accentuate its size; the corner is less than halfway to the eye. Teeth are small and in a single row. Anal fin with 4–6 (usually 5) stout spines. Preoperculum serrated. (See also coloration.)

Coloration   Usually greeny-brown or reddish on the back, lighter on the sides and yellowish on the belly. Males have conspicuous blue spots on the vertical fins and on the sides of the head. The tail has a dark, crescent-shaped mark with a light band in front and at the edge of the fin.

Size   Attains 15 cm (6 in.), usually up to about 12 cm (4¾ in.).

Remarks   A little-known wrasse which is local in its distribution. It lives in shallow water from 2–25 m (1–14 fathoms) amongst algae-covered rocks and in eel-grass beds. The young are found in the shallower depths, and may very rarely be caught near extreme low-tide level. It is said to eat small crustaceans, and from the frequency with which it is taken in prawn traps it may scavenge on the bait, although it could as easily be attracted by the amphipods which swarm round pot baits. It is also known to act as a cleaner-fish, picking parasites off larger fishes, and is one of the very few temperate water fishes to show this behaviour. It is also known as the small-mouth wrasse.

Rainbow wrasse   *Coris julis*

Distinguishing features   A long, slender-bodied wrasse with very small scales (more than 60 in the lateral line) which do not extend on to the head. Dorsal spines thin and flexible, 8–9 in number. Teeth protrude forwards from the mouth.

Coloration   Variable with sex and age, also with living depth. Females and young males orange-brown above with a yellow-white stripe on sides; adult males greenish above with a zig-zag blue-edged orange band on sides. Both have a bright blue spot on the edge of the gill cover.

Size   Males to 25 cm (10 in.), females to *c.* 18 cm (7 in.).

Remarks   Excessively rare in northern European seas; it has occurred at most twice, and records of eggs identified as belonging

Rainbow
wrasse
◄

►
Goldsinny

to this species may be doubted. In the Mediterranean and on the warmer Atlantic coasts it is very common, living in shallow water of 3–120 m (1½–65½ fathoms) close to rocks and among sea-grass beds. Active during the daytime, and probably buries itself in sand at night. This wrasse changes sex, from female to male, and often lives in small, loosely organized male-dominated communities.

Goldsinny   *Ctenolabrus rupestris*

Distinguishing features   Relatively slender-bodied with a pointed head and small mouth. The scales are large, 35–39 in the lateral line; the preoperculum finely serrated on its rear edge but not ventrally; anal fin with only 7 or 8 branched rays. Teeth in front of jaw curved and large; in 2 rows. (See also coloration.)

Coloration   Brown or reddish-orange with dusky spots on dorsal fin membrane between the first and fifth spines, and on the top of the tail just in front of the fin.

Size   Attains a maximum length of 18 cm (7 in.), usually around 12 cm (4¾ in.).

Remarks   The goldsinny is one of the more common small wrasses in northern European seas although it is only abundant locally, despite its wide distribution. It lives close to algal-covered rocks in 11–50 m (6–27 fathoms), and among eel-grass beds, and in extreme low-water tidal pools on rocky shores which may be no more than 1 m deep. It is usually found in proximity to deep water, and may migrate offshore. Its bold markings resemble those of other wrasses known to act as cleaner fish, but this behaviour has not yet been recorded for the goldsinny. Its biology is generally little known.

Baillon's wrasse   *Crenilabrus bailloni*

Distinguishing features   Relatively deep-bodied, with large to moderate scales, 33–38 in the lateral line, and 4 scales between it and the dorsal fin ray bases. Two or 3 rows of scales on the cheek. Edge of preoperculum is serrated on rear and lower faces.

Coloration   Dull greeny-brown with dusky spots on the dorsal fin membrane between the first branched rays, and on the tail in front of the tail fin and below the lateral line. A blue arc on the base of the pectoral fin.

Baillon's wrasse

◄

►
Corkwing wrasse

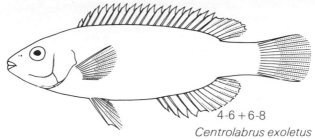

4-6 + 6-8

Centrolabrus exoletus
rock cook

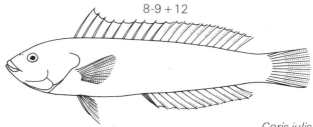

8-9 + 12

Coris julis
rainbow wrasse

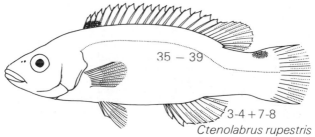

35 — 39

3-4 + 7-8

Ctenolabrus rupestris
goldsinny

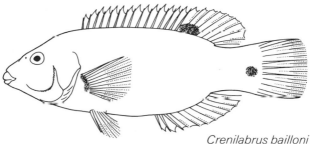

Crenilabrus bailloni
Baillon's wrasse

Size   Attains a length of 20 cm (7.9 in.).

Remarks   An excessively rare wrasse in northern European seas which has been recorded on very few occasions; it is not common even to the south, where it has been reported more frequently. It is believed to live near rocks covered with algae and in eel-grass beds, but its biology is virtually unknown.

Corkwing wrasse   *Crenilabrus melops*

Distinguishing features   A deep-bodied wrasse with large scales (32–36 in the lateral line) extending on to the head and cheeks, where there are several rows. It has 3 anal spines, 8–10 branched rays. Preoperculum edge serrated on rear and lower edges. Pelvic fins are long and reach almost to anus. Teeth in single series except in large specimens.

Coloration   Variable with habitat; usually green or greeny-brown, sometimes reddish. The males have bluish lines on the lower sides of the head and belly. Dusky, comma-shaped spot behind the eye, and a pupil-sized spot on the tail before the fin and on, or below the lateral line.

Size   Exceptionally reaches 25 cm (10 in.), usually around 15 cm (6 in.); may attain a weight of 453 g (1 lb).

Remarks   This is the most common of the smaller wrasses in northern European seas. It is particularly abundant among rocks, both between tide marks, where it is a common inhabitant of heavily weedy rock pools, and below tide level down to 30 m (16 fathoms); it is also found in eel-grass beds, especially when young. In winter it moves into deeper water. Its food is mainly molluscs and small crustaceans, but the young fish have been observed to act as cleaners. It builds a nest among algae in early summer, usually between rocks, guarded by the male. After hatching, however, the fry are planktonic and by the autumn have drifted inshore.

Weevers

A small family of marine fishes (Trachinidae) confined to the inshore waters of the eastern Atlantic from Norway to West Africa. Most species are small with a rather elongate body, a deep, compressed head and anterior body. The mouth is oblique, the eyes placed on top of the head, and the body scales lie in oblique rows. The habit of weevers is to bury themselves in sandy bottoms with only the eyes exposed. The first dorsal fin and the gill cover have venom glands at the bases of the spines, wounds from which are very painful and may be serious (due mainly to shock and secondary infections); they are not directly fatal.

Four species are known in European seas; only 2 occur in northern European waters.

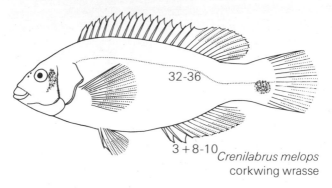

32-36

3 + 8-10 *Crenilabrus melops*
corkwing wrasse

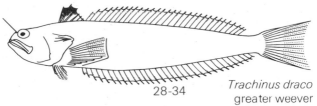

28-34

Trachinus draco
greater weever

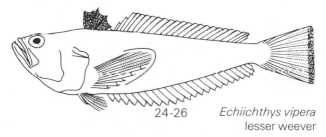

24-26

Echiichthys vipera
lesser weever

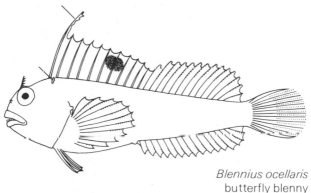

Blennius ocellaris
butterfly blenny

Greater weever   *Trachinus draco*

Distinguishing features   A slender-bodied species with a relatively small head. Short spines in front of and above each eye, and
pointing downwards above the front of the upper lip. Scales in
oblique rows on body; small scales on cheek. Pectoral fin outline
notched at upper edge. Second dorsal fin rays 29–32; anal rays 28–
34.

Coloration   Yellowish-brown above, lighter on the sides and
belly with characteristic dark streaks on sides following scale rows.
First dorsal fin partly heavily pigmented.

Size   Attains 41 cm (16 in.) in length.

Remarks   Like all members of the family, it is a bottom-living
fish which lies buried in the sandy sea-bed during daylight and
emerges to forage at night. It lives in relatively deep water of 30–
100 m (16–55 fathoms), but may be taken on occasions as shallow as
8 m (4½ fathoms). Because of its burrowing and preference for deep
water, it is not often caught in trawls and has been regarded as rare,
whereas it is probably fairly common, at least locally.

  It feeds almost entirely on bottom-living animals, particularly
crustaceans and fishes, the latter comprising sandeels, dragonets, and
gobies especially. It is landed and marketed as a food-fish on the
continent of Europe, and its flesh is rather well flavoured.

Lesser weever   *Echiichthys vipera*

Distinguishing features   A short-bodied weever, the head and
anterior body deep (depth more than a quarter of the length without
tail fin). The mouth is strongly oblique. No spines close to eyes or
above upper lip; no scales on cheek. Outline of pectoral fin
smoothly rounded. Second dorsal fin 21–24 rays; anal fin 24–26 rays.

Coloration   Yellow-brown on back (usually matches sand it is
living in), the sides and particularly the head with darker blotches;
lighter ventrally. First dorsal fin mostly black.

Size   Attains 14 cm (5½ in.) in length.

Remarks   The weever occurs in shallow water on clean sandy
bottoms from low-tide mark to 50 m (27 fathoms). It also occurs
between tide marks, moving on to the beach with the advancing
tide and retreating as the tide ebbs, and occasionally becoming

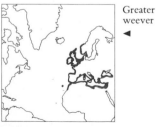

Greater
weever

◄

►

Lesser
weever

stranded in pools of water on the shore. It burrows in the sand, using its pelvic and pectoral fins which move the sand out from underneath, assisted by the water forced out of the gill chamber as the fish respires. When disturbed it tends to bury itself deeper, but also erects its dorsal fin spines which have venom-producing tissue along their underside. If trodden upon by a bather or paddler, the wound is at once extremely painful, with local swelling of the affected limb. Many weevers are caught in shrimp trawls, and stings from the gill cover and dorsal spines are a constant hazard when sorting the catch. The most widely recommended treatment is to soak the area of the wound in very hot water as soon as possible after the injury, as heat destroys the toxic quality of the venom.

The weever's food consists mainly of small bottom-living organisms, especially crustaceans such as amphipods and young brown shrimps, and fishes such as sandeels and gobies, and worms. It spawns in summer.

It has no value to fishermen or anglers, and its chief impact on man is in being one of very few dangerous fishes in European seas. It is locally abundant in some sandy areas, but by no means common elsewhere.

Blennies

A very large family (Blenniidae) of mainly small fishes found world-wide in temperate and tropical seas, with a few species living in freshwater. Many live in intertidal pools or under rocks on the shore; others are found in the shallow sea. Their life style is low-key, relying on obliterative coloration among algae and rocks; many breed in crevices in such situations. Their abundance, and the numerous species recognized illustrate their importance as members of the shallow sea community.

Blennies all have scaleless skins, numerous close-packed small teeth in the jaws, and two long rays in each pelvic fin, placed well-forward on the throat. Many species have small lappets of skin on the head. About 17 species are recognized in European seas, only 4 of which occur in northern Europe.

Butterfly blenny   *Blennius ocellaris*

Distinguishing features A rather stout-bodied blenny with a large eye. A flattened, bushy tentacle on the head above each eye; small fleshy flaps at the base of the first dorsal fin ray, and the upper edge of the pectoral fin. Dorsal fin rays very high, especially the first unbranched rays; fin deeply notched. (See also coloration.)

Coloration Greenish-brown, or warm brown with 5 to 7 darker bars running across back and sides; a conspicuous eye-spot on the dorsal fin, black with a pale blue to white encircling ring.

Size Attains a maximum length of 20 cm (8 in.).

Remarks The butterfly blenny is the only blenny to be found at any depth in European seas. It inhabits depths from 10–100 m (5½–55 fathoms), usually on shell bottoms or where the encrusting algae *Lithothamnion* is abundant. It also lives on sandy bottoms where it seeks shelter in empty mollusc shells and human debris such as broken pottery, crockery, cans, and hollow marrow bones. It breeds in spring and summer, the eggs being deposited in such hollow receptacles, or in rocky crevices, and are guarded by the male. The newly-hatched young are planktonic for a short while. The blenny feeds on small crustaceans, worms, and small fishes, but its diet has not been closely studied.

Tompot blenny   *Parablennius gattorugine*

Distinguishing features A stoutly-built blenny with a uniformly high dorsal fin, the anterior rays of which are stiff and spiny, and separated from the soft-rayed dorsal by a shallow notch. A flattened branched tentacle above each eye.

Coloration Yellowish-brown to medium-brown with 7 or more dark brown bars running across the sides. The eye is reddish-brown.

Size Attains 30 cm (11¾ in.); rarely exceeds 20 cm (8 in.).

Remarks The tompot is a common blenny in the immediately sub-tidal region in European seas. Small specimens are found occasionally in the lowest shore pools on rocky shores amongst kelp, but the adults are most common from 1–12 m (3–39 ft) below low-tide level. This fish favours rocky areas where it conceals itself on ledges or between stones. It spawns in mid-March to April, the eggs being deposited in a crevice and guarded by the male. Its food is composed principally of small crustaceans, but its diet has not been fully studied. It is occasionally caught in crab pots on the south and west coasts of the British Isles.

Shanny   *Lipophrys pholis*

Distinguishing features The only European blenny to lack a tentacle on the top of the head; the forehead is smoothly rounded except that in large fish a fleshy ridge develops in the mid-line. Dorsal fin uniform in height with unbranched and branched rays separated by a shallow notch.

Butterfly blenny

Tompot blenny

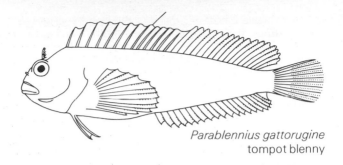

Parablennius gattorugine
tompot blenny

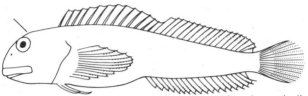

Lipophrys pholis
shanny

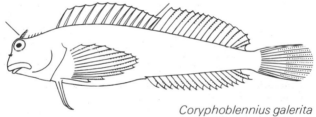

Coryphoblennius galerita
Montagu's blenny

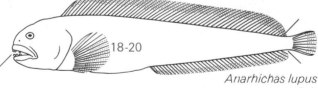

18-20

Anarhichas lupus
catfish

21-22

Anarhichas minor
spotted catfish

Coloration   Variable with habitat, usually dull brown, dark green, or greeny-grey, blotched indistinctly with darker colours; a dark spot between the first and second dorsal fin rays.

Size   Attains a length of 16 cm (6¼ in.).

Remarks   An extremely common shore fish which is very adaptable. Although it is most abundant on rocky coasts, it will colonize sandy and muddy pools provided they contain stones, or wood or metal pilings which allow green algae to grow. On rocky shores it can be found in pools or under stones from high-water neap-tide level down to extreme low water; it is most abundant from mid-tide level down. It occurs down to a depth of 30 m (16 fathoms).

It feeds on a wide range of smaller animals, most notably barnacles, small crabs and other crustaceans. The young fish specialize in nipping-off the limbs of barnacles when they are protruded in feeding movements, but also eat small amphipods and copepods. It spawns throughout spring and summer, and the eggs are laid on the underside of a large stone or the roof of a crevice. They are guarded and aerated (by fanning with the pectoral fins) by the male. Exceptionally the shanny may live for as long as 10 years.

Montagu's blenny   *Coryphoblennius galerita*

Distinguishing features   A small blenny with a characteristic fleshy flap across the forehead between the eyes; the free edge is fringed and a line of small fine tentacles runs along the centre line of the nape. A conspicuous notch between the unbranched and branched rays of the dorsal fin.

Coloration   Greeny-brown in background colour with darker markings and small blue-white spots on head and body. Adult males are strongly marked with these spots and have a yellow fringe to the crest on the head; the lip at the mouth corner is orange.

Size   Grows to a length of 8.5 cm (3½ in.).

Remarks   On the Atlantic coasts of Europe found on rocky shores in pools at around mid-tide level. It is particularly common in pools with little cover other than the coralline alga, *Corallina*, and the encrusting species, *Lithothamnion*. In the Mediterranean it is found in extremely shallow water, again close to rock faces. It feeds mainly on the encrusting barnacles which live on nearby rocks, and bites off

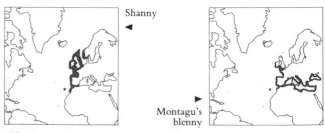

Shanny ◄

► Montagu's blenny

their appendages when they are extruded from their shell; it also eats small copepod crustaceans. It lays its eggs in crevices in the rock, usually on the ceiling, and they are guarded by the male. It spawns in July in British waters.

Catfishes or Wolf-Fishes

A small family (Anarhichidae) of marine fishes related to the blennies (and not to the true catfishes). They are confined to the temperate and boreal waters of the northern hemisphere. They are long-bodied, rather large fish which lack pelvic fins and have huge dog-like teeth in the front of the jaws and rounded crushing teeth in the sides and on the palate. They mostly live close to the sea-bed in moderately deep water on the lower continental shelf. Some species are fished for commercially and occasionally are caught by sport fishermen, but they are not much exploited for either purpose.

Three species occur in northern European seas.

Catfish *Anarhichas lupus*

Distinguishing features   Typical of the family, with long dorsal and anal fins (free of the tail fin in this species), huge head with strong teeth in the jaws. The length of the tail fin is twice the depth of the caudal peduncle; the pectoral fin is moderately large, its length about 3.5 times into the snout to anus distance. Pectoral fin with 18–20 rays. Teeth on the vomer (central row in the roof of the mouth) large, the length of the row considerably longer than that of the palatine teeth (either side of it also in the roof of the mouth). (See also coloration.)

Coloration   Body is brownish or bluish-grey with 9–12 darker cross-bars extending onto the dorsal fin.

Size   Grows to a maximum of 1.25 m (49¼ in.) and a weight of *c.* 12 kg (26 lb 7 oz); the majority of specimens caught today are less than 1 m (39½ in.).

Remarks   In the seas off Iceland, the Faroes, and Norway this fish is found in abundance and in relatively shallow water from 20–30 m down to 300 m (11–16 to 164 fathoms), and young ones even in immediately sub-tidal situations. To the south (as round the British Isles) it lives in 60–300 m (33–164 fathoms). It lives mostly on hard

Catfish

bottoms, sometimes on mud, and spawns in the winter, the eggs being deposited as a ball-like clump on the sea-bed. The larvae stay on the bottom until their yolk reserves are used up, then briefly are found in the mid to surface layers, but by late autumn are bottom-living. The adults feed on crabs, sea urchins, mussels, whelks, and scallops. It is a slow-growing fish which is quickly affected by heavy fishing.

Its flesh is well flavoured and firm, but this fish is not caught in great quantities. Its skin can be prepared as leather. This species is the one most frequently caught by anglers.

Spotted catfish   *Anarhichas minor*

Distinguishing features   Similar to the preceding species in general build with the tail fin long (twice the depth of the body before the fin) and pectoral fin length about 3 times into the snout to vent distance. In this species the dorsal fin ends in a series of low rays which continue up to the tail fin rays. Pectoral fin rays 21–22. Teeth on vomer (centre of the roof of mouth) rather arched or pointed, the row equal in length to the rows of palatine teeth either side of it. (See also coloration.)

Coloration   Yellowish-brown with numerous, distinct rounded spots on dorsal fin, back, and sides. Juveniles [up to 10 cm (4 in.)] have faint bars which break into spots with growth.

Size   Attains a maximum size of *c.* 135 cm (53 in.), but is rarely longer than 120 cm (47¼ in.); maximum weight up to 20 kg (44 lb 2 oz).

Remarks   This is an Arctic species which is found mainly in the cold deep water of the Norwegian Sea and the Barents Sea, and to some extent replaces the more southerly catfish. It lives at depths of 20 m (11 fathoms) in the northern parts of its range, down to *c.* 500 m (273 fathoms); it is most common between 100–200 m (55–109 fathoms). It feeds on sea urchins, brittlestars, crabs, and molluscs. Its breeding habits are similar to the preceding species except that the eggs are laid in deeper water, 110–250 m (60–137 fathoms).

This is the most important of the catfishes to the fishing industries of the USSR and other northern countries; its flesh is of good quality and the skin can be used for leather. It is, however, slow growing and stocks can quickly become exhausted.

Spotted catfish

Distinguishing features Typically catfish-like, but the body deeper and more gross than the other species, the head pointed, and the tissues soft and watery (feels jelly-like when handled). The pectoral fin is small, its length 4 or more times in snout to vent length; 20–22 pectoral rays. Length of the tail fin rays less than 2 times in the depth of the caudal peduncle. Teeth in row in centre of palate rounded or pointed, the length of the row less than the length of the rows of palatine teeth either side.

Coloration Dark greyish-brown or chocolate with faint, blurred markings forming obscure bars on sides.

Size Grows to 130 cm (51¼ in.) and a weight of 20 kg (44 lb 1 oz); usually around 90 cm (35½ in.) and up to 15 kg (33 lb 1 oz).

Remarks An Arctic form which is moderately common in the Norwegian Sea northwards, and is known from such areas as the Skaggerak and northern North Sea only from single occurrences. It lives mainly on soft bottoms of silty mud in depths of 60–970 m (33–530 fathoms), and feeds on crustaceans, sea urchins, and brittlestars. Its watery flesh means that it has little value as a food-fish, although it is caught in considerable quantities.

Three-Fin Blennies

A large family (Tripterygiidae) found mostly in tropical and warm temperate seas. Most are small fishes living close to the sea-bed in shallow water, usually among rocks and coral. They differ from blennies by possessing scales, from gobies by having two-rayed pelvic fins, and from both by having 3 separate dorsal fins; both groups occur in similar habitats.

Three species are found on the coasts of southern Europe; one other is known from northern Europe.

Black-face blenny *Tripterygion atlanticus*

Distinguishing features Characteristic among northern European fishes because it has 2-rayed pelvic fins, a body covered with rough-edged scales, and 3 dorsal fins. It is distinguished from its

Jelly cat

Mediterranean relatives by having 42–48 scales in the lateral line; anal rays 26 or 27; second dorsal rays 16–18; third dorsal rays 12–14. (See also coloration.)

Coloration   Pale brown with 5 oblique darker stripes across the body, head with dusky patches, yellowish ventrally. In the breeding season males are black anteriorly, extending back to include the pelvic fins, the pectoral fin base, and the first dorsal fin; the remainder of the body is deep yellow or orange with dusky bars.

Size   Grows to 6.8 cm (2¾ in.).

Remarks   This species was described only as recently as 1975 and was first found in 1972. It has so far been captured only in the English Channel, although it may also have been found off the northern Spanish Atlantic coast. It lives on the low shore among stones on fine gravel with algal covering, and occurs as deep as *c.* 20 m (11 fathoms). Its secretive nature and habit of hiding in crevices on rock faces and on wrecks are probably the reasons why it was not discovered earlier; it has been seen by divers on a number of occasions on the southern English coast.

Arctic Blennies

Representatives of 2 families of fishes found in the cooler seas of the northern hemisphere, and resembling blennies in certain features, are described together here as a matter of convenience. Both are particularly well represented in the North Pacific. Their members are long-bodied slender fishes with long-based, wholly spiny dorsal fins, and pelvic fins which are often reduced to small stumps, sometimes are moderately long, and at others are absent. Most species of these 2 families are inshore or shallow sea inhabitants. The butterfish (family Pholidae) is much more common than the 3 members of the family Stichaeidae.

Yarrell's blenny   *Chirolophis ascanii*

Distinguishing features   Long slender body, but rather deep anteriorly. The dorsal fin is composed entirely of fairly long spines; the pelvic fins are small and flap-like, nearly as long as a dorsal spine. A large fringed tentacle above each eye, smaller tentacles on the top of the head, and on the first dorsal fin spines.

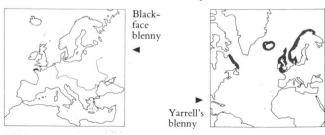

Black-face blenny ◀

Yarrell's blenny ▶

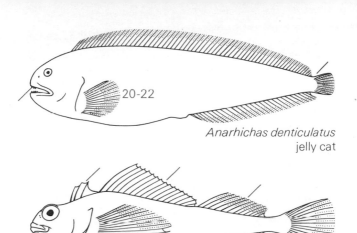

Anarhichas denticulatus
jelly cat

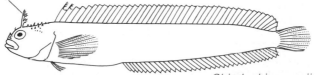

Tripterygion atlanticus
black-faced blenny

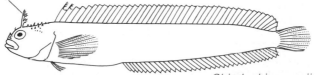

Chirolophis ascanii
Yarrell's blenny

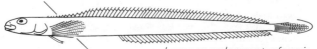

Lumpenus lampretaeformis
snake blenny

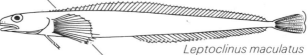

Leptoclinus maculatus
spotted snake blenny

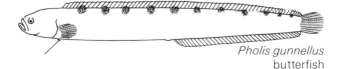

Pholis gunnellus
butterfish

Coloration Yellowish-brown with darker transverse bands forming double bars across the back; a dark ring around the eye continues across the cheek as a stripe.

Size Grows to 25 cm (10 in.).

Remarks A bottom-living species which is found in shallow water usually on rocky grounds within the seaweed zone, or below, to about 175 m (96 fathoms). It lives at a depth as shallow as 20 m (11 fathoms), but does not occur on the shoreline. It inhabits crevices in rocks and, in British waters at least, is more often caught in crab-pots and traps than in any other way. Its eggs are laid on the sea-bed (probably in crevices guarded by an adult—but this is not certain); the postlarvae are found in the plankton in May–June off Iceland, and January–April in the western Channel. Its food consists of benthic molluscs and worms, but has been little studied.

Owing to its habitat preferences and geographical range it is common only locally south of Scandinavia.

Snake blenny   *Lumpenus lampretaeformis*

Distinguishing features Very long slender body, almost eel-like, and with the tail fin long and pointed. The dorsal fin is long-based, the elements all spiny, those in front and at the end low. Pelvic fins longer than dorsal spines; pectoral fins rounded, all the rays enclosed in the fin membrane. Body in front of the anal fin shorter than the anal fin base.

Coloration Pale brown shading to blue on the sides, ventrally greenish-yellow; a series of irregular brown spots on sides.

Size Grows to 49 cm (19¼ in.) in length; rarely more than 25 cm (10 in.) in European waters.

Remarks A bottom-living fish found on muddy grounds in 30–200 m (16–109 fathoms), but most common between 40–100 m (22–55 fathoms). It is probable that this fish lives in burrows in the mud. Occasionally, as in late spring (in British waters) it has been caught in large numbers, but usually it is captured in small numbers only. It spawns in December and January on the bottom; postlarvae are pelagic and found mainly from February to April. Its food consists of small crustaceans, molluscs, brittlestars, and worms; it is eaten by both cod and halibut.

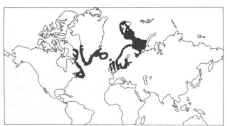

Snake blenny

Spotted snake blenny   *Leptoclinus maculatus*

Distinguishing features   Body moderately long but rather stouter than the preceding species. Dorsal fin entirely spiny, those in front distinctly low; pelvic fins long and slender, longer than the dorsal spines; pectoral fins long, the lower rays long with their tips free of the fin membrane; tail fin square cut. Snout to anal fin distance equal to anal fin base.

Coloration   Yellowish-brown with numerous brown spots; 5 darker large blotches on the back and upper sides.

Size   Attains a maximum length of 20 cm (8 in.), more usually up to 17 cm (6¾ in.).

Remarks   A northern species which is found on mud and stone bottoms, or gravelly ground in depths of 15–250 m (8–137 fathoms). The eggs are shed on the bottom in shallow water in winter; the postlarvae are pelagic and are found in June. This blenny is said to feed on worms and small crustaceans, and creep along the sea-bed using the free lower pectoral rays.

Butterfish   *Pholis gunnellus*

Distinguishing features   Long slender body, strongly flattened from side to side; head short, the lips fleshy. Dorsal fin long, running from the back of the head to the tail fin; anal fin about half the length of the dorsal; pelvic fins minute and spiny. (See also coloration.)

Coloration   Usually a warm brown, sometimes greenish, with indistinct vertical bars on sides, a dark stripe through the eye to the corner of the mouth. A row of white-ringed black spots along the base of the dorsal fin, 9–15 (usually about 12) in number.

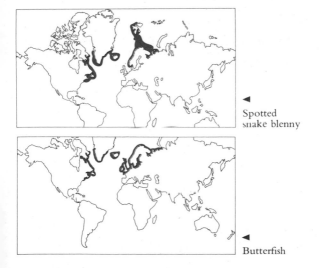

◄
Spotted
snake blenny

◄
Butterfish

Size   Attains 25 cm (10 in.) in length.

Remarks   A common fish on the seashore and below tide marks to *c.* 100 m (55 fathoms). It is found mainly on rocky shores from mid-tide level downwards and occurs in intertidal pools, under stones, and amongst loose algae. In deeper water it is common among rocks and on rough ground, but can be caught in trawls on mud and sand (presumably where loose stones and shells provide shelter). It spawns in January to February on the British coast, earlier further north, the eggs being laid in clumps between stones or inside shells on the shore and guarded by both parents, often by the female alone. The postlarvae are pelagic. The butterfish feeds on worms, small crustaceans, and molluscs. Because it is so abundant in littoral waters, it must play a large part in the food-chains of the area, but few observations are available on its predators. It is a frequent intermediate host of the sea-bird parasitic worm *Cryptocotyle*, which encysts to form black blisters in the skin.

Sandeels

A family (Ammodytidae) of rather small marine fishes, found mainly in the northern hemisphere and most abundantly in the North Atlantic. Relatively few species are known; 6 occur in European waters, of which 1 is confined to the Mediterranean. They are superficially similar, being slender-bodied with a sharply protuberant lower jaw, long dorsal and anal fins. They burrow in clean sand and shell grounds, but also swim actively in huge schools in mid-water. At all times of their lives they are preyed upon by other fishes and sea-birds, and as a group they play an important role in the food-webs of the shallow sea.

Sandeel   *Ammodytes tobianus*

Distinguishing features   A typical sandeel with long, slender body, long dorsal fin which slots into a groove, a rather shorter anal fin, small pectoral fins, a forked tail fin, and no pelvic fins. The upper jaw can be swung forwards to form an extended tube; no large teeth in the roof of the mouth. Lateral line pores open along the canal, not on branch canals; scales present on body and on the base of each tail fin lobe. 50–56 rays in the dorsal fin; 61–66 vertebrae.

Sandeel

Coloration Yellowish-green on the back, the sides are yellow, the belly silvery.

Size Grows to a maximum length of 20 cm (8 in.).

Remarks An extremely common inshore fish in northern European seas, living from about mid-tide level to depths of *c.* 30 m (16 fathoms). It is always found close to clean, rather fine sand in which it burrows with great rapidity, or swimming over the sand often in a head-down posture. Two spawning races are recognized, spring spawners and autumn spawners, which are locally dominant in any one place, but have been found in several parts of their range. Both races deposit their eggs in the sand and these stick to the sand grains. It is an extremely important food-fish to a wide variety of other fishes, e.g. mackerel, herring, gadoid fishes in general, and bass, and sea-birds. It is a popular bait-fish for anglers. Large quantities are also captured for reduction to fish meal.

Raitt's sandeel   *Ammodytes marinus*

Distinguishing features Virtually identical with the preceding species, having a freely protrusible upper jaw, and no 'teeth' in the roof of the mouth. It differs in having the belly scales in irregular rows and having no scales on the base of the tail fin lobes. Dorsal rays 55–67; vertebrae 66–72.

Coloration Greeny-blue on the back, the sides bluish fading to silver which continues onto the belly.

Size Grows to 24 cm (9½ in.).

Remarks An extremely abundant offshore species which usually lives in depths of 30–150 m (16–82 fathoms). It is also occasionally found in inshore waters, even in river mouths. It burrows in sand and fine gravel, and also swims in large schools in mid-winter. Its food consists mainly of planktonic crustaceans, fish larvae, and worms; in turn it is eaten by other fishes as well as sea-birds. It lives for up to 5 years, and spawns in winter (January to March) in the English Channel, later further north.

Smooth sandeel   *Gymnammodytes semisquamatus*

Distinguishing features Closely similar to the preceding species with a protrusible upper jaw, and no 'teeth' in the palate. The lateral

Raitt's sandeel

line has short canals branching above and below the main canal (typically 2 above for every 3 below). Body scaleless except on the posterior half. A short groove below the pectoral fin is only a little longer than that fin. Dorsal rays 56–59; anal rays 28–32; vertebrae 65–70.

Coloration Greenish-brown above, even golden on the back, the sides yellowish, and the belly silvery.

Size Attains 23.5 cm (9¼ in.).

Remarks This is one of the less well-known sandeels of northern Europe and is also more southerly in its distribution. It usually lives in offshore areas in depths of 20–200 m (11–109 fathoms), over coarse sand or shell gravel. Its distribution is rather local on account of this preference. It spawns in winter (English Channel) and March–August (North Sea), the eggs being laid among the shell gravel. It feeds in mid-water on copepods, planktonic crustaceans, and fishes. It lives for up to 5 years.

Greater sandeel   *Hyperoplus lanceolatus*

Distinguishing features Elongate and slender-bodied like all the sandeels, but this species does not have a protrusible upper jaw, and in the roof of the mouth it has a pair of conspicuous teeth. Scales present over the body but not on the head; lateral line not branched. A shallow fold of skin on each side of the belly reaches back to the first third of the anal fin. Dorsal 52–61 rays; anal 28–33 rays; vertebrae 65–69. (See also coloration.)

Coloration Back and upper sides bluish-green, the belly silvery-white; a distinct black blotch on the side of the snout.

Size Grows to 32 cm (12½ in.).

Remarks An inshore sandeel which is found from low-tide level (young specimens) down to *c*. 150 m (82 fathoms), on sandy bottoms. It breeds during spring and summer in 20–100 m (11–55 fathoms), the eggs being shed in sand, although the larvae and postlarvae are pelagic. It feeds on a wide range of planktonic crustaceans, fish eggs and larvae, but as it grows it eats larger crustaceans and fishes, including the other sandeel species. This is the largest species of sandeel known, and although it is not so abundant as the smaller species it is quite common. Like the others, it is preyed upon by numbers of larger fishes and even small cetaceans.

Smooth sandeel ◄

► Greater sandeel

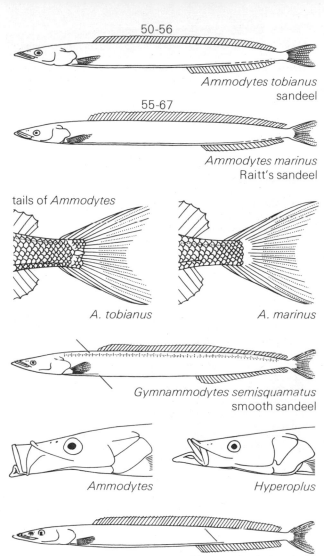

50-56

Ammodytes tobianus
sandeel

55-67

Ammodytes marinus
Raitt's sandeel

tails of *Ammodytes*

A. tobianus

A. marinus

Gymnammodytes semisquamatus
smooth sandeel

Ammodytes

Hyperoplus

Hyperoplus lanceolatus
greater sandeel

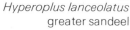

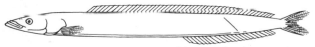

Hyperoplus immaculatus
Corbin's sandeel

Corbin's sandeel · *Hyperoplus immaculatus*

Distinguishing features A large sandeel closely similar to the preceding species and sharing its features of a non-protrusible upper jaw and a pair of large teeth in the upper jaw. A shallow fold of skin along the lower sides of the belly is interrupted, but runs to the tail fin. Dorsal fin rays 59–61; anal fin rays 31–34; vertebrae 70–74.

Coloration Back and sides dark bluish-green, the belly white or silvery. The snout is uniformly dark with no pronounced dark spot.

Size Attains 30 cm (11¾ in.).

Remarks An offshore large sandeel which lives on coarse sand or shell-gravel bottoms. Its depth range is from *c.* 50–300 m (27–164 fathoms), although young specimens are occasionally captured in much shallower water. It spawns in winter and spring, and the larvae and postlarvae are found in the plankton mainly in May (off western Scotland) and January to March (English Channel). The biology of this fish is relatively little known.

Dragonets

A small family (Callionymiidae) of marine fishes found mostly in shallow inshore waters, although a few are found on the lower continental shelf. All are rather flattened from above, their heads being almost triangular, with broad expanded pelvic fins, and a restricted gill opening on the top of the head. This is associated with the life style of many of them, as they lie buried in the sea-bed with just the top of the head and back exposed. Dragonet males are brilliantly coloured, especially in the spawning season, and spawning is accompanied with quite elaborate courtship displays.

Dragonets are widely distributed in tropical and warm temperate seas, but become more sparse in cool temperate waters. Six species occur in European seas, but only 3 live in the northern area.

Dragonet · *Callionymus lyra*

Distinguishing features The largest, most abundant dragonet. The body is flattened above and below, the tail rounded in cross-

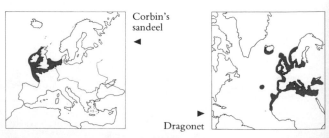

Corbin's
sandeel
◄

►
Dragonet

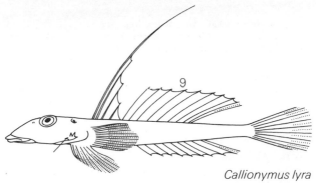

Callionymus lyra
dragonet ♂

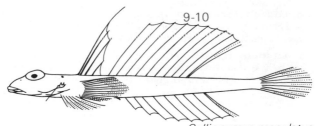

Callionymus lyra
dragonet ♀

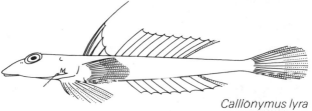

Callionymus maculatus
spotted dragonet ♂

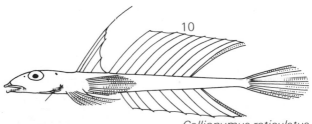

Callionymus reticulatus
reticulated dragonet ♂

section; head large, the snout long. Four sharp spines on the preoperculum, the first one pointing forwards, the other 3 pointing backwards or upwards. Second dorsal fin with 9 rays. (See also coloration.)

Coloration Females and immature males pale brown above with a series of 6 brown blotches on the sides and 3 conspicuous saddles across the back; the dorsal fins are not very high. Males have enormously long dorsal fin rays and a long tail fin, the membrane yellow with greeny-blue stripes. The head and body are yellowish to brown with numerous blue stripes and blotches.

Size Males attain 30 cm (11¾ in.), females 20 cm (8 in.) in length.

Remarks The dragonet is extremely common in certain areas, particularly over sandy or muddy bottoms and in depths of 20–100 m (11–55 fathoms), extending downwards as far as 200 m (109 fathoms). Its food consists of polychaete worms, small crustaceans, and molluscs. Spawning takes place in February to March, continuing on the west coast of Ireland into June, and is preceded by elaborate display of the colourful fins by the male. The eggs and postlarvae are pelagic. Males live for up to 5 years, females a little longer.

Spotted dragonet   *Callionymus maculatus*

Distinguishing features Similar to the preceding species but smaller, living in deeper water, and differently coloured. Its body is compressed anteriorly, rounded in cross-section at the tail. The preopercular bone has 4 sharp points, the lower being rather small, and pointing forwards, the other 3 all pointing upwards. Nine to 10 rays in the second dorsal fin. (See also coloration.)

Coloration Females and young males are brownish-yellow on the back with 2 rows of conspicuous brown spots on the sides and scattered smaller blue spots. Four dark brown saddles across the back are distinct but with irregular margins. Males are similarly coloured but have very high dorsal fins and a longer tail fin; the former has 4 rows of conspicuous dark-centred spots interspersed with pale, blue-white spots.

Size Males attain 14 cm (5½ in.), females 11 cm (4¼ in.) in length.

Remarks A deeper water species than the preceding one, it is most

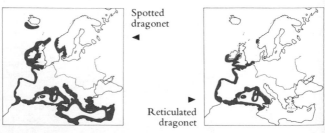

Spotted
dragonet

Reticulated
dragonet

abundant from 70–300 m (38–164 fathoms), usually on sandy grounds. It is an inhabitant of the offshore banks rather than close inshore. It breeds from April to June; the eggs and larvae are pelagic, but are found over deeper water than those of *C. lyra*. Its biology is virtually unknown.

Reticulated dragonet	*Callionymus reticulatus*

Distinguishing features Typical of other members of the family, but has only 3 spines on the preoperculum, all 3 pointing back and upwards; no spine at the base. Second dorsal with 10 rays.

Coloration Females and young males are orange-brown on the back, creamy-white below. Males are the same colour but have dark-centred rounded spots and dark-margined, blue-white wavy lines and spots on the dorsal fins. Both sexes have pale blue spots on the sides and sharply defined dark-edged brown saddles across the back.

Size Males grow to *c.* 10 cm (4 in.), females to 8 cm ($3\frac{1}{4}$ in.).

Remarks Locally distributed and relatively uncommon in northern waters, and living on clean sandy bottoms from the low shore to *c.* 40 m (22 fathoms). It is believed to spawn between April and September in the English Channel. The postlarvae occur there in the plankton from May to September. Its biology is virtually unknown, but in the North Sea considerable numbers are eaten by the tub gurnard.

Gobies

The gobies represent one of the most successful families (Gobiidae) of bony fishes in terms of number of species known. They are abundant in temperate and tropical seas in inshore waters, and many species are found in estuarine conditions and in freshwater. They are typically small fishes [the largest grows to a length of 27 cm ($10\frac{1}{2}$ in.)], rather elongate, but with a broad head and cylindrical front part of the body; the cheeks and lips are swollen and the eyes large and close together. They have 2 dorsal fins (the first with 6 stiff rays in most species), a single anal fin, and a rounded, large tail fin; the pectoral fins are large, and the pelvic fins are fused to form a broad palm-like disc which has a weak adhesive power and enables the fish to cling to the substrata in still or slow-moving water. They have scales with toothed edges on the body, but do not possess a lateral line on the body; instead they have sensory pores in characteristic rows on the head.

Gobies are difficult to identify, especially as there are 18 species known from nothern European waters. Their identification is simplified by a knowledge of their habitat and life style, and for convenience they are divided into several groups under habitat headings and size attained.

Large gobies—12 cm (4¾ in.) or more in length:

    living on rocky shores   *Gobius cobitis, G. paganellus*

    living in inshore waters
      —on mud or sand   *G. niger*
      —on rocks   *G. cruentatus, Thorogobius ephippiatus*

Medium gobies—7–11 cm (2¾–4¼ in.):

    living on stony shores
      and inshore   *Gobius couchi*

    living offshore below
      15 m (50 ft)   *G. gasteveni, Buenia jeffreysii, Lesuerigobius friesii*

Small gobies—less than 8 cm (3¼ in.);

    pelagic   *Aphia minuta, Crystallogobius linearis*

    living on or close to
      shore   *Gobiusculus flavescens, Pomatoschistus microps, P. pictus, P. minutus*

    living offshore in *c.* 30 m
      (100 ft)   *P. norvegicus, Lebetus* spp.

Giant goby   *Gobius cobitis*

Distinguishing features   A large goby with a large head and deep caudal peduncle. The space between the end of the dorsal fin and beginning of tail fin about two-thirds the head length. Pelvic fin with distinct lobes at the edges of the membrane; pectoral fin with free upper rays; scales between pectoral fin base and tail fin 59–67; nape scaly but scales do not extend to eye edge. Anterior nostril with several finger-like processes.

Coloration   Brownish-olive, or greyish, with 'pepper and salt' speckling and rounded blotches on sides; ventrally cream; narrow light edges to the dorsal, anal, and tail fins.

Size   Grows to 27 cm (10½ in.).

Remarks   This is the largest goby in European seas, but its distribution is very restricted in northern seas. In the Channel it is found in rocky shore pools from extreme high-water level down to mid-tide level, often in pools where salinity is low owing to freshwater run-off. It prefers pools with bare rock bottoms, or those where loose rocks are exposed on the bottom and which contain green filamentous algae. It feeds extensively on this algae, but also eats crustaceans, particularly gammarids and shore crabs.

Rock goby   *Gobius paganellus*

Distinguishing features   Moderately large with body deep in front of the tail fin and caudal peduncle (end of second dorsal to tail fin distance) about half head length. Anterior membrane of pelvic

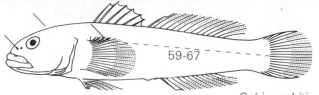

Gobius cobitis
giant goby

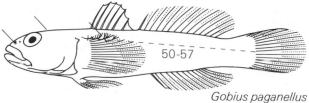

Gobius paganellus
rock goby

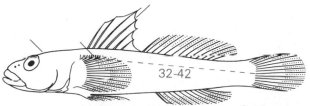

Gobius niger
black goby

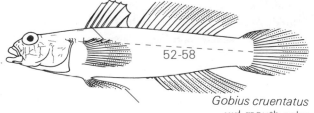

Gobius cruentatus
red-mouth goby

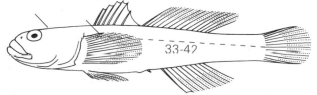

Thorogobius ephippiatus
leopard-spotted goby

fin well developed, no lateral lobes or at most weak lobes; pectoral fin with the upper rays free, much divided, and reaching back nearly to the level of the dorsal origin. Scales between pectoral fin base and tail fin 50–57. Nape scaly, scales extending forward to the edge of the eyes. Anterior nostril with 5 or 6 finger-like branches.

Coloration   Brown with darker mottling and lateral blotches; upper part of first dorsal fin with pale edge. Adult males deep purple-brown, first dorsal fin with conspicuous orange band.

Size   Grows to 12 cm (4¾ in.).

Remarks   Confined to rocky habitats and best known on rocky shores, where it lives in pools or under stones with dense algal cover, mainly from mid-tide level and below, and continuing downwards to 15 m (49 ft). Like other gobies it spawns in crevices or under loose rocks, the eggs being attached to the roof in a close-packed, single layer. Breeding takes place from April to June in northern European waters. It feeds on a wide range of smaller animals, particularly small crustaceans, young fishes, and a little algae. It may live for up to 10 years.

Black goby   *Gobius niger*

Distinguishing features   A stout-bodied goby with the tail in front of the fin deep and the caudal peduncle short (less than two-thirds head length). Scales large, 32–42 in a series between pectoral fin and tail. Anterior membrane of pelvic fin well developed but with no lobes either side; upper pectoral fin with short, free rays. Nape scaly. Anterior nostril with a simple flap on the rim. First dorsal fin rays elongate in adults, particularly so in males.

Coloration   Variable with habitat and maturity; usually medium to dark brown with darker blotches on back and sides. Underside of head dark.

Size   Attains a maximum length of 17 cm (6¾ in.).

Remarks   Widely distributed, living on muddy and sandy bottoms, especially in eel-grass beds from 2 to *c.* 70 m (1–38 fathoms). The black goby is particularly common in estuaries and low salinity areas such as the Baltic Sea and coastal lagoons. It feeds primarily on small crustaceans, including small shore crabs, small molluscs, worms, and some small fishes. It spawns from May to August, the eggs being laid inside a cavity, such as under loose

Giant goby ◄

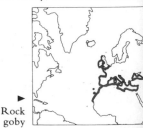

► Rock goby

rocks, roofing tiles, or the shells of the larger molluscs. As with other gobies the eggs are elongate and laid in a dense patch in a single layer; they are guarded by the male.

Red-mouth goby   *Gobius cruentatus*

Distinguishing features   A stout-bodied goby with a deep caudal peduncle, the length of which (last dorsal ray to the origin of the tail fin) is about two-thirds of the head length. Anterior membrane of pelvic fin well developed but without lobes at the sides, rear margin of the pelvic disc slightly concave; upper rays of pectoral fin free. Scales 52–58 in series between pectoral fin base and tail fin; scales present on nape, upper part of gill cover, and rear part of cheek. Anterior nostril with a simple tentacle. (See also coloration.)

Coloration   Warm brown, almost reddish with darker blotches on sides; lips and cheeks with vivid red markings. Lines of black papillae on head.

Size   Attains 18 cm (7 in.) in total length.

Remarks   An exceedingly rare goby in northern waters which was first discovered in 1968 among museum specimens collected in the 1930s. A third specimen was collected in 1960, and another, probably this species, was seen more recently. All were caught in the Republic of Ireland, in shallow inshore water. In the Mediterranean, this fish lives on stones and sandy ground amongst eel-grass. Captures of further Atlantic specimens would be of the greatest interest.

Leopard-spotted goby   *Thorogobius ephippiatus*

Distinguishing features   A relatively slender goby with a rather deep but long caudal peduncle (distance between last ray of second dorsal and tail fin equals head). Anterior membrane of pelvic fins well developed but with no lateral lobes; no free rays on upper edge of pectoral fin. Scales 33–42 in series from pectoral base to tail fin; no scales on head, nape, or anterior to dorsal fin. Anterior nostril with a raised rim but no flap or tentacle.

Coloration   Pale fawn with conspicuous orange to brick-red blotches on head and body, and a black spot near the edge of the first

Black goby ◄

► Red-mouth goby

dorsal fin. Breeding males are dark with a conspicuous light edge to the second dorsal fin.

Size   Attains a maximum length of 13 cm (5 in.).

Remarks   This species has a wide distribution but was very difficult to capture before the use of scuba diving equipment became widespread. As a result, it is little known. It lives from 6–40 m (20–131 ft) below the surface, in vertical rock faces, hiding in crevices in the rock. Very rarely it is found in deep rock pools near low-water level. It spawns from May to July in the Channel. Its food comprises mainly amphipod crustaceans and polychaete worms. This species was formerly known as *Gobius forsteri*.

Couch's goby   *Gobius couchi*

Distinguishing features   A moderately elongate goby with a deep caudal peduncle, the length of which is about two-thirds of the head; head large, cheeks and lips protuberant. Scales large, 35–45 in line from pectoral fin base to tail; scales on nape and on upper edge of gill cover but not on cheek. Uppermost pectoral rays free at tips for up to one-quarter of their length; pelvic fins with well-developed anterior membrane, but not lobed at sides. Anterior nostril with a triangular flap of skin. (See also coloration.)

Coloration   Fawn-brown or grey with coarse reticulations on the back; paler on sides with yellow or gold flecks and 7–9 dark brown blotches on the sides; a dark brown or black spot at the upper rays of the pectoral fin near the base with a pale rear border.

Size   Probably attains 8 cm (3¼ in.).

Remarks   A recently described species (1974) which is so far known only from Helford, Cornwall, and Lough Ine, Co. Cork. At Helford it lives in small pools of water beneath flat stones or among green and red seaweeds growing on pebbles on the low shore at extreme low-tide level. It is presumed to live in deeper water below low-water mark also. Its food is composed of polychaete worms, small crustaceans, molluscs, and algae. This fish is estimated to live for up to 6 years, but much of its life history is, as yet, unknown.

Steven's goby   *Gobius gasteveni*

Distinguishing features   Rather elongate, but caudal peduncle

Leopard-spotted goby ◀

► Couch's goby

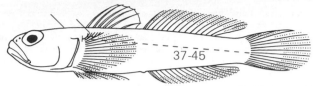

Gobius couchi
Couch's goby

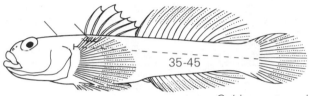

Gobius gasteveni
Steven's goby

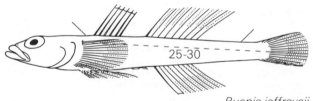

Buenia jeffreysii
Jeffreys's goby

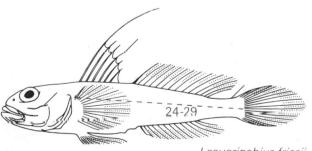

Lesuerigobius friesii
Fries's goby

compressed and deep, shorter (last dorsal fin ray base to tail fin ray base) than two-thirds of head length. Scales large, 37–45 in a row between the base of the pectoral fin and the tail; scales extend onto nape and a few on the upper edge of the gill cover; cheeks are naked. The 2 top rays in the pectoral fin divided and free at their tips for about a quarter of their length; pelvic fin disc with an anterior margin, but with no lateral lobes, posterior edge rounded or concave. Anterior nostril with a thin, finger-like lobe.

Coloration   Pale grey above, white below with a series of lateral reddish-brown blotches, white spots on cheek and gill cover, on the latter set in orange. A conspicuous dark, triangular spot on the pectoral fin at the bases of the upper rays.

Size   Attains 12 cm ($4\frac{3}{4}$ in.) in length, but rarely exceeds 10 cm (4 in.).

Remarks   An offshore goby which has been found in the English Channel at about 36–74 m (20–40 fathoms). It is known only from the Channel and off Madeira, but may be expected to occur both between these localities in suitable depths, and possibly in the Mediterranean also. It has been captured on bottoms described as muddy sand, and shell and small stones. It was formerly confused with the Mediterranean species *Gobius auratus*.

Jeffreys's goby   *Buenia jeffreysii*

Distinguishing features   A rather slender-bodied goby with a narrow caudal peduncle, its length (last dorsal ray to tail fin rays) almost equal to head length. Pelvic fin has anterior membrane with no lateral lobes; upper pectoral fin rays not free of membrane or much branched. Scales large, 25–30 in series from pectoral fin base to tail fin origin, none on nape. Anterior nostril with a raised rim but no lobe. Cheeks without vertical rows of sensory papillae.

Coloration   Pale browny-grey with coarse reticulation flecked with rusty brown dots, paler saddles across back opposite dusky spots on sides. Dorsal fins with dusky spots.

Size   Attains at least 6 cm ($2\frac{1}{2}$ in.).

Remarks   A little-known offshore goby which has been captured in isolated areas on the Atlantic coasts of northern Europe in 10–330 m ($5\frac{1}{2}$–108 fathoms) on sand, mud, shell-gravel, and gravelly bottoms. It breeds from March to August. The eggs have been

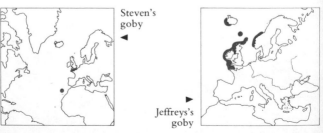

Steven's goby ◄

► Jeffreys's goby

found in mollusc shells and are no doubt guarded by the male as in other gobies.

Fries's goby   *Lesuerigobius friesii*

Distinguishing features A stout-bodied goby with a moderately slender but short caudal peduncle. The first dorsal fin rays are elongate, the tail fin is pointed; no free pectoral fin rays; pelvic fins form a disc with an anterior membrane but without lateral lobes. Scales large, 24–29 in a series from the pectoral fin base to the tail fin; nape covered with scales. Papillae on head large and conspicuous. (See also coloration.)

Coloration Pale fawn or grey with conspicuous golden yellow blotches on head, body, dorsal, and tail fins.

Size Grows to a length of 11 cm (4¼ in.).

Remarks A bottom-living goby found in moderately deep water in 20–350 m (11–191 fathoms), although possibly most abundant between 40–150 m (22–82 fathoms). In places this goby has been observed to live in association with the Norway lobster, *Nephrops norvegicus*, in whose burrows the goby conceals itself. As the fish has been captured elsewhere where the crustacean is common, it is probable that the association is widespread. The goby appears to act as a watchdog for the crustacean, but the precise relationship and much of the fish's biology, is not known.

Transparent goby   *Aphia minuta*

Distinguishing features Slender-bodied, and compressed from side to side; eyes lateral. Pelvic fin disc well developed with anterior membrane; pectoral fins with no free rays at top. Mouth large and oblique. Scales large, 24–25 in row on side, but very fragile and easily lost. Body completely transparent except for pigmented eyes, silvery swim-bladder, and gut.

Coloration Colourless; minute speckles of pigment on head, dorsal and anal fins.

Size Males grow to 5.1 cm (2 in.); females to 4.6 cm (1¾ in.). Males have larger, higher fins and larger teeth than females.

Remarks This little fish is pelagic in inshore waters from the surface down to a depth of *c.* 60 m (33 fathoms). It lives in huge

Fries's goby ◄

► Transparent goby

schools, but on occasions may be found in groups of 30–50. It occurs over a variety of sea-beds, sand, mud, and also in estuaries. Its food consists of small planktonic organisms, especially the larvae of crustaceans and molluscs. Despite its normally near-surface life style, it breeds on the sea-bed from May to August when each female lays up to 2000 eggs in an empty bivalve shell. Adults die soon after spawning, at an age of 1 year plus.

The transparent goby is common in most of northern Europe's seas, but owing to its small size and pelagic life is not often captured.

Crystal goby   *Crystallogobius linearis*

Distinguishing features Totally transparent except for the eye and a few dark points on chin, and the bases of the fins. Body slender and compressed; eyes lateral; pectoral fin normal with no free tips to the upper rays; pelvic fin a deep funnel in males, rudimentary or absent in females. Mouth strongly oblique; male with larger jaws and canines in lower jaw, female with smaller mouth and teeth. Scales absent.

Coloration See above.

Size Males have 2 rays in the first dorsal fin and attain 4.7 cm (2 in.); females usually lack a first dorsal fin and grow to 3.9 cm (1½ in.).

Remarks A surface-living fish in offshore waters over depths of between 20–80 m (11–44 fathoms), exceptionally as shallow as 5 m (3 fathoms) and as deep as 400 m (219 fathoms). On the Atlantic coasts of northern Europe it is seasonally extremely abundant; literally thousands can be taken in a single short haul of a fine-meshed net. It feeds on plankton.

It breeds from May to August on the sea-bed, the eggs being laid in the empty tubes of large worms such as *Chaetopterus* in *c.* 30 m (16 fathoms). The males guard the developing eggs, but the larvae live in the plankton soon after hatching. Its total life span only just exceeds 1 year.

Two-spotted goby   *Gobiusculus flavescens*

Distinguishing features A rather slender-bodied goby, compressed from side to side; eyes lateral, widely spaced. Pelvic fin with an anterior membrane, pectoral fins without branched upper rays.

Crystal
goby

◄

►

Two-spotted
goby

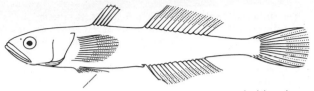

Aphia minuta
transparent goby

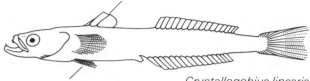

Crystallogobius linearis
crystal goby ♂

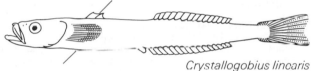

Crystallogobius lincaris
crystal goby ♀

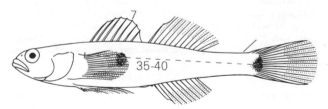

Gobiusculus flavescens
two-spotted goby

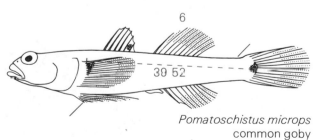

Pomatoschistus microps
common goby

The tail, between the end of the dorsal rays and the tail fin, is long and slender, almost as long as the head. Seven rays in the first dorsal fin. Scales 35–40 in lateral series. (See also coloration and remarks on habitat.)

Coloration   Body reddish-brown with darker reticulations and a series of pale saddles along the nape and back, the sides with alternate black and pale blue marks. A highly characteristic large black spot with a pale edge at the tail fin base; males have a similar spot on the side, beneath the first dorsal fin.

Size   Attains 6 cm ($2\frac{1}{2}$ in.).

Remarks   An active, inshore goby which lives in small schools adjacent to algae from near the surface down to depths of 15 m (8 fathoms). It is relatively common in rock pools on the shore where larger brown algae grow. It also lives amongst eel-grass. It is semi-pelagic in its life style, except when breeding from May to July, when males are guarding the eggs laid in the hollow holdfasts of the brown algae. It feeds on planktonic organisms, especially crustacean and mollusc larvae and copepods.

Common goby

Pomatoschistus microps

Distinguishing features   A moderately stout, small goby with a rather long tail (last dorsal ray to tail fin distance nearly equals head). Pelvic fin with an anterior membrane smooth-edged, without minute projections. Six rays in the first dorsal fin. Scales moderate in size, 39–52 in a lateral series; no scales present on head, nape, or breast.

Coloration   Light grey to sandy fawn with reticulations of fine dots and faint pale saddles across the back. Dusky marks on sides which, near the tail fin base, are conspicuous, as is the triangular mark on the pectoral base. Males have a dark spot on the rear of the first dorsal fin membrane, dark thin bars across the sides and a dusky throat.

Size   Attains a length of 6.4 cm ($2\frac{1}{2}$ in.).

Remarks   An abundant small goby which is found close inshore in intertidal pools, in estuaries, and slightly brackish drainage ditches and rivers. It is particularly common on muddy, marshy shores, but is also found in high shore pools on sand. In winter most migrate into deeper water. It spawns from April to August, the eggs being

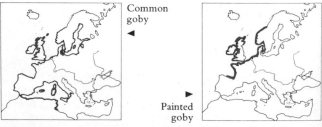

Common goby ◄

► Painted goby

laid on the hollow surface of an overturned bivalve shell such as a cockle or a clam. Several broods of eggs are produced by each female, each guarded within the shell by the male. By the end of the breeding season sheltered saltings pools will contain thousands of small gobies. It feeds mainly on small crustaceans and their larvae. By its very abundance it must be an important link in the food-chains of the muddy and sandy littoral zone, but there is little information available on its predators.

Painted goby
Pomatoschistus pictus

Distinguishing features   A relatively stout-bodied small goby with a moderately long caudal peduncle, nearly as long as the head. Pelvic disc well developed with an anterior membrane which is smooth edged. Six rays in the first dorsal fin. Scales large, 36–43 in a lateral series, none on head or nape. (See also coloration.)

Coloration   Warm brown to fawn with a network of darker spots on the scale edges, a line of 4 double dark spots along the sides and large paler saddles on the back reaching down the side. Dorsal fins with a row of black spots with orange banding across the fin membranes. Males are more brightly coloured.

Size   Attains 9.5 cm (3¾ in.), usually only around 6 cm (2½ in.).

Remarks   A moderately common goby in northern European seas which is rather restricted by its choice of habitat. It is found in inshore waters from around low-tide mark down to a depth of 50 m (27 fathoms), but mainly on gravel, shell, or coarse sand mixed with shells and stones. It occurs also on sand in close proximity to rocks, and in eel-grass beds. Occasionally found in intertidal pools with stony bottoms. It does not enter estuaries.

It breeds from April to July, the eggs being laid in a bivalve mollusc shell and guarded by the male. Newly-hatched larvae are *c.* 3 mm long and are pelagic until they reach a length of *c.* 12 mm.

Sand goby
Pomatoschistus minutus

Distinguishing features   A relatively slender goby with a long caudal peduncle, nearly as long as the head. The pectoral fins are rounded, their upper rays not free of the fin membrane. The pelvic disc and anterior membrane is complete; the latter is edged with small villi (short finger-like processes). First dorsal fin usually with 6 rays. Scales small, 58–70 in a lateral series (pectoral base to tail), scales present on the nape and on the breast.

Coloration   A light sandy-brown with a fine network of dark dots and faint saddles across the back. Males have a conspicuous dark blue to black, white-rimmed spot on the posterior edge of the first dorsal fin and 4 narrow dark cross-bars.

Size   Attains 9.5 cm (3¾ in.), usually only around 6 cm (2½ in.).

Remarks   An extremely common goby on inshore sandy grounds from about mid-tide level to 20 m (11 fathoms). It is possibly most common in depths of 30 cm (12 in.) below low-tide level down to 10 m (5½ fathoms), and is caught in great quantity by shrimp nets and trawls. It enters the mouth of estuaries, but is rarely found in low salinity water. It moves into deeper water in winter. It breeds from March to July, the female laying her eggs in empty bivalve shells where they are guarded by the male. After hatching, the young are pelagic until they reach a length of *c.* 17 mm. Few specimens live longer than one year. Its food is composed mainly of small crustaceans, particularly copepods, amphipods, and young brown shrimps. It is preyed upon by a number of bottom-living fishes, especially the bull-rout, codling, pouting, and even bass. It is also taken by terns.

Norway goby   *Pomatoschistus norvegicus*

Distinguishing features   Closely similar to the preceding species, but lives in deeper water. Scales small, 55–58 in a lateral series, no scales on the nape or the throat. Second dorsal fin with 8–10 branched rays; anal fin with 8–10 branched rays.

Coloration   Pale sandy-brown with fine reticulation of dark dots and dusky spots on sides. Males have 5 to 6 very narrow dark vertical bars on the sides.

Size   Attains a maximum length of 6.5 cm (2½ in.).

Remarks   The Norway goby has often been confused with the sand goby which it closely resembles. It lives in deeper water, however, from 30–280 m (16–153 fathoms), being most abundant in northern European waters between 50–120 m (27–66 fathoms). It is usually found on coarse sand and muddy bottoms, less often on shell. Its biology has been little studied.

Another similar species of goby, *Pomatoschistus lozanoi*, has been recognized in the North Sea and elsewhere. Both physically and in depth distribution it falls between the Norway goby and the sand goby. Its certain identification can be established only by study of the sensory papillae on the cheeks.

Diminutive goby   *Lebetus scorpioides*

Distinguishing features   A very small but relatively stout-bodied goby which is set apart by the pelvic fin disc lacking an anterior margin, while the posterior end is concave. The dorsal fins

Sand goby

Norway goby

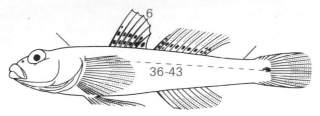

Pomatoschistus pictus
painted goby

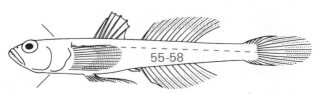

Pomatoschistus minutus
sand goby

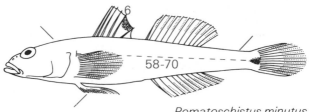

Pomatoschistus norvegicus
Norway goby

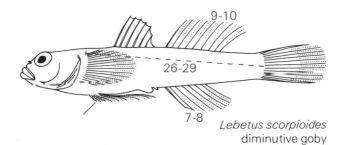

Lebetus scorpioides
diminutive goby

are high, but short-based, second dorsal fin with 9–10 full length rays; anal fin with 7–8 full length rays. Scales large, 26–29 in a lateral series from pectoral fin base to tail fin base; no scales on nape.

Coloration Males yellowish to dusky-grey, underside reddish-orange; sides with vertical bars and a sharp-edged pale band across tail stalk. First dorsal fin yellowish with a white edge, second dorsal with a jet black edge and oblique yellow and white bands. Female pale brown with deep brown cross-bars, the first dorsal fin with oblique yellow to orange-red bands with a dark spot at the rear end; the second dorsal has a narrow dark edge and thin oblique orange-red bands.

Size Attains a length of 3.9 cm (1½ in.).

Remarks This minute goby is widely distributed in the eastern North Atlantic but in isolated areas. This is probably due more to the difficulty of catching so tiny a fish in the depths it inhabits than to true scarcity of the species. It lives in depths of *c.* 30–375 m (16–205 fathoms) on coarse grounds, mainly sand and gravel, sometimes on muddy sand, and often where calcareous algae encrust stones and shells. It spawns between February and September (in the Channel—postlarvae are captured in the plankton between February and October). Its food consists of small crustaceans and worms.

Guillet's goby   *Lebetus guilleti*

Distinguishing features Closely similar to the preceding species, but distinguished by having 7–9 full-length rays in the second dorsal fin and 5–6 rays in the anal fin. It also has 25–26 vertebrae. (*L. scorpioides* has 27–29.) (Fish not illustrated.)

Coloration Similar to the preceding species but paler. The adult male colouring has not yet been described.

Size Possibly up to 30 mm (1¼ in.), the maximum observed size is 24 mm (1 in.). This is probably the smallest species of fish in European seas.

Remarks The biology of this species is virtually unknown. Although it was described as long ago as 1913, it is only since 1971 when two forms of postlarvae of *Lebetus* were recognized in the English Channel that it has been accepted as an inhabitant of the

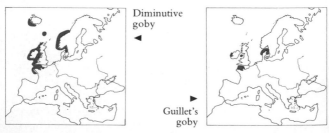

Diminutive
goby
◄

►
Guillet's
goby

European coastline. It is believed to live in shallower water than its relative, probably from 2 to 30 m (1–16 fathoms), mainly on the *Lithothamnion* alga-encrusted stones and shell ground of well-lit water. Postlarvae have been recorded from June to September, which must reflect the breeding season closely.

The distribution map shows areas in which this species has been identified; it is probably as widespread as its relative.

Snake Mackerels

A small family (Gempylidae) of moderate to large marine fishes which are widely distributed in the tropical and warm temperate oceans of the world. They are fast-swimming, predatory fishes found near the surface of the sea and in mid-water. Generally they are slender-bodied and streamlined (superficially like elongate tuna), possessing large teeth in the jaws, but lacking lateral keels on the sides of the tail.

Several species are exploited as food in the warmer oceans, but in northern European waters only 2 species occur as rare visitors.

Johnson's scabbardfish   *Nesiarchus nasutus*

Distinguishing features   Moderately long, compressed body with a long pointed snout and a strongly protuberant lower jaw ending in a fleshy tip. Teeth large and fang-like. Two small finlets behind the dorsal and anal fins.

Coloration   Dark brown or black on the back with violet tints on the sides; fins and inside mouth black. Lateral line white.

Size   Attains 130 cm (51¼ in.).

Remarks   An active predatory fish which lives from the surface down to a depth of *c.* 1000 m (547 fathoms), always in the open sea. It eats a wide range of mesopelagic fishes and squids, while the young mainly eat crustaceans and young fishes. Young fish live nearer to the surface, and are much more frequently captured than the fast-swimming adults. They have been caught in all the warmer oceans and this fish is assumed to be circumtropical in its range. It is a rare vagrant in the eastern North Atlantic. Only Atlantic distribution is shown on the map.

Johnson's
scabbardfish

Distinguishing features Somewhat elongate body but rounded in cross-section, the head is smoothly rounded, the lower jaw prominent but not pointed; teeth moderate in size, sharp and strong. First dorsal fin composed of short spines; 2 small finlets behind the dorsal and anal fins. Body covered with sharp spiny scales giving the body a rough surface.

Coloration Dark purplish-brown, lighter on the sides and ventrally (fades to dull brown after death). Inside of mouth brown.

Size Attains a length of 2 m (6 ft 7 in), and weight of *c.* 45 kg (100 lb).

Remarks An active predatory fish found world-wide in tropical and warm temperate seas, and which usually lives in mid-water in depths of 183–732 m (100–400 fathoms). It is found only in open oceans, never coming into inshore waters. In the eastern North Atlantic it is very rare. It feeds on a wide range of mid-water fishes and squids, but its biology has been little studied. Its flesh is very oily; the oil has a purgative effect.

The map shows its range in the Atlantic Ocean.

Scabbardfishes

A moderately small family (Trichiuridae) of marine fishes of world-wide distribution in tropical and temperate seas. Most live near the surface or in the middle depths of the open ocean down to *c.* 1000 m (547 fathoms). They are all long-bodied fishes with elongate heads and jaws with formidable teeth. The dorsal fin runs the whole length of the body; the tail fin is absent in some species but small in the remainder. Most have no pelvic fins.

Some 30 species are known, although only 4 occur in the eastern North Atlantic, and only 1 of these is at all common. Several species grow to *c.* 1.5 m (5 ft) in length and are valuable food-fishes locally.

Hairtail *Trichiurus lepturus*

Distinguishing features Long and slender-bodied with a pointed head and moderately long teeth in the jaws, supplemented with huge fangs. Dorsal fin long, its origin in front of the pectoral fins and

Oilfish

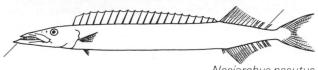

Nesiarchus nasutus
Johnson's scabbardfish

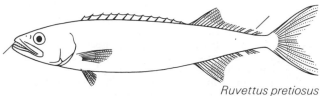

Ruvettus pretiosus
oilfish

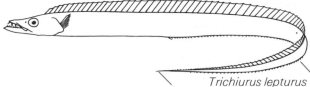

Trichiurus lepturus
hairtail

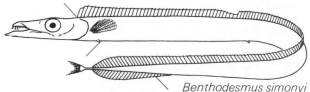

Benthodesmus simonyi
frostfish

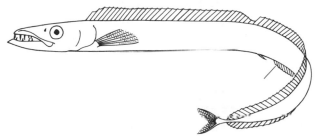

Aphanopus carbo
black scabbardfish

continuing to the tail tip. No tail fin. Anal fin comprising a single long spine and a series of hair-like rays. Head profile steep behind eye.

Coloration Bright silvery overall; tip of the jaw and dorsal fin edge dusky.

Size Grows to 1.5 m (5 ft).

Remarks A very rare fish in the seas of northern Europe and caught only occasionally as far north as the British Isles. Usually it lives from the near surface down to 350 m (191 fathoms) over the outer continental shelf, but occasionally comes closer inshore, as off West Africa. It feeds actively on smaller fishes and squids. Off the Portuguese coast and southwards it is a frequently captured, and locally important, food-fish.

It is world-wide in distribution in tropical and subtropical seas, seasonally entering cool temperate zones. The map shows Atlantic distribution only.

Frostfish   *Benthodesmus simonyi*

Distinguishing features Extremely slender and long-bodied, with a long-based dorsal fin and a short anal fin. Pelvic fins minute in adults, small in young, tail fin small but deeply forked. Dorsal fin with 45–46 slender spines confluent with 102–109 rays.

Coloration Silvery but with dusky shading on back and fins.

Size Attains 90 cm (35½ in.) in length.

Remarks A rare deep-water fish which lives over the continental slope in 200–400 m (109–219 fathoms). Off the Portuguese coast and in the tropical Atlantic it is more common, but nowhere has it

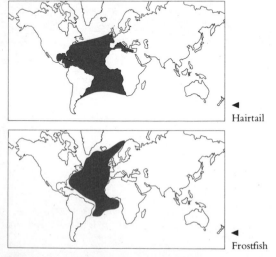

◄
Hairtail

◄
Frostfish

been found abundantly. Its biology is little known. It is known also in the Pacific and Indian Oceans, each possessing a distinct subspecies; the Atlantic subspecies is formally known as *Benthodesmus elongatus simonyi*.

Black scabbardfish   *Aphanopus carbo*

Distinguishing features   Slender and long-bodied with a small but well-developed tail fin, and dorsal fin composed of 38–40 slender spines, distinguished by a dip from the second dorsal fin of 53–56 rays. Anal fin well developed with a dagger-like spine in front. Pelvic fins absent in the adult. (See also coloration.)

Coloration   When freshly caught, dark with dull coppery iridescence on the sides; when dead, jet black, the skin tending to slough off leaving dead white flesh exposed.

Size   Grows to 110 cm (43 in.).

Remarks   The most common of the scabbardfishes in the eastern North Atlantic, although it is not often captured. Off southern Europe it lives in mid-water at depths of 183–640 m (100–350 fathoms), coming closer to the surface at night, although in northern waters it tends to live deeper than this; *c.* 300–900 m (164–492 fathoms). It feeds on a wide range of smaller fishes, shrimps, and squids. Off Madeira, and to a lesser extent Portugal, it is an important food-fish and is captured in large quantities on special deep-water lines. To the west of the British Isles it is captured occasionally, but it can be captured in numbers in rather deeper water than is usually trawled.

Scabbardfish   *Lepidopus caudatus*

Distinguishing features   Long and slender-bodied, with a pointed snout and a dorsal profile which is smoothly rounded, then steeply curved at the nape. Dorsal fins well developed and continuous, tail fin small but conspicuous, anal fin low and very short, pelvic fins small. A small flattened spine just behind the vent. (See also coloration.)

Coloration   Entirely silvery, dusky on the edges of the fins and on the head.

Size   Attains 203 cm (80 in.).

Black
scabbardfish

Remarks An uncommon fish in the eastern North Atlantic, although relatively common off the Portuguese coast where it is fished for commercially on sandy bottoms at depths of 100–250 m (55–137 fathoms). Further north it tends to live deeper, down to 400 m (219 fathoms). It is occasionally stranded on shore in large numbers, presumably as the result of upwelling deep water carrying schools into cooler shallower water, but this rarely happens in Europe. Its food consists mainly of fishes, but shrimps are eaten as well. It is widely distributed in the tropical and warm-temperate Atlantic, Indian, and south Pacific Oceans.

Mackerels and Tunnies

A large family (Scombridae) of marine fishes found in tropical and warm temperate seas around the world, with relatively few species moving seasonally into cool temperate seas, such as those of northern Europe. These fish are often large and predatory, and live in the surface waters of the sea, making considerable migrations which in some cases involve crossing ocean basins. They are spindle-shaped with a pointed snout, round-bodied in cross-section, with a tapering tail. The dorsal fin is composed of stout rays (which slot completely into a groove on the back in the larger species); the second dorsal and anal fins are well developed and stout, ending in a series of separate finlets; the tail fin is high and deeply forked (or lunate). The whole body plan is that of a fast and powerful fish, streamlined to attain the maximum efficiency from its swimming movements. Tunnies are among the few fishes to have a body temperature higher than the surrounding water. This can be seen as another contribution to their swimming efficiency.

Tunnies are heavily exploited as food-fish. Although fisheries in the Mediterranean are known to have been in existence for more than 2000 years, it is only in the second half of the twentieth century that oceanic exploitation has become so heavy that some stocks have become severely depleted. Most of the large tunnies and several of the smaller species have now been overfished.

Some 50 members of the family are recognized, but of these only 10 occur in the seas of northern Europe, and all but 2 are rather rare stragglers here.

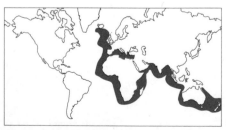
Scabbardfish

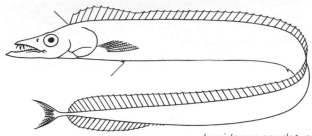

Lepidopus caudatus
scabbardfish

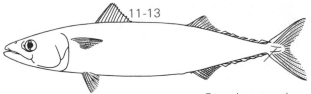

11-13

Scomber scombrus
mackerel

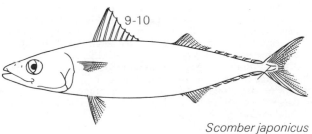

9-10

Scomber japonicus
Spanish mackerel

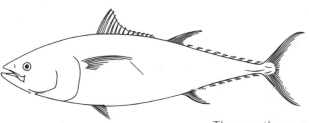

Thunnus thynnus
blue-fin tunny

Mackerel

Distinguishing features   Relatively slender-bodied but rounded in cross-section; second dorsal and anal fins followed by a series of 5 finlets. First dorsal fin with 11–13 slender spines, clearly separated from the second dorsal fin and having no deep groove along the back. The tail fin has 2 small keels at the bases of the fin lobes, but does not have a keel on the side of the tail. (See also coloration.)

Coloration   Back brilliant blue-green with black irregularly curving lines, which are sometimes broken into spots and curves. The lower sides and belly are white with pinkish and gold reflections. The blues and iridescent colours on the sides fade quickly after death.

Size   Attains a maximum length of 66 cm (26 in.) and weight of 3.3 kg (7 lb 4oz); rarely more than 1.8 kg (4 lb). The usual length today is *c.* 40.6 cm (16 in.) and weight *c.* 680 g (1 lb 8 oz).

Remarks   A common North Atlantic fish living near the surface of the sea in huge schools above the continental shelf. It is found seasonally close inshore, as well as over offshore banks, but is highly migratory—making inshore migrations as well as moving north in summer. The reverse movement occurs as the sea cools in winter. The fish spawns in summer, the season covering most months from May until August; the eggs and postlarvae float at the surface.

The food of the mackerel is varied. Young fishes eat planktonic crustaceans, their larvae, and fish larvae. The adults also eat large quantities of pelagic crustaceans and, in addition, they prey heavily on schools of smaller fishes, especially sprats, herring, and sandeels. In winter they fast partially, the mackerel schools retiring to the deeper water on the edge of the continental shelf, or in localized deeps. With the sparsity of planktonic food organisms, and smaller schooling fish in such places, they tend to lie quiescent near the sea-bed. At all seasons of the year, however, they are preyed upon by larger fishes, especially the more active sharks, and tunnies, and by dolphins and other small cetaceans.

The mackerel is an important food-fish. It is captured in different ways, including varied nets and feathered hooks. It is also a fine sporting fish. Because of its poor keeping qualities it was formerly not much marketed, but now large quantities are frozen before transport. It is also canned and smoked, and in these ways has assumed a much greater importance to the fishing industries of

Mackerel

northern Europe. However, it is a slow-growing fish (large specimens may be as much as 20 years of age), living at the extremity of its range, and is thus likely to be overfished quite quickly.

Spanish mackerel   *Scomber japonicus*

Distinguishing features   Closely similar to the mackerel with the 2 dorsal fins widely separated and no groove in the mid-line of the back. Small keels at the bases of the tail fin lobes; no lateral keel on the body. First dorsal spines 9–10; head larger than the mackerel (3 to 3.5 times in the body length); scales larger round pectoral fin base. (See also coloration.)

Coloration   Back greeny-blue with faint wavy dark lines extending down the sides; lower sides and belly silvery-white with an iridescent flush, and numerous rounded dusky spots on the sides.

Size   Attains 40 cm (15¾ in.) in length.

Remarks   World-wide in tropical and warm temperate seas, the Spanish or chub mackerel (as it is known in North America) is a rare visitor in the eastern North Atlantic. In the Mediterranean, however, it is common, as it is off Portugal, and is fished for commercially. It is a schooling fish common on the high seas, from the surface to 300 m (164 fathoms), and coming into inshore waters in summer. It feeds on pelagic crustaceans and whatever fishes are common locally, and in its turn is preyed upon by larger fishes, small cetaceans, and sea-birds. It is heavily fished in the North Pacific (California and Japan).

Blue-fin tunny   *Thunnus thynnus*

Distinguishing features   The only common large tunny in northern European waters. The body form is typical of the family with a series of finlets behind the second dorsal and anal fins. First dorsal fin high in front, the middle spines short and the fin outline concave, 13–15 spines in all; first dorsal fin separated from second by a very small space. Body completely scaled; the scales on the anterior body larger than the rest. Pectoral fin short, about equal to snout length. Gill rakers on lower limb of first arch, 24–28. (See also coloration.)

Coloration   The back is dark blue, shading to green on the upper

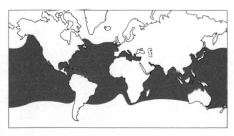

Spanish
mackerel

327

sides; the belly is white. The fins are grey-blue, but the second dorsal and anal fins are brown and the finlets are greyish-yellow.

Size Attains 4 m (13 ft 1½ in.) and a weight of 907 kg (2000 lb), but now rarely over 2.6 m (8 ft 6 in.) and 300 kg (661 lb 8 oz) in weight.

Remarks A wide-ranging fish in the Atlantic (in North America it is known as the blue-fin tuna), with close relatives in the Indian and Pacific Oceans. It is a surface-living, schooling fish, rarely found deeper than 100 m (55 fathoms), which lives over the outer continental shelf and makes seasonal migrations. In northern European waters it is mainly a summertime visitor, appearing in July and August, and rarely captured or seen later than September. It is very sensitive to water temperature and in cold summers may not appear. Most of these fishes are migrants from the south, off North Africa or possibly from the Mediterranean, but some make a trans-Atlantic journey. The regularity of their migrations into northern seas has been affected by overfishing both there and to the south.

The tunny feeds on planktonic animals, especially crustaceans, but also preys heavily on schools of smaller fishes, in particular herring, sprat, pilchard, whiting, and sandeels. It also eats large quantities of squids. The young feed on smaller prey but eat many young fish. It breeds in June in the Mediterranean and off Spain, the eggs and larvae being pelagic. Growth rate is fast, 6-year-old fish are *c.* 1.5 m (4 ft 11 in.) long, and the tunny may live for up to 30 years, but very few fish can survive so long today because of heavy fishing pressure.

Long-fin tunny   *Thunnus alalunga*

Distinguishing features Typical tunny-like body shape. The first dorsal fin is high in front, successive spines being slightly shorter so that the fin outline is concave; the first and second dorsal fins are close together. Body completely scaled, those in front larger than the rest. Pectoral fin very long, depressed it reaches beyond the second dorsal fin. 18–22 gill rakers on the lower limb of the first gill arch.

Coloration Deep blue above with a bluish iridescent band on the sides, the belly silvery-white. Fins dark, but the tail, second dorsal, anal, and the finlets have light trailing edges.

Blue-fin tunny

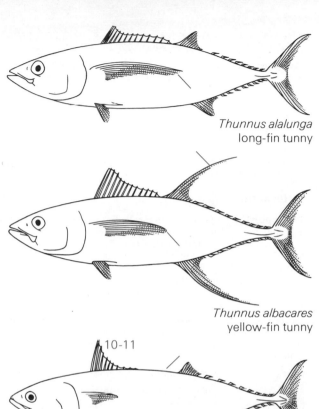

Thunnus alalunga
long-fin tunny

Thunnus albacares
yellow-fin tunny

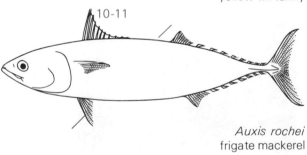

10-11

Auxis rochei
frigate mackerel

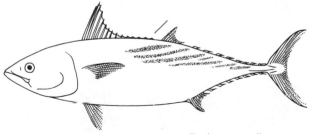

Euthynnus alletteratus
little tunny

Size Attains 130 cm (51 in.) in length, and certainly 23 kg (50 lb), possibly 43 kg (95 lb) in weight.

Remarks The long-fin tunny (albacore in North America and elsewhere) is world-wide in tropical and warm temperate seas. In northern European waters it is common in Biscay, but northwards is a rare vagrant, found only in warm seasons and usually singly. It is an important food-fish in southern Europe.

Its food is mainly fish, especially anchovy, skipper, lantern fishes, and hatchet-fishes; it also eats squids and planktonic crustaceans. It lives in the surface waters down to a depth of 50 m (27 fathoms) in large schools, spawns in May to June off the Portuguese and Spanish coasts, and later makes its feeding migration into northern waters.

Yellow-fin tunny   *Thunnus albacares*

Distinguishing features Typical of the tunnies in body shape and closely resembling the 2 preceding species. Like them, the first dorsal fin is high anteriorly with a strongly concave edge and almost joins the second dorsal fin. The body is fully scaled. The pectoral fin is moderately long, depressed it reaches beyond the level of the second dorsal fin origin. The lobes of the second dorsal and the anal fins are very long, exceptionally so in large fishes. (See also coloration.)

Coloration Bright blue above, yellowish on the sides, silvery-white ventrally. All the finlets are brilliant clear yellow, the lobes of the second dorsal and anal fins, and the outer edge of the tail pale yellow.

Size Attains 2 m (6 ft 6 in.).

Remarks A world-wide species in tropical and warm temperate

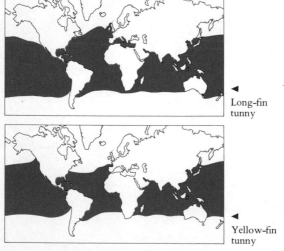

◀ Long-fin tunny

◀ Yellow-fin tunny

waters which has occurred once in northern European seas (on the North Wales coast in 1972). Its status anywhere north of southern Spain is that of an accidental vagrant. It is usually found in the surface waters with temperatures of 22–28°C, exceptionally down to 14°C, and like other large tuna is seasonally migratory. It is one of the few tuna to be found in inshore waters. It is an important food-fish in tropical seas.

Frigate mackerel   *Auxis rochei*

Distinguishing features   Very similar to a large mackerel, except in coloration. The first dorsal fin is high, and strongly concave, and widely separated from the second dorsal fin. Second dorsal and anal fins small. Small fleshy keels at the bases of the tail fin lobes and a larger one on each side of the tail. A large triangular flap of skin between the pelvic fin bases. Scales present on the front of the body only.

Coloration   Blue-green or dark blue on the back, silvery on the sides and belly; rather wavy, dusky lines run across the back obliquely from the lateral line upwards.

Size   Grows to 61 cm (24 in.) and a weight of *c*. 3 kg (6 lb 10 oz).

Remarks   The frigate mackerel is a pelagic, schooling fish of the open sea in tropical and warm temperate waters, which comes close inshore in warm seasons. In northern European waters it is rarely caught, although southwards, in Biscay, it is caught in some numbers. It feeds on smaller schooling fishes, especially pilchard, anchovy, and scad, small squids and crustaceans.

Little tunny   *Euthynnus alletteratus*

Distinguishing features   Typically tunny-shaped with the first dorsal fin high in front, then each spine successively shorter to give a concave edge. Scales on front part of the body form a distinct corselet which is very conspicuous. Anal fin origin beneath the first dorsal finlet.

Coloration   Steel blue above, with wavy and curved black lines on the posterior back. Creamy-silver on the lower sides and ventrally, an iridescent stripe in front. Several (5–7) dusky spots behind and below the pectoral fins.

Frigate
mackerel

Size Attains a length of 91 cm (36 in.), and a weight of 9 kg (19 lb 14 oz).

Remarks An extremely rare tunny in northern European waters which has been recorded 5 or 6 times only. To the south, however, it is very common; in tropical and warm temperate parts of the Atlantic it is the most common tunny in inshore waters. It forms tight compact schools near the surface, and feeds on all kinds of smaller fishes, squids, and crustaceans—often attracting flocks of sea-birds to the scene by the frenzy of their feeding. It is commercially exploited despite its small size, for its flesh is firm and tasty. It is also highly favoured by anglers.

Skipjack tuna *Euthynnus pelamis*

Distinguishing features Typically tuna-shaped, with a high first dorsal fin and each succeeding ray shorter, giving the edge a concave outline, and almost extending to the second dorsal fin. Moderate-sized scales are present anteriorly, but the posterior body is scaleless. Lower limb of first gill arch with 36–40 gill rakers. Distance between snout and first dorsal fin origin greater than distance between second dorsal fin origin and the last finlet. (See also coloration.)

Coloration The back is plain deep blue above shading to green on the side; the sides and belly are shining silver white. The belly has 4, 5, or 6 long broad stripes running from the scaly area to the tail.

Size Attains 1 m (39½ in.) in length and a weight of *c.* 22.7 kg (50 lb).

Remarks In northern European waters the skipjack tuna (which is also known as the oceanic bonito) is uncommon, but because of its

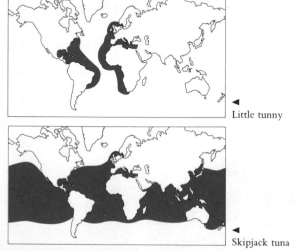

◄
Little tunny

◄
Skipjack tuna

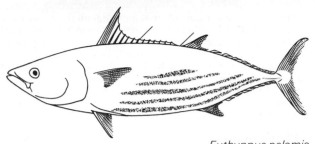

Euthynnus pelamis
skipjack tuna

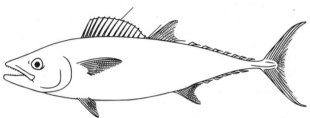

Orcynopsis unicolor
plain bonito

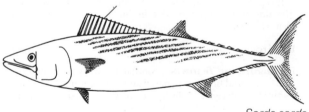

Sarda sarda
bonito

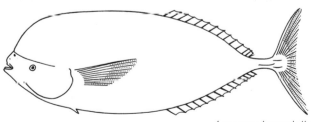

Luvarus imperialis
louvar

wide range and habit of making migrations it occurs more frequently than the other rare tunnies. It lives in both small and large schools world-wide in tropical seas and seasonally in temperate ones, usually offshore and on open ocean coasts. This tunny can be captured in mid–ocean. It feeds on a wide range of planktonic crustaceans, squids, and smaller fishes, especially smaller scombroids, lantern fishes, and young pilchards and anchovies, and their relatives. It is a very important food-fish, exploited throughout the world but most notably in the Pacific. Most of the catch is canned.

Plain bonito   *Orcynopsis unicolor*

Distinguishing features   Typically tunny-like in shape with a long-based first dorsal fin which touches the second dorsal at the base. Spines of the first dorsal fin long and slender, the second to sixth rays high and the outline convex. Scales present on the front of the body only. Teeth in jaws large, well spaced and canine-like.

Coloration   The back is steel blue, the sides blue-green, ventrally silvery-white. No dark spots or bars.

Size   Attains 1.5 m (60 in.).

Remarks   A little-known tunny which may live in deeper water than most. It is common only locally, as off the North African coast; elsewhere it occurs singly from time to time over a short period, then is not reported again for years. In northern European waters it has been caught only off Scandinavia on 3 occasions and must be regarded as very rare. It is believed to live in the open sea.

It is possibly confined to the Atlantic Ocean, but a similar species (the dog-tooth tuna) occurs in the Pacific Ocean and may be identical with it.

Bonito   *Sarda sarda*

Distinguishing features   Similar to the other tunnies in build. The first dorsal fin is long-based and almost joins the second dorsal; its outline is straight or slightly concave, the first 10 spines being the longest and of almost uniform height. The pectoral fin is short. The mouth is large and extends back to the rear edge of the eye. (See also coloration.)

Coloration   The back is steel blue to olive green with numerous (*c.* 10) oblique black lines running across it; sides silvery-yellow.

Plain bonito

Size Attains 91 cm (36 in.) in length and a maximum of 7 kg (15 lb 7 oz), but most caught are less than 4 kg (8 lb 13 oz).

Remarks A moderately regular visitor to northern European seas, and very common off southern Europe. It is migratory with the seasons, not living in water below 15°C and preferring temperatures around 22°C. It is a strong, swift, open-ocean predator travelling in tight compact schools and leaping clear from the water when in pursuit of its prey. In European seas the bonito eats anchovy, pilchard, sprat, whiting, mackerel, and scad, and squids. The schools are usually found offshore, 25–32 km (15–20 miles) off the coast.

It spawns mainly in early spring off the North African coast and in the Mediterranean. After spawning, the schools migrate to richer feeding-grounds, and in the Atlantic it is this migration which brings them into northern European waters. It forms an important part of the European tunny fisheries, and is fished for throughout the tropical Atlantic. It is also a fine sporting fish.

Louvar

A most striking fish which is placed in a family (Luvaridae) on its own. It has some resemblances to the members of the tunny family, especially in the tail fin which is high and the keel either side of the tail itself. It is world-wide in distribution in warm temperate seas, although it has not been reported in tropical waters either side of the equator. The adult is totally different from the young fish which goes through several characteristic stages of development. This has led to several of these stages being recognized at some time as distinct species, and even genera, of fishes. Only adults have occurred in northern European waters.

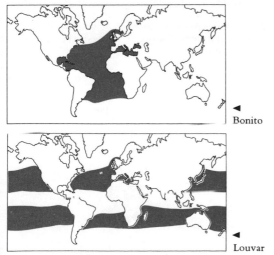

◀ Bonito

◀ Louvar

Distinguishing features Deep-bodied with a high, almost vertical profile; mouth small and toothless. Tail fin strong with high lobes, a small keel at the base of each and a large fleshy keel on the side of the tail. Dorsal and anal rays low but strong, few in number.

Coloration Brilliant, body pale pink, deep blue above; the fins are scarlet except that the tail fin is deep blue with reddish tinges.

Size Grows to 1.88 m (6 ft 2 in.) in length and a weight of 140 kg (309 lb).

Remarks A rare vagrant in northern European seas, where it is best known as a stranded fish, or is caught in shallow water on coasts close to the open sea. These are exceptional circumstances, however, as it is a mesopelagic inhabitant of the ocean. It lives from the surface down to about 1000 m (547 fathoms) and feeds on salps, medusae, and ctenophores (all pelagic animals which might be classed as jellyfishes). It is known to breed in the Mediterranean, where many of the highly variable young stages have been captured, but many details of its life history are as yet unknown.

Sailfish and Swordfish

The sailfish and the swordfish belong to 2 distinct, although closely-related families (Istiophoridae and Xiphiidae). Both have slender bodies with a pointed head and a long pointed snout forming a bill. The istiophorids have a slender bill, rounded in cross-section, and include the marlins and spearfishes, while the swordfish has a broad bill, flattened above and below. The swordfish is the only member of its family; the sailfish family contains perhaps 10 species. Both families are distributed world-wide in tropical and temperate seas, although the istiophorids favour warmer water. The swordfish is an uncommon fish in northern European waters; the sailfish is exceptionally rare (1 record).

Sailfish *Istiophorus platypterus*

Distinguishing features Rather slender-bodied with a high sail-like first dorsal fin, the middle rays are longest, longer than the depth of the body. Pelvic fins long and slender.

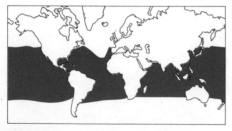

Sailfish

Coloration Generally dark blue above, fading to white or silver below; the sides often have dusky vertical bars or spots. Dorsal fin bright cobalt blue with round or oval black spots.

Size Attains 3.6 m (12 ft) and a maximum weight of *c.* 125 kg (275 lb), but the average is closer to 32 kg (70 lb).

Remarks Encountered once only in northern European waters (stranded on the English Channel coast of Devonshire in 1928), and rare even in southern European waters. It is found world-wide in tropical oceans at the edge of coastal waters and in the open sea, but is strongly migratory, travelling coastwise with seasonal warming of the water. Its food consists of smaller schooling fishes and squids, which are common in the surface waters of the sea. It is well known as a sporting fish (especially off the North American coast), and has been exploited by high-seas fisheries as a food-fish.

Swordfish · *Xiphias gladius*

Distinguishing features Heavy-bodied anteriorly, slender towards the tail, with a long pointed snout produced into a sword-blade (flat top and bottom). A single keel on the sides of the tail. No pelvic fins. The dorsal fin is high in front; in adult fish it is clearly separated from the second dorsal, but in young fishes both first and second dorsal fins, and the anal fins, are united to form single fins.

Coloration Grey-blue above, paler blue beneath, almost white on the belly; the fins are dark greyish.

Size Attains a maximum length of 4.9 m (16 ft), but the average is between 2 and 3 m (6 ft 7 in.–9 ft 10 in.) and weights of *c.* 60–120 kg (132–265 lb).

Remarks An open ocean migrant which is nowhere abundant in European waters, although distinctly more common off southern Europe than it is in the north. From Biscay northwards the swordfish is a rare vagrant. The adults appear to be solitary, but are occasionally seen in pairs, except when spawning in spring and summer, when large schools form. It is an active, strong swimmer which attacks schooling fishes, including mackerel, herring, sprat, pilchard, argentines, and rat-tails, as well as squids. It lives at the surface and as deep as 610 m (334 fathoms), and consequently its diet includes numbers of deep-water fishes.

For centuries the swordfish has been exploited as a food-fish in

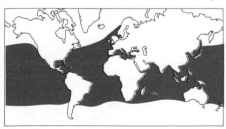

Swordfish

Europe and this may be the reason why it is comparatively scarce today. In North America it became a relatively popular food-fish more recently, and heavy catches were made, but the numbers landed have declined in recent years. It is a fine sporting fish for anglers.

Blackfishes

A moderately large family (Centrolophidae) of oceanic fishes found at the surface and in the middle depths of the sea. Most of them are found over the outer edge of the continental shelf and further out to sea, but occasional specimens stray into shallow water. Most are rather compressed with long dorsal and anal fins, but the fin spines are soft as is the skeleton in general, and these fish are usually flabby to handle. Young specimens are usually deeper-bodied than adults and many species live in association with medusae (jellyfishes); adults of some species eat medusae.

Three species only occur in northern European seas; others live off southern Europe.

Blackfish *Centrolophus niger*

Distinguishing features Slender-bodied but oval in cross-section, the snout blunt and profile gently curved. The head is moderately long, equal to the body depth at the anal origin. The dorsal fin origin is well down the back, about level with the end of the pectoral fin.

Coloration Deep brown, almost black, on the back, shading on the sides to grey and ventrally with silvery flecks. Fins all dark.

Size Attains a maximum length of 1 m (39½ in.); usually about 75 cm (29½ in.) in length.

Remarks An oceanic fish found on the edge of the continental shelf and probably most abundant between 100–600 m (55–328 fathoms), but in mid-water not on the bottom. However, numerous reports of this fish inshore, in shallow water, suggest that it is likely to occur almost anywhere in the northern European area. Whether this is due to migration by the fishes, or to movement of water masses in which they are living, is not known. It is relatively common off the western coasts of the British Isles at appropriate

Blackfish

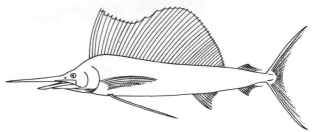

Istiophorus platypterus
sailfish

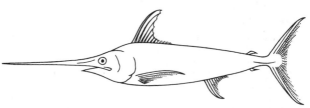

Xiphias gladius
swordfish

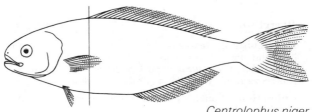

Centrolophus niger
blackfish

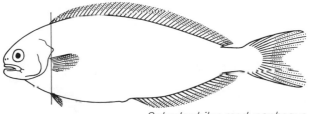

Schedophilus medusophagus
Cornish blackfish

depths. The adults feed heavily on deep-water jellyfishes, and also eat small fishes and crustaceans. The young live in association with medusae near the surface.

Cornish blackfish *Schedophilus medusophagus*

Distinguishing features   Rather deep-bodied and compressed from side to side (body with flattened sides in cross-section); the snout blunt and profile steep. Head short, its length about two-thirds of the body depth at the anal origin. Dorsal fin begins as short rays anteriorly set vertically in front of the pectoral fin base. Body flabby, the bones, even jawbones, flexible and elastic.

Coloration   Dull brown above with a violet sheen over the body cavity, and grey-brown ventrally.

Size   Attains 58 cm (23 in.) in length.

Remarks   Adults are found in the open sea at depths of 300–900 m (164–492 fathoms) in mid-water, not on the bottom. They are moderately common to the west of the British Isles and off the Portuguese coast on the edge of the continental shelf, but this species is only very rarely found in inshore waters, in contrast to its more abundant relative, *C. niger*. It appears to eat only the large dusky coloured deep-water medusa, *Atolla*. Young fish are deeper-bodied greenish-brown above and lighter below; they are frequently found at the surface of the sea accompanying jellyfishes and flotsam. Very rarely the young are found in northern European seas, as the result of oceanic surface drift.

Barrelfish *Hyperoglyphe perciformis*

Distinguishing features   Relatively deep-bodied; profile of head and body steep; body depth 2½ to 3 times in the length; preoperculum with weak teeth. Dorsal fin of 6–8 quite strong spines and 20–22 feeble rays. (Young specimens described.)

Coloration   Young are dark green above, shading to olive, white ventrally; adults are dark brown or black in colour.

Size   Attains 91 cm (35¾ in.); specimens in European waters to 33 cm (13 in.).

Remarks   A rare vagrant from the western Atlantic which owes its occurrence in northern European waters to the habit of the young

Cornish
blackfish
◄

►
Barrelfish

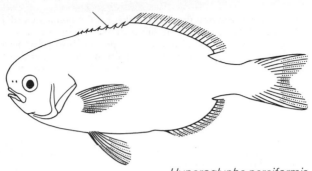

Hyperoglyphe perciformis
barrelfish

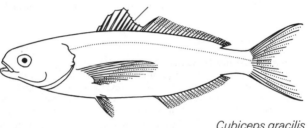

Cubiceps gracilis
longfin cigarfish

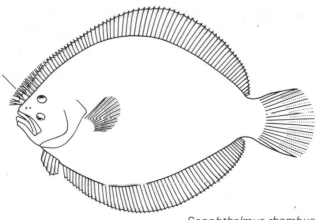

Scophthalmus rhombus
brill

fish of accompanying floating wreckage, or *Sargassum* weed, in the tropical Atlantic. Most occurrences have been of small fishes associated with floating boxes or logs, presumably drifted across the Atlantic by winds and currents. Adults are deep-water fish found along the edge of the continental shelf and have not been encountered in European seas.

Cigarfish

A small family (Nomeidae) of mainly tropical and warm-temperate oceanic fishes of world-wide distribution. They are closely related to the blackfishes (and may belong to that family). Like their relatives, they pass through a surface-living stage when young, but the adults are deep-water fishes found in the middle waters over the edge of the continental shelf.

Only 1 member of the family is found in northern European seas, and that very rarely; other members live in the tropical Eastern Atlantic.

Longfin cigarfish   *Cubiceps gracilis*

Distinguishing features   Slender and cigar-shaped body with a moderately large head and a blunt snout. Lateral line runs parallel to the back in a gentle curve. Pectoral fins long, much longer than the head length. First dorsal fin of 10–12 flexible spines, second fin longer and lower; anal fin similar to second dorsal. Scales large.

Coloration   Plain medium brown in colour; slightly lighter ventrally.

Size   Attains 90 cm ($35\frac{1}{2}$ in.), but in European seas usually around 25 cm (10 in.).

Remarks   Exceptionally rare in northern European seas and then mostly young fish which, presumably, have been carried northwards by currents and wind. The young live at the surface often associating with large medusae (jellyfishes), usually in the open sea, but occasionally being drifted close inshore. Adults live on the edge of the continental shelf and are free-living predatory fishes, although little is known of the biology of this species.

Closely related, if not identical, species are found in the Pacific and Indian Oceans.

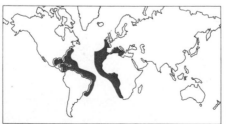

Longfin
cigarfish

Left-Eyed Flatfishes

A small family (Scophthalmidae) of flatfishes which have both eyes on the left side of the head (reversed specimens are rare). During larval development the right eye moves from the right side of the head and comes to rest close to the left eye. Members of the family are wide-bodied with large heads and well-developed pelvic fins, which are approximately the same size each side. The family is confined to the Atlantic basin and includes several valuable food-fish such as the turbot and brill, as well as a number of minor species. Seven species are included here.

Brill   *Scophthalmus rhombus*

Distinguishing features   A broad-bodied, heavy-headed flatfish, with a large curved mouth, and broad-based pelvic fins. The first rays of the dorsal are free of the fin membrane for up to half their length. Body covered with scales, small but distinct on the eyed (coloured) side, small and embedded in the skin in the blind side. Dorsal fin rays 73–83; anal fin rays 56–62.

Coloration   Dull sandy-brown with small darker flecks and lighter spots; the fins are lighter, the tail fin not spotted; underside creamy-white.

Size   Attains a maximum length of 75 cm (29½ in.), but not usually longer than 50 cm (19¾ in.). Usual weights are around 2.3–3.6 kg (5–8 lb) and the maximum is *c*. 7.2 kg (16 lb).

Remarks   The brill reaches the northern extremity of its range in northern Europe, and north of England and Denmark it declines in abundance quickly. It is common to the south of these countries. Adults are bottom-living in depths of 9–73 m (5–40 fathoms), but the young (about postage stamp size) are common close inshore and even in intertidal pools on sandy shores. It is most common on sandy bottoms, but is occasionally caught on gravel and mud.

It preys on a wide range of bottom and near bottom-living fishes, especially sandeels and whiting, and also eats squids and crustaceans in large quantities. It spawns in spring and summer; the eggs and larvae are pelagic. The larva hatches out at a length of *c*. 4 mm and becomes bottom-living at 20–35 mm (¾–1¼ in).

The brill is of some commercial importance; as food its flesh is less tasty than that of the turbot. A number are caught by anglers.

Brill
◄

►
Turbot

Distinguishing features Body extremely broad and rather thickset; head large; broad-based pelvic fins of virtually equal size; a large mouth. The first rays of the dorsal fin are branched, but only their extreme tips are free from the fin membrane. Body scaleless but with irregularly scattered large bony tubercles in the skin, sometimes present on the blind side only. Dorsal fin rays 57–71; anal fin rays 43–52.

Coloration Very variable to match the sea-bed; generally it is a dull sandy-brown with darker spots and speckles extending on to the fins, including the tail fin.

Size Attains a length of 1 m (39½ in.) and a weight of 25 kg (55 lb 2 oz); more usual lengths are 50–80 cm (19¾–31½ in.) and weights of c. 5–12 kg (11 lb–26 lb 8 oz). Females are larger than males.

Remarks Like the brill, the turbot is close to the extremity of its range in northern European waters and rapidly becomes scarce to the north, although it is common in the southern North Sea, Irish Sea, and the English Channel. The turbot lives in shallow inshore waters from just below the shoreline to about 80 m (44 fathoms) on shell-gravel, gravel, and sandy bottoms. Young fish live in shallower water than adults, which are particularly common on offshore banks; the young of less than 1 year are common in the breakers and tidal pools of sandy shores.

The turbot feeds very heavily on fishes. It is an active predator capturing large quantities of sandeels, sprat, herring, whiting, pouting, and less often other flatfish species, dragonets, and gobies. It spawns during spring and summer, the females producing up to 10 million eggs. The eggs and larvae are pelagic, and the postlarvae have a distinct swim-bladder which is lost when the young fish begins to live on the sea-bed at 2·5 cm (1 in.). The extended pelagic life, which may continue for 4–6 months, assists in the dispersal of the young turbot from the rather restricted spawning grounds.

This is one of the most valuable of marine food-fish and is ranked by many as the finest flavoured. It is caught in trawls, seines, and by lines, but is never sufficiently abundant to satisfy demand. It is one of the most promising sea fishes for intensive culture in the future.

Megrim *Lepidorhombus whiffiagonis*

Distinguishing features A rather narrow-bodied flatfish with a moderately large head, large eyes and mouth. The dorsal and anal fins end with the base of the last 2 rays on the underside. Eyes large, the lower one in front of the upper, their diameter just less than the snout length. Lower jaw distinctly prominent. Pelvic fins long-based, equal both sides. Dorsal fin rays 85–94; anal rays 64–74.

Coloration Pale yellowish-brown with dusky patches; ventrally dead white.

Size Attains 61 cm (24 in.); usually between 35 and 45 cm (14–17¾ in.).

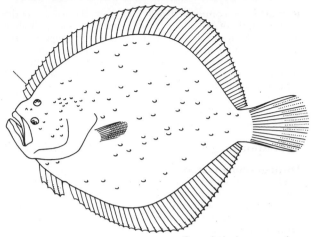

Scophthalmus maximus
turbot

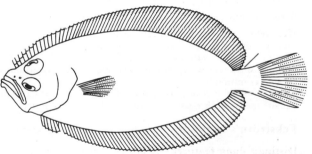

Lepidorhombus whiffiagonis
megrim

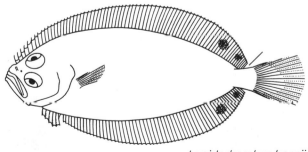

Lepidorhombus boscii
four-spot megrim

Remarks A common flatfish found on the lower continental shelf in depths of 50–300 m (27–164 fathoms), and most abundant on muddy bottoms, although not confined to that type of bottom. It spawns in spring in deep water, the eggs being transparent and pelagic. The postlarvae change to a bottom-living life at about 19 mm (¾ in.) in length. The megrim feeds mainly on fishes including scaldfishes, sandeels, dragonets, gobies, and the smaller members of the cod family. It also eats crustaceans and squids. It is taken in some quantity by trawling and is of moderate importance to the fishing industry, but its flesh is rather dry.

Four-spot megrim   *Lepidorhombus boscii*

Distinguishing features A narrow-bodied flatfish with a small head, large eyes, and mouth. The dorsal and anal fins end with the bases of the last 2 rays on the blind side. Eyes very large, level with one another, their diameter longer than the snout length. Lower jaw slightly prominent. Pelvic fins long-based, equal both sides. Dorsal fin rays 79–86; anal rays 65–69. (See also coloration.)

Coloration Pale yellowish-brown without dusky markings on back except for 2 rounded black blotches on the end of both the dorsal and anal fins. White on the blind side.

Size Attains 41 cm (16¼ in.); usually around 32 cm (12½ in.).

Remarks Lives in deeper water than the preceding species and is usually captured lower down the continental slope in depths of 293–1000 m (160–547 fathoms), although in the Mediterranean it is found in shallower water still. It is confined to muddy grounds, but is quite common.

It has only minor importance as a food-fish in northern Europe, but off the Spanish coast it is captured in some quantity.

Eckström's topknot   *Phrynorhombus regius*

Distinguishing features A broad-bodied flatfish with a rather small head, the snout deeply notched in front of the upper eye. The dorsal and anal fins continue on to the lower side of the body forming distinct lobes; pelvic fins long-based, both equal in size and not joined to the anal fin. Scales small, each with several strong spines on the eyed side, giving a rough feel to the body; on the blind side less strongly toothed and smaller.

Megrim

◄

► Four-spot megrim

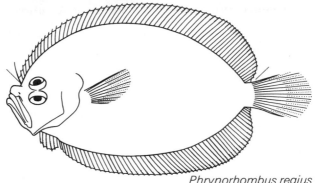

Phrynorhombus regius
Eckström's topknot

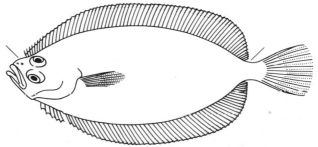

Phrynorhombus norvegicus
Norwegian topknot

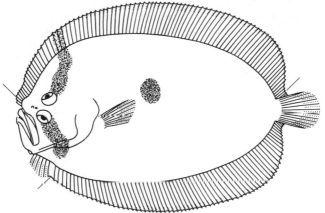

Zeugopterus punctatus
topknot

Coloration   Warm brown with irregular dusky patches, one distinct dark blotch in the middle of the side; dorsal and anal fins more regularly marked with dark stripes along individual rays.

Size   Attains 20 cm (8 in.).

Remarks   A relatively uncommon fish which seems to be confined to offshore waters on the western coast of Europe, and in the Mediterranean. It is found on rough grounds, and may cling to the underside of rocks, which would partially explain its apparent rarity. Its depth range is 9–55 m (5–30 fathoms). Occasionally specimens have been caught in sandy bays on the western coast of Britain. It spawns in April to June; the eggs and postlarvae are planktonic. Its biology is little known.

Norwegian topknot   *Phrynorhombus norvegicus*

Distinguishing features   Rather slender-bodied with a small head and a smooth profile to the snout. The dorsal and anal fins continue on to the lower side of the body to form distinct lobes; pelvic fins are long-based and equal in size; both are free of the anal fin. Scales are moderately large, on the eyed side having teeth on the edge making the body feel rough; ventrally these teeth are smaller.

Coloration   Yellowish-brown with irregular dusky marks on the head and back, also on dorsal and anal fins.

Size   Grows to 12 cm (4¾ in.).

Remarks   A moderately common flatfish, but one which is not often captured because of its small size and of its habit of living amongst rocks and on rough grounds. It lives at depths of 20–50 m (11–27 fathoms), but has been caught as shallow as 10 m (5½ fathoms) and as deep as 170 m (93 fathoms). Its biology has been little studied. Its food consists of worms, crustaceans, and young fishes, and it breeds in late spring and summer. The young fish lives on the sea-bed at a length of 13 mm (½ in.).

Topknot   *Zeugopterus punctatus*

Distinguishing features   A wide-bodied flatfish with a large head, the dorsal fin origin just behind the upper lip. The dorsal and anal fins end with a distinct lobe on the underside of the tail. Pelvic fins long-based, equal in size, and joined to the anal fin by a distinct

Eckström's topknot ◄

► Norwegian topknot

membrane. Scales with teeth on upper side which feel rough.

Coloration   Warm brown on the eyed side with irregular dusky mottling; a rounded dark blotch on the lateral line in the mid-body, dark lines running to the eyes.

Size   Attains a length of 25 cm (10 in.).

Remarks   An uncommon flatfish of rather restricted distribution. It lives among rocks and on rough grounds in 1–25 m ($\frac{1}{2}$–14 fathoms) and is occasionally captured on the low shore amongst algae. Those on the shore are usually found clinging to the sheltered side of boulders in the kelp (*Laminaria*) zone; they are usually young fish. Their food is said to consist largely of young fishes and crustaceans, but the diet has not been adequately studied. The topknot spawns in spring.

Scaldfishes

A large family (Bothidae) of flatfishes, closely allied to the left-eyed flatfishes and sharing their feature of having both eyes on the left side of the head. Family members are distinguished by having the dorsal fin beginning right in front of the eyes, and all rays segmented and none spiny; the pelvic fins are short-based, that on the eyed side being larger than the other. The family is widely distributed in tropical and warm temperate seas in all the ocean basins. Most live in shallow water, but 2 of the 3 northern European representatives are moderately deep-water fishes; others live in the Mediterranean.

Scaldfish   *Arnoglossus laterna*

Distinguishing features   Slender-bodied with a small head and a moderate mouth; eyes on the left side. The dorsal fin begins in front of the upper eye, its first rays free of the fin membrane but not elongate. Pelvic fin on blind side much shorter than the other. Dorsal fin rays 87–93; anal fin with 65–74 rays. Lateral line scales 51–56; body scales fragile and usually missing.

Coloration   Pale brownish-grey with diffuse darker spots and dark dots on the fins, the pelvic with a dusky spot.

Size   Attains 19 cm (7$\frac{1}{2}$ in.).

Topknot ◀

▶ Scaldfish

Remarks   A common fish in shallow water in northern Europe. It lives most abundantly on sandy bottoms at depths of 10–60 m (5½–33 fathoms), although occasionally it has been captured as deep as 200 m (109 fathoms). It spawns in spring and summer; the eggs and larvae are pelagic, and development often continues for a considerable time. They become bottom-living at a length of 16–30 mm (½–1¼ in.). Little is known of the life history of this fish. It is too small to have any value as a commercial species, but its abundance (as in the southern North Sea) suggests that it may be of importance in the food-chains of such areas.

Imperial scaldfish   *Arnoglossus imperialis*

Distinguishing features   Closely similar to the preceding species. The dorsal fin origin is in front of the upper eye, and the second to fifth rays are long and thickened (free of the membrane and very long in males; free at the tips and about twice the length of the remaining rays in females). Pelvic fin on blind side shorter than the other fin. Dorsal fin rays 95–106; anal rays 74–82. Lateral line scales 58–63; fragile and easily shed.

Coloration   Pale yellowish-brown with irregular small flecks on back. Conspicuous black patch on the rear edge of the pelvic fin (males), grey in females.

Size   Attains 25 cm (10 in.).

Remarks   Moderately common in deep water from 60–350 m (33–191 fathoms), but most abundant in 60–100 m (33–55 fathoms). It lives mainly on sandy or muddy grounds. Spawning takes place in spring, the planktonic larval stage is prolonged, and the young live on the bottom at *c.* 3–5 cm (1¼–2 in.) in length. The biology of this scaldfish is very poorly known.

Thor's scaldfish   *Arnoglossus thori*

Distinguishing features   Closely similar to the other scaldfishes; like them the pelvic fin on the blind side is much smaller than the other. The dorsal fin origin is in front of the upper eye, the first, third, and fourth rays a little longer and thicker than the remainder, the second very long with a fleshy flap on its edge. Dorsal fin rays 81–91; anal rays 62–67. Lateral line scales 49–56; fragile and easily shed.

Imperial
scaldfish

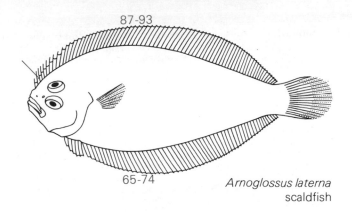

87-93

65-74

Arnoglossus laterna
scaldfish

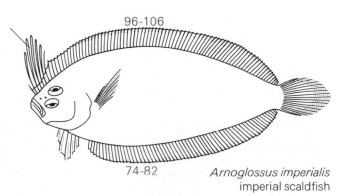

96-106

74-82

Arnoglossus imperialis
imperial scaldfish

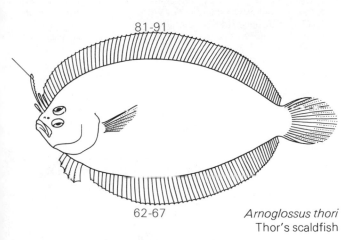

81-91

62-67

Arnoglossus thori
Thor's scaldfish

Coloration Brown or greyish above, with dusky spots and blotches, 2 of which (behind the curve in the lateral line, and near the tail fin) are conspicuous. Membrane on second dorsal spine very dark.

Size Grows to 18 cm (7 in.).

Remarks Of very restricted distribution in northern European seas. It lives in inshore waters of 15–92 m (8–50 fathoms) mainly on mud and sand bottoms, although it has been captured on rough grounds. It spawns in spring in southern Biscay, presumably later further north. The eggs, and characteristically deep-bodied post-larvae are planktonic, and the postlarval stage continues for a considerable time, as it does not live on the bottom until it is 20–25 mm (nearly an inch) in length. As with the other scaldfishes its biology is virtually unknown.

Right-Eyed Flatfishes

A large family (Pleuronectidae) of flatfishes which all have both eyes on the right side of the body, the left eye moving over the head during metamorphosis from postlarva to bottom-living young. Reversed examples, those which have both eyes on the left of the fish, are very common in some species, e.g. flounder, less common in others, e.g. plaice and dab, and relatively rare in the remaining species.

The family is widely distributed in the cool temperate waters of the Atlantic, Pacific, and Indian Oceans, being best represented in the first. Most are shallow-water, bottom-living fishes, but some are found in deeper water on the upper continental shelf. Some species, especially the Greenland halibut and to a less extent the halibut, live at least partly in mid-water and are active hunters of fish. These species have the upper eye closer to the edge of the head (which presumably allows a wider field of vision), and the teeth are strongly developed in both sides of the jaws.

Eight species are known from northern European seas; one of these (the flounder) also lives in freshwater but does not breed there.

Plaice   *Pleuronectes platessa*

Distinguishing features A typical flatfish, in normal specimens with both eyes on the right side of the head, head and jaws relatively

Thor's
scaldfish
◀

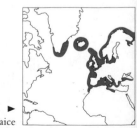

Plaice

352

front views of flatfishes

Scophthalmus   *Arnoglossus*   *Pleuronectes*   *Reinhardtius*   *Solea*

small, eyes moderate in size. Teeth best developed in the jaws of the blind side. Scales smooth-edged; lateral line straight; a line of 4–7 bony knobs on head between upper gill opening and eyes. Anal fin rays 48–59. (See also coloration.)

Coloration   Eyed side warm brown with large, bright red or orange spots; blind side is clear pearly white.

Size   Exceptionally grows to 91 cm (35¾ in.) in length and weighs 7 kg (15 lb 6 oz); more usually around 50 cm (19¾ in.) and 1.1 kg (2 lb 8 oz).

Remarks   The plaice is a bottom-living fish, most abundant on sandy bottoms, but also found on muddy bottoms and gravel in depths of 0–200 m (0–109 fathoms). It is most common in 10–50 m (5½–27 fathoms). Young fish, even newly metamorphosed plaice of *c*. 2 cm (¾ in.), live in the shallower depths from the shoreline to 10 m (5½ fathoms). It is not uncommon to find them in sandy intertidal shore-pools. Large fish also come into the tidal zone to feed at high tide on sand and mud flats. Plaice eat a wide range of bottom-living animals, especially molluscs, including burrowing species which often have their breathing siphons nipped off (the jaws with their teeth larger on the underside are well adapted to do this). They also eat large numbers of crustaceans and worms, and less often brittlestars and sandeels.

The plaice spawns in the early months of the year, mainly between January and March, throughout its range, but tending to be concentrated on certain areas in depths of 20–40 m (11–22 fathoms). The eggs float at the surface initially, hatching in 10–20 days depending on the temperature. The larvae and postlarvae are also surface-living for between 4 and 6 weeks, after which, with the eye now migrated to the right side and other internal changes completed, it becomes bottom-living at a length of 10–17 mm (½–¾ in.). By this time the young fish has usually drifted into shallow inshore water.

The plaice is the most important flatfish of the northern European fishing industry. It is caught mainly in trawls and Danish seines, but can be captured on lines and in set nets. Heavy fishing has resulted in the largest plaice now being very rare for it is a long-lived species becoming sexually mature at 3–7 years (females) and 2–6 years (males), and living for up to 30 years. It is also commonly caught by anglers.

Flounder   *Platichthys flesus*

Distinguishing features   Similar in general appearance to the preceding species, but lacks the line of bony knobs on the head. Small but sharp prickles along the bases of the dorsal and anal fins. Scales smooth-edged, lateral line straight; also prickly. Anal fin rays 35–46. Frequently 'reversed', so that the eyes and colouring are on the left side.

Coloration   Dull brown, even greenish-brown with indistinct reddish blotches on the eyed side; blind side opaque and dull white.

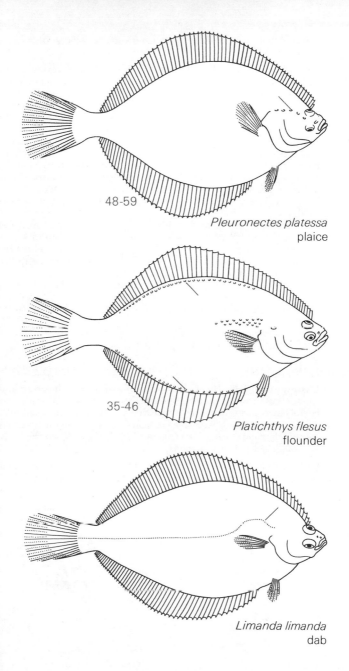

48-59

Pleuronectes platessa
plaice

35-46

Platichthys flesus
flounder

Limanda limanda
dab

Size   Attains 51 cm (20 in.) in length and a weight of *c.* 3 kg (6 lb 10 oz).

Remarks   A widespread European fish living from the tide line to 55 m (30 fathoms), and also penetrating into freshwater so that it is found in rivers and lakes in communication with the sea, even where the water seems entirely fresh. The flounder penetrates further into freshwater in more northern, cooler conditions than in the south. It lives on sandy and muddy bottoms.

It feeds on a wide range of bottom-living invertebrates, especially molluscs such as cockles, worms, and crustaceans (brown shrimps particularly). Young fish eat smaller crustaceans, for example, sandhoppers, fairy shrimps, and young brown shrimps. Close inshore the flounder makes migrations up the shore to feed at high tide, retreating as the tide falls. It is more active at night-time than by day.

It breeds in spring in depths of 25–40 m (14–22 fathoms), the eggs, larvae, and postlarvae being surface-living. The flounder lives on the sea-bed from a length of 1.5–3 cm ($\frac{1}{2}$–$1\frac{1}{4}$ in.). The very young live close inshore and, at about the size of a postage stamp, are very abundant in the tidal reaches of rivers.

The flounder is caught in some quantity in northern Europe, especially in the Baltic Sea, but it is not an important food-fish. It is rather more valuable as an angler's fish owing to its habit of living close inshore.

Occasionally it interbreeds with the plaice; the hybrid is intermediate in form between the parent species.

Dab   *Limanda limanda*

Distinguishing features   A small flatfish similar to the preceding species with a small mouth, but with a moderate-sized head. The lateral line is strongly curved above the pectoral fin on the eyed side. The scales on this side have fine teeth on their edges and the body has a distinctly rough feel; on the blind side only the edges of the body are rough. Anal fin rays 50–64.

Coloration   Usually warm sandy-brown, varying from light brown to grey-brown with small darker freckles on the eyed side; on the blind side white.

Size   Grows to about 42 cm ($16\frac{1}{2}$ in.) in length and 1.3 kg (2 lb 14 oz) in weight; not usually longer than 25 cm (10 in.).

Flounder ◄

► Dab

Remarks An extremely abundant fish especially in the North Sea, and on other shallow, sandy grounds in northern Europe. It lives mainly in depths of 20–40 m (11–22 fathoms), but small specimens are found as shallow as 2 m (1 fathom); adults have been caught at 150 m (82 fathoms). In addition to the young fish living in shallow water, adults move inshore in the summer in a seasonal migration. The dab spawns in spring and early summer, the eggs, larvae, and postlarvae being pelagic, while young fish live on the sea-bed from a length of 13–18 mm ($\frac{1}{2}$–$\frac{3}{4}$ in.). They become sexually mature at 2 (males) or 3 (females) years of age, and live for 10–12 years in all.

The food of the dab is variable with local conditions, but in general it eats almost any bottom-living invertebrate abundant locally which is small enough to be captured. Numerous kinds of small crustaceans, polychaete worms, and molluscs make up its bulk.

It is a moderately important flatfish to the fishing industry and is caught mainly in trawls and Danish seines. It is also popular with anglers, despite its small size, for it is common in inshore waters and takes a bait eagerly. When fresh, it has probably the best-flavoured flesh of all the flatfishes.

Lemon sole   *Microstomus kitt*

Distinguishing features Slightly less broad-bodied than the preceding species, but thick and fleshy. It has a small head (length about one-fifth of the body length) and very small mouth with protuberant lips. The scales are smooth-edged and the skin is smooth to the touch; there is a shallow curve in the lateral line above the pectoral fin.

Coloration Generally warm brown with irregular mahogany markings and flecks of yellow and green on the eyed side.

Size Attains a length of *c.* 66 cm (26 in.) and a weight of *c.* 1 kg (2 lb 3 oz).

Remarks A widespread flatfish in northern European waters where it seems to be common only locally. It lives on a wide range of bottoms from mud (exceptionally), and sand, gravel, even rocky grounds, in depths of 40–200 m (22–109 fathoms), particularly on offshore banks. Small specimens can, however, be caught close inshore. It spawns in spring and summer in depths of *c.* 100 m (55 fathoms), the eggs and larvae being planktonic, while the postlarvae are found in mid-water and become bottom-living at a length of *c.* 3 cm (1$\frac{1}{4}$ in.). It becomes sexually mature at 3–4 years (males), 4–6 years (females), and may live for 17 years.

The lemon sole is rather a specialized feeder on polychaete worms, but it also eats numerous crustaceans and molluscs, although its small mouth is the limiting factor in size of prey. It fasts during most of the winter months.

It is a moderately important food-fish, caught mainly in trawls; the British market takes most of the European catch. It is very rarely caught by anglers.

Distinguishing features   A very slender, narrow-bodied flatfish with the eyes on the right side of the head. Head small; eyes relatively large; mouth small. The lateral line is very slightly curved above the pectoral fin; scales are small, lightly toothed and very fragile, particularly on the eyed side. Blister-like cavities on the underside of the head.

Coloration   Eyed side a uniform grey or grey-brown with a dusting of darker points on the fins and a dusky pectoral fin. Blind side white.

Size   Attains a maximum length of *c.* 55 cm (21¾ in.); usually around 35 cm (13¾ in.).

Remarks   A moderately deep-water flatfish which lives on the lower continental shelf from 300–900 m (164–492 fathoms) and deeper. It appears to be confined to mud and mud-sand bottoms, and is especially common in the deep fjords of the Norwegian and Faeroese coasts. Its food consists of bottom-living invertebrates, especially small crustaceans and worms. It spawns in summer, and the eggs and young stages float near the surface. At a length of 4–5 cm (1½–2 in.) the young fish is living on the sea-bed. Its growth is rather slow, sexual maturity is attained in 3 to 4 years, and the witch may live for 14 years.

     It is of some importance as a food-fish in northern European waters, especially off Iceland, Faeroe, Norway, and Sweden. It is mostly captured in trawls.

Long rough dab   *Hippoglossoides platessoides*

Distinguishing features   A rather slender narrow-bodied flatfish with the eyes on the right side of the head, a rather small head, but with a large mouth (the edge of the jaws reaches the middle of the eye). Eyes large (diameter greater than snout length). Lateral line slightly curved over the pectoral fin. Scales relatively large, fine teeth on their edges giving the eyed side particularly a rough texture. Tail fin with middle rays longest.

Coloration   Uniform pale brown, sometimes with a russet tinge; ventrally white.

Size   May attain 48 cm (19 in.), usually around 30 cm (11¾ in.).

Lemon sole ◄

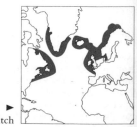

► Witch

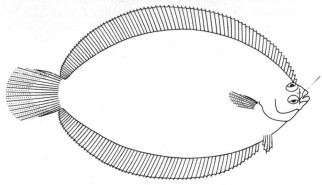

Microstomus kitt
lemon sole

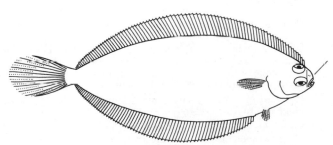

Glyptocephalus cynoglossus
witch

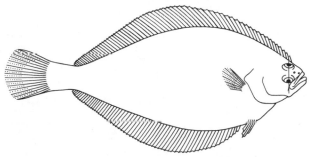

Hippoglossoides platessoides
long rough dab

Remarks A common flatfish which lives in moderately deep water on the lower continental shelf on fine sand or muddy bottoms. It seems to be most abundant at depths of *c.* 40–180 m (22–98 fathoms), although its extreme depth ranges are 4 to *c.* 400 m (2–218 fathoms). These greater depths are usually only in the southern parts of its range. It spawns in spring, the eggs and larvae being pelagic until the latter reach a length of 2–3 cm ($\frac{3}{4}$–1$\frac{1}{4}$ in.), when they live in mid-water. Postlarval development continues in deeper water and the young are bottom-living from 3.5–4.5 cm (1$\frac{1}{2}$–1$\frac{3}{4}$ in.). The long rough dab becomes sexually mature after 2 or 3 years, but in the far north after 7 to 10 years. It lives for some 17–20 years; but all such old fish are females.

Its food consists of crustaceans of various kinds, worms, molluscs, and brittlestars, and rather few fish. It has virtually no value as a food-fish as its flesh is watery and insipid.

The Greenland and North American populations are subspecifically distinct, *H. platessoides platessoides*; the European populations are *H. platessoides limandoides*.

Halibut
Hippoglossus hippoglossus

Distinguishing features A slender-bodied but thickset right-eyed flatfish, with a moderate-sized head and very large mouth. Lower jaw is prominent; both jaws have large teeth. The lateral line has a strong curve above the pectoral fin. Dorsal fin originates by the front edge of the upper eye; tail fin square cut or slightly concave. Scales small and embedded in the skin.

Coloration Dull greeny-brown, sometimes almost black; the blind side is pearly white.

Size Attains a maximum length of 2.54 m (8 ft 4 in.) and weight of 320 kg (706 lb); today rarely above 2 m (5 ft 7 in.). Records of halibut of 3–4 m (9 ft 10 in–12 ft) exist from the period before the stocks were heavily fished.

Remarks The halibut is a deep-water boreal flatfish found at depths of 100–1500 m (55–820 fathoms), but seasonally migratory and living at different depths at different times of its life. It is found on a wide range of bottoms, from sand, gravel, and rocky grounds, but it is not confined to the sea-bed, as are most flatfishes, for it is an active predator which forages in mid-water. Young halibut feed heavily on the deep-sea prawn, *Pandalus borealis*, and other crustaceans; they also eat squids, and fishes such as sandeels, and

Long rough dab

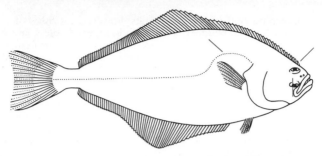

Hippoglossus hippoglossus
halibut

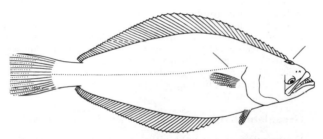

Reinhardtius hippoglossoides
Greenland halibut

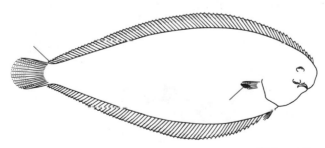

Solea solea
sole

deeper water flatfishes. The adults, however, eat fishes of many kinds: herring, haddock, cod, rat-tails, capelin, redfish, and small skates, squids, and some crustaceans. There are probably few fish species that are common in the depths inhabited by the halibut which are not eaten from time to time.

The halibut spawns in winter and early spring close to the sea-bed in depths of 400–1000 m (219–547 fathoms), on the edge of the northern continental shelf. The eggs (which are very numerous) drift in deep water until they hatch in 9–16 days. The postlarvae metamorphose into young flatfish at around 3–3.5 cm (1¼–1½ in.), and by a length of 4 cm (1½ in.); they are bottom-living. The young fish live close inshore for between 2 and 4 years, then gradually move into deeper water until they are sexually mature at 10–14 years. Mature females and the well-grown young are more common on offshore banks, but the mature males live on the edge of the continental shelf. The females move into deeper water to spawn, and both sexes make a northerly migration in summer to the richer offshore feeding-grounds, after spawning. Females are larger than males at all ages, and outlive them today to 35–40 years; formerly, before fishing pressure was intense, to possibly 50 years.

The halibut is an important food-fish caught mainly on hook and long-line, although a few are taken by trawl. Its flesh is firm and of excellent flavour. However, owing to its slow growth rate, and the relatively late age at which it becomes sexually mature, it is very vulnerable to overfishing and stocks are greatly diminished in the North Atlantic. The range is itself restricted compared with its original status.

Greenland halibut   *Reinhardtius hippoglossoides*

Distinguishing features Rather slender-bodied but thickset; eyes on the right side of the head. Head moderately large, jaws very large with long, fang-like teeth. Eyes large, the upper eye on the extreme edge of the body. Lateral line virtually straight from head to tail; scales small and embedded. The dorsal fin origin is beside the rear edge of the upper eye. Tail fin square-cut in adults, slightly concave in young fish.

Coloration Medium brown to dark greeny-brown on the eyed side; blind side dark, brown or bluish.

Size Maximum length *c.* 120 cm (47¼ in.), weight *c.* 45 kg (99 lb); usually 80–100 cm (31½–39 in.) and 11–25 kg (24–55 lb).

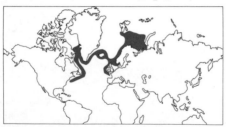

Halibut

Remarks The Greenland halibut is a boreal species which lives in deep water on the edge of the continental shelf in 200–2000 m (109–1093 fathoms), although north of the Arctic circle it may be caught in water as shallow as 500 m (273 fathoms). It is not a bottom-living fish and ranges in mid-water in search of food such as deep-sea prawns, cod, Arctic cod, eelpouts, capelin, and redfish, as well as squids. It is an active, mid-water hunter, as its near symmetry (when compared with other flatfishes) and colouring suggest.

It spawns in 700–1500 m (383–820 fathoms) in summer, and the eggs, larvae, and postlarvae are all found free-floating in deep water. Metamorphosis is completed at a length of 6–8.5 cm ($2\frac{1}{2}$–$3\frac{1}{2}$ in.); the young may be found then in the shallower regions inhabited by this flatfish.

The Greenland halibut is exploited by the fishing industries of the more northerly European countries, as well as by Greenland and North America. Most are captured on long lines. Its flesh is inferior to that of the halibut. It is also found in the North Pacific.

Soles

A family of flatfishes (Soleidae) of world-wide distribution in temperate and tropical seas, and usually found in shallow water. Like other flatfishes they pass through a metamorphosis in their development when one eye (the left in this group) migrates over the top of the head and comes to lie beside the other on the right side. Other adaptations follow; usually the nostrils are expanded and in many species small sensory barbels are present on the blind side. Reversed specimens are very rare. Soles are usually slender-bodied, the dorsal fin begins on the snout, and the preoperculum is covered by skin.

Many species are known, but in northern European waters only 4 are at all common, with another deep sea species occasionally reported.

Sole   *Solea solea*

Distinguishing features Slender-bodied, but thickset, the head small, mouth curved and set to one side; dorsal fin origin in front of upper eye. Pectoral fins moderate, that on the blind side only a little smaller than the other; the dorsal and anal fins joined to the tail fin

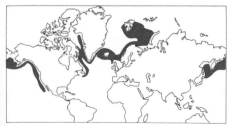

Greenland
halibut

base by a membrane. Nostril on blind side swollen, but not forming a conspicuous rosette.

Coloration Medium brown to dark brown with irregular dusky patches on the eyed side; pectoral fin with an elliptical black spot on its upper edge. Blind side creamy-white.

Size Attains *c*. 60 cm (23½ in.) and a weight of 3 kg (6 lb 10 oz); usually 30–40 cm (12–15¾ in.).

Remarks The most abundant member of the family in European seas, although it reaches the northern limit of its range to the north of the British Isles. It is common on sandy and muddy grounds from 10–100 m (5½–55 fathoms), occasionally occurring as deep as 160 m (87 fathoms), while very young specimens can be caught in intertidal pools on sandy shores and below tide level in 1–2 m (½–1 fathom). It feeds mainly on small crustaceans and worms, and will also eat small molluscs and sometimes fishes. It is normally a nocturnal feeder, but in conditions of dull weather and in murky water, such as in estuaries, it will feed in daylight. At night also it is active, often well clear of the sea-bed, and may even be captured at the surface.

It spawns in spring and early summer in shallow coastal water of 40–50 m (22–27 fathoms). The eggs and larvae are pelagic, but from 12–15 mm they metamorphose into young soles and live on the bottom, usually having drifted into shallow coastal, and frequently into estuarine water. The very young live in the breakers and on sandy shores. Adults migrate into shallow water during summer and into deeper water in winter; in very cold winters they accumulate in deep pits, for example those in the North Sea where the water is slightly warmer.

The sole is an important and valuable food-fish. It is caught mainly in trawls, but some are taken in set nets. It has little interest for anglers because of its rather specialized food requirements and nocturnal habits.

Sand sole *Pegusa lascaris*

Distinguishing features Body shape typically that of a sole. The front nostril on the underside of the head expanded into a broad rosette-like organ as large as the eye diameter. Pectoral fin on blind side only a little smaller than that on the eyed side. Dorsal fin origin in front of upper eye; dorsal and anal fins connected to the base of the tail fin by a low membrane.

Sole

Coloration Uniformly light brown with irregular dark spots and freckles on the eyed side; pectoral fin with a rounded black spot on the middle of the fin. Creamy-white on the blind side.

Size Attains 35 cm (13¾ in.).

Remarks A rare fish in northern European waters, and usually ranges no further north than the northern Irish Sea. It is found on muddy and sandy bottoms in depths of 30–350 m (16–191 fathoms) and appears to live in shallower water mainly during summer. It spawns in the western Channel in July, the eggs and larvae being pelagic. It does not apparently live close inshore, although a few occurrences have been reported as shallow as 8 m (4½ fathoms). The sand sole is said to eat large quantities of molluscs. Its biology has been very little studied in northern waters.

Solenette   *Buglossidium luteum*

Distinguishing features Typically sole-like in appearance but very small. Pectoral fins small, that on the blind side vestigial (a single long ray and two smaller ones). Eyes minute, their diameter much less than the snout length.

Coloration Sandy or light yellow-brown, freckled with brown spots; every fifth or sixth ray of the dorsal and anal fins black, almost to the tip. Yellowish ventrally.

Size Attains a maximum length of 13 cm (5 in.).

Remarks This minute sole, the smallest European species, is common on sandy bottoms offshore in depths of 5–40 m (3–22 fathoms), but a few live down to 83 m (45 fathoms). It feeds on small crustaceans and worms. It breeds during the summer, the eggs and larvae (which are 2 mm long at hatching) are pelagic and the

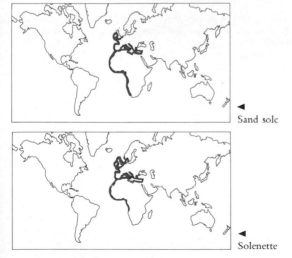

◄ Sand sole

◄ Solenette

young fish drifts down to the sea-bed at about 12 mm ($\frac{1}{2}$ in.) in length. It has no value to commercial fisheries or angling because of its small size.

Thickback sole   *Microchirus variegatus*

Distinguishing features   Typically sole-like in appearance, but body thickset and deep. Pectoral fins small, that on the blind side minute. Anterior nostril on the blind side tubular, not expanded into a rosette. Eyes moderately large, the diameter greater than the snout distance; space between the eyes equal to eye diameter.

Coloration   Chestnut brown on the back with 5 darker brown cross-bands ending in dark patches on dorsal and anal fins. White ventrally.

Size   Attains 33 cm (13 in.) in length.

Remarks   An offshore species of sole, living in depths of 37–92 m (20–50 fathoms), but with extremes of its depth range from 18–400 m (10–219 fathoms). It lives on sand, and sand and gravel bottoms. In northern European waters it is rather rare and its biology is little known. Spawning takes place in the English Channel in spring and early summer in deep water, the eggs, larvae, and postlarvae being pelagic at first, but as the postlarvae grow they live deeper down. From about 12 mm ($\frac{1}{2}$ in.) the young fish seek the bottom, although they may be more than 18 mm ($\frac{3}{4}$ in.) before they live on the sea-bed.

In northern waters this fish is too rare to contribute much to fisheries, but its flesh is of good quality.

Trigger-Fish

A family (Balistidae) of mainly tropical and warm temperate fishes found in the shallow sea, although a few are oceanic. Some trigger-fishes move into temperate seas with seasonal warming of the water, one such occurring in northern European waters. Elsewhere they are especially well known as colourful inhabitants of coral reefs, but some species rely on their dull coloration and compressed shape to frustrate predators by mimicry of algae or driftwood.

The trigger-fishes have an interesting development of the spines in the first dorsal fin, the first spine being strong and stout, while the

Thickback sole

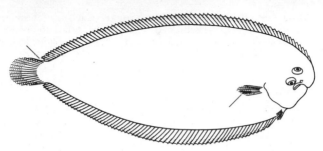

Pegusa lascaris
sand sole

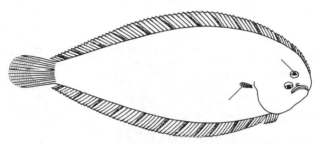

Buglossidium luteum
solenette

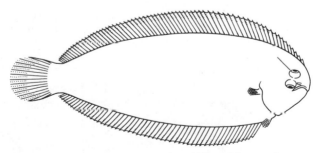

Microchirus variegatus
thickback sole

slender second spine acts as a lock or trigger which has to be released before the first can be depressed. These fish have the habit of taking refuge in a crevice in the rock or coral and, with the spine locked in position, wedging themselves in, face an attacker with their sharp, rat-like teeth.

Trigger-fish   *Balistes carolinensis*

Distinguishing features   Deep-bodied, with a long snout, small eye, and small mouth; teeth sharp and incisor-like. First dorsal fin with 3 spines, the first strong and robust; second dorsal and anal fins well developed; pelvic fins absent, replaced by a rough-edged spine. Two or 3 enlarged bony plates behind the gill opening.

Coloration   Olive brown or greyish; the dorsal and anal fins with basal blue lines.

Size   Attains 41 cm (16 in.).

Remarks   An uncommon visitor to northern European seas, being found mainly in summer or early autumn as the result of migration or, more likely, drift in ocean currents. In some years (as in 1973) common on the Atlantic coast and occasionally penetrating into the North Sea. It is more usual for only 1 or 2 to be reported annually. This is an open sea species, the young living in *Sargassum* weed in the tropical Atlantic, while the adults often accompany floating wreckage. The adults are said to eat crustaceans of various kinds, and are occasionally taken in baited crab-pots, and by anglers. In general its biology is little known.

Puffer-Fish

A relatively numerous family (Tetraodontidae) of mainly tropical or warm-temperate marine fishes, although several freshwater species are known in tropical Africa and Asia. Most are stout-bodied, rather rounded fishes with small fins (lacking spiny-rayed fins) and large eyes. Most have fine spines in the skin which stand erect when the body is puffed up with water. They have 4 teeth in the jaws.

   Puffer-fishes are typically found in shallow, inshore waters around coral reefs, in sea-grass beds, and in estuaries, but a few (including the only form found in northern Europe) are oceanic in

Trigger-fish

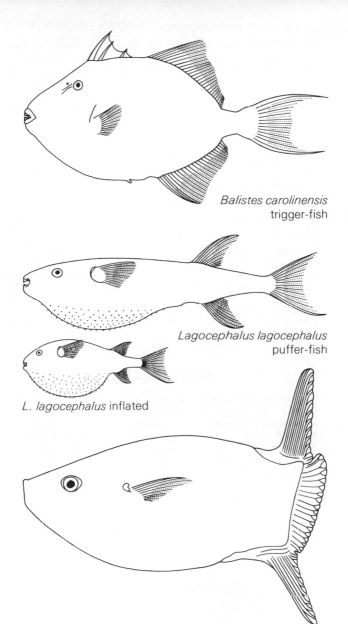

Balistes carolinensis
trigger-fish

Lagocephalus lagocephalus
puffer-fish

L. lagocephalus inflated

Ranzania laevis
slender sun-fish

life style. They have no economic importance except in Japan, where they are known as fugu and are eaten after special preparation, for their blood, liver, and gonads contain a virulent toxin which, if ingested, can cause painful and even serious illness.

Puffer-fish   *Lagocephalus lagocephalus*

Distinguishing features   Stout-bodied but with a slender tail, with small dorsal and anal fins, and a forked tail fin. Four teeth in the jaws form a parrot-like beak. Skin on the back smooth; on the extensible belly-pouch small spines are embedded which become erect when the pouch is inflated. The lateral line is a raised fold of skin along the lower side.

Coloration   Back bright blue to steel blue, the belly pure white; small dusky spots along the lower side.

Size   Attains 61 cm (24 in.).

Remarks   A rare vagrant in northern European waters which is captured or stranded from time to time mostly in late summer. It is a pelagic species which lives in the open sea in the tropical Atlantic, and in the Indian and Pacific Oceans as well. Its presence in northern waters is presumably due to drift from the south-west in ocean currents. Its biology has been little studied, but some specimens have contained squids' beaks in their stomachs and their skin was scarred by squids' sucker discs; crustacean remains have also been found.
 The map shows Atlantic range only.

Sun-Fishes

A small family (Molidae), world-wide in distribution in the upper layers of the oceans in tropical and warm temperate zones, with some seasonal migration into temperate seas. They include some of the largest fishes of the open sea, but despite this their biology is poorly known or even the number of species in the family. They resemble their relatives, the puffer-fishes, in having small mouths with well-developed beak-like teeth in each jaw. (They are fused in the mid-line so that each half looks very like a bird's bill.) Their most striking feature is the apparent absence of a tail, the body ending with the vertical dorsal and anal fins with a frill-like fin which represents the tail fin.
 Only two species occur in northern European waters.

Puffer-fish

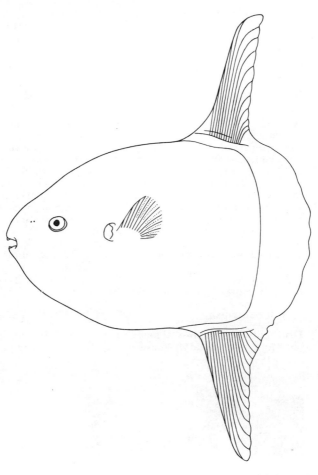

Mola mola
sun-fish

Sun-fish   *Mola mola*

Distinguishing features A huge round-bodied fish with dorsal
and anal fins near the end of the body, and a rounded lobed tail 'fin'
between the 2. The eye is small, the gill opening is restricted, the
mouth is small; the pectoral fins rounded; pelvic fins absent.

Coloration Blueish or greyish-brown; darker above, light on the
belly.

Size Attains 4 m (13 ft) in length and a weight of *c.* 1500 kg
(3300 lb).

Remarks The sun-fish is an open ocean species of world-wide
distribution, found in the upper waters at depths of 183–366 m
(100–200 fathoms). Many reports of sightings of fish at the surface,
often with their subsequent capture, have led to the belief that they
bask on their sides at the surface; it seems more probable that these
are simply sick or disabled fish. Very occasionally they are caught in
shallow, inshore water due presumably to passive drift in currents.

The food of the sun-fish consists mostly of planktonic organisms,
especially jelly-fishes, salps, and comb-jellies, but fish larvae and
crustaceans are also eaten. A number of specimens have been caught
on anglers' baits. They have no value as a food-fish; the flesh is soft
and insipid, and this and the gut are frequently infested with worm
cysts.

The status of this fish in northern European waters is that of a
relatively widespread but uncommon fish.   •

Slender sun-fish   *Ranzania laevis*

Distinguishing features Elongate but deep and compressed in
body form. Dorsal and anal fins high, similar in shape and placed

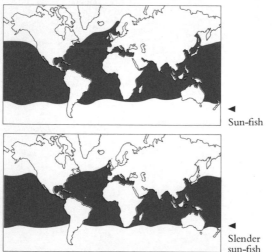

◄
Sun-fish

◄
Slender
sun-fish

opposite one another; pectoral fins small but elongate, pelvic fins absent, tail fin greatly modified. The mouth is small and compressed so that when closed it is a vertical slit. (See illustration on p. 369.)

Coloration Deep blue on the back, metallic silver on the sides with brilliant silvery, black-edged stripes curving across the head and belly.

Size Attains 80 cm (31 in.) in length.

Remarks An oceanic sun-fish which is found in all the tropical and warm temperate oceans. It probably lives in the upper 200 m (109 fathoms) of the sea, feeding on medusae, comb-jellies, and other planktonic life forms, but very few observations have been made on specimens captured in their natural habitat. Most of our slight knowledge of its biology is derived from stranded fish or those caught in inshore waters, which are an alien habitat. Its status in northern European seas is that of a very rare visitor mostly in later summer.

Index

377

379

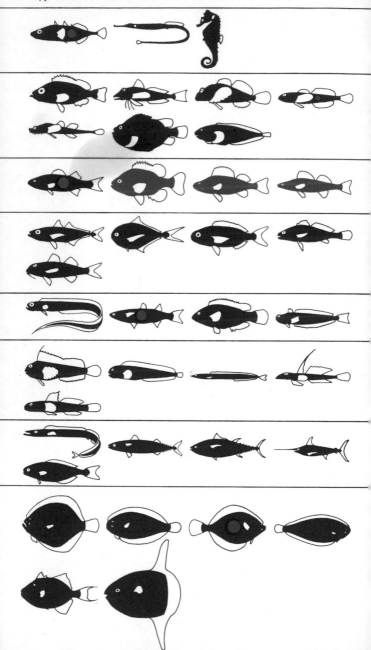